GLOBAL POLITICS

GLOBAL POLITICS

STEPHANIE LAWSON

OXFORD

UNIVERSITY PRESS

OXFORD
UNIVERSITY PRESS

Great Clarendon Street, Oxford, OX2 6DP,
United Kingdom

Oxford University Press is a department of the University of Oxford.
It furthers the University's objective of excellence in research, scholarship,
and education by publishing worldwide. Oxford is a registered trade mark of
Oxford University Press in the UK and in certain other countries

Published in the United States of America by Oxford University Press
198 Madison Avenue, New York, NY 10016, United States of America

British Library Cataloguing in Publication Data
Data available

Library of Congress Control Number: 2020949220

ISBN 978-0-19-884432-7

Printed in Great Britain by
Bell & Bain Ltd., Glasgow

To Liisa Adele, James Kofi,
Thomas Grainger, Annabel Grace,
Kaito Maximus, and Mina Matilda

PREFACE

This book introduces key topics and themes in the study of contemporary global politics—a field that encompasses the traditional discipline of International Relations (IR) but which is more expansive in scope, seeking insights from a range of relevant disciplines and transcending the narrower focus on relations between sovereign states in an international system of states. It deals with a wide range of practical issues in the global political sphere while also providing the conceptual and theoretical tools necessary for their explanation, interpretation, and understanding. While all the topics dealt with are of current relevance, a feature of the book is the way in which it provides the reader with a historical and contextual understanding of the subject matter, from the development of states as political communities over time to the nature of contemporary global order, along with the political ideas and theories that have accompanied these developments.

The book is very much concerned to provide not just factual information about historical and contemporary issues and ideas but also the critical intellectual skills required for their analysis. It is especially important that, regardless of one's pre-existing orientation to the world of politics, one takes the time to consider seriously all the various approaches to global politics set out in this book, from those at the more conservative end of the spectrum to the more critical and innovative perspectives that have emerged over the last few decades. All have something interesting and important to say about the state of global politics, whether we agree with their particular lines of argument or not.

Although the book does not champion any particular ideology or theoretical approach, it does take a critical stance on some of the most dangerous ideologies, especially racism, as well as on issues such as 'fake news', 'alternative facts', anti-science, conspiracy theories, and the like. The latter all undermine what serious social science and genuine intellectual enquiry is about.

The book is also sympathetic to the view that the study of global politics, especially in conventional IR approaches has, to date, been highly Eurocentric and needs to expand its horizons to encompass a wider range of world views and perspectives.

The book is organized so as to take the reader through from a broad explanation of the field of global politics and the way in which it has been theorized to more specific concerns with security, international organizations, international law, diplomacy and foreign policy, and global political economy—all fairly standard topics for an introductory textbook. The penultimate chapter, however, devotes space to one of the greatest challenges of our times—the state of the global environment in an era increasingly recognized as the 'Anthropocene'. This particular topic raises many issues for debate among the present generation of students and young people who are, after all, the ones who will be living with the consequences of large-scale environmental degradation well into the future. The final chapter brings into focus many of the general issue areas discussed throughout the book and which have implications for the broad normative questions facing students of global politics in the present period. These are bound to generate some lively debates.

In producing this book, I should point out that at least some of the material draws directly from two other publications with Oxford University Press that I have been involved in. The first is *Introduction to Politics*, co-authored with Robert Garner and Peter Ferdinand and now in its fourth edition (2020), which contains discrete sections on Concepts and Ideologies, Comparative Politics, and Global Politics. It was therefore designed to meet the requirements of a course of study, often taught over a full year, that covers the three major fields. The second publication, with the same co-authors, is *Politics* (2019). This was designed for courses in the discipline of politics that do not specifically include global politics or international relations.

The present book draws from my contributions to both these publications, but is designed as a stand-alone introductory textbook on global politics. In expanding to twelve chapters (from seven in *Introduction to Politics*) it also adds much more material on a number of important topics, including additions to the theory sections, which now have sections on race, culture, and sexuality as well as a new chapter on international law.

ACKNOWLEDGEMENT

Acknowledgement is due to my co-authors on the previous publications, Robert and Peter, together with the OUP team of editors, especially Sarah Iles and Sam Ashcroft. They have all been a pleasure to work with over many years and this book would not exist without them. Special thanks to Robert and Peter for allowing me to use some of their glossary entries. Family, friends, and colleagues—Carolyn, Preston, Mike, Cathie, Judith, Sigrid, Brigitte, Alan, Karin, Graham, Carol, Fred, Jonathan, Lavina, and Noah among them—have been, as always, a great support network. Finally, my thanks to all the reviewers who gave invaluable feedback on earlier drafts of the chapters. Needless to say, any errors of omission or commission are my responsibility alone.

The publishers and author would like to thank the lecturers who helped with reviewing early versions of the manuscript, including Suvi Alt, University of Groningen; Alan Apperley, University of Wolverhampton; André Gerrits, Leiden University; Ali Burak Güven, Birkbeck, University of London; Jeremy Moses, University of Canterbury, New Zealand; Andrea Schapper, University of Stirling; Taku Tamaki, Loughborough University; and Carla Winston, University of Melbourne.

DETAILED CONTENTS

LIST OF FIGURES

LIST OF BOXES

ABBREVIATIONS

AL	Arab League
ALP	Australian Labor Party
APEC	Asia-Pacific Economic Cooperation
ASEAN	Association of Southeast Asian Nations
ASEM	Asia-Europe Meeting process
AU	African Union
CCP	Chinese Communist Party
CFSP	Common Foreign and Security Policy
CHOGM	Commonwealth Heads of Government Meeting
CIA	Central Intelligence Agency
CND	Campaign for Nuclear Disarmament
COP	Conference of the Parties
CSTO	Collective Security Treaty Organisation
CT	Critical Theory
DFAIT	Canada's Department of Foreign Affairs and International Trade
ECOSOC	The Economic and Social Council
EPA	Environmental Protection Authority
ESDP	European Security and Defence Policy
FAO	Food and Agricultural Organization
FCDO	Foreign, Commonwealth and Development Office
FIFA	Fédération Internationale de Football Association
GATT	General Agreement on Tariffs and Trade
GCC	Gulf Cooperation Council
GFC	global financial crisis
GMO	genetically modified organism
GPE	Global Political Economy
GWOT	global war on terror
HRC	Human Rights Commission
HRC	Human Rights Council
IAEA	International Atomic Energy Agency
IBRD	International Bank for Reconstruction and Development
ICC	International Criminal Court
ICCPR	International Covenant on Civil and Political Rights
ICESCR	International Covenant on Economic, Social and Cultural Rights
ICISS	International Commission on Intervention and State Sovereignty
ICJ	International Court of Justice

ICTY	International Criminal Tribunal for the former Yugoslavia
IGO	intergovernmental organization
IHL	International Humanitarian Law
ILO	International Labour Organization
IO	international organization
IPCC	Intergovernmental Panel on Climate Change
IPE	International Political Economy
IR	International Relations
IS	Islamic State
ISAF	International Security Assistance Force
ISIL	Islamic State in Iraq and the Levant
ISIS	Islamic State in Iraq and Syria
IWEIA	International Work Group for Indigenous Affairs
LGBTQIA	lesbian, gay, bisexual, transgender, queer or questioning, intersex, and asexual
MAD	mutually assured destruction
MDG	Millennium Development Goal
MERCOSUR	Southern Common Market
MNC	multinational corporation
MOU	memorandum of understanding
NAFTA	North American Free Trade Agreement
NGO	non-governmental organization
NIEO	New International Economic Order
NPT	Nuclear Non-Proliferation Treaty
OAS	Organization of American States
OECD	Organization for Economic Cooperation and Development
OIC	Organization of Islamic Cooperation
OPEC	Organization of Petroleum Exporting Countries
OUA	Organization of African Unity
PCIJ	Permanent Court of International Justice
PIF	Pacific Islands Forum
QUANGO	quasi-autonomous NGO
SACB	Saudi Arabian Cultural Bureau
SALT	Strategic Arms Limitation Treaty
SDG	sustainable development goal
SMR	small modular reactor
TCO	transnational criminal organization
TED	Technology, Entertainment, Design
TNC	transnational corporation
TPP	Trans-Pacific Partnership
UDHR	Universal Declaration of Human Rights
UN	United Nations

UNAIDS	United Nations Programme on HIV/AIDS
UNCLOS	UN Convention on the Law of the Sea
UNDP	United Nations Development Program
UNEP	UN Environment Program
UNESCO	United Nations Educational, Scientific and Cultural Organization
UNFCCC	UN Convention on Climate Change
UNFPA	United Nations Population Fund
UNPFII	UN Permanent Forum on Indigenous Issues
USAGM	US Agency for Global Media
USMCA	United States-Mexico-Canada Agreement
VCLT	Vienna Convention on the Law of Treaties
VOA	Voice of America
VRS	Army of Republika Srpska
WHO	World Health Organization
WTO	World Trade Organization
XR	Extinction Rebellion

GUIDED TOUR OF THE TEXTBOOK FEATURES

This textbook is enriched with a range of learning features to help you navigate the text and reinforce your understanding of politics. This guided tour shows you how to get the most out of your textbook.

Reader's Guides

at the beginning of each chapter set the scene for the themes and issues to be discussed, and indicate the scope of the chapter's coverage.

Key Concepts boxes

throughout the text draw out and clearly explain important ideas.

Key Debates boxes

in each chapter highlight key areas of contention and challenge you to think critically about important issues in the text.

Key Quotes boxes

throughout the text draw out important and influential statements.

Case Study boxes

demonstrate how political ideas, concepts, and issues manifest in the real world.

Short Biographies

provide you with more information on key political thinkers and their ideas.

Key Points

at the end of each section draw out the most important points and arguments from the text.

Glossary terms

appear in colour throughout the text and are defined in a glossary at the end of the book, helping you expand your vocabulary and aiding your exam revision.

Key Questions

at the end of every chapter help you to check your understanding of core themes and issues and critically reflect on the chapter material.

Further Reading

lists are provided at the end of each chapter to help you take your learning further and to locate the key academic literature relevant to the chapter topic.

GUIDED TOUR OF THE ONLINE RESOURCES

 www.oup.com/he/lawson1e

The Online Resources that accompany this book provide students and instructors with a range of ready-to-use teaching and learning resources.

Lawson, Global Politics

Description

Global Politics is a concise and engaging introduction to international relations. Lawson presents key theories and concepts, demonstrating how they apply to everyday life. Using examples from around the world, both historical and contemporary, the textbook presents a truly global picture of politics.

⬇ CC v1.0

⬇ Simple CC v1.0

Resources for Global Politics

Global Politics 1e Instructor Resources

Lawson

Instructor resources to accompany *Global Politics*, which feature:

- PowerPoint slides
- Essay questions

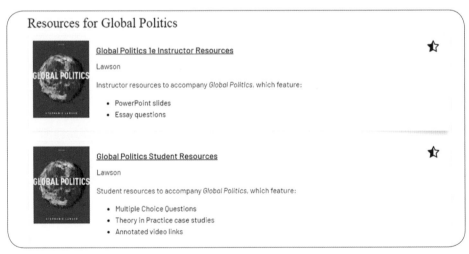

Resources for Global Politics

Global Politics 1e Instructor Resources

Lawson

Instructor resources to accompany *Global Politics*, which feature:

- PowerPoint slides
- Essay questions

Global Politics Student Resources

Lawson

Student resources to accompany *Global Politics*, which feature:

- Multiple Choice Questions
- Theory in Practice case studies
- Annotated video links

FOR STUDENTS

Multiple-choice questions

Self-marking multiple-choice questions have been provided for each chapter of the text to enable you to test your understanding of key themes and act as an aid to revision.

Extended case studies

Extended case studies help you think critically about the ways in which theory can be applied in practice.

Links to videos

Videos illustrate contemporary issues in International Relations, building on the knowledge you gain from each chapter.

FOR INSTRUCTORS

Essay questions

Chapter-specific essay questions promote students' critical reflection on core issues and themes.

PowerPoint presentations

Fully customizable PowerPoint slides complement each chapter of the book, providing a useful resource to instructors preparing lectures and in-class handouts.

WORLD MAP

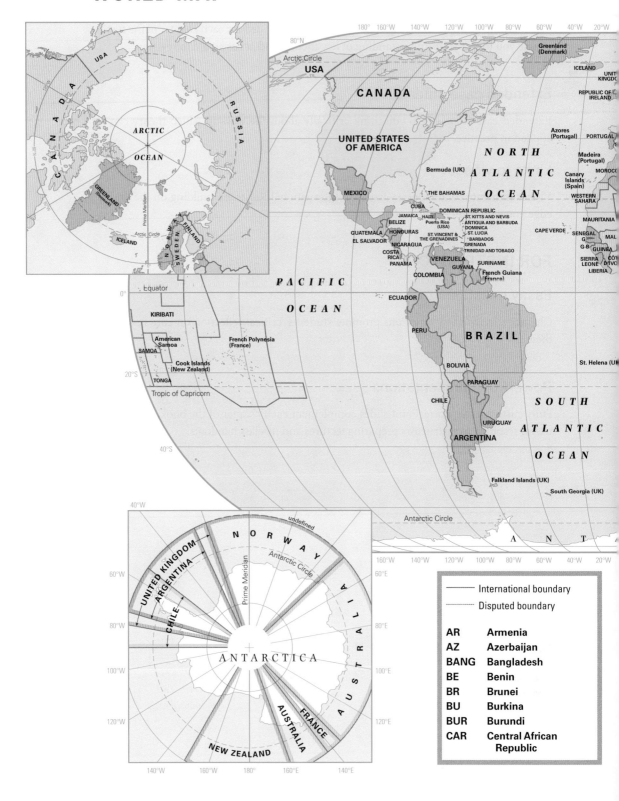

Inset map (Arctic):

CANADA
USA
RUSSIA
ARCTIC OCEAN
GREENLAND (Denmark)
NORWAY
SWEDEN
FINLAND
ICELAND
Arctic Circle
Prime Meridian

Main map:

80°N
Arctic Circle
Greenland (Denmark)
ICELAND
UNITED KINGDOM
REPUBLIC OF IRELAND
USA
CANADA
UNITED STATES OF AMERICA
Azores (Portugal)
PORTUGAL
Madeira (Portugal)
MOROCCO
Bermuda (UK)
NORTH ATLANTIC OCEAN
Canary Islands (Spain)
WESTERN SAHARA
MEXICO
THE BAHAMAS
CUBA
DOMINICAN REPUBLIC
JAMAICA
HAITI
ST. KITTS AND NEVIS
ANTIGUA AND BARBUDA
DOMINICA
BELIZE
Puerto Rico (USA)
GUATEMALA
HONDURAS
ST. LUCIA
EL SALVADOR
ST. VINCENT & THE GRENADINES
BARBADOS
GRENADA
NICARAGUA
TRINIDAD AND TOBAGO
COSTA RICA
PANAMA
VENEZUELA
SURINAME
COLOMBIA
GUYANA
French Guiana (France)
ECUADOR
MAURITANIA
CAPE VERDE
SENEGAL
G.
G-B
GUINEA
SIERRA LEONE
CÔTE D'IVO
LIBERIA
MAL
PACIFIC OCEAN
KIRIBATI
American Samoa
French Polynesia (France)
SAMOA
Cook Islands (New Zealand)
TONGA
PERU
BRAZIL
BOLIVIA
St. Helena (UK)
PARAGUAY
CHILE
SOUTH ATLANTIC OCEAN
URUGUAY
ARGENTINA
Falkland Islands (UK)
South Georgia (UK)
Antarctic Circle
ANT
0° Equator
20°S Tropic of Capricorn
40°S

160°W 140°W 120°W 100°W 80°W 60°W 40°W 20°W

Inset map (Antarctica):

ANTARCTICA
UNITED KINGDOM
ARGENTINA
CHILE
NORWAY
AUSTRALIA
FRANCE
NEW ZEALAND
undefined
Antarctic Circle
Prime Meridian
40°W
60°W
80°W
100°W
120°W
140°W
160°W
180°
160°E
140°E
120°E
100°E
80°E
60°E

Legend:

——	International boundary
----	Disputed boundary

AR	Armenia
AZ	Azerbaijan
BANG	Bangladesh
BE	Benin
BR	Brunei
BU	Burkina
BUR	Burundi
CAR	Central African Republic

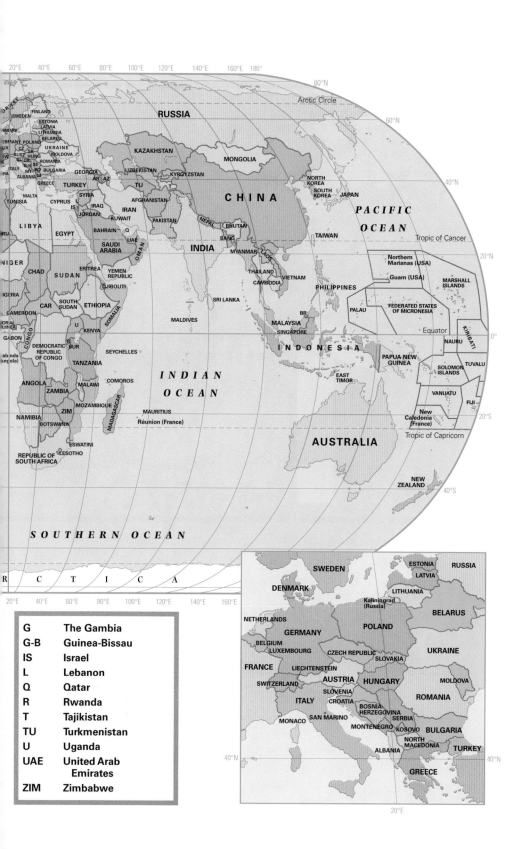

20°E 40°E 60°E 80°E 100°E 120°E 140°E 160°E 180°

80°N

Arctic Circle

60°N

RUSSIA

SWEDEN
FINLAND
ESTONIA
LATVIA
LITHUANIA
BELARUS
DENMARK
GERMANY **POLAND**
LUX UKRAINE
CZ SK MOLDOVA
AUST HUNG
SLO CR ROMANIA
SW B/H SE
ITALY BULGARIA
ALBANIA M GEORGIA
GREECE
MALTA **TURKEY**
TUNISIA **CYPRUS** SYRIA
IS IRAQ
JORDAN KUWAIT
BAHRAIN Q UAE
LIBYA **EGYPT**
SAUDI
ARABIA
OMAN

KAZAKHSTAN

MONGOLIA

UZBEKISTAN KYRGYZSTAN
TU T
AFGHANISTAN
IRAN
PAKISTAN NEPAL BHUTAN
INDIA BANG
MYANMAR LAOS

CHINA

NORTH
KOREA
SOUTH
KOREA **JAPAN**

**PACIFIC
OCEAN**

Tropic of Cancer

TAIWAN

20°N

40°N

Northern
Marianas (USA)

Guam (USA)

**MARSHALL
ISLANDS**

NIGER CHAD SUDAN ERITREA YEMEN
REPUBLIC
DJIBOUTI
IGERIA
CAR SOUTH
SUDAN ETHIOPIA
CAMEROON
ORIAL
GUINEA U KENYA
GABON
CONGO DEMOCRATIC
REPUBLIC
OF CONGO BUR
ab nda
nçola) TANZANIA
ANGOLA ZAMBIA MALAWI
ZIM MOZAMBIQUE
NAMIBIA BOTSWANA
ESWATINI
REPUBLIC OF LESOTHO
SOUTH AFRICA

THAILAND VIETNAM
CAMBODIA
PHILIPPINES
SRI LANKA
MALDIVES
BR
MALAYSIA
SINGAPORE

INDONESIA

PALAU FEDERATED STATES
OF MICRONESIA

Equator

NAURU KIRIBATI

0°

TUVALU

PAPUA NEW
GUINEA
EAST
TIMOR
SOLOMON
ISLANDS

VANUATU FIJI

New
Caledonia
(France)

20°S

**INDIAN
OCEAN**

SEYCHELLES

COMOROS
MADAGASCAR
MAURITIUS
Réunion (France)

AUSTRALIA

Tropic of Capricorn

NEW
ZEALAND

40°S

SOUTHERN OCEAN

R C T I C A

20°E 40°E 60°E 80°E 100°E 120°E 140°E 160°E

G	The Gambia
G-B	Guinea-Bissau
IS	Israel
L	Lebanon
Q	Qatar
R	Rwanda
T	Tajikistan
TU	Turkmenistan
U	Uganda
UAE	United Arab Emirates
ZIM	Zimbabwe

SWEDEN **ESTONIA** **RUSSIA**
LATVIA
DENMARK LITHUANIA
Kaliningrad
(Russia) **BELARUS**
NETHERLANDS
GERMANY **POLAND**
BELGIUM
LUXEMBOURG CZECH REPUBLIC **UKRAINE**
SLOVAKIA
FRANCE LIECHTENSTEIN
AUSTRIA **HUNGARY** MOLDOVA
SWITZERLAND SLOVENIA
ITALY CROATIA **ROMANIA**
BOSNIA-
HERZEGOVINA
MONACO SERBIA
SAN MARINO MONTENEGRO KOSOVO **BULGARIA**
NORTH
MACEDONIA
ALBANIA **TURKEY**
40°N 40°N
GREECE

20°E

1

INTRODUCING GLOBAL POLITICS

- The Nature of Global Politics
- Globalization Past and Present
- Theories, Norms, and Methods
- Conclusion

Reader's Guide

This introductory chapter presents an overview of global politics starting with an account of the global political sphere as a specialized area of study—more conventionally known as the discipline of International Relations (IR)—and including an explanation of the distinction between the 'global' and the 'international'. It also addresses the extent to which the world is 'globalized', even as some pundits herald a halt to globalization and a return to the closed politics of nationalism. Next we explore the history of globalization which provides an essential backdrop to our understanding of the phenomenon in the present, and the challenges to it. This includes attention to the interweaving of globalization's political, economic, social and cultural dimensions and some of the implications for the current state-based world order. In the final section we move on to a different set of issues which are essential to the basic question of *how* we study global politics and any of the phenomena associated with it. We consider the role of theory and method, including concerns raised by the notion of a 'post-truth' world. The conclusion references contemporary debates about the critical intellectual skills needed to face future challenges in the study of the global political sphere.

THE NATURE OF GLOBAL POLITICS

If politics in the national sphere is a multifaceted activity that resists easy definition, this is no less the case in the global sphere. But at the very least we can characterize global politics as involving the distribution and utilization of power and resources on a worldwide basis, accompanied by questions of what is right or wrong, just or unjust, in this distribution. Historically, it involves state formation, technological development, the projection of power beyond the state, and the rise of an intricate network of global relations in which almost every human community is enmeshed. At a practical level, key contemporary issues in global politics include a plethora of social, economic, and political activities, ranging from the distribution of wealth and poverty, civil and interstate warfare, migration, the fate of refugees, transnational criminality, finance and trade, and diplomatic negotiations, to the management of pandemics, the global environment, and the role of both the **state** and global institutions in addressing all such issues. These may also involve further questions of **identity politics**—of how national, racial, ethnic, religious, and gender identities play out in political terms.

All the issues and questions sketched above, which are discussed in more detail in later chapters, may generate disagreement and contestation. In the 'real world' of global politics, this does not necessarily precipitate violence in the form of warfare, and indeed the history of our species points to an enormous capacity for cooperation and peaceful negotiation within and between communities, as well as the ability to deploy political power to achieve positive goods. Even so, the tendency to violence along with the abuse of power seems an ever-present danger, constituting a central concern for individuals and communities.

A major challenge for politics, and what politics is in fact largely about, is how to devise ways of resolving or managing conflict and disagreement without resorting to violence. In the national or domestic sphere, conflict and disagreement is dealt with by governments which, by and large, possess sovereign power and authority in accordance with a constitutional set-up or regime. This is so whether they are authoritarian or democratic, or somewhere in between. Where governments fail to manage conflicting positions either within the state or between states, violence in the form of civil war—as in the case of contemporary Syria—or interstate war—as illustrated by the World Wars of the twentieth century and the wars in Afghanistan and Iraq in the twenty-first century—is usually the result.

Among the most frequently used terms in discussions of global politics is **sovereignty** which is taken to be the defining feature of the modern territorial state. Regardless of their constitutional form states are characterized as possessing sovereign authority within their territorial boundaries and, in an international system of states, are therefore regarded as sovereign entities. *Unlike* the national or domestic sphere, the resolution or management of conflict in the international or global sphere must be carried out in the absence of an overarching sovereign authority capable of enforcing laws and punishing transgressors. We shall see later that the United Nations, while constituting the prime organ of **global governance**, is not a world govern*ment* in the sense that it possesses sovereign authority and the capabilities that go with it.

Because there is no world government, the global sphere is generally described as anarchic, which means, literally, 'no government'. The term **anarchy** is nowadays commonly associated with violent groups who are given to destroying property during times of political protest. In the present period, this occurs most often at meetings of global organizations such as the World Trade Organization (WTO), as discussed in Chapter 10, with the protests often characterized as 'anti-globalization'. But this is not what is meant by anarchy in the global sphere more generally, and it certainly does not mean that the global sphere is necessarily chaotic. It does, however, have implications for global order and security. And it certainly has implications for how global politics is theorized, as we see in later chapters.

Another important point to note at this stage is that although we often distinguish between the domestic and the global spheres, they cannot be firmly marked off from each other. Although many traditional IR scholars have tended to treat these spheres as entirely separate entities, contemporary scholars are much more likely to accept that domestic political and indeed social, economic, cultural, and other concerns interact constantly with the international or global sphere and vice versa.

The Emergence of Global Politics as a Field of Study

While there have always been strong incentives for avoiding warfare as a means of settling differences, and adopting non-violent political strategies instead, the stakes became far higher during the twentieth century as the extent of death and destruction during the two World Wars demonstrated. Indeed, the scale of violence during the First World War of 1914–18, with some 20 million military and civilian deaths and a similar number injured, gave a significant impetus to the formal study of politics in the global sphere. The first Department of International Politics was established at the University of Wales, Aberystwyth, in the UK, together with the first endowed professorship, called the Woodrow Wilson Chair of International Politics. It was named after US President Woodrow Wilson in recognition of his contributions to world peace and security, manifest largely in his efforts to establish the League of Nations in the immediate aftermath of the war.

➡ **See Chapter 3 for further discussion of Woodrow Wilson and liberal theory.**

In the US, especially in the aftermath of the Second World War and the early years of the Cold War, there were renewed calls to promote the study of politics in the international sphere in a specialized discipline which became more commonly known as International Relations (IR). Here we may note that while 'IR' (capitalized) denotes the formal discipline, the lower case 'international relations' is generally used to refer to its substantive domain of study—that is, *the practice* of relations between nation-states, or what is increasingly being called 'global politics' (Eun, 2019: p. 84). With respect to the founding of the discipline of IR, given that it was nation-states that had been at war and wrought such destruction over the period 1914–18, it is scarcely surprising that interactions between such units, and the desire to secure peaceful relations between and among them, remained the primary focus of the new discipline.

On the practical side, much hope was invested in a novel experiment in world governance in the form of the League of Nations, designed to settle international disputes and avoid violence. But if there had been lessons to learn from the First World War and the nature of the peace settlement that followed, it seems that these were elusive. The next horrific episode of interstate violence from 1939 to 1945 saw four times as many people die as a direct or indirect result of the war. This time, the vast majority were civilians rather than military personnel, and indeed from early in the twentieth century to the present time, civilian deaths and injuries (including women, children, and the elderly) have come to far outnumber those of combatants in both civil and interstate warfare. An estimate of civilian deaths in the Second World War (including death from disease and starvation as a direct result of the war) puts the total at around 55 million while military deaths were up to 25 million (https://worldpopulationreview.com/countries/world-war-two-casualties-by-country/).

Rather than discarding the idea that an overarching institution of world governance could contribute effectively to global peace and security, political leaders once again invested hopes in the development of an overarching international institution, and the United Nations was established in 1945. This time, its membership was far more extensive and it is now truly global in the sense that virtually every sovereign state in the world is a member.

The Second World War also gave rise to the development of nuclear weapons technology and the first atomic bombs, designed and built in the US, were dropped on the Japanese cities of Hiroshima and Nagasaki in August 1945, ending the war in the Pacific. The **Cold War** between the two superpowers—the Union of Soviet Socialist Republics (otherwise known as the USSR or Soviet Union) together with its allies on the one hand, and the US and its allies on the other—followed almost immediately after the end of the Second World War. In this context, more countries—including Britain, France, the Soviet Union, and China, and later India and Pakistan—acquired nuclear war technologies capable of obliterating the entire human race as well as most other animal species. The focus for academic study therefore remained largely on relations between states and the causes of war and the conditions for peace between them, acquiring even greater urgency given the possibility of absolute devastation arising from interstate nuclear warfare. With the prospect of annihilation on a global scale entering the imagination, the idea of the necessity for *global* solutions became more widespread in political discourse.

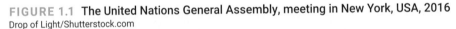

FIGURE 1.1 The United Nations General Assembly, meeting in New York, USA, 2016
Drop of Light/Shutterstock.com

It is relevant to note here that the destruction of human life from nuclear warfare was anticipated to occur not so much from direct casualties, enormous though these would be, but from the longer-term environmental consequences. A significant proportion of humanity could be also assumed to die eventually from radiation poisoning, and there was much evidence from the fallout from Hiroshima and Nagasaki to confirm this. But even more alarming was the expectation that nuclear warfare could result in a 'nuclear winter'. In a worst-case scenario, scientific modelling showed that global cooling, due to enormous quantities of atmospheric dust and smoke emanating from large-scale nuclear warfare blocking out light and heat from the sun, could eliminate almost all biological life on the planet.

The possibility of nuclear warfare of course remains a serious concern in the contemporary period, but by far the most prominent issue now is climate change induced by global warming. We discuss some of the controversies surrounding these issues in Chapter 11. An important point to be noted here is that these are truly global issues, transcending state boundaries in every sense of the word. Even so, it is states (through their governments) that are expected to implement and enforce specific policies at the local level to effectively address global environmental concerns. This underscores the saying 'think globally, act locally', although it is not suggested here that individuals and non-state actors and institutions do not also have an important role to play. This will become evident when we come to consider the role of social movements in global politics in later chapters.

➡ See **Chapter 11** for further discussion of climate change.

➡ See **Chapter 7** for further discussion of social movements.

Global Political Studies in the Contemporary Period

Since the end of the Cold War in 1989, the study of relations between states, and the ever-present possibility of large-scale interstate warfare, has of course remained a key focus for many scholars, with state security and the 'anarchy thematic' still occupying much conceptual space within the discipline. But the field has opened up to the study of the many different dimensions of politics that go beyond the state, the interactions of state actors, and the problem of anarchy. And so the terms 'world politics' or 'global politics' have been used increasingly to indicate a broader sphere of political interactions and dynamics that include but also transcend states. In other words, whereas the term 'international' refers primarily to relations between state entities encased in national boundaries, 'global' implies a more dynamic, unbounded world in which the role of both state and non-state entities and actors is taken into account. Along with the term 'global politics', we also encounter the terms 'global governance', 'global order', 'global society', 'global security', 'global trade', 'the global environment', and so on, much more frequently in the contemporary period, at least compared with earlier decades when the term 'international' was more commonly used in these pairings.

Even so, there are spheres of politics which transcend the national but to which the term 'global' cannot be readily applied. One of these consists in regional relations which are quite obviously restricted literally to a certain region—for example, to Europe, or southern Africa, or South Asia, or the island Pacific, or Latin America—rather than the global sphere as a whole. Regional relations are, almost by definition, multilateral, and they may or may not involve both state and non-state actors. Either way, their member-ship is not 'global' and their interactions are therefore probably better described in terms of 'international' relations. There is also the sphere of bilateral relations in which virtually all states are engaged—for example, relations between China and Russia, between South Africa and Zimbabwe, between Peru and Spain, between Fiji and Papua New Guinea, or between Mexico and the United States, and so on. Then there are a number of 'special relationships', such as that between the UK and the US. These may also be more accurately described as 'international' relations. All these bilateral interactions, however, take place within the more general sphere of global politics, which therefore remains an appropriate overarching term.

In addition to multilateral regional relations and state-to-state-and bilateral relations as described above, other types of relations fall well short of the 'global'. Examples include what might be called clubs of like-minded states, or states that share certain characteris-tics. The 'Group of 7' or G7, consisting of the UK, the US, Canada, France, Germany, Italy, and Japan, is an organization of states with advanced economies and particular interests in common which meets on an annual basis. Another example is BRICS—a club consist-ing of the emerging economies of Brazil, Russia, India, China, and South Africa. These clubs are forms of international organizations which we discuss further in Chapter 7. The point here is that it is not possible to dispense altogether with terms such as 'international relations' or 'international politics' in describing the interactions of entities which fall short of 'global' membership.

Another grouping of states worth noting here consists in the 'Anglosphere'. This includes, for the most part, Anglophone countries in which a set of common cultures and values predominate, namely Australia, New Zealand, and Canada as well as the UK and the US. These countries, incidentally, constitute a substantial part of 'the West', an entity which also includes other European countries and which may be described in both geopolitical and cultural/civilizational terms. 'The West' appears frequently in discussions of global politics, especially to the extent that it is often seen as exercising **hegemony**, dominating not just the political sphere but also social, cultural, and eco-nomic spheres.

The status of the West, and relations with the 'non-West', raises further issues concern-ing the more traditional notion of IR as a discipline. In recent years, the dominance of the West in constructing the discipline itself has been challenged on intellectual and cultural grounds by a movement seeking to raise the profile of non-Western contributions. The term deployed in this approach is 'global IR'—as explained further by one of its principal proponents in Box 1.1. The term 'Global North' is also frequently used as a substitute for the West, while the term 'Global South' is often used in place of the 'non-West' or 'Third World', especially when discussing development issues and the distribution of wealth and poverty (although the categories can be misleading). The issues raised by the promotion of global IR—along with the West/non-West or Global North/South—are also relevant to the field of postcolonial theory and the 'decolonization of the curriculum' discussed in Chapter 5.

One other objection to the term 'international relations' as applied to the sphere of world political interactions is that it is not actually 'nations' that are formally interact-ing, but rather 'states', as represented by their governments. We look in more detail at the distinction between state and **nation** in Chapter 2. For the time being, we may simply note that the term 'global politics' is useful precisely because it transcends both states and

BOX 1.1 KEY QUOTE

Global IR

The idea of a global IR challenges traditional IR's neglect and marginalization of the voices and experiences of the non-Western world, or the Global South. The principal aim of global IR is to 'bring the Rest in'. It calls for greater participation from scholars from the Global South in the IR discipline and the broadening of the way IR is taught and written in the dominant centres of knowledge in the West. The purpose of global IR is to ensure the transformation of the discipline into something that actually captures and explains the relationships among states and societies in all parts of the world: East, West, North, South. A global IR perspective on IR theory does not seek to displace existing theories but challenges them to broaden their horizons and acknowledge the place and role of the non-Western world.   (Acharya, 2017)

nations and encompasses a variety of entities that contribute to the sphere of relevant interactions in a more holistic sense.

A final point to consider here is the extent to which security issues have, at least since the end of the Cold War, also 'gone global', in contrast with an approach that is limited to conventional interstate military threats. Security, like politics itself, is multifaceted and needs to be conceptualized in terms which transcend the state and state-sponsored forces. Terrorist organizations, for example, present a serious material threat, but they are essentially *non-state* actors and cannot be confronted or contained by conventional military methods alone, or by state agencies alone. They are now widely recognized as a *global* threat requiring a *global* response. One obvious example is the fact that the actions of relatively small but resourceful and determined non-state actors in the form of Al-Qaeda, Boko Haram, Al-Shabab, and Islamic State (IS) (which despite its name and aspirations remains in the non-state category) have reverberated throughout the global system, triggering both major warfare and insurgencies as well as a plethora of changes in the securitization of international travel, financial processes, and many other areas. Of course, state-based agencies are involved in countering terrorism, but coordination on a global scale is often required for an effective response. Other important non-state global actors include transnational corporations as well as a myriad of non-government organizations (NGOs), not to mention criminal organizations of all kinds which engage in many different activities from smuggling (weapons, drugs, people, etc.) to cyber crime (e.g. data theft and espionage). The activities of all these groups tend to transcend state boundaries, contributing to a highly pluralistic global system characterized by multiple overlapping interactions and dynamics.

In addition to security threats in the form of physical violence, whether emanating from state or non-state forces, humans have always faced the most basic challenges in securing the essentials for survival, including sustenance and shelter. Today, food security, water security, health security, and energy security, among others, remain serious concerns for very many people whose access to these most basic of security goods is far from adequate. These basic security needs, along with the overarching issue of global environmental security, are entangled in turn with issues concerning the right to development and the global division of wealth and poverty. We consider all these matters from both empirical and conceptual/theoretical perspectives in more detail in Chapter 6.

GLOBALIZATION PAST AND PRESENT

Although globalization as a historic process may be seen as occurring over a very long period, it became much more prominent as a phenomenon following the end of the Cold War, an event marked by the breakdown of communist rule in Eastern Europe and the collapse of the Soviet Union. The apparent defeat of communism as a viable ideology and political system was, almost inevitably, accompanied by a renewed faith in the power of **capitalism** and **liberal democracy**. It was in this environment that globalization very quickly became a conspicuous theme in public discourses promoting a new paradigm for global order which could transcend the existing state system.

The question of when globalization began to develop historically is not a settled one, but if we were to search for a specific starting point, it may well be when the Atlantic Ocean was crossed by Christopher Columbus in 1492, opening what was, for Europeans, a whole new world and signalling the beginning of centuries of exploration and colonization; or it may be traced to the first circumnavigation of the globe completed in 1521, a feat usually credited to the Portuguese captain Ferdinand Magellan; or to the founding of the city of Manilla in 1571 when Spanish traders inaugurated it as a base for their trans-Pacific galleons. These examples put Europe at the centre of global historical developments, and imply that developments elsewhere are not especially relevant. However, it is just as plausible to claim that the beginnings of globalization may be marked by the establishment of the transcontinental Silk Road which saw the first Chinese goods appear in Europe as early as the first century AD, followed by the European adaptation of Chinese technologies, such as printing and gunpowder. This elevates the role of China in the process and, considering the important role played by South Asian and Middle Eastern merchants whose territories were traversed by the Silk Road, highlights their crucial role as well.

Contributions to ever more extensive relations were made by the establishment of other trans- and intercontinental routes by Islamic empires reaching south into Africa and across to South East Asia. One legacy of this is the fact that many modern states, situated far from the original homeland of the Prophet Muhammad in Saudi Arabia (born AD 571), are predominantly Muslim. Indonesia, for example, is half a world away from Saudi Arabia, but is the largest majority Muslim state in the world with a population of around 260 million people. This also illustrates the extensive spread of cultural values, of which religious beliefs are a subset, in the pre-modern period. All these instances, and many others, could well be included on an historical map of globalization, which would therefore highlight not just the fact of ever wider and denser trade relations but increasing cross-cultural contact as well.

Another major contributing factor was the growth and global spread of the modern European empires—mainly Spanish, Portuguese, British, French, Dutch, and German—which also saw the spread of Christianity and other aspects of European culture and which have contributed to the perceived dominance of the West. In political terms, the European colonial empires eventually gave rise to the globalization of the European state system itself, as we see in Chapter 2. The expansion of the European colonial empires was also accompanied by scientific, industrial, and technological development as well as the rise of capitalism, which, based on private ownership of the means of production, distribution, and exchange, as well as the principles of free trade, was to underpin the dominant global economic system. It is this system which is now taken as characterizing contemporary globalization, although there is much more to the phenomenon in the contemporary period than its economic and financial aspects, as highlighted in Box 1.2.

BOX 1.2 KEY CONCEPT

Globalization

Numerous definitions of globalization appear in the literature, but common themes include the compression of time and space and an observable increase in interdependence, integration, and interconnectedness on a global scale, signalling the development of some kind of global awareness and what might well be dubbed a worldwide 'web of significance'. The material aspects of globalization include flows of capital, goods, services, and people, all facilitated by increasingly sophisticated communications, transport, and financial infrastructure. Thus globalization is a complex process rather than a fixed 'thing', and one that appears to be ongoing. And although there is a tendency to emphasize its economic aspects, globalization is multidimensional in the sense that it embraces political, social, and cultural dynamics as well.

Another important element is **hierarchy**. A globalized world is by no means one in which all actors are equal—some occupy very powerful positions within the global system while others languish at the bottom. This is obviously implicated in the distribution of wealth and poverty mentioned in the opening section, and raises issues of justice and fairness.

The term 'global' also implies not just the crossing of borders but their transcendence and possibly even their erasure. This contrasts with conventional ideas about the concept of the 'international' which denotes a world separated into discrete bounded entities—namely sovereign states or nation-states—with political interaction occurring primarily between those entities.

'Transnationalism' is a closely related term which has come into more common usage in recent years, and is often used as a synonym for globalization. But whereas 'transnationalism' still references 'the national' (and therefore may not take us much further than 'internationalism'), 'globalization' transcends this sphere more comprehensively, at least in its more literal sense.

In the contemporary period, there has been much talk about **deglobalization**. National economic **protectionism** has come to the fore, especially in the US under the Trump administration. There has also been a resurgence of **nationalism** across other parts of the world, with calls for a return to a greater measure of social, cultural, and political insularity. 'Brexit' was driven largely by such factors—not by the prospect of economic gain as Britain will almost certainly suffer a downturn as a result.

(Continued)

The recent Covid-19 pandemic has also brought into focus both positive and negative aspects of globalization. In the short term, it necessarily saw the closure of borders, which limited the movement of not only people but also certain goods, leading to breaks in vital supply chains. Much attention focused on the lack of local production facilities for medical and other supplies, with many calling for the reinvigoration of nationally based manufacturing industries. But the protection of national industries can lead to other problems, not least the fact that goods that were previously produced elsewhere at much less cost become significantly more expensive and therefore out of reach of lower socio-economic groups. Downturns in trade are a key factor in recessions, both nationally and globally. In addition, it seems that global cooperation in some areas is more important than ever, with scientific and medical research teams linking up around the globe to work on producing both an effective vaccine and treatments. And the work of the World Health Organization (WHO), for all that we may find fault with some of its procedures, has become more important than ever.

But the lessons of history seem hard to learn. As one commentary notes, 'During pandemics, societies have often scapegoated individuals, blamed foreigners and put up barriers to the outside world.' The choices concerning the way ahead now seem quite stark. Either 'find a way to harness globalisation to a common purpose, or retreat into **isolationism** and nationalism that will crash the world economy and increase international tensions. In the past, the US was the only country with the political and economic clout to organise a global response. Without strong US leadership, the prospects look much bleaker' (Schifferes, 2020).

How the tensions between globalization and deglobalization play out in the longer term remains to be seen. In the meantime, the phenomenon of globalization has been a key theme in the study of global politics, and will remain so for the foreseeable future.

The Concept of Modernity

It is not possible to examine globalization in historic perspective—or indeed almost any aspect of contemporary global politics—without also looking at least briefly at the concept of **modernity** which is implicated in the exploration of continuity and change in the international system (Shilliam, 2017). The first point to note is that it is partly a temporal notion in the sense that the 'modern period' is seen as coming after earlier epochs which European thought has categorized as 'pre-historic', 'ancient', and 'medieval'. Exact dates marking the transition from one period to another are not possible, but a common assumption is that modernity was emerging by the end of the sixteenth century, although earlier developments contributed to its rise. It is usually associated with certain scientific and technological achievements, intellectual and cultural movements, and economic change—mainly in Europe but with influences from elsewhere. These include:

- the Renaissance, from about 1400 to 1600, during which the 'rebirth' of classical learning and aesthetics from ancient Greece and Rome occurred, along with important inputs from the Arab/Islamic world;
- the Protestant Reformation, which arose in the 1500s and broke up the monopoly over religious matters held by the Catholic Church while introducing concepts of individualism, personal responsibility, and autonomy;
- the emergence and consolidation of ideas about sovereignty and statehood in the seventeenth century in the context of violent contestations between Catholics and Protestants;

- the intellectual movement known as the **Enlightenment** in the eighteenth century, in which traditional authorities were critically questioned and ideas of scientific rationality and secularism promoted;
- the French and American Revolutions, also in the eighteenth century, which, inspired by Enlightenment ideas, again sought to break from traditional authority and promote democratic ideas;
- the **Industrial Revolution**, beginning in the mid-eighteenth century, in which technological development saw the growth of mechanization, factories, and, as a by-product, urbanization;
- the rise of capitalism, which flourished in an age in which liberal ideas about freedom, progress, and individual advancement had challenged traditional orders, and which went hand in hand with industrialization and imperialism.

The rise of modernity encompasses all of the above, and of course goes beyond them in its subsequent development. But if one were simply to note these particular events and developments as constitutive of modernity, and explore no further, one would miss the fact that so many of them—in addition to colonialism—are interconnected not just within Europe but with many other parts of the world. For example, and as noted above, technologies such as gunpowder and printing (among others) were first developed in China while important advances in mathematics, medicine, and chemistry were transmitted from the Arab/Islamic world in the medieval period. Arab scholars were also responsible for preserving, translating, and developing the work of ancient philosophers such as Aristotle, which later became so influential in European/Western philosophy. A detailed study would illuminate many other contributions from the indigenous populations of Africa, South Asia, the Americas, the island Pacific, and so on. What we call modernity, and 'Western civilization' for that matter, therefore owes a great deal to the achievements of people around the world, making it much more 'global' in origin than most may at first suspect.

Another point to note is that contemporary modernity itself may take different forms depending on location. If we did a detailed study of modernity in Japan, Italy, the United Arab Emirates, Malaysia, Sri Lanka, Brazil, Zimbabwe, etc., we would find that it takes different forms. In this case we could talk about multiple modernities (in the plural), rather than a single universal form. It is also common to see modernity, or 'the modern', contrasted with 'the traditional', and sometimes it is difficult to do otherwise. But to set up these categories in such a simple dichotomy can be misleading—just as the dichotomous construction of the West/non-West can be highly problematic. These points raise some quite complex conceptual matters for the study of global politics, some of which we encounter in later chapters. The main point in outlining the concept of modernity here, however, is simply to raise awareness of its constitutive features so that when it is referenced later in this text, or in other readings on global politics, it may more readily be understood.

The Rise of Global Consciousness

Another important aspect of contemporary globalization is increased public awareness of developments on a global scale, facilitated by technological developments such as the proliferation of the Internet—a massive global networking infrastructure. This includes ever-expanding online social media and global news networks communicating news and events, opinions and analysis almost instantaneously. This has enabled the emergence of a global consciousness simply not possible in earlier periods when information could take days, weeks, and even months to circulate. The negative side of this is the 'dark net' used for criminal activities and illicit marketplaces (for drugs, sex workers, paedophiles, and private data and identity theft, among other things), which can only be accessed using special encryption tools. These illicit industries, too, are well and truly globalized.

On an altogether different level, global awareness is an important factor in the extension of concerns beyond the borders of one's own political community and social networks. This is embodied in the concept of **cosmopolitanism**, which incorporates the idea of the 'global citizen'. It therefore emphasizes the notion that we all belong to 'one world' rather than simply one country, and that humanity shares common problems, common interests, and a common fate, all of which transcend particular political communities and their borders. Cosmopolitanism also represents a different *ethical* vision of international order. Rather than limiting one's moral concerns to whatever goes on within the boundaries of one's own state, cosmopolitanism implies a moral concern for the world and its people as a whole. Images of humanitarian disasters around the globe, for example, whether wrought by natural causes or induced by human activity, invariably bring responses in the form of both state-sponsored and private aid and relief efforts to victims of floods, fires, earthquakes, tsunamis, epidemics, social and political violence, and outright warfare, wherever these may occur. Cosmopolitanism also underpins the idea of universal human rights—rights held equally, at least in principal, by every human regardless of their particularities with respect to gender, sexuality, age, religion, ethnicity, nationality, occupation, disability, and so on. These issues are discussed in more detail in Chapter 12.

Cosmopolitanism is often contrasted with **communitarianism** and nationalism. These each have distinctive elements, but both express a much more focused concern with one's own community or national group. This can very often (but not necessarily) take a form which is hostile to other communities or national groups, expressed in an antipathy to foreigners or people who do not share the same ethnicity, language, religion, etc. The latter attitude is more common in the ideology of nationalism, as discussed in Chapter 2. Communitarianism is not exactly the same. It focuses neither on the individual nor on humanity as a whole but sees life as intimately connected with those with whom we share immediate cultural or social bonds, while treating the concept of universally applicable moral values and human rights with suspicion. Elements of both communitarianism and nationalism are therefore at odds with the cosmopolitan approach. Again, these issues are discussed in more detail in Chapter 12, but it is important to introduce the terms here because global politics, as indicated in the opening section of this chapter, involves the distribution and utilization of power and resources on a worldwide basis and these are inevitably accompanied by questions of what is right or wrong, just or unjust, in this distribution.

Globalization, Ideology, and Culture

Another point relevant to the discussion of globalization is that the phenomenon is not simply an objective process that can be described in mechanical terms. Globalization—or more especially **globalism**—is also an ideology, or is at least implicated in the formation of ideologies, and very powerful ones at that (see Box 1.3). In the contemporary period, the economic aspects of globalization are often linked closely to a neoliberal agenda. Certainly, the increasing power of capital and the institutions through which it operates (corporations, banks, and other financial institutions) at a global level appears to be a very

---

BOX 1.3 KEY QUOTE

Globalization as Ideology

[G]lobalization contains important *ideological* aspects in the form of politically charged narratives that put before the public a particular agenda of topics for discussion, questions to ask, claims to make . . . The social forces behind . . . competing accounts of globalization seek to endow this concept with norms, values, and meanings that not only legitimate and advance specific power interests, but also shape the personal and collective identities of billions of people.

(Steger, 2010: p. vii)

---

tangible phenomenon, and one which has tended to dominate discussions of globalization and the global economy. These issues are discussed in Chapter 10.

Globalization has also been discussed extensively in terms of its impact on the cultural dimensions of contemporary social and national life, although this is not unrelated to its economic aspects. The spread of certain products—Coca Cola, Levi's, McDonald's, Starbucks, Nike—and various chain stores which seem to have a presence in modern shopping malls right around the globe, along with the dominance of 'culture industries' such as the Hollywood movie machine and the American pop music industry, have given rise to images of a homogenizing (and largely US-dominated) global culture, linked in turn to the machinery of global capitalist production which is set to obliterate myriad local cultural practices.

Is this a genuine possibility, or a grossly exaggerated scenario? Even if we concede that some sort of 'global culture' is developing, is it necessarily the case that the principal vehicle will be American or 'Western' popular culture? And is it possible to think of 'culture' in other ways, and not just in terms of the commodification of certain goods that can be manufactured, packaged, sold, and consumed? There is certainly much more to culture than this. We can envisage, for example, the development of global cultural norms supportive of human rights, including the rights of women and minority groups. Here some may argue that contemporary norms associated with human rights are also a product of 'Western culture', or a 'Western cosmopolitan outlook', and simply another imposition on non-Western people who may have very different values. On the other hand, while we may concede that many of the norms associated with human rights have their origins in the West, they do have strong resonance elsewhere.

The discussion of human rights in terms of culture also highlights the fact that 'culture' is not a 'thing' to be bought, sold, or used. Nor is it associated simply with music, art, clothing, food, language, religion, and so on, although it may encompass any or all of these things. Culture is, more than anything else, a process through which people organize their group lives, establishing rules and norms of behaviour as well as ways of dealing with the environment in which they find themselves, as discussed further in Chapter 5. At the same time, culture as a process does not just involve discrete groups and interactions within such groups—it is also essential to inter-group relations. If we consider that almost all human groups on the planet are now connected in one way or another, it is clear that a global web of interaction has formed, and is still forming. This is essentially a cultural process and a key aspect of globalization. But meaningful interaction—whether political, social, economic—requires a language of communication, and language is itself a cultural artefact. This raises some interesting issues relating to the dominance of the West and, in particular, of the Anglosphere, as explored in Box 1.4.

BOX 1.4 CASE STUDY

Language and Cultural Hegemony in a Globalized World

Discussions of Western hegemony in a globalized world tend to focus on its political and economic aspects, but there are important cultural issues that need to be considered as well, and of these language is a central component. Membership of the West includes the countries of the Anglosphere in addition to virtually all of Europe. In the latter region, one will find hundreds of different languages still spoken, in addition to the twenty-four 'official languages' of the EU. But it is English that has become effectively globalized as the dominant language of international communication, leaving other widely spoken European languages such as French and Spanish far behind. And, arguably, it is the Anglophone group of countries—the US and the UK in particular—that have achieved a certain cultural dominance in the global sphere.

One example of this dominance is the extent to which the international higher education industry is centred largely around universities in the Anglosphere, with the UK, the US, and Australia leading the field. This may change as numbers in the UK and the US are expected to experience relative decline due to Brexit and President Trump's anti-immigrant stance, with Canada, Australia, and New Zealand (also predominantly Anglophone countries) becoming major beneficiaries.

Universities in other non-English speaking countries that wish to 'internationalize' usually teach at least part of the curriculum in English. It is already established as the medium of instruction in many Indian universities and virtually all African, Pacific, and Caribbean countries with a history of British colonialization. The majority of scientific and technical papers are also published in English. And English is the principal language of international academic conferences, as it is of almost any international professional conference.

The international aviation industry requires competent English to be spoken by all pilots and air traffic controllers. The common language of many international organizations is English. The Association of Southeast Asian Nations (ASEAN), whose membership does not include any Anglophone country, is a prime example. English is also the language of most international sporting associations and events, including the Olympics, although French is technically a second official language. The Fédération Internationale de Football Association (FIFA) has four official languages—English, French, German, and Spanish—but in practice referees use English.

So although English is spoken by fewer than 400 million people as a first language, it is widely spoken as an additional language, especially among educated middle classes. It is therefore difficult to escape the conclusion that the English language is hegemonic in the sense that it dominates the global social and political context. But we should also note that wherever it has been adopted, it has also usually undergone local adaptations, giving rise to much variety in spoken English and very many different colloquial vocabularies and accents.

The dominance of the international higher education industry by the principal Anglosphere countries, as well as the ascendancy of English as a medium of instruction in many non-English-speaking countries, once again raises issues relevant to the development of 'global IR'. It must be noted, however, that Anglophone curricula do not focus only on ideas emanating from the English-speaking world. In traditional IR, the curriculum has long embraced political thought from the ancient Greek and Roman worlds as well as prominent European philosophers from Germany, France, Italy, Denmark, Hungary, and many other countries—some of whom we encounter in the theory chapters. But to date there has been little exploration of ideas from elsewhere, or an appreciation of the fact that the world simply does not look the same from every location around the globe. These matters are closely related to a broader trend in 'decolonizing the curriculum' across the humanities and social sciences in particular—a trend calling for greater representation of non-Western contributions, and challenging often unconscious Eurocentric biases in mainstream ideas, perspectives, and assumptions.

In summary, English is likely to endure as the predominant language of international communication for the foreseeable future, and 'Western culture' more generally will remain a powerful influence around the globe. But other developing trends are likely to bring a more diverse array of cultural forces to bear on global politics and society, and to widen current approaches to research, scholarship, and teaching in the field. Most importantly, greater awareness of the diversity of culturally attuned perspectives highlights the fact that people see and experience the world in different ways according to where they are located in the global system.

KEY POINTS

- Globalization is often seen as a contemporary phenomenon, but its origins stretch back over many centuries of ever-increasing global connections through the extension of trade networks, colonial ventures, and cross-cultural interactions.

- Accounts of globalization tend to emphasize its economic aspects but it embraces a range of complex political, social, and cultural dynamics as well, evident in both historical and contemporary processes, including modernity itself.

- Despite the homogenizing tendencies of globalization, and the hegemonic status of the West, the world remains heterogeneous across all the dimensions noted above.

THEORIES, NORMS, AND METHODS

Although Chapters 3, 4, and 5 will deal with particular theoretical approaches to global politics, it is important to introduce here the role of theory, the different approaches to methods used in the study of global politics, the nature of evidence, and the status of objective knowledge. These issues, which are common across all academic disciplines, have become increasingly important in contemporary political debates about 'fake news', the proliferation of conspiracy theories, and what has been described as a 'post-truth' world.

The first clue to understanding what theory is about may be found in the original Greek term *theoria*, which means contemplation or speculation. In this sense, theory has a strong 'ideational' component, although it certainly has a close relationship to the practical and the material, as set out in Box 1.5. To explain briefly, everything that arises in the world of ideas—including concepts, theories, definitions, etc.—may be described as belonging to the category of the 'ideational'. This is contrasted in turn with the 'material'. In other words, there is a distinction between ideas (which are by definition abstract) and things (material objects). The ideational and the material, however, work together in the social world, and cannot really be separated. For example, the *idea* that we have moral obligations beyond our borders, or that we should act to alleviate humanitarian crises wherever they occur, is essential to the delivery of *material* aid at a practical level.

BOX 1.5 KEY QUOTE

On Theory and Practice

As an intellectual enterprise, theory is often contrasted with action or practice, sometimes in a negative sense as reflected in the rather clichéd stock phrase, 'it's all very well in theory but it doesn't work in practice'. . . . This suggests that theories stand to be tested in light of practice, or in competition with other theories, and succeed, fail, or undergo modification on that basis. Even when theory does fail in some sense, the value of theoretical speculation should never be underestimated. Nor should 'the abstract' be set up in opposition to 'the real', as if they were completely unrelated. While theorizing is indeed a mental process rather than a physical action or event, it is intimately related to practice. It aims to make sense of actions, events, or phenomena in the physical or natural world as well as the social world, of which politics is a significant part. Some go so far as to propose that theories actually create realities. At the very least, thinking generally precedes action and, indeed, we are usually enjoined to think before we act. Whether those thinking processes always result in what we might consider desirable outcomes is another matter.

(Lawson, 2015)

Theory is a vital part of virtually any field of study or branch of knowledge, from the natural sciences through to the humanities and social sciences. In the latter fields, theory is not necessarily testable in the same way that it is in the natural sciences and therefore remains more speculative. But that does not mean that it has no value. In the study of global politics, theory is best conceived as a way of organizing the basic elements of our thinking about the world around us, offering a framework for asking questions about why particular political and social orders are as they are, whether they are just or unjust, and whether it is indeed possible to make the world a better place. We may not get final answers to these questions, or an objective truth about the state of the world we live in, but we cannot even begin to address these questions without some kind of theoretical framework in which the 'facts' of global politics are made sense of.

Issues in Methodology

Theoretical developments also raise important issues of methodology involving the search for objective knowledge on the one hand, and the place of norms and values on the other. The study of politics and society, from ancient times to the present, has always involved different kinds of analyses and methodologies. In both the national and global spheres, political studies are often divided into two distinct fields according to their aims and methods—political science and political philosophy. The latter is concerned primarily with ideas and values, asking questions about what is right and fair, about human freedom, about the role of values, and about rights and obligations. It is therefore strongly normative in its focus not just on how the world is but also on how the world *ought* to be.

Political *science*, on the other hand, is more concerned to elucidate the world *as it is*. It therefore takes as its major task the production of accurate descriptions of the political world based on objective **empirical analysis** of political institutions and practices. The latter approach became more common in the study of both national and global politics following the Second World War, especially in the US where virtually all the social sciences became heavily influenced by the notion that they needed to be more truly 'scientific'. It was therefore necessary to eschew the more normative (and therefore subjective) approaches by adopting methods that were largely quantitative, involving the production of statistical analyses of political practices, trends, policy impacts, voter behaviour, and so on. The knowledge produced by the latter is simply factual, and says little or nothing about values, or what ought to be done in politics. So while a statement of what *ought* to be is described as a *normative* statement, and is by definition value-laden, a statement of what *is* constitutes a *positive* statement and is therefore held to be value free.

Other terms associated with a quantitative approach (which by definition involves statistical data) include behaviouralism—so called because of an emphasis on how people actually behave in politics and society rather than how they ought to behave; and positivism—a term reflecting an ambition to produce a neutral, universally valid, body of positive knowledge about subjects such as politics, usually based on statistical analysis, but going beyond empiricism in seeking to build theories. Positivism therefore aspires to produce knowledge via the same methodology deployed in the natural sciences, including not only the collection of empirical facts but also the formulation and testing of hypotheses, the identification of relevant variables, and the determination of cause and effect which should lead in turn to some measure of predictability in politics.

Critics of positivist approaches tend to preference an *interpretive* approach to the study of politics. Rather than viewing political realities as singular and objective, let alone amenable to quantification, interpretive approaches examine political issues within their social and historical contexts while highlighting the intersubjectivity of human experience. They also tend to use *qualitative* methods including participant observation, interviews, focus groups, and documentary research (e.g. archives, newspapers, websites, etc.).

Here we should note that while normative and interpretive approaches do not develop knowledge via the testing of hypotheses and the accumulation of 'facts' through positivist methodology, they may nonetheless be undertaken as modes of systematic investigation and theory construction based on reasoning and intuition. Thus if 'science' is simply taken to refer to the systematic accumulation of knowledge—and this is in fact its ordinary meaning (from the Latin *scientia*, knowledge)—then normative theory and interpretive methodology, when undertaken in a rigorous, organized manner, may be regarded as no less scientific than theories generated via positivist methods. In any event, the data produced in positivist or quantitative methods always needs to be *interpreted*. After all, facts rarely speak for themselves.

It may seem that empirical and positivist approaches on the one hand, and normative analysis and interpretivism on the other, are quite separate and even at odds with each other, with the former holding itself out as objective while the latter is highly subjective. But this is not necessarily the case. Some approaches to theory and knowledge reject a hard and fast distinction between them, and indeed insist that both are needed in producing useful or meaningful analysis in the field of global politics.

Another point to note is that knowledge produced by positivist methodologies is never completely objective in any event, and the results it produces often reflect the subjective biases of the scientists concerned (whether these are natural or social scientists). There are many examples where bias is fairly obvious—for instance, when scientific studies commissioned by major coal or oil producers show that fossil fuels are *not* implicated in global warming, or when tobacco companies sponsor research to show that smoking does *not* cause cancer.

Even where no vested interest is obvious, it is difficult to maintain that any study in any field is entirely free of subjective biases. Even so, facts, as far as we can ascertain them, are vitally important in providing evidence for important policy choices—climate change and energy policy being obvious areas. But even though the scientific evidence for **anthropogenic** climate change (that is, climate change produced by human activity, and industrialization in particular) appears overwhelming, an influential minority in politics and the media has branded the science of climate change a conspiracy or 'fake news'. And many people believe this to be the case. The politics of climate change will be discussed further in Chapter 11, but for the moment it is worth noting the findings of one researcher that 'attitudes about climate are informed not by an understanding of science but by world views, values, political identification, social and cultural conditioning and gender identity' (Huntley, 2020).

Knowledge and Belief

Why some people believe things that are not true, and for which there is no real evidence, or why they disbelieve something for which there is actual, solid evidence, is an interesting question. It is at least partly because people tend to believe what they want to believe—that is, they will prefer to believe something that reinforces their preconceptions about the world or which favours their sense of identity, their interests, and their preferences. Some will therefore be inclined to (mis)interpret data, select only those 'facts' that fit their preferred schema, and reject anything that contradicts or falsifies it. This is called 'confirmation bias'—a tendency in human thought that has been observed from ancient times through to the present, as reflected in the quote in Box 1.6 by celebrated North African/Arab historian, Ibn Khaldun (1332–1406). Although he lived and wrote almost seven centuries ago, his observations remain compelling in the present period.

Because confirmation bias very often rejects what it might seem more rational to accept (on the basis of evidence), it may be likened to an entirely subjective, emotional response. Certainly, people often get very defensive and angry when their beliefs are challenged. And because emotions are just as important in the dynamics of politics as rationality, if not more important, the study of emotions in politics, including global politics, has become an increasingly important field of study over the past decade or so, bringing in insights from neuroscience and psychology. Studies focusing on subjective feelings of pride, anger, and fear as well as honour, love, and empathy—and much else in between—contend with theories and approaches which see humans as ultimately *rational*

BOX 1.6   KEY QUOTE

Ibn Khaldun on Confirmation Bias

If the soul is impartial in receiving information, it devotes to that information the share of critical investigation the information deserves, and its truth or untruth thus becomes clear. However, if the soul is infected with partisanship for a particular opinion or sect, it accepts without a moment's hesitation the information that is agreeable to it. Prejudice and partisanship obscure the critical faculty and preclude critical investigation. The result is that falsehoods are accepted and transmitted.

(Khaldun, 1969: p. 35)

FIGURE 1.2 **Statue of Ibn Khaldun in Bejaïa, Algeria** MohamedHaddad/Shutterstock.com

actors who deal with the world objectively. Such studies bring the disciplines of neuro-science and psychology into play as well. While we cannot deal with these in a relatively brief introductory textbook, they are certainly worth noting as interesting and important contributions to the field.

Epistemology and Ontology

We now come to two important philosophical terms related to issues of theory and meth-od in global politics—**epistemology** and **ontology**. Epistemology concerns the study of knowledge, of how we know what we know; of what we do not, or cannot, know; of how we can justify claims to knowledge (e.g. through the presentation of evidence); of what is truth and falsehood; and so on. Those subscribing to a positivist epistemology will claim that objective, value-free, positive knowledge is possible within both the natural and social sciences, at least if a proper scientific method is followed. Others may insist that objec-tive knowledge is unattainable in any sphere—a position often called 'postpositivist'. Does this mean that we live in a 'post-truth world' of conspiracy theories and fake news where facts count for little and we are guided less by reason than by passions, prejudices, and emotions? (see Box 1.7).

Finally, we come to ontology—a branch of **metaphysics** concerned with the nature of existence or being. It may seem logical that we can only have knowledge of something that actually *exists*; that constitutes a reality in some material sense of the term. But reality itself

---

BOX 1.7 KEY DEBATE

Do We Live in a Post-Truth World?

Debates over the extent to which expert evidence, statistics, and factual narratives embody an objective truth, or at least something close to it, has come under much scrutiny in recent decades. This has led some to declare that we live in a 'post-truth' world in which appeals to emotion and prejudice prevail over appeals to 'the facts'. This tendency aligns with all kinds of conspiracy theories, some more bizarre than others. The more fantastic include: that the world is, in reality, ruled by alien reptiles disguised as humans; that NASA faked the moon landing; that Barack Obama was born in Kenya (and that he's secretly a Muslim); and that the 5G network is responsible for spreading the COVID-19 virus. Former Soviet dictator Joseph Stalin encouraged a belief that Adolf Hitler had survived the Second World War and remained a threat.

Conspiracy theories, focusing mainly on sinister foreign operations, have been rife in Russia throughout the Putin era, while in China a popular belief is that genetically modified organisms (GMOs) are part of a Western plot to control China's food supply as well as to cause cancer. Various 'deep state' theories have emerged in authoritarian states such as Turkey and Pakistan where shadowy figures are accused of undermining the government. In the contemporary US, 'deep state' operatives in the FBI, the CIA, and the Department of Justice allegedly provide cover-ups of the nefarious activities of Democrats, in particular, and were encouraged by former President Trump himself. It is also interesting to note that those who believe in such conspiracy theories are also more inclined to be climate change deniers.

Of course, there are such things as conspiracies. It is quite clear that the attacks of '9/11' were the result of a highly successful conspiracy—and all the available evidence points to Al-Qaeda operatives. But a conspiracy *theory* is another thing altogether. The latter, which is almost always designed to cast doubt on factual, mainstream accounts or explanations of important events, is generally based on no real evidence, or a complete distortion of evidence. People who subscribe to conspiracy theories often think they are more 'clever' than regular chumps around them because they have access to privileged knowledge or think they possess superior insights. The sad truth is that they are usually the real chumps.

Another perspective on truth and falsehood worth mentioning here has been provided by the German/American philosopher Hannah Arendt whose famous work on *The Origins of Totalitarianism* had this to say: 'The ideal subject of totalitarian rule is not the convinced Nazi or the convinced Communist, but people for whom the distinction between fact and fiction (i.e., the reality of experience) and the distinction between true and false (i.e., the standards of thought) no longer exist' (Arendt, 1968: p. 172).

Serious social scientists, and indeed serious academic studies of any kind, have a great deal of respect for evidence, even while warning that we are advised never to take things at face value, and to interrogate the facts as presented to us by our governments, our fellow academics, the media, and so on. Sometimes 'news' is indeed fake or at least has a heavy 'spin' on it that makes facts speak in particular ways to particular audiences. And conspiracies do indeed exist. This may leave us to wonder:

1 Is there any such thing as a solid truth?

2 What does genuine evidence consist of?

3 How can we muster reliable facts about the world?

4 What constitutes genuine 'knowledge'?

FIGURE 1.3 **Hannah Arendt** dpa picture alliance/Alamy Stock Photo

is not so straightforward. Realities exist not simply as sets of objects or things that have a material form and can therefore be seen or touched. Identities, for example, are ideational, but they *exist*. And they can be extraordinarily powerful politically, as exemplified by national/nationalist identities, gender identities, class identities, ethnic identities, and linguistic identities, among others. There has also been increasing interest in the concept of 'ontological security' through which scholars have explored, among other things the consequences of collective trauma in situations of ethnic or religious-based violence, forced migration, asylum-seeking, and so on (see Kinvall and Mitzen, 2017: p. 3).

- Theorizing about global politics is essentially an ideational exercise but it is inextricably related to the material and practical aspects of the subject matter and provides a means through which the facts of global politics can be organized and interpreted.
- Positivist and normative approaches often appear to be at odds, but both are important in the analysis of global politics and they can complement each other.
- The idea of a 'post-truth' world has achieved prominence in recent times, raising many questions about the relationship between objectivity and subjectivity, the role of emotions, the nature of evidence, the status of genuine knowledge, and so on.

CONCLUSION

This chapter has sought to provide a broad overview of global politics as a specialized field of study. This field has been more conventionally known as International Relations or IR, although many scholars now see this as denoting a rather state-centric approach to the subject matter. The term 'global' is clearly more expansive, transcending the state and encompassing a wider range of phenomena and actors that seems more appropriate to the contemporary period. Even so, the state remains a key actor, and relations between states (or their governments) are an important focus. Further, because 'IR' is still commonly used to designate the discipline, it will sometimes be used interchangeably with 'global politics' in this book. It is also worth emphasizing that although we can distinguish the national or domestic sphere of politics from the international or global, and identify certain distinguishing dynamics within each sphere, they cannot be treated as completely separate. The interactions between these spheres constitute in fact a vital element of global political studies. Also of note is the term 'global IR'—which may seem an odd combination of terms. But 'global IR' has acquired its own resonance in seeking to encompass more fully the range of global political actors outside the West and to account for their concerns and contributions.

The overview of globalization provided in this chapter has also introduced a variety of issues of historic and contemporary importance, including the rise of modernity, the emergence of the European empires, the development of 'global awareness' and a cosmopolitan outlook, and some aspects of the role of culture in global politics. Once again, we have noted the hegemony of the West and, in terms of language at least, the role of the 'Anglosphere'. The final section on theories, norms, and methods has introduced some basic issues underlying approaches to knowledge and interpretation in politics generally and some contemporary concerns about politics in a 'post-truth' world. This raises questions concerning the critical intellectual skills needed to face future challenges in the study of the global political sphere. It is the aim of this book to encourage the development of such skills.

KEY QUESTIONS

1 In what sense does the study of 'global politics' go beyond traditional IR in accounting for the role of non-state actors and processes?

2 How does the idea of a 'global IR' challenge Eurocentrism in the study of global politics?

3 What are some of the ideational aspects of globalization?

4   What is the relationship between modernity and globalization?

5   How important is the role of culture in globalization?

6   Is globalization really the defining condition of our time?

7   Why are theory and method so important to the study of global politics?

8   Is it possible to obtain objective truths about the state of global politics?

FURTHER READING

Axford, Barry (2013), *Theories of Globalization* (Cambridge: Polity Press).
> Provides a wide-ranging, critical introduction to a complex topic from a variety of disciplinary perspectives as well as raising issues and themes such as governance, democracy, intervention, and empire.

Darian-Smith, Eve and Philip C. McCarty (2017), *The Global Turn: Theories, Research Designs, and Methods for Global Studies* (Oakland, CA: University of California Press).
> An interdisciplinary approach to theory and method in global studies generally which also seeks to 'de-centre' Eurocentric approaches.

Erikson, Thomas Hylland (2014), *Globalization: The Key Concepts* (London: Bloomsbury Academic, 2nd edn).
> Outlines the principal debates and controversies surrounding globalization, providing an anthropological perspective on the subject matter which looks at the phenomenon both 'from above' as well as 'from below'.

Holslag, Jonathan (2018), *A Political History of the World: Three Thousand Years of War and Peace* (London: Penguin).
> Offers a very broad overview of the various factors underlying the causes of war and the quest for peace. Examples range from ancient Egypt and Rome to China, the Middle East, the USA, and Europe.

Lamb, Peter and Fiona Robertson-Snape (2017), *Historical Dictionary of International Relations* (Lanham, MD: Rowman & Littlefield).
> Provides a general guide to theory and practice in relations between states, and between states and other actors on the world stage. A number of key thinkers are also discussed.

McIntyre, Lee (2018), *Post-Truth* (Cambridge, MA: MIT Press).
> There are many new books on the phenomenon of post-truth, fake news, and science denial. This is one of the more scholarly accounts.

WEB LINKS

http://www.history.ac.uk/resources/e-journal-international-history
> This free electronic journal 'aims to promote an understanding of the breadth, depth and policy relevance of international history by examining how the politics, societies, economies and traditions of countries have shaped and influenced international relations since circa 1500'.

http://www.globalization101.org
> This website is maintained by the Levin Institute of the State University of New York and 'is dedicated to providing students with information and interdisciplinary learning opportunities on this complex phenomenon'.

https://www.e-ir.info/
> E-International Relations is a reputable open access website for students and scholars of international politics where you will find blogs, articles, and books on all aspects of global politics.

http://libguides.fhda.edu/c.php?g=597101&p=4132590
> This is a website put up by De Anza College which provides a list of reliable fact-checking sites that can help us to distinguish factual information from misinformation, half-truths, and outright lies.

 For additional material and resources please visit the **online resources** at: www.oup.com/he/lawson1e.

2

STATES, NATIONS, AND EMPIRES

- States and Nations in Contemporary Global Politics
- States and Empires in Global History
- Modernity and the State System
- The Globalization of the State System
- Conclusion

Reader's Guide

This chapter provides an overview of what is often regarded as the central institution, not only of domestic or national political order but also of current international or global order—the state. Alongside the state, we must also consider the idea of the nation and the ideology of nationalism—perhaps the most powerful political ideology to emerge in the modern world. States understood in terms of political communities have existed since humans began to establish settled communities and an appreciation of their long-standing history leads to a more nuanced analysis than one focusing simply on the modern sovereign state and its European origins. There is, however, another form of international political order that has actually been far more common throughout history, and that is empire. Indeed, empires have emerged on almost every continent and due attention to these once again affords a deeper understanding of the phenomenon. With the rise of modernity from around the beginning of the seventeenth century, we also encounter the rise of the modern state and state system in Europe along with ideas about sovereignty, citizenship, the nation-state, and democracy. The discussion moves on to the effective globalization of the European state system through modern imperialism and colonialism and the extent to which these have been productive of contemporary global order. Against this background, in the final section we consider challenges to the state and state system under conditions of globalization as well as the resilience of nationalist ideology and important manifestations of nationalism, populism, and anti-globalization in the present period. The concepts, ideas, and developments dealt with in this chapter also provide a basis for approaching some of the more theoretical aspects of global politics covered in the next three chapters.

STATES AND NATIONS IN CONTEMPORARY GLOBAL POLITICS

The terms 'state' and 'nation' are often used synonymously or joined together to produce 'nation-state', but they refer to two distinct entities. By itself, the 'state' is given several different dictionary meanings. But for present purposes, the 'state' refers to a distinctive political community that has its own set of formal rules and practices and which is more or less separate from other such communities. The state is therefore virtually synonymous with the structure of rule and authority, and the institutions which regulate these within a particular geographical space. In the global sphere, 'the state' refers specifically to the modern sovereign state which is recognized as possessing certain rights and duties. This kind of state is distinct from the states that generally make up a **federal system**, such as the individual states of which the United *States* of America is composed—or of India, Malaysia, Nigeria, South Africa, Germany, Russia, Canada, or Australia, and others which are also federal systems.

The sovereign state has been given a clear legal definition by the 1933 Montevideo Convention on the Rights and Duties of States. Of the sixteen articles adopted in this convention, the most important are the first eleven, and of these, Article 1 provides the most succinct understanding of the criteria for a modern sovereign state, namely: *a permanent population; a defined territory and a government capable of maintaining effective control over its territory: the capacity to conduct international relations with other states.*

A particularly important provision highlighting the sovereign aspect of international statehood is Article 8, which asserts the right of states not to suffer **intervention** by any other state. Article 10 emphasizes the conservation of peace as constituting the primary *interest* of all states. Article 11 reinforces both these messages in no uncertain terms (Box 2.1). Thus the state in global politics is envisaged as a *formally constituted, sovereign political structure encompassing people, territory, and institutions.* As such, a state interacts with similarly constituted structures in an international system of states which, ideally, is characterized by peaceful, non-coercive relations, thus establishing a similarly peaceful international order conducive to the prosperity of all. One might well say, if only it was so! The last century saw horrific manifestations of large-scale interstate war, putting paid to the notion that a sovereign state system would guarantee peace.

On the other hand, interstate warfare has been on the decline with most large-scale violent conflicts now taking the form of civil wars. The latter, however, very often involve

---

BOX 2.1

Article 11, Montevideo Convention on the Rights and Duties of States, 1933

The contracting states definitely establish as the rule of their conduct the precise obligation not to recognize territorial acquisitions or special advantages which have been obtained by force whether this consists in the employment of arms, in threatening diplomatic representations, or in any other effective coercive measure. The territory of a state is inviolable and may not be the object of military occupation nor of other measures of force imposed by another state directly or indirectly or for any motive whatever even temporarily (https://www.jus.uio.no/english/services/library/treaties/01/1-02/rights-duties-states.xml).

other states as well. A notable example in the present period is the Syrian civil war which started in 2011 and in which Russia and Iran have supported the government of President Bashar al-Assad while the US and various other state actors including Turkey, France, and Saudi Arabia have intervened as well.

The Nation as 'a People'

We look in more detail at the historic emergence of the state in a later section, but for now let us consider the nation, a term which refers specifically to 'a people' rather than a formal, territorial entity. The idea of the nation as we understand it today developed largely in the modern era. Indeed, its origins lie in the same state-building dynamics that emerged in post-Westphalian Europe, discussed shortly, as well as in emergent ideas about democracy. Some of the ideas surrounding the French Revolution of 1789 were especially important. The democratic impulse of the revolution required a distinct body of people—citizens—to constitute *a sovereign people* and it is this body which came to be conceptualized as 'the nation'. Although the record of democratic development in Europe remained very patchy until quite recent times, the idea of the nation caught on rapidly. The subsequent development of the modern state and state system brought together the three prime characteristics of the modern state—*sovereignty, territoriality*, and *nationality*.

The term 'nation' derives etymologically from the Latin *natio*, literally 'birth' or 'to be born', from which the words 'native', 'nativist', 'nativity' also derive. It refers specifically to 'a people' rather than a formal, territorial entity or structure of authority, although there are certainly territorial associations. There is no widely agreed definition of what constitutes 'a people' or 'nation' beyond the fact that it denotes an entity that claims a collective identity, usually grounded in a notion of shared history (preferably a long and glorious one) and a shared culture which may include language and religion, art and artefacts. One influential formulation of the nation has been provided by Benedict Anderson who describes it as an 'imagined community', as set out in Box 2.2.

BOX 2.2 KEY QUOTE

Benedict Anderson on the Nation as an 'Imagined Community'

[The nation] is *imagined* because the members of even the smallest nation will never know most of their fellow-members, meet them, or even hear of them, yet in the minds of each lives the image of their communion. . . .

The nation is imagined as *limited* because even the largest of them encompassing perhaps a billion living human beings, has finite, if elastic boundaries, beyond which lie other nations. No nation imagines itself coterminous with mankind. . . .

It is imagined as *sovereign* because the concept was born in an age in which Enlightenment and Revolution were destroying the legitimacy of the divinely-ordained, hierarchical dynastic realm. . . . [N]ations dream of being free . . . The gage and emblem of this freedom is the sovereign state. . . .

Finally, it is imagined as a *community*, because, regardless of the actual inequality and exploitation that may prevail in each, the nation is always conceived as a deep, horizontal comradeship. Ultimately it is this fraternity that makes it possible, over the past two centuries, for so many millions of people, not so much to kill, as willingly to die for such limited imaginings.

(Anderson, 2006: pp. 6–7)

Nationalism as an ideology generally supports the claim that each nation is entitled, in principle, to enjoy political autonomy within a sovereign state of its own. Since the early twentieth century, this has been based largely on the apparently democratic principle of national **self-determination**. Nationalism also entails principles of inclusion and exclusion. Some conceptions of the nation based on civic and liberal ideals are more pluralistic than others, allowing it to embrace diverse elements. More conservative right-wing versions, however, may seek the exclusion of alien elements from an existing state to safeguard the 'authenticity' of its national character. Perceptions of national identity based on religion, language, skin colour, or some other ethnic or cultural factor come into play here, and are often implicated in debates about immigration and border protection, discussed further below. In economic terms, nationalism also stands opposed to some of the principal elements of globalization which favour more open borders for the movement of goods and services, as discussed in Chapter 10.

Nationalism and Territoriality

Spokespeople for a nation often claim that it has a very long and continuous history, usually in association with a particular territory. As the quotes in Box 2.3 indicate, a link to a specific ancestral territory is also a key element in defining the nation, providing it with a spatial foundation and legitimate locale while also specifying the boundaries between one's own nation and others. To designate it as ancestral is to give it a historic dimension which strengthens the legitimacy of the territorial claim. *Political* control of a specified territory linked in turn to a specified people is what constitutes a 'nation-state'. This is the ideal that lies at the heart of the ideology of nationalism. In the process of asserting claims to territory, therefore, nationalist movements place particular interpretations on spaces or places—interpretations which serve to legitimate claims not just to ownership in an ordinary sense but to sovereignty in terms of establishing political power and control over the territory in question.

The focus on territory invites consideration of the contributions of political geography with respect to how 'landscapes of power' are constructed in the context of nationalism. Landscapes of power involve, among other things, landscapes of control, especially over national frontiers. These are often marked by barriers in the form of walls or fences and sometimes by militarized spaces such as minefields. In virtually all cases, there will at least be checkpoints controlling entry and exit (see, generally, Jones, Jones, and Woods, 2004). The Great Wall of China is one notable historic example of a structure designed to keep out menaces from the north. Sometimes, however, the barriers are designed to keep people in rather than out. The

---

BOX 2.3

The Territorial Dimensions of Nationalism

Whatever else it may be, nationalism is always a struggle for control of land; whatever else the nation may be, it is nothing if not a mode of constructing and interpreting social space.

(Williams and Smith, 1983: p. 502)

The nation's unique history is embodied in the nation's unique piece of territory—its 'homeland', the primeval land of its ancestors, older than any state, the same land which saw its greatest moments . . . time has passed but [it] is still there. (Anderson, 2015: p. 24)

FIGURE 2.1 Great Wall of China fotohunter/Shutterstock.com

infamous Berlin Wall, which divided Germany throughout much of the post-Second World War period, is one such example, and its breach in 1989 still stands as the symbolic moment of the end of the Cold War. But even as some walls come down, others go up.

The best-known contemporary example of an attempt to build a massive wall of exclusion is US President Trump's call for a barrier of nearly 2,000 miles between the US and Mexico. 'Border security' is also now a stock phrase of politicians in contemporary Australia where asylum seekers attempting to arrive by boat have been intercepted and incarcerated in offshore facilities and held for years. 'Brexit' was at least partly about stemming the flow of foreigners onto British soil. While it would be wrong to brand all or even most of those favouring the departure of Britain from the EU as motivated primarily by racist attitudes, given a range of other factors involved, aspects of the Brexit experience highlight a link between **racism** and nationalism, which we consider next.

Nationalism and Racism

If a 'nation' is assumed to be synonymous with 'a people' who share certain characteristics, including not simply a common set of cultural practices but also common biological descent and relatedness, then it shares some conceptual ground with the idea of 'race'. We deal with issues of race and racism in more detail in Chapter 5, but given some of the associations of nationalism with racism, it is important to consider certain aspects of the phenomenon here. This is especially so given the extent to which 'white nationalism' appears to have been on the rise in recent times, as illustrated Box 2.4, and has implications for migration, citizenship, and refugees in the global system.

A World of Multinational States

However defined, 'nations' are assumed to populate sovereign states and are very often described in singular terms. The state of France, for example, is occupied by a singular 'French nation', Japan by the 'Japanese nation', Turkey by the 'Turkish nation', and so on. These examples indicate the commonly accepted conflation of state and people that produces the familiar term 'nation-state', which again reflects the principle of national

BOX 2.4 CASE STUDY

'White Nationalism'

The most notorious historic example of the relationship between nationalism and racism is provided by Nazi Germany where notions of white (Aryan) racial supremacy led, during the Second World War, to the extermination of millions of people considered racially inferior. Jewish people were particular targets but other non-Aryan 'races', including Gypsies or Roma, along with homosexuals, were subject to elimination as well.

Another historic example is the system of apartheid practised in South Africa between 1948 and 1994 which entailed the political, social, and economic subordination of the majority black African population and other non-white minorities. The history of slavery and of the denial of civil rights in the US, along with the fate of indigenous populations in white settler colonies, including Australia and New Zealand, provide further examples.

Attitudes of racial superiority underpinning such practices are manifest in contemporary expressions of white nationalism and are linked directly to 'hate crimes'. Extreme right-wing versions of nationalism have been evident among some pro-Brexit factions in Britain, accompanied by a steep rise in 'race hate crime' following the Brexit referendum (*Independent*, 2016), lending credence to the association between nationalism and racism.

Milder forms of nationalism may also seek the exclusion of alien elements from an existing state, allegedly to safeguard its national character and identity. These can also play into fears that immigrants pose a danger to physical security as well.

The latter issues were especially prominent in US President Trump's policies on immigration and related issues. Trump consistently portrayed Muslims and Mexicans, in particular, as posing a security threat, linking the former to terrorism and the latter to drugs, rape, and other crimes. Trump's opponents claim that this led to a rise in hate crimes, including a massacre in El Paso, Texas, on the border with Mexico in which twenty-two people died and another twenty-four were wounded in August 2019.

While many terror attacks have been linked to Islamist extremism (with most incidents actually occurring in Africa, the Middle East, and South Asia), 'white nationalism', a far-right ideology based on a belief in the superiority of a Christian/Caucasian heritage, also poses a significant danger in Western countries.

Violent 'hate' attacks by white nationalists may target not just migrants but other minority groups within the state, or simply those opposed to their ideology. Notorious incidents include a massacre in Norway in July 2011 when a white nationalist killed eighty-five people and injured over a hundred more (mostly other white Norwegians), while in New Zealand, in March 2019, fifty people worshipping at a mosque in March 2019 were killed by a white nationalist from Australia.

A report released in January 2019 showed that from 2009 to 2018, right-wing extremists were responsible for 73 per cent of 'hate' killings in the US, compared with 23 per cent for Islamists and 3 per cent for left-wing extremists. 'In other words, most terrorist attacks in the United States, and most deaths from terrorist attacks, are caused by white extremists' (Serwer, 2019).

While the examples introduced above show the very significant dangers posed by an extensive history of white nationalism around the world, we must nonetheless recognize that it is not the only form of nationalism based on the denigration and exclusion of others who are considered inferior in some way. The treatment of the minority Rohingya Muslim population of contemporary Myanmar, which is distinguished on the basis of a darker skin colour as well as along religious lines (Myanmar has a majority Buddhist population), provides another example. More than three quarters of a million Rohingya have been driven from Mynamar into neighbouring Bangladesh since 2016. Violence against Rohingya by the Myanmar military includes mass sexual violence against women and girls.

All these examples illustrate extreme versions of nationalist ideology informed by racial prejudice and hatred and legitimating acts of gross political violence.

self-determination. However, only a moment's critical reflection is needed to recognize that the matching of state and nation is seldom so neat and unproblematic. Rather, it is an ideal that has rarely, if ever, been achieved. There is virtually no state in the world encompassing a single homogeneous nation. The 'French nation' is an historic amalgam of numerous groups, many speaking different languages. Japan is often described as a 'pure' nation-state but it has an indigenous minority—the Ainu—and also encompasses the people of Okinawa who consider themselves distinct from mainstream Japanese. Turkey is home to a substantial minority of Kurds who also claim nationhood as a people, and who have sought political recognition for many years—as do Kurds in other parts of the Middle East. Kurds are in fact a prime case of 'a nation without a state'.

Many states are made up of two or more 'nations'. The contemporary British state, for example, is comprised of recognized substate national entities: the Welsh, Scots, English, Northern Irish, and Cornish. In 2014, the Scottish 'nation' voted on whether or not to establish Scotland as a sovereign state, failing by just under 6 per cent. But all the national subgroups within the UK are multilayered, especially since immigration over the centuries has brought dozens of different 'nationalities' to the British Isles, thereby producing the 'multicultural' and indeed 'multinational' Britain of the contemporary period.

A close inspection of other national entities in Europe will show similar stories. And what started out as British settler colonies, which are a legacy of modern empire and of mass migration—both aspects of globalization—are now among the most 'multinational' in the world today—the US, Canada, Australia, and New Zealand in particular. But if we look to places like Nigeria, India, and China, it is also evident that these states are made up of many different groups speaking different local languages and possessing different cultural practices. Even relatively small states can be incredibly diverse. Papua New Guinea, for example, has a population of just over 6 million, yet there are more than 850 different languages spoken and each language group could theoretically consider itself to be 'a nation'. It is often because of such diversity that states like Papua New Guinea are considered to be 'weak states' or 'fragile states'. On the other hand, Somalia, often considered a classic example of a 'failed state', is relatively culturally homogeneous but social order, to the extent that it exists, has been extremely fractious.

Although most states are acknowledged as containing many more than one nation, the identity of the state will to some extent be equated with a dominant majority. Thus in the US, Canada, Australia, and New Zealand, for example, a dominant white English-speaking majority constitutes a mainstream. In China, the category of 'Han Chinese' constitutes more than 90 per cent of the population, although these speak numerous different dialects and are therefore scarcely homogeneous. China also encompasses Tibet and the Tibetans, who are clearly distinct from the dominant majority, as are the Uigar people of the north-western Xinjiang region. Both areas have given rise to secession or independence movements which have been heavily suppressed by the Chinese state. In other cases, secessionist movements, usually based on a claim by a minority to a distinct nation-hood that can be properly accommodated only by the establishment of a sovereign state of its own, have led to civil wars or insurgencies. Although such conflicts are technically *intra*state, they invariably have significant repercussions in the global sphere, from the generation of large numbers of asylum seekers to the fuelling of illicit trade in weapons.

This brief discussion of the basic distinctions between 'state' and 'nation'—and some of the political dynamics associated with the relationship between the two entities—provides some indication of how simple terms attempt to capture complex realities. It also high-lights how modern sovereign states are often seen as constituted through and by a 'nation'. Sometimes these nations claim a very long and continuous history, usually in association with a particular territory. Other nations have been much more recently 'constructed' and are sometimes described as 'artificial' for that reason. The contemporary 'Australian nation', for example, may be seen as a construct with its origins in the relatively recent past—that is, from the beginning of British settlement in 1788, although it also encom-passes indigenous Australians whose ancestors have occupied the land for up to 60,000 years as well as more recent immigrants from all around the world.

Whatever their historic status and the manner of their formation, nations are seen as integral to, and indeed constitutive of, the modern state. The term 'nation-state' is there-fore likely to endure as a category in global political order for the foreseeable future, even though the constitution of particular nations and the political claims made in their name remain deeply contested.

KEY POINTS

- The terms 'state' and 'nation' tend to be used synonymously but are distinct entities.
- The 'nation' in a 'nation-state' is often assumed to be homogeneous in terms of culture or ethnicity but this is rarely the case.
- The relationship between 'state' and 'nation' is complex and often gives rise to deep politi-cal contestation including race-based versions of nationalism.

STATES AND EMPIRES IN GLOBAL HISTORY

Global history is an important adjunct to the study of contemporary global politics, bring-ing depth to the understanding of how any given historical moment, including our own, has been shaped by broad-scale transformations occurring over substantial periods of time. This section provides at least a brief account of key developments in earlier periods, includ-ing those that occurred outside Europe and the West more generally. This highlights the fact that although the latter have dominated the modern era to date, developments in other parts of the world are equally important. A global history approach therefore helps to modify the tendency to Eurocentrism evident in conventional accounts of the global political system.

In this section we consider in particular the variation in state forms and the phenome-non of empire throughout history. This illustrates that international systems are highly vari-able and that the sovereign state system with which we are familiar today may very well be replaced by a different kind of system at some point in the future. Certainly, proponents of

globalism believe that a transformation is under way in which state boundaries and controls will become increasingly meaningless. Others believe that we are entering a new era of empire, although there are differing views as to where its principal centre of power may lie. Yet others seek to reinforce the existing state system and its boundaries, emphasizing the importance of 'the nation', its integrity, and indeed its security. As mentioned above, this has been especially noticeable in recent debates about immigration in Britain and some other European countries as well as in the US and Australia where conservative politicians and their supporters have tended to portray migrants as a security threat, as discussed in Chapter 6.

Note that in this section I use the term *international* system when referring to phenomena that are not truly global. For example, empires throughout history may be described as a form of 'international' system in the sense that they encompass different states (and/or nations), but empires are not generally 'global' in the sense that they gather in all such entities around the world under a single centre of power. Whether a true 'global empire' is ever likely to come about is another question.

Let us begin with the concept of the state understood simply as a political community. The earliest of these date more or less from the time that human groups first developed settled agricultural and/or animal husbandry practices about 8,000–10,000 years ago. These required an ongoing association with a particular part of the earth's surface as well as a way of organizing the people and their resources and generally protecting themselves. As we have seen, the definition of the modern state includes a relationship between a permanent population and a certain defined territory. This part of the definition can therefore be extended back in time to cover numerous historic cases without running too much risk of anachronism.

Having said that, there have also been 'stateless societies' throughout history—typically those with a nomadic lifestyle which have therefore lacked the same fixed attachment to, or control over, a particular territory. But there have also been small settled societies lacking in a central authority or hierarchy, and these sometimes existed alongside more hierarchical formations. In pre-colonial Nigeria, for example, some Igbo people lived in small, autonomous villages without hereditary chiefs but rather with a council of elders assisted by a headman chosen by them. The neighbouring Yoruba, on the other hand, were highly centralized and hierarchical (Mentan, 2010: p. 23). Both are now largely encompassed within the modern state of Nigeria (with some also in neighbouring states), itself a product of European imperial state-making, which we come to shortly. The formation of states, incidentally, has also given rise to 'state systems' or 'international orders' which denote the ways in which political communities have systematically organized their relations with other such communities either in their immediate geographical area or further afield.

Historical Antecedents of Statehood and International Orders

Since the study of global politics is, by and large, based on a discipline that has developed largely in the West, it is scarcely surprising that the historical antecedents of statehood and international orders have been sought in the 'cradle of Western civilization'—that is, the eastern Mediterranean region where the ancient Greek and Roman civilizations flourished from about the eighth century BC. These, however, had close connections with the civilizations of northern Africa and the Near East, and both Greece and Rome drew on the rich sources of knowledge and aspects of cultural practices from both regions. In turn, the communities of northern Africa and the Near East were connected to other communities, and so processes of cross-cultural learning, including political practices, were transmitted from much further afield as well.

The form of the state in ancient Greece was the *polis*, often translated as 'city-state', although that is not its exact literal meaning. The *polis* consisted in a body of citizens along with its customs and laws—the political community—as well as both an urban centre (city) and the surrounding rural or agricultural territory. The largest and best known was the Athenian *polis*—also often referred to as providing the archetypal model of classical democracy. The political philosophy of certain leading thinkers who gathered in Athens—many of whom did not actually favour democracy—has also underpinned much subsequent political theory concerning the nature and purposes of the state. Aristotle (385–323 BC), for example, saw the *polis* or state as the *natural* habitat for humans rather than an artificial construct separating them *from* nature. When he famously described 'man' as a *zōon politikon* (political animal) he did not mean that humans were naturally scheming, devious creatures, as the term is often taken to imply. Rather, he meant that the human is a creature designed *by nature* to live in a *polis* (Aristotle, 1981: bk 3).

Athens for a time also headed another important form of political organization, an empire, although the best known of these in the ancient world is undoubtedly the Roman Empire which can be dated from around the third century BC until the second half of the fifth century AD. Developments in Rome are important to the historical growth of the West, especially in relation to theories of republicanism as well as the legal system of parts of Europe. It is also partly due to the Roman Empire that Christianity became firmly established in Europe, a development with significant consequences for the subsequent development of political ideas and practices.

In considering empire as a form of international system, it is important to note that, like states, empires have existed at various times throughout most of the world and have taken different forms. What they tend to share in common is the fact that they are relatively large-scale political entities made up of a number of smaller political communities (generally states) with a central controlling power. Empires are therefore hierarchical and are usually held together by force. Some states may also be held together by force, but it is more characteristic of empires. And although empires constitute a kind of international

FIGURE 2.2 **The Acropolis of Athens** milosk50/Shutterstock.com

order, this is quite different from the current international state system, underpinned as it is by a theory of sovereign equality among its constituent members. In contrast, empires are characterized by formal relations of domination and subordination. The brief tour of historical empires set out in Box 2.5 also gives a better sense of the diversity of our world and the fact that not everything of historical significance happened in Europe.

Modern Imperialism

While most historical empires have left important legacies of one kind or another, those which have had the most profound impact on the structure of the present international system and the nature of contemporary global order are the modern European empires. The largest and most powerful of these was the British Empire, although it had other rivals in Europe. France, Spain, Portugal, Holland, Denmark, Belgium, Italy, and Germany were all colonizing powers at one time or another, but none acquired the same power and influence as the British.

BOX 2.5   CASE STUDY

Empires in Global History

The earliest known empires were situated around the river systems of the Tigris, Euphrates, and the Nile, their geographical location suggesting a certain correlation between the conditions required for successful agriculture and the establishment of settled political communities with extensive networks of relations between them. This broad region saw the rise of the Sumerian, Egyptian, Babylonian, Assyrian, and Persian Empires between about 4,000 BC and 400 BC. The methods of domination used by the controlling powers of these empires varied from direct control over small-er subject communities to more indirect methods which allowed some autonomy to local groups provided that regular tributes were forthcoming (Stern, 2000: p. 57; Lawson, 2017: ch. 2).

Africa also produced a number of empires, spanning ancient, medieval, and modern periods. These included the Ghana, Mali, and Songhay Empires in West Africa which thrived between about the sixth and sixteenth centuries AD. The most significant city within both the Mali and Songhay Empires was Timbuktu, which became a great centre for learning as well as trade and commerce and is still famed for its precious ancient manuscripts.

The Ottoman Empire, with its capital in Istanbul, emerged in the fourteenth century and lasted until the early 1920s, giving it a lifespan of around 600 years. At its height in the sixteenth and seventeenth centuries the Ottoman Empire ruled over some 14 million people and stretched from the deserts of central Asia to parts of central Europe, northern Africa, and southern Spain (see, generally, Duducu, 2018).

Further east, the ancient kingdoms of the Indus Valley formed a broad civilizational entity, with Hinduism and Sanskrit providing some basic cultural cohesion over much of the region. Even so, political communities within the region evinced much variety, with both oligarchies and republics in evidence. The region's best-known empire was established in the north in 300 BC. Although it lasted less than a century, its reputation was assured largely because one of its leading figures, Kautilya, produced a highly sophisticated text on statecraft, the *Artha'sastra*, which set out the ways and means of acquiring territory, keeping it, and reaping prosperity from it. It is comparable to Machiavelli's writings on statecraft, although some see it as presenting a far harsher picture of the struggle for domination (Boesche, 2002: pp. 253–76).

(Continued)

The Islamic Mughal Empire also emerged in the Indian subcontinent and held sway over much of the region until its decline in the late fifteenth and early sixteenth centuries. More generally, the legacy of Islamic empires—cultural, political, and military— remain today in significant parts of Africa, Central Asia, South Asia, South East Asia (especially present-day Malaysia, Indonesia, Brunei, and parts of Thailand and the Philippines) as well as sizeable parts of Eastern Europe.

In the Americas, the Aztec, Mayan, and Inca civilizations which flourished before the advent of Europeans were synonymous with imperial power. The Aztec and Inca Empires emerged from a period of political fragmentation and military conflict in the thirteenth and fourteenth centuries, which ended with the establishment of strong centres of power with control over significant territories and peoples (see Lockard, 2008: p. 347). These, however, collapsed in the face of other imperial incursions, especially those of the Spanish who soon overwhelmed the local empires through military power as well as the spread of diseases to which the indigenous people had no immunity. This was to be a fate endured by many indigenous people around the world.

One of the most extensive and durable empires of all was the Chinese, which lasted from the time of the Shang dynasty in the eighteenth century BC, until the early twentieth century, although there was a substantial interlude during which it disintegrated into a number of warring states. It was during a period of chaos and violence that the ancient philosophy of Confucius, which is largely concerned with setting out political and social arrangements conducive to good order under strong leadership and authority, is thought to have developed (see Lawson, 2006: p. 155). This is comparable to the conditions under which European theorists of sovereignty, which is ultimately concerned with the same problems, were to develop their ideas.

There are numerous other examples of empire throughout the world, from ancient through to modern times, showing just how common this form of international system has been. Indeed, they have been far more common than state systems.

FIGURE 2.3 Statue of Confucius in China Gautier Willaume/Shutterstock.com

Given the extent to which imperialism and colonialism facilitate cultural spread, it is scarcely surprising that British—or more particularly English—culture gained significant ground around the world. This is partly manifest in the fact that English, as we saw in Chapter 1, now prevails as the major international language although French and Spanish are also widely spoken, the latter in Central and South America in particular. Cultural spread, however, goes both ways and contemporary Britain, and significant parts of Europe, have absorbed cultural influences in turn, including many from their former colonies.

More generally, the history of empire, which encompasses exploration, trade, proselytization, and migration and the transfer of social and political practices, is also part of the history of globalization. The networks and movements of people prompted by the global reach of the modern European empires, in particular, along with technological innovations and the development of financial and economic systems that accompanied these, established much of the basis on which contemporary global interdependence rests. These developments, and others, have raised a number of interesting issues for debate, as illustrated in Box 2.6 which discusses, among other things, a new imperial order characterized by the power of transnational and multinational corporations, which are also mentioned briefly in Chapter 7 in the context of international organizations.

BOX 2.6 KEY DEBATE

Globalization and the New Imperialism

The phenomenon of globalization has been linked to a new form of empire which, it is argued, is replacing the traditional form of state sovereignty with a different kind of sovereignty. This is said to rely neither on a territorial centre of power nor on fixed boundaries or barriers. Nor does the US occupy a singularly privileged position in this new imperial configuration, simply taking up where the old European empires left off. Rather, the new imperial order is characterized by the power of transnational corporations (TNCs) or multinational corporations (MNCs), and forms of production owing no allegiance to territorial entities and which in fact seek to supplant their sovereignty (see Hardt and Negri, 2000: pp. xi–xiv). By the turn of the twenty-first century, it was noted that the 300 largest TNCs owned or controlled about a quarter of productive assets around the entire globe, while their total annual sales were comparable to, or greater than, the GDP of most countries. Sales by Itochu Corporation, based in Japan, exceeded the GDP of Austria, while those of Royal Dutch/Shell equalled Iran's (Greer and Singh, 2000). Much of the focus of critique has been on Western (i.e. European or US-based corporations) but, as the example just mentioned shows, Japanese corporations have been equally prominent.

More recently, there has been a significant growth in Chinese corporations operating in Africa and the Pacific. One highly critical opinion piece on the new 'Chinese imperialism' says that: 'Chinese corporations are all over Africa. In June 2017 a McKinsey & Company report estimated that there are more than 10,000 Chinese-owned firms operating in Africa. . . . The reason Chinese corporations are in Africa is simple; to exploit the people and take their resources. It's the same thing European colonists did during mercantile times, except worse. The Chinese corporations are trying to turn Africa into another Chinese continent [and] squeezing Africa for everything it is worth' (Mourdaukoutas, 2018). Some may see this version of 'empire' as an exaggerated scenario, but at the very least its proponents provide a basis for critical reflection on key aspects of the phenomenon of globalization and the growing power of deterritorialized corporations, both Western and non-Western, as non-state actors.

(Continued)

Some other recent commentators *do* regard the US as exercising genuine imperial control at a global level, although its political leaders reject any such connection. In his analysis of US **hegemony**, Niall Ferguson (2003a) quotes prominent US politicians as emphatically denying that the global role of the US today is an imperial project. George W. Bush, for example, claimed in 2000 that 'America has never been an empire ... We may be the only great power in history that had the chance, and refused.' He continued with this theme when declaring a victory in Iraq in May 2003 over the forces of Saddam Hussein, insisting that while other nations had 'fought in foreign lands and remained to occupy and exploit', Americans, in contrast, 'wanted nothing more than to return home' (quoted in Ferguson, 2003a). Ferguson concludes another major book on the subject of the British Empire with the observation that Americans have taken on the global role formerly played by Britain, yet without facing the fact that an empire comes with it. In short, the US is 'an empire in denial' (Ferguson, 2003b: p. 370).

A contrary argument has been put by Paul Schroeder who says that much of the hype about an American empire is based on a misleading and unhistorical understanding of the term which ignores crucial distinctions between empire and other forms of power and order in the international system. A *real* empire, he says, requires effective final authority whereas the power of the US is more correctly understood as hegemony. The latter, he says, consists of acknowledged leadership and dominant influence by one unit within a community of units which do not come under a single authority, whereas an imperial power actually rules over subordinates in a formalized hierarchical system (Schroeder, 2003).

Similarly, hegemony in the context of global politics has been defined as 'the ability of an actor with overwhelming capability to shape the international system through both coercive and non-coercive means' (Norrlof, 2015). Examples include the UK in the nineteenth century and the US in the twentieth and twenty-first centuries as well as 'a cohesive political community with external decision-making, such as the European Union'. Furthermore, rule under hegemony is sustained through influence over other states 'rather than by controlling them or their territory' (ibid.).

Another commentator says that the contemporary world has some very large political units which, although technically sovereign states, or composed of sovereign states, may be usefully analysed in terms of empire. In addition to the US, these include the EU, Russia, and China. This further suggests an expansive understanding of empire and the fact that they can be democratic, **authoritarian**, or mixed in character. In view of this, he says, it is time to bring the concept of empire back into the study of politics (Colomer, 2017).

This may leave us to wonder:

1 Do transnational corporations constitute a new form of empire?
2 Is there a real difference between hegemony and empire?
3 Is the US a genuine imperial power in the contemporary period?

KEY POINTS

- States as political communities have existed for thousands of years and have taken a wide range of forms in terms of size and institutional features. There have also been non-state societies, mainly egalitarian in form and lacking the kind of centralized and hierarchical authority characteristic of states.
- Empires as a form of international order have occurred in ancient, pre-modern, and modern periods and throughout most parts of the world, and take different forms according to time and place.

MODERNITY AND THE STATE SYSTEM

Empires have clearly been a dominant form of international system throughout history, often encompassing states in a wider system of order characterized by hierarchy. With the exception of the imperial state, other states in such systems have generally been subordinate entities lacking a certain integrity and capacity. The modern sovereign state and state system, however, appear to have a very different character. We now examine the historical emergence of the sovereign state and state system in Europe against the background condition of modernity. As we saw in Chapter 1, this is a complex phenomenon associated with the rise in Europe of science and technology leading to industrialization, increased military power, and, with it, enormous political and social change, including diminishing religious authority.

We must also recall, however, that the rise of modernity in Europe did not occur in isolation from other influences. Not only were important ideas and inventions transmitted from China and Arabia but significant aspects of Greek and Roman learning were also recovered through the work of Islamic scholars, thus enabling scholars of medieval Europe, and later, to study the ancient philosophers and develop their insights further. The 'discovery' of new worlds in the Americas and the Pacific also served to acquaint Europeans with a seemingly endless array of widely varying states and societies, all of which prompted new comparisons and questions for the study of politics and society (Lawson, 2006: p. 60).

Development of the European State System

In the year 1500—often used as a convenient marker for the beginning of the modern age—the historian Paul Kennedy says that it was scarcely apparent to anyone that a cluster of rather insignificant states in Western Europe 'was poised to dominate much of the rest of the earth' (Kennedy, 1989: p. 3). Chinese civilization at the time seemed vastly superior to any other. Technological innovation, including moveable type printing, gunpowder, paper money, and massive ironworks, had contributed to an expansion of trade and industry, further stimulated by an extensive programme of canal building. China also possessed an army of over a million. All this, together with an efficient hierarchical administration run by an educated Confucian bureaucracy, made Chinese society 'the envy of foreign visitors' (Kennedy, 1989: p. 5). More generally, as we saw earlier, empires elsewhere were thriving and so there were many other important centres of power at the beginning of the modern period.

There had been no political organization of Europe as a whole in the Renaissance or early modern periods to match the Chinese or Ottoman Empires. Rather, medieval Europe consisted of a rather chaotic patchwork of overlapping jurisdictions and fragmented authorities, scarcely resembling a coherent state system or international order. The only institution providing any sort of unity was the Christian (Catholic) Church based in Rome, from where it imposed some religious authority on the rest of the continent. However, the Protestant Reformation, described briefly in Chapter 1, would challenge the supremacy of the established church, triggering a massive theological and political fallout.

Key aspects of the development of European states and the state system are often seen as arising out of a devastating struggle between Catholic and Protestant forces, ending with the Peace of Westphalia in 1648. This is conventionally understood to have resulted in the consolidation of certain characteristics of the modern state that are central to aspects of IR theory, as set out in Box 2.7. These characteristics included not only the principle of religious coexistence

BOX 2.7 CASE STUDY

The Peace of Westphalia

The Thirty Years War between Catholic and Protestant forces in Europe ended in 1648 with the Peace of Westphalia. This was achieved through complex diplomatic negotiations over a period of five years, ending when the Treaties of Osnabrück and Münster were signed to form a comprehensive agreement covering matters of law, religion, and ethics as well as numerous practical issues.

Some of the principles enshrined at Westphalia, such as the authority of rulers to determine the religious affiliations of their subjects, were very similar to an earlier agreement, the Peace of Augsburg of 1555, so the ideas underpinning the 1648 treaty were not entirely new. On the matter of subjects following the religion of the ruler, it is also interesting to note that Ibn Khaldun had observed, around 300 years earlier, that the institutions and customs of people, including their religion, depended on those of their rulers (Khaldun, 1969: p. 25).

Westphalia was infused with emergent ideas about a kind of international law which could transcend religious differences and therefore be applied universally—that is, to Catholic and Protestant states alike. The foremost thinker along these lines was the Dutch jurist Hugo Grotius (1583–1645) whose influential work, *De Jure Belli et Pacis* (*Laws of War and Peace*) confronted the problem of conflicting moralities and the need for toleration as well as setting out minimum standards for conduct. Most importantly for the development of the state system and international order, it granted co-equal juridical status to states.

Westphalia has been described as the first, and perhaps the greatest, of the modern European peace treaties and is considered to have established the legal foundations of modern statehood. Its principal feature in this latter respect concerns the right of rulers to conduct their affairs within their own territories free from outside interference, thus establishing the principle of autonomous political authority which underpinned the development of the doctrine of sovereignty.

The articulation of principles and doctrines, however, does not mean that practice always accords with their intent. There has been little to prevent violations of both the letter and spirit of the Westphalian Peace, as the subsequent history of Europe itself shows only too clearly. The Westphalian model nonetheless provides a benchmark for both critics and supporters of the sovereign state system as well as for those who predict its eventual demise due to the irresistible state-transcending forces of globalization.

but also the monopoly claims by the state over such matters as declarations of war and the negotiation of peace, diplomatic representation, and the authority to make treaties with foreign powers (Boucher, 1998: p. 224). For these reasons, Westphalia was long regarded as the founding moment of the modern *sovereign* state. One scholar says: 'Most scholars . . . see the seventeenth century, and particularly the Peace of Westphalia . . . as the best historical reference point for symbolizing that fundamental turn in European political life' (Jackson, 2018: p. 44).

That assessment, however, has come under challenge and some regard it as little more than a 'foundation myth' with the principal driver of the rise of the modern state being best located in capitalist development in England in particular (Teschke, 2003; see also Clark, 2005). The finer points of that particular debate are beyond the scope of an introductory text. Whether myth or not, it is nonetheless important to look at what the idea of the 'Westphalian moment' is based on, given that it was to become such a key reference point for the emergence of the modern sovereign state and cannot be dismissed entirely as a factor in its historical development.

Sovereignty in Principle and Practice

The principle of sovereignty came to be regarded by some theorists as effectively enclosing states within a 'hard shell', with the shell corresponding to the territorial borders. It was meant to guarantee non-intervention in the internal governmental arrangements or any other domestic affairs of a state. The theory possessed an attractive simplicity. Rulers within states could follow the religious, political, and moral principles of their choice, and could also require their subjects to conform. The protective shell of sovereignty guaranteed the complete independence of each state—or rather the ruling elements within each state—to arrange their domestic affairs as it suited them, regardless of what any external actor might think and no matter the relative standing of the state in terms of size, power, and capacity. As pointed out in Chapter 1, the state is sovereign in the sense that it is the supreme law-making body within a particular territory with the ultimate power of life and death over individuals. The juridical sovereignty possessed by individual states remains a basic principle of international law today.

While admirable in its theoretical simplicity, the principles of state sovereignty in the international sphere have been far less straightforward in practice. This has been demonstrated in part by the fact that Europe appears to have been no less prone to warfare among its constituent states for much of the 300-year period following Westphalia. The extent to which this can be attributed to the rise of nationalism along with the modern state system has been much debated. Whatever the historical reasons for war, it is really only in the post-Second World War period that Europeans seem finally to have struck on a formula for peaceful relations. That this was achieved via a regional supra-state framework in the form of the EU is something of an irony because although the principle of state sovereignty was initially formulated to prevent warfare, it seems that a more lasting peace has been acquired through significant modification of its basic elements.

Another factor to be considered is the moral conundrum raised by the actions of states with respect to the treatment of their own citizens or any others within their borders, whether visitors, migrants, or refugees. A strict interpretation of the theory of state sovereignty prohibits any action by actors outside the state even in cases of genocide or other forms of human rights abuses. In the present period, however, there has been much discussion of an assumed right of **humanitarian intervention**, a nascent doctrine which seeks to trump the sovereign rights of states—or rather their rulers—to do as they please within their own borders.

This accords with another recently promoted notion—that the possession of sovereignty by a state confers on it the **responsibility to protect** its inhabitants, not to cause them harm. The intervention in Libya in 2011, authorized by the UN Security Council, reflects the failure of the Libyan regime to safeguard unarmed civilians during the uprising. The 'responsibility to protect' in this instance shifted to the international community. But this has not happened to date with respect to the Syrian crisis, largely because of the politics of the UN Security Council, which we consider in Chapter 6. Even so, the international community does assume major responsibility for the millions of displaced persons or refugees generated by such conflicts, even if this often seems inadequate in execution.

Here we should note that the theory of state sovereignty faces two ways, possessing both external and internal dimensions. As Evans and Newnham (1998: p. 504) put it, the doctrine makes a double claim: 'autonomy in foreign policy and exclusive competence in internal affairs'. The latter depends on there being an ultimate authority within the state that is entitled to make decisions and settle disputes. Thus 'the sovereign', who may be either a person (such as a monarch) or a collective (such as a parliament representing the sovereignty of the people) is the highest and final power in the state's political system and cannot be subject to any other agent, domestic *or* foreign (Miller, 1991: pp. 492–3). As far as the external or international sphere goes, this produces, somewhat paradoxically, a condition of anarchy—which means, literally, 'without a ruler'. For if all states are sovereign, and therefore the final arbiters of their own destinies, there can be no higher authority placed outside and above the individual states in an international system of states (see Evans and Newnham, 1998: p. 504).

The rise of the modern European state system was accompanied by the ideology of nationalism. We noted earlier the assumption implicit in the principle of self-determination that each 'nation' is entitled to a state of its own, which is highly problematic given that there are thousands of groups around the world that could make some credible claim to constituting a nation. Despite the practical difficulties, the idea that nations and states go together seems very persuasive. But like the sovereign state itself, the idea of the nation is a relatively recent one. Indeed, its origins lie in the same state-building dynamics that emerged in post-Westphalian Europe as well as in emergent ideas about democracy, as noted earlier.

Another significant development came in the wake of the Napoleonic Wars. This was the Concert of Europe, a term designating a series of irregular conferences focused on resolving diplomatic crises between states. Beginning with the Congress of Vienna in 1815, it lasted until the mid-1850s and, although the meetings were eventually discontinued, the art of diplomacy within Europe matured to a significant extent and became an important instrument of the state system. At the beginning of the nineteenth century, however, the modern European state system still existed more in theory than in practice, and it was still far from being regarded as a 'nation-state' system. But the *national* idea was becoming more prominent in the rhetoric of state-making movements throughout the century which saw the emergence of new 'national' states in Greece (1830), Belgium (1831), Italy (1861), Germany (1871), and Romania, Serbia, and Montenegro (1878).

By the beginning of the twentieth century, the modern state system with its principles of sovereignty, nationality, and territoriality was reasonably well entrenched in Europe, as well as in much of the Americas. But it scarcely existed in other parts of the world. This brings us next to the subject of European colonization and decolonization, for it is largely due to the legacy of empire that the European state system became effectively globalized in the twentieth century, thus giving rise to the present global system.

KEY POINTS

- Modernity is a phenomenon associated initially with social, political, intellectual, and technological developments in Europe which brought significant changes to the political landscape.

- The Peace of Westphalia is conventionally regarded as the founding moment of the doctrine of state sovereignty and therefore of the modern state and state system in Europe, although its importance in this respect is contested.

- Nationalism as a form of political/cultural identity is also closely associated with the rise of the modern sovereign state and state system.

THE GLOBALIZATION OF THE STATE SYSTEM

We have seen that numerous empires existed in ancient times and in many different parts of the world. The modern period did not spell the end of empires and, if anything, imperialism and colonialism not only continued with the rise of the sovereign state in Europe but also thrived under it. Furthermore, it is through the European empires that the sovereign state system was effectively transported to the rest of the world. Early Spanish, Portuguese, and Dutch explorers and traders were followed by the British, French, Belgians, and Germans. Shipping routes and trading posts encircled the world, the latter providing a base for subsequent colonization. It was not long before almost the entire world came under the direct control of one or other of the European powers. After the Second World War, however, there was significant normative change concerning the legitimacy of colonial rule. The principle of self-determination, originally developed in relation to Europeans in the aftermath of the First World War, was now invoked as a right of colonized people everywhere and drove a decolonization movement which saw almost all former European colonies achieve independence by the end of the twentieth century.

The establishment of colonial states with their relatively clear boundaries, administrative centres (capitals), and more or less permanent, settled populations followed the structure of European states. When decolonization came, the transition from colonial state to sovereign state, in an international system of similarly structured states, seemed relatively simple from a technical point of view. Sovereignty was simply transferred from the colonizing power to an indigenous elite. In the decades following the end of the Second World War—that is, from 1945 through to the 1990s—most of the former colonial states from the Atlantic and Africa, Asia and the Pacific acquired sovereign statehood on the basis of existing boundaries and with structures of governance—parliaments, electorates, a civil service, etc.—reflecting European practices.

Virtually all former colonies therefore became part of an international system of states based largely on the European state system, a development which effectively ensured the globalization of that system. Even those states which had not been colonized, such as Japan and Turkey, Thailand and Tonga, adopted the European state format. But independent sovereign statehood has not been an outstanding success for a number of countries. While few postcolonial states have actually collapsed altogether, a number have experienced major difficulties in maintaining the basic elements of effective statehood. This suggests that the modern sovereign state is a poor fit in these places. These problems therefore bring into question both the assumed benefits of the globalization of the European state system and its long-term prospects as an effective system of international order. Furthermore, the deepening and widening of the EU, as a project in regionalization that at once incorporates as well as transcends sovereign states, has raised questions about the future of the traditional sovereign state in its original heartland. Conversely, the resurgence of nationalism in parts of Europe in recent years—as manifest in anti-EU parties in many EU countries, including Italy, Germany, France, the Netherlands, Austria, Poland, Spain, and Hungary, not to mention Brexit—indicates a trend in the opposite direction (see Judis, 2018).

> **KEY POINTS**
>
> - It is largely due to the global reach of the European empires and their political legacies that the European state system became the basis for the current international state system and international order.
> - Formal sovereign statehood has not always delivered significant benefits, especially in the Global South where a number of weak or failing states provide little in the way of benefits to their citizens.

CONCLUSION

This chapter has provided an account of the evolution of the global political system, focusing on the formation of states and empires from the earliest times to the present era of globalization. Setting the rise of the contemporary global order against this background helps to illustrate not only the variety of state forms and international systems in history but also the fact that while some systems have achieved an impressive longevity, no system has ever achieved permanence. It would therefore be mistaken to assume that the present system, based largely on sovereign states, will necessarily remain as it is over the longer term. This is especially so given the challenges of globalization, however that phenomenon is conceived, and the various pressures it exerts on all aspects of sovereign statehood.

Even so, the possible passing of states as political communities, and the sovereign state form in particular, raises a further question: if states cease to fulfil their function as a major basis for national and global political organization, what would replace them? Would we see a return of empire in one form or another? Others seriously question the wisdom of dismissing the importance of the state, and relations between states, both now and in the foreseeable future, even as other actors come to play increasingly important roles. We have also looked briefly at important historic ideas such as the nation and the ideology of nationalism. It is this ideology that has come to underpin the modern sovereign state and, given its continuing power, it is one reason why the sovereign state may continue well into the future as a principal unit of political organization even as new forms of empire come and go.

KEY QUESTIONS

1. What constitutes a nation on the one hand and a state on the other?
2. What is the relationship between states and nations?
3. What is meant by the term 'imagined community'?
4. What are the key features of empires?
5. Under what circumstances did the idea of sovereign statehood arise in Europe?
6. What are the distinguishing features of the modern sovereign state?
7. How did the European state system become globalized?
8. Are there really new forms of empire emerging in the present period?

FURTHER READING

Bremmer, Ian (2018), *Us vs Them: The Failure of Globalism* (London: Penguin).

> Deals with the recent rise of populist nationalism around the world and the challenges it poses for the values of international cooperation, free trade, and democracy itself.

Breuilly, John (ed.) (2013), *The Oxford Handbook of the History of Nationalism* (Oxford: Oxford University Press).

> This book comprises a significant collection of essays by leading scholars of nationalism, global in scope and with much historical depth. It looks at different forms taken by nationalist ideology from Europe to the Middle East, Asia, and the Americas.

Burbank, Jane and Frederick Cooper (2010), *Empires in World History: Power and the Politics of Difference* (Princeton, NJ: Princeton University Press).

> Examines numerous historic empires from ancient Rome and China across Asia, Europe, the Americas, and Africa, focusing attention on strategies of conquest, consolidation, and rivalries together with an emphasis on how empires handled the considerable differences among populations.

Rÿser, Rudolph C. (2012), *Indigenous Nations and Modern States: The Political Emergence of Nations Challenging State Power* (New York: Routledge).

> This is a more specialized study, looking at the phenomenon of what the author calls 'bedrock nations'—indigenous people who many once thought would be absorbed and assimilated by modern societies but whose identities have survived to take up a role as assertive political actors in many contemporary states.

Spencer, Phillip and Howard Wollman (eds) (2005), *Nations and Nationalism: A Reader* (New Brunswick, NJ: Rutgers University Press).

> Another interesting collection of essays by key commentators on the subject matter, providing an overview of the origins, different types and concepts of nationalism, issues such as race, gender, and ethnicity, and the impact of globalization and migration as well as debates about citizenship and self-determination.

WEB LINKS

https://opil.ouplaw.com/view/10.1093/law:epil/9780199231690/law-9780199231690-e1472

> An entry on the website of *Oxford Public International Law* providing an account of the legal aspects of sovereignty.

https://plato.stanford.edu/entries/colonialism/

> The online *Stanford Encyclopedia of Philosophy* provides an excellent scholarly account of both colonialism and imperialism.

https://plato.stanford.edu/entries/nationalism/

> Again, the online *Stanford Encyclopedia of Philosophy* has a high-quality entry on the ideology of nationalism, including moral debates.

http://www.the-american-interest.com/2016/07/10/when-and-why-nationalism-beats-globalism/

> A contemporary commentary on the nationalism/globalism debate, and why nationalism seems to be on the rise.

http://blog.oup.com/2016/12/nationalism-brexit-identity-referendum/

> OUP blog site discussing the role of nationalism in the Brexit vote.

 For additional material and resources please visit the **online resources** at: www.oup.com/he/lawson1e.

3

TRADITIONAL THEORIES IN GLOBAL POLITICS

- Early Liberal Approaches

- Classical Realism

- The English School

- Neoliberalism and Neorealism

- Contemporary Discourses of Moral Realism

- Conclusion

Reader's Guide

Whenever we think about the world around us, we do so through a certain set of assumptions concerning the reality of that world. Different theorists obviously see the world in different ways and will interpret facts accordingly. This also highlights the point that facts do not simply speak for themselves. Two major bodies of theory—liberalism and realism—which constitute much of the traditional theoretical terrain of studies in international politics, offer competing interpretations of the facts and therefore competing explanations and solutions addressing the causes of war and the conditions for peace. Here we should note, again, that traditional theories, while offering universally valid explanations of political behaviour, have been developed largely in the West and therefore draw mainly on European and North American experiences and concepts such as sovereignty and anarchy. These theories also developed at a time when racism, imperialism, and masculinist ideas were widespread. It follows that the theorists most often singled out as key figures in the development of IR theory (and political and social theory more generally) throughout much of the twentieth century, and studied on that basis were, almost exclusively, male figures from countries associated with Western imperialism, including the US. They are therefore seen to have developed their ideas on the basis of a relatively limited and privileged world view and to have beem deeply

(Continued)

imbued with ethnocentrism. This does not mean, however, that there is nothing of interest or importance in these ideas. After all, both realist and liberal views have found much support in locations around the world. Another preliminary point is that the more conventional term *international* politics or relations is used frequently in this chapter because traditional theorists conceived of their work as largely addressing relations between states and rarely conceptualized it as 'global' in the more diffuse sense in which the term is used now. An exception is the later generation of liberals whose theories—especially in the economic realm—have informed contemporary discourses of globalization.

EARLY LIBERAL APPROACHES

It has often been assumed that the formal academic study of international politics emerged in the wake of the First World War, for although scholars had frequently focused on political issues in the international sphere before that time, they had tended to do so from within disciplines such as history and law rather than political science. But as with the notion that Westphalia produced the modern sovereign state system, the idea that IR as a discipline suddenly appeared after the First World War has been branded as another foundational 'myth'. An alternative viewpoint regards 'thinking about international relations' as having become a primary academic activity only after 1945, and even later than that in the Third World (Acharya and Buzan, 2019: p. 6), while others see it as really dating only from the 1980s (Ashworth, 2018). Whatever the 'real' origins of the discipline, it is certainly the case that the unprecedented scale of what became known as the 'Great War' prompted an urgent search for a new, more stable international order providing for lasting peace and security.

Key Figures in Liberal Thought

Under the influence of certain key figures, including US President Woodrow Wilson (1856–1924) (see Box 3.1), the quest for a more stable, secure, and peaceful world order saw a cluster of liberal ideas, known as **liberal internationalism** and **liberal institutionalism**, develop. As the terms suggest, these envisaged a prime role for international institutions in underpinning such an order.

Liberal international theorists of the early twentieth century drew on a pre-existing body of philosophy in constructing their notion of order. Ancient philosophers had emphasized the capacity of individual human reason for delineating the 'good life', and had also advanced ideas about cosmopolitanism, but it was modern liberal thinkers who advocated concrete political action in achieving reform when the existing order was found wanting. Among the most important contributors to liberal ideas specifically in international politics are Hugo Grotius (1583–1645) and Samuel Pufendorf (1632–94), both of whom experienced the Thirty Years War, discussed in Chapter 2.

BOX 3.1 SHORT BIOGRAPHY

Woodrow Wilson (1856–1924)

Thomas Woodrow Wilson was born in Staunton, Virginia, just five years before the start of the Civil War. He showed little early promise, failing to learn to read before ten or eleven years of age and experiencing difficulties all his life due, probably, to dyslexia. His later achievements as both a scholar and a politician, becoming first a professor at Princeton University and then US president for two terms from 1913 to 1921, therefore stand out as representing a triumph over personal adversity.

As a Democrat, Wilson gained a reputation for promoting an expanded role for government and pursued progressive liberal policies on a number of fronts, reflecting the abandonment of nineteenth-century *laissez-faire* dogma which had promoted the idea that government had almost no role to play in socio-economic matters. Reforms included the abolition of child labour, the introduction of an eight-hour day in the private sector, a graduated income tax, and the establishment of the Federal Reserve to steer the economy. Other innovations saw regular press briefings— previously unheard of in US presidential politics. Wilson was also the first Southerner to be elected president since the Civil War. Unfortunately, he proved to be very much a product of his time and place when it came to race issues, supporting segregation and other regressive policies within the US administration which amounted to white supremacism.

Internationally, Wilson is best known for his role in bringing the US into the First World War in 1917, 'to make the world safe for **democracy**', and later for his efforts at the Paris Peace Conference of 1919, held in the Palace of Versailles, which brought the League of Nations into being. He is also credited with articulating the general principle of the right to **self-determination**, although this was to be exercised initially within Europe rather than extended to the still colonized world. The latter reflected not only Wilson's attitudes to non-white

FIGURE 3.1 President of the United States of America 1913–1921, Woodrow Wilson Library of Congress

(Continued)

peoples but those prevailing among European leaders of the time more generally when ideas of racial superiority were rife.

Despite failing to persuade an **isolationist** US Congress to join the new international institution, in which hopes for a more stable and peaceful world order were vested, he was nonetheless awarded the Nobel Peace Prize in 1919 in recognition of his leading role in promoting world political organization. In the same year the first academic chair of International Politics was established at the University of Wales, Aberystwyth, and named in honour of Wilson.

Grotius argued for the possibility of universal moral standards against which the legitimacy of actions in pursuit of self-preservation could be judged. This has featured in liberal international thought ever since. He also formulated some of the earliest ideas in the modern period about the 'sociability' of the international sphere which were highly influential in the development of later ideas about **international society** (Dunne, 1998: pp. 138–9). Pufendorf, whose work was immensely influential, incorporated a basic natural law of self-preservation in his work on universal jurisprudence and the law of **nations**. He too promoted the essential sociability of humans, which served to counter ideas about excessive self-interestedness.

Another major figure is Immanuel Kant (1724–1804) whose seminal work, *Perpetual Peace*, was published in 1795. In order to secure lasting peace among states, he devised a set of propositions for a law of nations founded on a federation of free states—ideas which have remained highly influential in peace theory. Kant further proposed that under republican forms of government the individual concern for self-preservation, which was entirely rational, would ensure that citizens effectively vetoed warmongering. This is one of the rationales behind the influential **democratic peace** thesis. Woodrow Wilson also endorsed the idea that democracies are inherently peaceful, both within themselves and in their relations with each other, and believed that if all countries were governed democratically, then warfare would be virtually eliminated. He certainly believed that, if all European countries had been democracies in 1914, war would have been avoided (see Lawson, 2015: pp. 89–93).

One problem with the Kantian approach, and with much liberal thought more generally, is the assumption that individuals will usually act rationally and in a way best calculated to serve their own individual self-interest and, especially, to enhance prospects for their own self-preservation. Recent work on the role of emotions and passions in politics shows that such assumptions cannot be sustained (see, for example, Jeffery, 2014; Hutchison, 2016). Kant himself, however, did recognize that there were limits to human reason, and that reason itself should be subject to critique.

Peace, Prosperity, and Progress in Liberal Thought

A major theme uniting liberal thinkers from Grotius onwards, and which helps to distinguish liberal from realist thought, is an optimistic view of the possibilities for peaceful relations, which in turn contributes to greater prosperity. This derives from a positive view of **human nature**, at least to the extent that people can learn from their mistakes, some of which are undoubtedly dreadful. Beyond this, liberals believe that rationally chosen, self-regarding courses of action by individuals tend to lead to better outcomes for all, or at least for a majority. Thus over time humans can *progress* towards a better state of existence as individuals within their political communities and in relations between communities. But none of this comes about by itself. People (agents) need to make it happen. So just as human rationality *and* agency are required to build a satisfactory social and political order within a state, so they are required just as much, if not more, in the construction of international institutions designed specifically to overcome the negative effects of anarchy and to contain tendencies to war. This style of thinking was crucially important in underpinning developments in the immediate aftermath of the First World War.

President Wilson led his country into war in the belief that, once the forces responsible for the war were defeated, a strong international organization dedicated to preserving international peace and security could flourish. He proposed a general association of nation-states to make mutual guarantees concerning economic and political independence and territorial integrity, regardless of each state's size or capacity. This was operationalized through the 1919 Treaty of Versailles which embodied the Covenant of the League of Nations. However, the treaty also imposed harsh reparations on Germany for loss and damage caused by the war and has been described as 'one of the best examples of a peace treaty creating the pre-conditions of a future war' (Evans and Newnham, 1998: p. 559). We consider further aspects of the League in Chapter 7, but for present purposes this provides a useful case study of how theory and practice are interwoven (Box 3.2).

BOX 3.2 CASE STUDY

Liberal Theory and the League of Nations

It is often said that the League of Nations was a failure because it did not prevent the outbreak of the Second World War. Certainly, the liberal internationalism which underpinned it was derided, at least by realists, as a form of idealism or utopianism bound to fail when faced with the realities of power politics (*Machtpolitik*) in an anarchical international sphere. But is this to mistake cause and effect? Although some provisions allowed too much leeway in the application of sanctions, the institutional design of the League itself was workable enough, and the United Nations (UN) is still based on many of these. As the first major attempt to set up a mechanism for collective security on such an extensive international scale it must have been hailed as a considerable achievement. Other factors were far more important in undermining its chances for success. Thus when the League, and the principles of liberal internationalism on which it was based, stand accused of failing to check the aggression of Germany, Italy, and Japan, we must remember the failure of the US to join, the refusal to allow Communist Russia to join, the aggression of France itself when, along with Belgium, it invaded a German industrial area in an attempt to exact reparation dues, the failure of Britain to condemn this violation of League rules—all combined with the vengeful nature of the treaty's reparations provisions. A humiliated Germany was ripe for the rabid, populist right-wing nationalism that Hitler came to espouse while the geopolitical landscape of swathes of Eastern Europe was highly vulnerable to the aggression of a remilitarized Germany. The question then is: did the League of Nations fail; or did state leaders of the time fail the League of Nations?

The Idea of Self-Determination

Another important aspect of liberal international theory promoted by Wilson and others in the wake of the First World War was the principle of self-determination, a term which has several nuances. First, self-determination can refer to the right of states freely to determine their own policies and practices. Second, it can refer to the right of citizens to determine their own government and therefore a preferred set of policy options—a defining characteristic of **liberal democracy**. And third, it can refer to the quest of a nationalist movement to secure political autonomy, which can include an act of **secession** to form a new sovereign state. This right to *national* self-determination further strengthens the legitimacy of the nation-state idea discussed in Chapter 2.

Historically, the principle of the self-determination of 'peoples' (understood as 'nations') was not extended to include the colonized world until after 1945, as noted above. Indeed, the League entrenched European colonial domination through its mandate system which was designed to ensure that 'advanced nations' would continue to administer 'peoples not yet able to stand by themselves under the strenuous conditions of the modern world', on the principle that the well-being and development of such peoples was a 'sacred trust of civilization' (Pederson, 2015: p. 1). When the doctrine of national self-determination was applied to the colonial world after 1945 by the newly established United Nations, it became a powerful ideology underpinning the entire decolonization movement. Here we should note that the idea of self-determination is an inherently liberal one with deep roots in European political thought. **Nationalism** is also irredeemably European in origin. But this has scarcely diminished the near-universal appeal of national self-determination and its efficacy in demolishing the legitimacy of **colonialism**.

One country that provided an exception to the general treatment of non-Western countries was Japan, which had attended the Versailles conference as one of the five great powers, having supported the alliance of forces opposing Germany in the war. Japan had taken possession of Germany's former colonial territories in Micronesia (located in the northern Pacific Ocean) and continued to hold these under a League mandate. Japan had also initiated a 'racial equality proposal' at Versailles which was intended to apply, not to all non-Western people, but to members of the League only. In other words, it was designed to give Japan only (and Japanese people only) equal 'racial status' with Europeans. The proposal was vigorously opposed by the US and Australia—the latter having adopted an explicit 'White Australia Policy' to prevent Asian immigration. It was in fact Australia which most strongly opposed Japan's proposal and ensured its defeat even though most European countries were sympathetic to Japan's position (see, generally, Imamoto, 2018). Japan's failure to have the proposal adopted served to weaken its attachment to the League and was perhaps a factor in its subsequent strategic choices leading up to the Second World War. One lesson to be learnt from this is that although liberal theory promotes human equality as a core value, the liberal impulses underpinning international developments at this time, including self-determination and issues of race, continued to be tainted by deeply ingrained prejudices.

In the meantime, liberal international theory reached a high point in the interwar years. Among the prominent liberal scholars of the time was Norman Angell, awarded the 1933 Nobel Peace Prize on the basis of his extensive writings on the futility of war. It is also notable that thinkers such as Angell, although believing that humans could change for the better, were scarcely blind to their follies and self-destructive behaviour, for if humans were so inherently good and peaceful, he said, devices such as the League of Nations would hardly be necessary (Angell quoted in Sylvest, 2004: p. 424). Subsequent developments, however, saw liberal ideas overshadowed as realism rose to prominence and its proponents denounced the idealism they believed to be implicit in liberal international theory and the perceived ineffectiveness of international institutions in the face of what they thought were the realities of power politics.

Whatever criticisms they may have attracted later, the early twentieth-century liberals have been recognized widely as key figures in the founding of an academic discipline devoted to the study of international or global politics. As we shall see, liberalism was to make something of a comeback in the latter part of the twentieth century, and remains highly influential in international/global theory. In practical terms, its precepts underpin an extensive system of international law as well as the principal political institutions of contemporary global governance embodied in the UN system. In other words, liberalism underpins the theory and practice of a **rules-based international order**, a concept that has been invoked increasingly in recent times. We discuss this, and related issues, in Chapter 8. We also discuss, more specifically, economic aspects of liberalism in Chapter 10.

KEY POINTS

- A significant impetus for liberal international theorists of the early twentieth century was the devastation wrought by the First World War and a determination to identify the causes of war and the conditions for peace.

- Liberal international theory is characterized by an optimism concerning the prospects of a peaceful international order. It accepts that sovereign states are the key actors in international affairs but proposes that their behaviour, even under conditions of anarchy, can be modified through international institutions and a strong rules-based international order.

- Liberal internationalism is also generally supportive of the trends underpinning globalization while standing opposed to such ideologies as populist nationalism and trade protectionism.

CLASSICAL REALISM

The Treaty of Versailles not only failed to resolve a number of Europe's political problems but also exacerbated others. New states had been created in Eastern Europe partly in an attempt to apply the principle of national self-determination. Strategically, they were also supposed to serve as 'buffer states' between Western Europe and the emergent communist empire further to the east. The USSR's own brand of internationalism at the time was committed to the overthrow of the dominant capitalist economic order by means of worldwide revolution. Throughout the 1920s, however, relative peace was the order of the day and even Germany had joined the League of Nations. But none of this was to prevent the rise of Adolf Hitler, who set about building the Third Reich on an ultra-nationalist basis.

Developments in other parts of the world were significant too, especially the rise of Japan which had achieved extraordinary industrial growth over the previous half-century. Although Japan had been a member of the League of Nations, and some Japanese remained committed to internationalism, aggressive militarism and imperialism succeeded in a period when the effects of the Depression enhanced the influence of ultra-nationalists, as it had in Italy and Germany. The German invasion of Poland in 1939 led the world into its second large-scale war. Japan had already invaded China but it was not until 1940 that Japan became part of the 'Axis Alliance' with Italy and Germany and, in the following year, brought the US into the war by attacking Pearl Harbor.

Over the period 1939–45, at least 50 million people were killed as a direct result of the Second World War—more than five times the number killed in the previous World War. The death camps of Nazi Germany, in which some 6 million people were murdered, also highlighted the consequences of racialist nationalism. The Holocaust, which refers primarily to the mass murder of Jews in this war, stands as the most notorious act of genocide in human history. Given that the study of international politics had been founded by people dedicated to the prevention of war, and the death, destruction, and suffering it caused, this war must be seen as a devastating setback. Here is where political realism enters the picture as a theory designed to explain how the world *really* is rather than how it *ought* to be.

Realism, Power Politics, and the Struggle for Survival

While there is no single, concise theory that goes under the name of 'realism', virtually all realist approaches take the struggle for power and security by sovereign states in the anarchic sphere of international politics as their central focus. And although realism emerged as an explicit theory of international politics only in the twentieth century, many of its proponents claim that they are part of a much longer tradition. An account of the Peloponnesian War, which took place between Athens and Sparta from 431 to 404 BC, by the ancient Greek historian Thucydides, contains a dialogue commonly taken to illustrate two cardinal principles of political realism. The 'Melian Dialogue', set out in Box 3.3, suggests, first, that power politics is the name of the game in relations between states, and second, that issues of morality are irrelevant in the sphere of power politics. This sphere is therefore *a*moral in the sense that no moral rules can be applied, rather than *im*moral which indicates the transgression of an existing moral rule.

Another significant figure in classical realist thought is Niccolò Machiavelli (1467–1527) who developed a pragmatic approach to politics, eschewing idealist imaginaries and moralizing. A particularly important idea, often traced to Machiavelli, is *raison d'état* (reason of state), which is reflected in the more common contemporary phrase 'national interest'. Although Machiavelli did not use the precise term 'reason of state', he urged that, where the safety of the country is at stake, a ruler ought not to consider what is just or unjust, merciful or cruel, but rather what will secure 'the life of the country and maintain its liberty' (Machiavelli, 2009, 3: p. 41).

Perhaps the most important figure claimed for the realist tradition is Thomas Hobbes (1588–1679). Hobbes starts by positing a state of nature as well as a certain human nature, both assumed to be universal; that is, *constant for all times and all places*. Hobbes's state of nature is devoid of all that is necessary for the good life. It lacks security, justice, and any sort of morality. And it lacks these elements precisely because there is no sovereign power to enforce them. The essential characteristic of this condition of nature

BOX 3.3 HISTORY

The Melian Dialogue

The inhabitants of the island of Melos were neutral in the war between Athens and Sparta and would not submit to Athens. The Athenians first sent envoys with terms for a Melian surrender and Thucydides records the dialogue:

> **Athenians:** [W]e shall not bulk out our argument with lofty language, claiming that our defeat of the Persians gives us the right to rule . . . So keep this discussion practical, within the limits of what we both really think. You know as well as we do that . . . questions of justice only arise when there is equal power to compel: in terms of practicality the dominant exact what they can and the weak concede what they must.
>
> **Melians:** So can we not be friends rather than enemies? Would you not accept our inactive neutrality?
>
> **Athenians:** Your friendship is more dangerous to us than your hostility. To our subjects friendship indicates a weakness on our part, but hatred is a sign of our strength.
>
> **Melians:** Do you not think that our alternative offers you security? Since you have diverted us from talk of justice and want us to follow your doctrine of expediency, we must try again by another route and state our own interest, which might convince you if it happens to coincide with yours. At present there are several neutrals: do you want to make enemies of them all?
>
> **Athenians:** You are not in an equal contest, so questions of honour maintained or shame avoided have no relevance. You should be thinking more of your survival, and that means not resisting a force much stronger than you.
>
> **Melians:** We can assure you that we do not underestimate the difficulty of facing your power and a possibly unequal fortune. Yet, as for fortune, we trust that our righteous stand against injustice will not disadvantage us in divine favour . . .
>
> **Athenians:** . . . we know it for sure of men, that under some permanent compulsion of nature wherever they can rule, they will. We did not make this law; it was already laid down, and we are not the first to follow it; we inherited it as a fact, and we shall pass it on as a fact to remain true for ever; and we follow it in the knowledge that you and anyone else given the same power as us would do the same . . . You seem to forget that interest goes hand in hand with safety, while the pursuit of justice and honour involves danger [and] what reassures potential parties to a conflict is obviously not mere sympathy with those who have invited them but some clear superiority in practical strength.
>
> (Extracts from Thucydides, 2009, 5: pp. 302–6)

Thucydides further records that the Melians refused to surrender. The Athenians laid siege to the city and eventually forced a surrender, whereupon they put to death all males of military age, and enslaved the women and children.

is anarchy. Fear and insecurity dominate people's consciousness, driving individuals to seek the means of their own preservation above all else. And since domination is the only viable means of achieving one's preservation, the inevitable result is the war of each against all. This scenario prompted Hobbes to pen his most famous line; namely, that life in the anarchic state of nature is solitary, poor, nasty, brutish, and short!

To dispel anarchy and escape this scenario into a realm of peace and security, individuals must contract together to live under a single, indisputable political authority—a sovereign power—who can enforce order and obedience to a set of laws. People retain only a fundamental right to self-preservation, since it is for this purpose that they submit to the sovereign authority in the first place. Political communities for Hobbes are therefore artificial constructs devised to alleviate the miserable, insecure conditions of the state of nature. As for relations between states, exactly the same conditions apply as for individuals in the state of nature. Since no overarching sovereign authority holds sway in the international sphere, states are condemned to exist in a realm of perpetual anarchy where survival is the name of the game—and this is achieved only through domination and the pursuit of pure self-interest. As for justice and morality, these simply have no place in such an environment (Lawson, 2015: pp. 33–5).

Thucydides, Machiavelli, and Hobbes are just some among a longer list of key figures who are generally included in the 'classical realist canon' and are, for all intents and purposes, considered European (although it is somewhat anachronistic to call Thucydides 'European'). But because classical realism aspires to provide a universally valid theory of international politics, it has also looked outside the usual European line-up to substantiate its credentials as a transhistorical and transcultural canon of reasoned political thought. It has therefore claimed at least two non-European figures as part of the canon: the ancient Chinese strategist Sun Tzu (*c*.545–470 BC) and Kautilya, the ancient Indian commentator on statecraft mentioned in Chapter 2, whose treatise, the *Arthashastra*, has often been compared to Machiavelli.

Sun Tzu's *The Art of War* gives sage advice to rulers on how power should be used to ensure their own interests and survival (Tzu, 2017). Kautilya's work, authored sometime in the first millennium BC (but impossible to date accurately), deals with similar themes, but is more extensive in its treatment of political themes, including political economy (Kautilya, 2016). Both advise that war should be avoided wherever possible, and that a clever leader is one who can win without fighting. This accords with the approach taken by most twentieth-century realist theorists who, far from being warmongers, generally argue for the use of force as a last resort.

Realism and the Critique of Liberalism

Also central to the development of basic theories of realism in international politics, from the 1930s up until about the late 1960s, was a critique of liberal ideas. Indeed, at least in its classic formulation, realism is essentially a conservative response to liberal international thought. One of the most prominent critics, E. H. Carr, is often described as a disillusioned liberal who believed the peace settlement following the First World War was a fiasco. He regarded the principal defect of liberalism as an almost complete blindness to the power factor in politics which he likened to a law of nature, rather like Hobbes.

One of Carr's principal arguments holds, first, that no political society, whether national or international, can exist unless people submit to certain rules of conduct. He further asserts the primacy of politics over ethics, arguing that as a matter of logic rulers rule because of superior strength, and the ruled submit because they are weaker. Political obligation thus derives from the recognition that 'might is right'. This accords with the logic of Thucydides' Athenian generals noted in Box 3.3 above. In preparing the ground for a theory of realism, Carr also asserts that this theory is in fact a reaction to utopianism and cites Machiavelli as initiating a revolt against utopianism in political thought in his own time (Carr, 1948: ch. 4) (see Box 3.4).

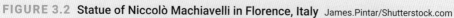

Machiavelli on the 'Real' versus the 'Ideal'

. . . it appears to me more appropriate to follow up the real truth of a matter than the imagination of it; for many have pictured republics and principalities which in fact have never been seen and known, because how one lives is so far distant from how one ought to live that he who neglects what is done for what ought to be done sooner effects his ruin than his preservation.

(Machiavelli quoted in Carr, 1948: p. 63)

FIGURE 3.2 **Statue of Niccolò Machiavelli in Florence, Italy** James.Pintar/Shutterstock.com

NICCOLÒ MACCHIAVELLI

Carr's broader view of politics, however, does not concede the entire ground to realism. He was also concerned to point out that it is just as likely to be found lacking the cold objectivity claimed for it by its proponents as any other way of thinking (ibid.: p. 89). This led him to conclude that sound political thinking must be based on elements of both utopia and reality, for when utopianism 'has become a hollow and intolerable sham, which serves merely as a disguise for the interests of the privileged, the realist performs an indispensable service in unmasking it'. Pure realism, on the other hand, offers 'nothing but a naked struggle for power which makes any kind of international society impossible' (ibid.: p. 93). As we see later in this chapter, the idea of international society was to become a central theme in the English School's contribution to theory.

Post-War Developments in Realist Thought

After the Second World War, and with the onset of the Cold War, the study of global politics developed rapidly in the US and acquired a distinctive realist tone. The principle figure in post-war American theorizing was Hans Morgenthau whose ideas have been compared with those of Thucydides by contemporary authors. Richard Ned Lebow (2007: pp. 52–70), for example, says that both Thucydides and Morgenthau see politics, in any time and any place, as subject to a basic human instinct revolving around power. Realism, like conservatism, therefore claims *not* to be an 'ideology'. This epithet is reserved for doctrines such as liberalism and socialism, which are grounded in idealist suppositions. Realism, on the other hand, claims to provide an account of how things 'really are', and thus asserts an essential objectivity. Morgenthau posits more or less eternal laws of politics rooted in an essential human nature which, he says, have not changed since the classical philosophies of China, India, and Greece endeavoured to discover them (Morgenthau, 1978: p. 4).

Realism also sees politics in the domestic sphere as much the same as politics in the international sphere in so far as it is driven by power politics. The crucial difference is of course the fact that a sovereign authority resides within states and therefore makes domestic order possible. Some order is possible in the anarchic international sphere, but this is achieved only through rather fragile mechanisms. These mechanisms include, first and foremost, a **balance of power** among constituent elements of an international system. In realist theory, this has a **deterrence** effect so long as states behave in a rational manner and do not allow greed and ambition to cloud their judgement.

More sophisticated versions of realism allow for the possibility of a deterrence effect also to arise from certain elements of sociability in an international system. In other words, if a group of states acknowledges a 'community of interests' or is otherwise bound by some common elements of culture, conventions, personal ties, and so on, then competition for power is greatly modified and less likely to generate warfare. Some states, however, aggressively pursue what they perceive to be their own interests regardless. This characterizes both unilateralism and militarism. Thus certain states, such as Athens during the period of the Peloponnesian War, or leaders like Napoleon and Hitler in later times, cannot be deterred. Lebow further quotes Morgenthau's wry observation that a balance of power 'works best when needed least' (Lebow, 2007: p. 58) (see Box 3.5).

Another point to note about the classical realism of Morgenthau, among others, is that it does not deny a role for moral judgement in global politics, although it does recognize a tension between morality and successful politics. Morgenthau is rather a critic of moral*ism*—of an abstract moral discourse that fails to acknowledge political realities and which can lead to *im*prudent action. In contrast, realism assigns supreme value to successful political action based on prudence. Right action therefore involves rational consideration of the likely consequences of any given course of action, and the ability to adopt the most prudent course. Morgenthau's political realism 'considers a rational foreign policy to be good foreign policy; for only a rational foreign policy minimizes risks and maximizes benefits and, hence, complies both with the moral precept of prudence and the political

> **BOX 3.5 KEY QUOTE**
>
> **Hans J. Morgenthau on Power Politics**
>
> International politics, like all politics, is a struggle for power. Whatever the ultimate aims of international politics, power is always the immediate aim. Statesmen and peoples may ultimately seek freedom, security, prosperity, or power itself. They may define their goals in terms of a religious, philosophic, economic, or social ideal. They may hope that this ideal will materialize through its own inner force, through divine intervention, or through the natural development of human affairs. But whenever they strive to realize their goal by means of international politics, they do so by striving for power.
>
> (Morgenthau, 1948: p. 13)

requirement of success'. In his further critique of moralism, Morgenthau highlights the tendency of states to equate their own aspirations with universal moral laws, and to conceal their ambitions behind such a façade. Even more pernicious, he says, is the claim that God is on one's side (Morgenthau, 1978: pp. 3–12). Here it is instructive to note that both George W. Bush and Osama bin Laden, in the crises precipitated by the attacks of 9/11, operated on the assumption that they had God on their side and declared as much to anyone willing to listen.

> **KEY POINTS**
>
> - 'Realism' as a general approach to the study of politics purports to analyse things as they *really are* rather than as they *ought to be*, and in this way marks itself off from the idealism of liberal thought.
> - In developing their ideas, classical realist scholars of the mid-twentieth century have claimed thinkers such as Thucydides, Machiavelli, and Hobbes as belonging to their tradition.
> - Realism comes in different forms, but virtually all realist theory in the global sphere of politics takes the struggle for power and security of sovereign states in conditions of anarchy as its central focus.

THE ENGLISH SCHOOL

While Morgenthau's version of classical realism was making its mark, especially in the US, another group of scholars based on the other side of the Atlantic developed a different approach. This group first gathered in London in 1959, constituting themselves as the 'British Committee' for the purpose of probing fundamental questions of international theory (Dunne, 1998: p. xi). It was to become known as the 'English School' although various of its members hailed from Australia, South Africa, and Canada as well as the UK. One member, Martin Wight, thought the entire field of international politics was theoretically underdeveloped compared with the study of domestic politics. He proposed that, just as political theory asks fundamental questions about the state, so international theory must ask fundamental questions about the international sphere which they conceived as constituting a 'society of states' (Wight, 1966: p. 18). While individual members of the group adopted varying positions, some giving emphasis to realist perspectives while others subscribed to more liberal ideas, they shared a common interest in historical and normative approaches, thereby rejecting the scientism or behaviouralism which had come to characterize much academic work in the US.

The Concept of International Society

As suggested in Wight's remarks, much of their theorizing revolved around the concept of international society articulated earlier by Grotius. This was understood as a society of sovereign states formed under conditions of anarchy. While English School theorists agreed that such conditions are inherently less stable than those in the domestic sphere, their emphasis was on the extent to which a stable order can nonetheless be achieved. A prominent member of the school, Hedley Bull, while accepting the basic premises of realism, proposed that state behaviour could be significantly modified through the adoption of rules and institutions. These generated an international environment and process of socialization in which norms, values, and common interests came to play an important role in influencing state behaviour (see Box 3.6).

The concept of international society, while obviously applicable at a global level, can also operate at a regional level. The EU provides an example of a formal, regionally-based international society. It declares values that are common to member countries which have come together to create 'a society in which inclusion, tolerance, justice, solidarity and non-discrimination prevail' and which are 'an integral part of our European way of life' (EU, 2018). It therefore projects a distinctive identity both to itself and to others. Another example of a regionally-based organization evincing features of an international society is ASEAN. But its six official 'fundamental principles' give the highest priority to state sovereignty and, while emphasizing cooperation, say nothing about integration. Its principles are: '1. Mutual respect for the independence, sovereignty, equality, territorial integrity, and national identity of all nations; 2. The right of every State to lead its national existence free from external interference, subversion or coercion; 3. Non-interference in the internal affairs of one another; 4. Settlement of differences or disputes by peaceful manner;

BOX 3.6 KEY QUOTE

Hedley Bull on the Society of States

[A] society of states (or international society) exists when a group of states, conscious of certain common interests and common values, form a society in the sense that they conceive themselves to be bound by a common set of rules in their relations with one another and share in the working of common institutions.   (Bull, 1997: p. 13)

FIGURE 3.3 **12th ASEAN+3 Summit in Hua Hin, Thailand, 2009** Republic of Korea/www.flickr.com/people/koreanet/

5. Renunciation of the threat or use of force; and 6. Effective cooperation among themselves' (https://asean.org/asean/about-asean/overview/).

Other regional bodies such as the African Union (AU) and the Arab League (AL) also share certain characteristics of a regional international society—often declaring values held in common and which indicate a sense of a shared political culture and identity—but, like ASEAN, they hold much more strongly to the doctrine of state sovereignty than EU members, and come nowhere near to allowing comparable levels of freedom of movement, trade, harmonization of laws, and so on. Even so, all these may be taken as 'real world' exemplars of the concept of international society.

Diversity in International Society

Despite general agreement among the early English School theorists on the basic principles of international society at a global level, there were diverging views on the extent to which a common core of norms could be established among all states which, after all, operated on differing value systems. Bull, Wight, and others were living in an era of decolonization, and states very different from those of Europe were emerging around the world (see Box 3.7). Could a theory as Eurocentric as theirs apply universally? Could the norms of a society of European states really be exported to the rest of the world? These questions highlighted the issue of cultural difference in world politics and the fact that much theorizing to date had been characterized by ethnocentrism or, more especially, Eurocentrism. Even so, to use the example of ASEAN again, it can claim to be a prime example of a regional international society along pluralist lines (as discussed in Box 3.7) which, despite various pressures and difficulties, has achieved an impressive longevity in the global political sphere. It might be more ethnocentric to say that because ASEAN is not European, it cannot meet exactly the same criteria.

BOX 3.7 KEY DEBATE

Pluralism versus Solidarism in the English School

Within the English School, opinion became divided over the extent to which norms, especially with respect to human rights and notions of justice, could be simply exported to other parts of the globe, and especially the former colonial world. Some, including Bull, adopted **pluralism** as the basis of their approach to this issue. This approach recognized that different people (understood in terms of different 'cultures') invariably have different norms and values and, therefore, different standards of justice. If each state is a repository of those standards of justice, one must conclude that there can be no universal yardstick against which standards can be evaluated.

This argument tends strongly towards a notion of ethical *relativism* based on the idea that individual states have not only no legitimate sovereign power above them but no moral authority above them either. The absence of a universal standard for 'right conduct' does not preclude the formation of an international society, but it does mean that it is fairly minimalist. International society is therefore held together simply by agreement on the importance of international order itself, and a normative commitment to supporting the goal of peaceful *coexistence* (Dunne, 1998: p. 100). This position accords more or less with **communitarianism**, as discussed in Chapter 1. According to this approach, morality arises *within* particular communities and basically holds good only *for* those communities. In the sphere of global politics, these moral communities are, in effect, states.

Others, however, adopted a 'solidarist' approach which recognizes the inherent plurality of values among states in the international sphere, but seeks a more robust commitment to shared norms of both domestic and international behaviour, especially when it comes to human rights. **Solidarism** therefore reflects not simply a solidarity among states making a commitment to forming a peaceful international society bound by a commitment to non-**intervention** but a broader commitment to the solidarity of humankind itself. This amounts to a form of ethical *universalism* which contrasts with the tendency to relativism in the pluralist approach. So while a norm of non-intervention may be taken as a standard feature of the society of states in the ordinary course of events, a solidarist position allows, in principle, for this norm to be overtaken by an *extra*ordinary turn of events, such as when a population group within a state becomes a target for genocide. Solidarism therefore shares common ground with **cosmopolitanism** which, as we saw earlier, contemplates the transcendence of state boundaries. For pluralists, however, the solidarist position with its cosmopolitan leanings moves too far away from an international society, understood as a society of bounded states, towards something of a world or global society which de-emphasizes state boundaries and indeed the notion of a state system as such (Buzan, 2004: esp. pp. 139–60). This debate raises some interesting questions:

- Should values and norms be considered as arising only within, and having relevance for, particular cultural groups such as 'nations'?

- If so, what are the implications for universal human rights?

English School theory has experienced a significant revival in recent years. As two prominent authors have remarked, the importance of the English School's concern with the relationship between international or global order and human justice is at the heart of current debates about the relationship between state sovereignty, human rights, and pressures for humanitarian intervention, as well as the phenomenon of failing or fragile states. In light of these concerns, the English School—or at least its solidarist component—is now also associated with the (re)interpretation of sovereignty as the **responsibility to protect**, mentioned in Chapter 2. Questions of clashing world views in a multicultural international society—a concern for some of the early theorists—also seem more urgent than ever in the post-9/11 world. Furthermore, ideas of international society as articulated by earlier English School theorists are seen as highly relevant not only for the analysis of regional integration projects but also for the problems of the global environment as well as aspects of global political economy (Linklater and Suganami, 2006: p. 2; see also Buzan and Schouenborg, 2018).

Another study of legitimacy in international politics argues that, apart from underscoring the very existence of international society, questions of legitimacy have become increasingly urgent in the present period. Bodies such as the UN are seen as an essential repository of much legitimacy in the international sphere, especially in relation to intervention, humanitarian or otherwise (see Clark, 2005). In addition, important aspects of English School theorizing resonate with emergent theories of social constructivism which have become especially prominent in the present period and which we explore further in Chapter 4.

KEY POINTS

- The English School, while accommodating both realist and liberal perspectives, promotes the idea of a society of states underpinned by a set of common norms and values.

- The 'pluralist' approach within the English School seeks to accommodate varying norms, values, and standards of justice of different states within a framework of coexistence based on respect for sovereignty.

- 'Solidarism', in contrast with the pluralist approach, promotes a common set of norms and standards including respect for human rights and, in exceptional circumstances, a right of humanitarian intervention.

NEOLIBERALISM AND NEOREALISM

Further developments in the post-war period saw revisions of both liberalism and realism, resulting in the two 'neos'. **Neorealism** also goes by the name of 'structural' realism because it focuses on the structure of the international system itself. **Neoliberalism**, on the other hand, is sometimes referred to as 'pluralism' for its much broader focus on the multiple forces at play in that system (Little, 1996: p. 66). The use of the term 'pluralism' here, incidentally, is not identical with the way in which it is used by English School theorists. Both usages invoke a concept of diversity, but whereas the English School usage was more concerned with the diversity of culture and values embodied within states, neoliberal pluralism refers to a plurality of actors and institutions in the global or international system. Here we should note also that *economic* neoliberalism, which is the focus of much contemporary discussion of globalization, refers to an approach emphasizing the role of global markets and free trade together with the minimization of state intervention, and so focuses on somewhat different issues.

Liberalism in the Post-War Period

Liberalism's period of renewal occurred after the Second World War when the international sphere underwent significant changes, especially with the founding of the UN as another attempt at creating an international institution capable of regulating global order and of keeping a check on aggressive power politics. The UN incorporated many of the League's features, including a General Assembly and a Secretariat presided over by a Secretary General, a Court of Justice, and an executive Council. In addition, specialized agencies were formed to assist in the task of building a global order with a strong economic and social framework.

The period after 1945 also saw substantial formal decolonization in Africa, the Middle East, and the Asia-Pacific, thus 'globalizing' the liberal idea of self-determination and, as we have seen, the sovereign state system itself as a vehicle for self-determination. As a result, the UN's membership base was much more extensive than that of the old League. Now, virtually every state in the world is a member and so it has become more truly global. All these developments were underpinned by liberal ideas and the aspiration to make the world a better place.

In terms of intellectual development, the renewal of liberalism in the post-war period challenged what was seen as realism's simplistic approach to the nature of the international system. Like realism, liberalism accepted the anarchic character of the international sphere as well as the central role played by sovereign states. Unlike realists, liberals not only accorded international institutions (such as the UN) a crucially important role in ameliorating the negative effects of anarchy and power politics but also came to regard the role of non-state actors as important. These include organizations ranging from transnational corporations to NGOs such as the Red Cross/Red Crescent, the International Chamber of Commerce, the World Council of Churches, and so on. These bodies are said to constitute a form of global **civil society** which operates alongside the state system and the set of regional and international institutions based on that system, to be discussed in Chapter 7.

The Idea of Interdependence

In addition to its attention to the plurality of actors in the international system, neoliberalism also applies a finer-grained analysis to sovereign states. Whereas realists tend to regard states as unitary actors in the international sphere, neoliberals acknowledge a variety of state characteristics and modes of behaviour often influenced by domestic political constraints. Some of the earliest neoliberal ideas were formulated by Robert O. Keohane and Joseph S. Nye (1977) in terms of a new **interdependence** model of international relations which highlighted linkages between various actors as well as their sensitivities to the effects of actions by others in the system, both state and non-state.

Interdependence is generally seen as much more complicated than the relations generated by mere security alliances, especially since the processes of industrialization, modernization, and globalization have produced many more dynamics than can be accommodated in realist theory. Thus neoliberals began to talk of 'complex interdependence' to describe the principle characteristic of a modern international system with its multiple actors, agencies, and forces. Nye said a different kind of world from that depicted by realists could be imagined simply by reversing their key postulates. Thus we can see a world where states are not the only significant actors but operate alongside many others; where force is only one instrument among others, which include economic manipulation; and where the dominant goal is not security, understood in traditional terms, but welfare (Nye, 2005: p. 207).

As we have seen, liberalism has also been closely associated with ideas about creating positive conditions for peace. The link between theory and practice here occurs not just in the construction of institutions but also in the work of the peace movement more

FIGURE 3.4 Recipients of the 2018 Nobel Peace Prize Denis Mukwege (left) and Nadia Murad (centre), with Naledi Pandor, Minister of International Relations and Cooperation of the South African Government, in New York, 2019 lev radin/Shutterstock.com

generally. Further intellectual support has been developed in specialist peace studies programmes in universities and other institutions throughout the world, from the home of the Nobel Peace Prize (established in 1901) in Sweden to Japan, where peace activism, peace museums, and peace studies have had a strong profile since the Second World War.

The Neorealist Turn to Structure

With neoliberalism appearing to provide a plausible alternative account of the international system, *neorealism* in turn restated the prime importance of power in an anarchical international sphere while modifying certain assumptions of classical realism. In refining the latter's ideas, neorealism also sought to produce a more *parsimonious* theory of international politics—that is, a theory stripped down to the essentials. This was meant to provide testable hypotheses in accordance with a more scientific approach. Critics would argue that this came at the expense of gross oversimplification.

The key neorealist figure in the 1970s was Kenneth Waltz whose major work, *Theory of International Politics* (1979), was highly influential in establishing the *structure* of the international state system as determining the behaviour of individual states, and not the other way around. Thus although states remained the principal actors, it was the structural attributes of the system as a whole that determined how states interacted with each other and therefore how the dynamics of the international political sphere worked. And if structure is the key determinant of state behaviour, individual agency has little impact. Furthermore, this structure remains essentially anarchic regardless of how many international institutions attempt to modify its effects.

In an earlier work Waltz (1959) had already laid some of the groundwork for the neorealist or structural realist enterprise through his delineation of three distinct spheres or 'images' of politics: (1) individuals, (2) the state, and (3) the international system of states. In the first image, warfare among individuals is driven by negative aspects of human nature—greed, stupidity, hubris, and misdirected aggression. In the second image, conflict is mediated by the internal (domestic) organization of states. The third image takes anarchy as the essential attribute of the structure of the international system, one which makes warfare much more likely to occur because of the absence of restraints under conditions of anarchy. For Waltz, the third image provides the exclusive subject matter for international politics while political activity within the first or second image exerts little influence on the international sphere because it does not affect its essential structure. In addition to strengthening the dividing line between the domestic and the international, this move effectively eliminates the influence of human nature on international politics. Instead, the struggle for power is determined by the structure of the system itself.

A leading contemporary realist, John Mearsheimer, says that the anarchic international system, in which no higher authority sits above the great powers, and in which there is no guarantee that one will not attack another, means that each state is moved by good sense to acquire sufficient power to protect itself: 'In essence, great powers are trapped in an iron cage where they have little choice but to compete with each other for power if they hope to survive' (Mearsheimer, 2010: p. 78). However, the action by one state to enhance its security vis-à-vis other states, for example by building up its military forces, invariably provokes other states to enhance their military capabilities in turn, thus making them more dangerous than they were before. This is, effectively, a feedback loop which results in a **security dilemma**, a concept developed much earlier in the Cold War period when the arms race was a prominent feature of power politics (see Herz, 1950). It also illustrates the key realist concept of the balance of power in so far as each state strives to adjust its capabilities to balance any change in the capabilities of other states, or at least those states considered relevant to the equation. This at least partly explains why North Korea—with an eye to the projection of military power by its prime 'enemy', the US, in its own East Asian region—has developed an independent nuclear weapons capability. These actions, according to neorealism, are all determined by the *structure* of the international system.

Waltz's ideas do not exhaust the range of ideas about structural realism. Other influential writers include Joseph Grieco (1988) who has elaborated on the idea of relative and absolute gains among states in terms of power and influence. Whereas liberals believe that states are content to make an absolute gain (measured against their own existing capacities rather than relative to other states), realists hold that states always seek both absolute and relative gains. Furthermore, states may well cooperate to enhance their overall position within the state system, but realists believe that states will engage in cheating behaviour if their leaders think this will yield greater power or if continued cooperation appears likely to weaken their position.

Offensive and Defensive Realism

Yet another branch of structural realism distinguishes defensive and offensive varieties and relates these to the concept of **hegemony**—a situation in which there is a dominant centre of power. Offensive realism holds that states constantly seek to enhance their power vis-à-vis others in the system, which is a perfectly rational means of guaranteeing survival. A state that acquires hegemonic status enjoys the greatest measure of security precisely because of its superior power. Defensive realism, on the other hand, views hegemonic ambitions in terms of the security dilemma because the pursuit of hegemony by one state will invariably provoke a reaction in others. Moreover, the combined power of other states may well be greater than that of the aspiring hegemon, leading ultimately to its defeat. However, realists of all varieties can see the dangers of expansionism and other ill-advised adventures abroad. Mearsheimer notes that almost every realist opposed the Iraq War of 2003, which turned into a strategic disaster for the US and the UK (Mearsheimer, 2013: p. 91).

The Critique of Liberal Hegemony

In reflecting on developments over almost three decades since the end of the Cold War, when liberalism appeared to be in the ascendance, Mearsheimer has recently identified a cluster of problems which he associates with 'liberal hegemony'—a state of affairs which he says runs contrary to the core logic of structural realism as well as the insuperable ideology of nationalism. In the end, he suggests that realism and nationalism

---

BOX 3.8   KEY QUOTE

John Mearsheimer on Liberal Hegemony

Liberal hegemony is an ambitious strategy in which a state aims to turn as many countries as possible into liberal democracies like itself while also promoting an open international economy and building international institutions. In essence, the liberal state seeks to spread its own values far and wide. . . . Liberal states have a crusader mentality hardwired into them that is hard to restrain. . . . The liberal state is likely to end up fighting endless wars, which will increase rather than reduce the level of conflict in international politics . . . Moreover, the state's militaristic behaviour is almost certain to end up threatening its own liberal values. Liberalism abroad leads to illiberalism at home.   (Mearsheimer, 2018: pp. 1–3)

---

will always trump liberalism, and any worthwhile foreign policy must recognize this. At the same time, he argues that those who pursue a militarist liberal foreign policy abroad must be aware of the threats this poses for the very values it seeks to promote at home (see Box 3.8).

Ideas about absolute and relative gains, offensive realism and defensive realism, along with the critique of liberal hegemony, are just some of the variations on the neorealist theme. Some of these ideas may appear as abstract elements of an oversimplified theory of global politics, limited in its ability to ask deeper questions about the state of the political world and what the future might hold. Critics of neorealism also hold that it has little to say about a range of pressing problems which go beyond the concerns of military security, from the condition of the global environment to imbalances in resource allocation and consumption around the world. Neorealism certainly says nothing about questions of **global justice**. There is now an emergent school of *neo*classical realism which seeks to broaden the scope of realist theory to attempt once again a more comprehensive theorization and analysis of the mass of variables which contribute to the dynamics of the global sphere (see Ross-Smith, 2018). We may well see another variety of realism develop more fully along these lines in the future. Another variant is moral realism discussed in the final section below.

A further problem with both neorealism and neoliberalism is that their assumptions are based almost exclusively on the dynamics generated by 'great powers', thus relegating less powerful states—which include much of the **Global South**—to virtual irrelevance in the wider scheme of things. With specific reference to Africa, it has been pointed out that theorists of both the 'neos' have located Africa on the margins of global politics, and portrayed African actors as possessing little agency of their own. It has been assumed that because African states lack 'hegemonic power' they cannot be included in great power theorizing, except to the extent that the continent generally 'suffers the whims of the stronger global players'. And when attention has been directed to the continent, thinking has been dominated by 'development theories aimed at reproducing Western economic, political and cultural ideals' (Dunn, 2001: p. 3).

KEY POINTS

- Important neoliberal ideas include 'complex interdependence' which recognizes multiple actors, agencies, and forces at work in the international system and more porous boundaries between domestic and international spheres—conditions favourable to globalization.

- States remain significant actors in neoliberal thought, but they operate alongside many others while economic power is just as significant as force.

- Neorealism takes *structure* as the prime determinant of behaviour in the international sphere, which is quite separate from the state's domestic sphere of politics and must be studied on its own terms.

- The idea of the 'three images' of politics in neorealist thought also eliminates human nature and individual agency as relevant factors. This narrows the scope of international politics and produces a more parsimonious theory which its proponents say can generate testable hypotheses. Neorealism has now split into a variety of approaches as well as being contested by neoclassical realism.

- A shortcoming of both the 'neos' is that they base their principal assumptions on the behaviour of 'great powers', thus excluding much of the Global South.

CONTEMPORARY DISCOURSES OF MORAL REALISM

Another variation on the realist theme has come from a school of thought in China promoting 'moral realism'. Drawing on aspects of ancient Chinese thought (mainly various schools of Confucian thought), this school has been concerned largely with developing a new theoretical perspective on China's rising power and status in global politics. The major point of contrast is generally with the behaviour of the US as a hegemonic power. A principal figure in this school, Yan Xuetong, has argued that the way in which the US conducts its foreign affairs is characterized by a double standard. It is a hegemon which 'presents norms as the principle for dealing with its friends, but power politics as a principle for dealing with its enemies' (Yan, 2012: p. 4). This style of hegemony means that it will rarely find fault with the behaviour of its allies, but will almost always find fault with its enemies, thus reinforcing and perpetuating relations of enmity which undermine harmony.

China, on the other hand, may be able to provide a very different kind of leadership in global politics—that of a 'humane authority'—although this would still be underpinned by significant material power. 'Humane authority', as the name suggests, requires a leading power to practise humane norms both domestically and internationally and to take on significant responsibilities in the global sphere. And in contrast with the US, which promotes international norms based on 'equality, democracy, and freedom', a Chinese approach could improve on these by adopting the guiding principles of 'fairness, justice, and civility'. Further, a humane authority will judge the behaviour of other states, not according to whether the personal relationship is one of 'friends' or 'enemies' but according to international norms of correct moral behaviour (ibid.).

More generally, Yan highlights that realism itself is not amoral and, like Morgenthau, considers morality to be an important aspect of power and an essential element of a state's capabilities. He goes on to note that in ancient Chinese thought there was a very close relationship between morality and interstate order, especially at the level of leadership, although some held that violence may be justified to uphold order. Other ancient thinkers, however, believed that violence is at odds with morality, and that it should not be necessary under proper moral leadership. Interestingly, there is a clear role for 'soft power'. If leaders display 'benevolent virtue' that proves attractive to 'distant people', the latter will be more likely to submit and so violence will be unnecessary (Yan, 2011: pp. 39–40). Yan does not say that this is how China *will* behave as its power grows but rather that this is how it can *choose* to behave and *ought* to behave. The more states that are attracted to a humane authority, the stronger the position of that authority.

This position is not very different from another take on moral realism set out in a conservative US publication:

> Morality in foreign affairs . . . is not found in a set of abstract rules of behavior for nation-states, nor is it found in deploying military power to advance some progressive, idealistic cause. Morality can be found only in the souls of righteous statesmen who, under complex international circumstances, act not out of malice or hatred, nor out of greed or pure self-interest, but who find a path to peace that is compatible not only with the interest of their own nations but that of the others. Such a policy cannot be sketched out in the abstract in advance; it can emerge only through the moral leadership of genuine statesmen who act to find a specific solution in a set of complex, concrete circumstances. This is one of the great lessons of classical political philosophy: justice is not an abstraction but found concretely in the soul of the just man (Smith, 2018).

Returning to the question of contemporary China and whether it can actually 'rise peacefully' (and exercise 'humane authority'), this raises some important issues. John Mearsheimer says that his theory of offensive realism predicts that China will attempt to dominate Asia in much the same way that the US dominates the Western hemisphere and, further, that the US will go to enormous lengths to prevent China from achieving regional hegemony. In addition, most countries in that region, including India, Japan, Singapore, South Korea, Russia, and Vietnam, will join with the US in containing Chinese power. 'The result will be an intense security competition with considerable potential for war. In short, China's rise is unlikely to be tranquil' (Mearsheimer, 2014). Others reject this argument, reverting to a more classical realist position that warns against any attempt by the US to damage China's economy and thus provoke a virulent anti-US nationalism in China that could well spill over into violence (Kirshner, 2010: p. 71).

The point about the dangers of Chinese nationalism in the present period was evident in criticisms of China by the Trump administration not just in relation to trade but in the spread of what that administration was determined to call the 'Chinese virus'—that is, COVID-19. Another view on the rise of China has been proposed by G. John Ikenberry (2008: p. 24) who says that such a power transition would not necessarily repeat past patterns because China faces a Western-centred system which is 'open, integrated, and rules-based' and which would be hard to overturn, but easy to join.

KEY POINTS

- Some contemporary schools of thought in China have expanded on the role of morality in realist thought, drawing on a variety of sources in ancient Chinese thought.

- Ideas of moral realism have been applied in particular to the rise of China in contemporary global politics with arguments suggesting that China could and should become a 'humane authority' in the global sphere. This is at odds with Mearsheimer's offensive realism which sees only danger in China's rise.

CONCLUSION

This chapter has shown how, and under what circumstances, two major competing bodies of international theory developed to provide a substantial framework for the discipline. It has also shown that, although much of the explicit theorizing about international politics did not begin until the twentieth century, both liberalism and realism have drawn on long-standing ideas in the history of political thought to address basic problems of international order. So too has the English School which, while encompassing aspects of both liberalism and realism, has focused much more attention on the *social* character of international or global relations, elaborating in particular the notion of international society and its normative underpinnings.

While most theorizing has been carried out largely, but not exclusively, on the basis of Western philosophical ideas, a new Chinese school of moral realism draws from ancient Chinese thought. More generally, both liberalism and realism have been modified over the years with competing strands developing within them, so neither can be taken as a single body of theory. At the same time, both liberalism and realism assume that certain propositions are universally valid—the 'fact' of international anarchy being a prime example. These and other assumptions, as well as the positivist approaches to methodology developed in the post-war period, have been challenged by some of the more recent bodies of theory, which we consider in Chapter 4.

KEY QUESTIONS

1 How do norms and methods inform the development of theory?

2 What were the major factors behind the rise of liberal international theory in the early twentieth century and what did early theorists hope to achieve?

3 In what way does the right to national self-determination strengthen the legitimacy of the nation-state idea?

4 Why did E. H. Carr describe early liberals as utopians, and was this description fair?

5 What are the distinguishing features of classical realist thought?

6   How does the idea of 'international society' contribute to our understanding of global politics?

7   How could the English School accommodate both realism and liberalism and remain coherent?

8   In what ways does neorealism differ from classical realism?

9   What is 'pluralist' about neoliberalism and how does pluralism relate to the concept of complex interdependence?

10   Is neorealism's parsimony a strength or a weakness?

11   Do liberal states really have a 'crusader mentality'?

12   Is 'moral realism' a contradiction in terms?

FURTHER READING

Angell, Norman (1934), *The Great Illusion* (London: W. Heinemann).
Originally published in 1910, this book is an early influential statement of Idealism which argues against the notion that national prosperity depends on a preponderance of military power. A sample of the text is available at http://net.lib.byu.edu/~rdh7/wwi/1914m/illusion.html.

Bell, Duncan (ed.) (2008), *Political Thought and International Relations: Variations on a Realist Theme* (Oxford: Oxford University Press).
Examines the complexities of realist theory in international thought and the ebb and flow of its appeal to scholars, and rejects assessments of realism that portray it as little more than a form of crude *realpolitik*.

Brown, Chris and Robyn Eckersley (eds) (2018), *The Oxford Handbook of International Political Theory* (Oxford: Oxford University Press).
Provides a substantial and sophisticated collection of essays by leading scholars on all aspects of theory in the field of global or international politics.

Buzan, Barry and Laust Schouenborg (2018), *Global International Society: A New Framework for Analysis* (Cambridge: Cambridge University Press).
Adopts a novel framework for analysing 'global international society', drawing on classical sociology, liberalism, constructivism, and postcolonialism.

Moses, Jeremy (2014), *Sovereignty and Responsibility: Power, Norms and Intervention in International Relations* (Basingstoke: Palgrave Macmillan).
Provides an in-depth analysis, supported by case studies, of the notion of sovereignty as responsibility as well as sovereignty as the expression of power.

Sleat, Matt (ed.) (2018), *Politics Recovered: Realist Thought in Theory and Practice* (New York: Columbia University Press).
A collection of scholarly commentaries covering various aspects of the quest to study politics 'realistically' while also looking at the role played by morals, values, and emotions as well as facts.

WEB LINKS

https://www.irtheory.com/list.htm

The International Relations (IR) Theory website is described as an online resource for students, scholars, and other professionals interested in international relations theory.

https://www.e-ir.info/category/blogs/murray/

This link is to the E-International Relations section on theory and practice in global politics.

https://www.e-ir.info/tag/realism/
https://www.e-ir.info/tag/liberalism/

These links will take you more specifically to entries on realism and liberalism on the E-International Relations website.

http://www.e-ir.info/2011/07/02/realism-and-liberalism-in-modern-international-relations/

This is a sample of a short student essay, again on the E-International Relations website, comparing realism and liberalism and their value in the study of international relations.

 For additional material and resources please visit the **online resources** at: www.oup.com/he/lawson1e.

4

CRITICAL APPROACHES TO GLOBAL POLITICS

- Marxism and Critical Theory

- Historical Sociology and World-Systems Theory

- Social Theory and Constructivism

- Postmodernism and Poststructuralism

- Conclusion

Reader's Guide

While liberal and realist theorists probe each other's ideas for faults and weaknesses, both operate within the same paradigm—an international order composed of sovereign states engaging each other under conditions of anarchy. Neither have challenged capitalism and its implications for social, economic, and political order. Marxism, on the other hand, which developed around the mid-nineteenth century, has provided very different perspectives and presents a significant challenge for mainstream approaches to global order in both theory and practice. Post-Marxist Critical Theory, along with historical sociology and world-systems theory, emerged in the twentieth century, giving rise to schools of thought which continue the critique of capitalism and the social and political forces underpinning it. In the meantime, ideas arising from social theory, such as the extent to which our perceptions of reality are socially conditioned and indeed 'constructed', achieved greater prominence following the end of the Cold War, an event which prompted many scholars to start asking new questions about global politics and the assumptions on which traditional theories rested. Constructivism, postmodernism, and poststructuralism remain concerned with issues of power and justice but provide different lenses through which these issues may be viewed in the sphere of global politics.

MARXISM AND CRITICAL THEORY

Marxist theory derives from the thought of Karl Marx (1818–83) and his close collabora-tor, Friedrich Engels (1820–95). It aims to provide a radical critique of capitalist society and, indeed, of earlier modes of social, economic and political organization, primarily through the analysis of class relations. The themes of power, ideology, and **hegemony**, and especially the way in which ruling classes maintain control and promote the legiti-macy of capitalism, are central to Marxist thought. Marxist ideas have had a major influ-ence on critical approaches to virtually all aspects of politics in both domestic and global spheres. In this chapter we examine several major strands of Marxist-influenced theory of direct relevance to global politics, including Gramscian theory (after its founding the-orist, Antonio Gramsci) and Frankfurt School theory (after its home base in Germany) which constitute distinctive approaches to contemporary Critical Theory (CT).

The strands discussed here are all variants of or draw from 'Western Marxism'. This distinguishes the legacy of Marx and Engels from the way in which their thought has been theorized in authoritarian communist regimes, especially in China and the former USSR where it underpinned distinctive revolutionary traditions (see Chan, 2003; Marik, 2008). In both cases, however, it was also transformed into a version of **authoritarianism**, although it was never inevitable that implementing Marxist ideas in practice would nec-essarily entail an authoritarian political system. As one commentator has noted, Marx has not always been well served by his followers (Rockmore, 2018: p. 2). Dependency and world-systems theory are also related to the Marxist tradition while historical sociology, although not necessarily Marxist, at least shares with that tradition a critical approach to large-scale patterns of social, political, and economic development over time.

Key Marxist Ideas

Among the main elements of Marxist thought is the notion of ideology as 'false consciousness'. This is especially important in analysing how the interests of any ruling class are presented as natural, inevitable, and desirable, even for subject classes. Although Marx never used the specific term 'false consciousness' in association with ideology, it has nonetheless been taken to characterize the tendency of ruling classes to distort the objective realities about their positions of privilege vis-à-vis working classes. This works to mask actual relations of domination and subordination.

These ideas are elaborated through Marx's notion of **historical materialism** which is based on a distinctive notion of 'reality' reflected in turn in the *material* conditions of life under the capitalist mode of production. Capitalism in this view constitutes the eco-nomic structure of society upon which all legal and political institutions and practices are based. This insight led Marx to declare that: 'It is not the consciousness of men that determines their existence, but their social existence that determines their consciousness' (Marx, 1950). In this we find an explicit formulation of the interrelationship between the ideational and the material as explained in Chapter 1. Some of these ideas were more fully developed, but with less of an emphasis on the material aspects, by Antonio Gramsci through his theory of hegemony which we come to shortly.

Here we should also note the Marxist emphasis on the role of the **bourgeoisie**, generally defined as a merchant and/or propertied class wielding essential economic power. The opening passages of the *Communist Manifesto* (1848), quoted in Box 4.1, describe how the

BOX 4.1   KEY QUOTE

Marx and Engels on Capitalism and Colonialism

The discovery of America, the rounding of the Cape, opened up fresh ground for the rising bourgeoisie. The East Indian and Chinese markets, the colonization of America, trade with the colonies, the increase in the means of exchange and in commodities generally, gave to commerce, to navigation, to industry, an impulse never before known . . .

Modern industry has established the world market, for which the discovery of America paved the way. This market has given an immense development to commerce, to navigation, to communication by land. . . .

The need of a constantly expanding market for its products chases the bourgeoisie over the entire surface of the globe. It must nestle everywhere, settle everywhere, establish connexions everywhere.

The bourgeoisie has through its exploitation of the world market given a cosmopolitan character to production and consumption in every country. . . . All old-established national industries have been destroyed or are daily being destroyed. They are dislodged by new industries . . . that no longer work up indigenous raw material, but raw material drawn from the remotest zones; industries whose products are consumed, not only at home, but in every quarter of the globe.

In place of the old wants, satisfied by the production of the country, we find new wants, requiring for their satisfaction the products of distant lands and climes. In place of the old local and national seclusion and self-sufficiency, we have intercourse in every direction, universal inter-dependence of nations. . . .

The bourgeoisie keeps more and more doing away with the scattered state of the population, of the means of production, and of property. It has agglomerated population, centralized the means of production, and has concentrated property in a few hands. The necessary consequence of this was political centralization. Independent, or but loosely connected provinces, with separate interests, laws, governments, and systems of taxation, became lumped together into one nation, with one government, one code of laws, one national class-interest, one frontier, and one customs-tariff. . . .   (Marx and Engels, 1848)

FIGURE 4.1 **Karl Marx** Everett Collection/Shutterstock.com

needs of a constantly expanding market see the bourgeoisie in a competitive scramble for position and advantage all over the globe, thereby creating the phenomenon of modern global **imperialism**. Indeed, the *Manifesto* describes quite accurately the chief characteristics of modern **globalization**.

The first Russian communist leader, Vladimir Ilyich Lenin (1870–1924), developed a more elaborate critique of imperialism as the 'highest and final stage of capitalism' and highlighted its parasitic exploitation of peripheral countries characterized by an increasing gap between rich and poor countries and also leading to wars over control of territory and resources (Lenin, 1986). Implicit in Lenin's analysis of imperialism was also its tendency to generate anti-colonial or national liberation movements which indicated, among other things, the limits of imperialism in international relations (Arrighi cited in Callinicos, 2018: p. 476).

Another key figure in the Marxist tradition is Rosa Luxemburg (1871–1919), both an activist and a philosopher. She was notable, among other things, for her sharp criticism of fellow socialists who adopted positions that constrained individual freedom. She wrote extensively on political theory, social history, sociology, cultural theory, and ethnography, contributing to a range of issues from feminism to **nationalism** and the idea of **self-determination** (Nettl, 2019: pp. ix–xi). With respect to the latter, Luxemburg argued that the 'formula of the right of nations' is a cliché which failed to take into account 'the wide range of historical conditions (place and time) existing in each given case' as well as 'the general current of the development of global conditions'. In addition, she said, this formula takes 'nations' to be homogeneous socio-political entities when they are clearly no such thing. Quite apart from the highly diverse ethnic heritage of most 'nations', Luxemburg argued that within each **nation**, there exist 'classes with antagonistic interests and "rights"' which undermines any case for conceiving of them as a 'consolidated "national" entity' (Luxemburg, 1976: p. 135).

As both a theorist and an activist, Luxemburg was concerned always to bring matters 'down from the clouds of abstraction to the firm ground of concrete conditions' (ibid.: p. 141), and she wrote in detail on these issues within the Russian empire of her time as well as on the experiences of European states and the general implications for the colonized world which she saw as operating as 'supply depots' for capitalist European nation-states. Furthermore, if the latter were the only ones considered as eligible entities for self-determination, then 'national self-determination' becomes 'a theory of the ruling races and betrays clearly its origin in the ideologies of bourgeois liberalism together with its "European" cretinism' (ibid.). In summary, Luxemburg believed that **nations** and nationalism were invented for the sole purpose of capitalist exploitation (see Worth, 2012: p. 144).

The influence of Marxist thought in global politics has been profound, both in the extent to which it came to underpin large-scale political movements in Russia, China, and many parts of the former colonial world in the twentieth century—despite its **Eurocentrism**—and in the reaction against its major precepts, especially in the US. The transformation of Marxism into a form of political authoritarianism sharpened the divide, and the profound 'clash of ideologies' between authoritarian communism and democratic capitalism produced the dynamics underpinning the Cold War from around 1945 to 1989.

The collapse of the Soviet Union and of communist regimes throughout Eastern Europe after 1989 was famously interpreted as signalling the 'end of history' in the sense

FIGURE 4.2 **Rosa Luxemburg** World History Archive/Alamy Stock Photo

that, after the failure of communism, there were no great challenges left to the pre-eminence of **liberal democracy** and capitalism as *the* political and economic systems *par excellence* (see Fukuyama, 1989). Marxism, however, continues to attract adherents, especially in a world where capitalist modes of production and governance continue to deliver enormous disparities in wealth and poverty as well as significant environmental threats.

Recent times have also seen the return and, indeed, strengthening of authoritarian rule around the world, from Russia to Turkey, Central Asia, China, and various countries of the Middle East and North Africa in particular. Contemporary authoritarianism, however, is rarely inspired by Marxist/communist ideals. Even in China, which remains under Chinese Communist Party (CCP) rule and an 'official' (albeit heavily revised) Marxist-Leninist ideology, a capitalist economic system has been adopted, with a burgeoning private sector driving spectacular economic growth while also producing vastly increased inequalities in the distribution of wealth.

Marxist-inspired Critical Theory (CT) has continued to develop, mainly in Western intellectual centres but with important contributions from elsewhere as well. CT has several branches although a common emphasis is on an ethical notion of **emancipation** from oppressive social and material conditions. Many contemporary proponents of CT have also moved away from the Marxist focus on economics and class struggle. And virtually all CT theorists reject political authoritarianism (as practised in the former USSR and in China) as a legitimate expression of socialist ideas. Here we should note that Marxism is not the only source of socialist ideas and that a robust tradition of democratic socialism, which was evolutionary rather than revolutionary, also developed from the early nineteenth century in Western Europe as a distinctive strand of thought. It is largely from this tradition that the social democratic welfare traditions of many West and North European democracies (including those of Scandinavia) draw, although key elements of Marxist critique have remained influential.

Gramscian Critical Theory

The Italian intellectual Antonio Gramsci (1891–1937) is often described as the leading European Marxist thinker of the twentieth century. He was both an activist and an intellectual who believed strongly in *praxis*, which links 'thinking' with 'doing' (see Box 4.2). One of Gramsci's most significant intellectual contributions was in highlighting the phenomenon of the *naturalization of power* in the creation of hegemony by elites. He argued that ruling classes maintained power and control, even in the absence of constant coercive force, because they make prevailing inequalities seem *natural, inevitable, and even right*.

Far from being 'natural', however, Gramsci pointed out that inequalities are the product of specific social, political, and economic circumstances. They are *made* to seem natural by those who have the *cultural* power to control 'hearts and minds'. These insights resonate with the Marxist conception of ideology as false consciousness, but the Gramscian approach focuses more on the consensual nature of support for hegemony. If people consider a particular social order to be natural, they are far less inclined to oppose it and will even effectively consent to it. Although Gramsci wrote mainly about domestic politics, he recognized that the dynamics of hegemony extended to the global sphere 'between complexes of national and continental civilisations' (Gramsci quoted in Schwarzmantel, 2009: p. 8).

Later figures, such as Canadian theorist Robert W. Cox (1926–2018), found Gramsci's insights highly pertinent in explaining the *hegemony of theories and ideas* in the global sphere. This differs from conceptions of hegemony which focus only on material (mainly economic and military) capabilities. Cox (1981: p. 128) is well known for declaring that 'theory is always *for* some one, and *for* some purpose'. Put another way, theories are never neutral in the selection and interpretation of facts—they are reflections of the subjective values and interests of those who devise them and, therefore, tend strongly to support those values and interests. It follows that *facts and values do not exist independently of each other*, so the idea that any theory can be 'value-free', or that knowledge can be totally objective, is insupportable.

Cox argued that **realism** is an *ideology of the status quo*, supporting the existing global order and therefore the interests of those who prosper under it. Furthermore, by presenting it as *natural*, the existing order is perceived as inevitable and unchanging in its essentials. Any difficulties that arise within the order are seen as problems to be solved within the parameters *of* that order. The order itself is never challenged. Rather, we are enjoined to accept it on the basis (to use a contemporary catchphrase) that *it is what it is*.

Cox and other Critical Theorists have insisted that no order is 'natural' or immune from change. All political orders, from that of the smallest community to the world at large, are humanly constructed and can in principle be reconstructed in a more just and

BOX 4.2 SHORT BIOGRAPHY

Antonio Gramsci

Gramsci was born in 1891 on the Italian island of Sardinia, growing up in impoverished circumstances. He won a scholarship to the University of Turin where he studied literature and linguistics and became acquainted with history and philosophy. He became a founding member of the Italian Communist Party, served as its secretary, and was elected a member of parliament in 1924. Despite having parliamentary immunity from prosecution, Gramsci was imprisoned in 1926 under the fascist regime of Benito Mussolini which had outlawed the Communist Party. Gramsci's impressive intellect had prompted his prosecutor to argue for a substantial prison sentence in order 'to stop this brain from functioning for twenty years' (quoted in https://mronline .org/2018/12/05/antonio-gramsci-and-the-modern-prince/#lightbox/0/). He died in prison in 1937. Despite very poor health and adverse conditions, Gramsci produced a fragmented but nonetheless impressive corpus of writings published posthumously under the title *Prison Notebooks* (see Gramsci, 1971). He is widely regarded as a founding theorist of the links between power, economics, and culture, including the power of cultural institutions such as the mass media (see, generally, Davidson, 2018).

FIGURE 4.3 **Antonio Gramsci** MARKA/Alamy Stock Photo

equitable manner. CT aims to provide the intellectual framework for *emancipation from unfair and unjust social, political, and economic arrangements that benefit the few at the expense of the many.* To the extent that liberalism participates in the perpetuation of injustices, especially through capitalism, it is subject to a similar critique. Cox became a key critic of globalization, arguing that the phenomenon is not simply the inevitable outcome of major, ongoing technical advances but is underpinned by a hegemonic ideology promoting deregulation of both capital and labour, to the considerable disadvantage of the latter (see Griffiths, Roach, and Sullivan, 2009: p. 169).

The Frankfurt School

The Frankfurt School of the 1920s and 1930s, which included figures such as Theodor Adorno, Herbert Marcuse, and Max Horkheimer, shared with Gramsci a concern for cultural and social factors, therefore placing less emphasis on economics. A more recent figure, Jürgen Habermas, has continued the Frankfurt School's tradition of critical enquiry through new forms of social theory. Habermas's theory of communicative action holds that, under the right conditions, a consensus about 'truth' may be reached. This relies on an epistemology which sees knowledge about the social world emerging through a process of continuous dialogue. Because the social sciences cannot proceed as the natural sciences do, they must instead see all action from the perspective of the actors involved (see Smith, 1996: pp. 27–8). Habermas rejects the notion of objective ethical truths that exist independently of any social world. They are made *within* a social world, but one which is wide enough to embrace everyone. This provides the basis for universally valid ethics and so Habermas's normative theory is clearly **cosmopolitan**.

Contemporary writers such as Andrew Linklater have extended Habermas's emancipatory concerns to the global sphere, especially with respect to how state boundaries tend to denote the limits of ethical concerns. The most creative Critical Theorists go beyond mere critique of existing theories and practices and put forward alternative visions of how the world *could* be (and *should* be). Linklater's ideas about transformative potentials for the way in which political communities are conceived and structured, for example, set out such a vision. Although **modernity** has a dark side, he argues that it still carries within it the seeds of the original aims of the **Enlightenment** which are, in the final analysis, about the emancipation of people from a range of constraints, prejudices, and exploitative practices. And while modernity gave us the Westphalian state system, the 'unfinished project of modernity' envisages a post-Westphalian world in which states as political communities no longer operate in the service of inclusion and exclusion. This transformation, he suggests, seems most likely to occur in the very region which gave rise to that system in the first place and which has since produced the EU, itself a project with considerable normative potential (see Linklater, 1998). Habermas too sees very similar possibilities in the European project (see Box 4.3). In light of more recent developments with Brexit and the rise of right-wing nationalist **populism** throughout the continent, however, it seems that the project has a very long way to go, and may well stall for some considerable time (see, generally, Martill and Staiger, eds, 2018).

Another important point is that CT just like realism and liberalism, is steeped in Eurocentrism. All its key figures from Marx to Gramsci, Habermas, Cox, and others, are operating within a critical tradition that is oriented almost exclusively to what has been happening in the West and, even when it does include attention to impacts in or on the non-West or Global South, the latter is often depicted as relatively passive. One author writes that in Gramscianism, for example, 'the global' turns out to be the 'provincial West writ large' (Hobson, 2012: p. 247). But if the solution is envisaged as producing specific

BOX 4.3 KEY QUOTES

Linklater and Habermas on the Transformation of Political Community

Alternative means of organising human beings . . . seem most likely to appear in Western Europe . . . where a lasting balance between the claims of the nation and the species may yet come to be struck . . . Whether Europe will be the first international region which is permanently transformed by peace rather than by war . . . is unclear. What is clear is that it is improbable that changes in the structure of European international society will be quickly emulated across the world as a whole . . . Promoting the ideal of a universal communication community in which insiders and outsiders recognise one another as moral equals is essential where the nature of political community has become problematical in the lives of its own members.

(Linklater, 1998: pp. 218–19)

It is undisputed that there can be no Europe-wide democratic will-formation capable of enacting and legitimating positively coordinated and effective redistributive policies without an expanded basis of solidarity . . . Sceptics doubt whether this can happen, arguing that there is no such thing as a European 'people' who could constitute a European state . . . On the other hand, peoples emerge only with the constitutions of their states. Democracy itself is a legally mediated form of political integration. It is a form that depends, to be sure, on a political culture shared by all citizens. But if we consider the process by which European states of the nineteenth century gradually *created* national consciousness and civic solidarity—the earliest modern form of collective identity—with the help of national historiography, mass communications, and military duty, there is no cause for defeatism. If this artificial form of 'solidarity among strangers' owes its existence to a historically influential abstraction . . . why should this learning process not continue on, beyond national borders?

(Habermas, 2003: pp. 97–8)

national or regional schools of studies in global politics like a 'Chinese School', an 'Indian School', or an 'African School', another scholar suggests that this may tend simply to reproduce an unproductive West/non-West binary. This is not to suggest that traditional sources of knowledge from non-Western sites have no place but rather to call for 'reorienting the discipline toward a *post*-Western era whose epistemological foundation is not hegemonic in nature' (Chen, 2011: pp. 1–2).

KEY POINTS

- The critique of capitalism by Marx and Engels provided a basis for later critiques of traditional theories in the field of global politics. Marx and Engels were also the first to observe how capitalism is implicated in the development of a global system.

- CT provides an intellectual and normative framework promoting a project of emancipation from social, political, and economic arrangements that benefit the few at the expense of the many through hegemonic control in a system of both coercion and consent.

HISTORICAL SOCIOLOGY AND WORLD-SYSTEMS THEORY

Historical sociology is concerned with the study of historical change with a focus on how complex, large-scale structures and patterns emerge over the longer term as products of particular social forces rather than as naturally occurring phenomena. Marx's approach to the systematic investigation of political, social, and economic relations over time is often described as a form of historical sociology. This does not mean that historical sociology is essentially Marxist in orientation, although some historical sociologists—such as the major proponents of world-systems theory which we examine shortly—may be.

Patterns of Historical Change

While historical sociology may be considered a fairly recent mode of enquiry, it has precursors in the work of earlier scholars. Ibn Khaldun, for example, mentioned in Chapter 1, produced the *Muqqddima* (Khaldun, 1967), an introduction to history with a strong sociological component and which considers issues concerning the nature of civilization and the rise and fall of states over time. It is therefore regarded as the earliest attempt by an historian to discover patterns of change in political and social organization (Dawood in Khaldun, 1967, p. ix; see also Alatas, 2014). Khaldun observed, among many other things, that 'history, in matter of fact, is information about human social organization, which itself is identical with world civilization', adding that it 'deals with such conditions as savagery and sociability, group feelings, and the different ways by which one group of human beings achieves superiority over another' (Khaldun, 1967: p. 35).

Recent figures in historical sociology include Michael Mann, who developed an analysis of complex social power (which incorporates political, military, economic, and ideological power) and whose seminal work spans four substantial volumes. His analysis investigates, among other things, the phenomenon of empires from ancient times, along with civilizations, the rise of **nation-states**, the development of capitalism, and, more broadly, the processes of globalization(s) which he sees as having taken more than one form. Mann has focused specifically on the 'centrality of ferocious **militarism** to our own Western society' (Mann, 1996: p. 221) which clearly has implications for global politics more generally. One of the lessons of Mann's approach is that there are many different ways in which people have organized themselves through time and space, as we saw in Chapter 2. This leads us to treat states, which may otherwise appear as natural and inevitable containers of politico-military organization, as just one possible form. Mann further asserts that realists are especially prone to reifying modern states, 'crediting them with a solidity, cohesion, autonomy and power in society that they rarely have' (ibid.: pp. 222–3).

Another prominent figure in the field is Andrew Linklater who has joined in discussion of the links between historical sociology and IR, once again noting the dissatisfaction expressed by both historical sociologists and critical IR theorists with the realist assumption that the basic driving principles of relations between states have not changed over millennia (Linklater, 2011: p. 194). In relation to the contemporary period, Linklater also notes the importance of sociological contributions to the analysis of global political and economic structures, citing in particular the work of sociologist Anthony Giddens (ibid.). The latter's key contribution focuses on the nation-state and violence and the dynamics of power and domination in the capitalist world economy (Giddens, 1985: p. 335).

Historical sociology as a methodological approach to the study of global politics attracts those IR scholars concerned to look for large-scale transnational and global patterns of change which transcend the traditional national/international divide. It also has the potential to transcend the West/non-West divide. It is especially useful in illuminating the fact that although aspects of human society, including particular configurations of power and privilege, may appear to occur 'naturally', a deeper historical and more extensive global perspective shows just how malleable societies are (Lawson, 2015: pp. 141–2).

Dependency and World-Systems Theory

This brings us to the sociological approaches developed around dependency theory and world-systems analysis by André Gunder Frank and Immanuel Wallerstein respectively. Frank's dependency theory and world-systems analysis uses a deep historical perspective, decentring Europe as the principal agent of historical change in the process. This approach distinguishes it from most versions of globalization which see Europe and the West more generally as at the centre of virtually all world-transforming dynamics. It also challenges the appropriateness of the Western path to modernity. As with postcolonial theorists, Frank sought to 'decentre' Europe and was critical of leading European philosophers, including Karl Marx, for their inherent Eurocentrism.

Frank's dependency theory is part of a larger critique of modernization and development theories applied initially to Latin America and then to the Global South in general. It explains underdevelopment in poor, peripheral countries as the exploitative legacy of Western imperialism and colonialism rather than local cultural factors to do with 'traditionalism'. Even after independence the underlying structures of exploitation remain while many postcolonial indigenous elites have simply colluded with the 'core' states (generally those of the industrialized North) in perpetuating relations of exploitation. A major focus of dependency theory is therefore on core–periphery relations and how these are embedded in the world system (Frank, 1967; Frank and Gills, 1996).

Wallerstein's world-systems approach critiques the totality of exploitative economic and political relations from a sociological as well as historical perspective. He embraces the basic assumptions of dependency theory, but his concept of *world* system is quite deliberate in not using *international*, for it depicts a capitalist world economy which transcends the nation-state model of separate political and economic units in much the same way as 'global' does. Further, his world system 'is a *social* system, one that has boundaries, structures, member groups, rules of legitimation, and coherence' (Wallerstein, 1976: p. 229, emphasis added). In addition, Wallerstein provides a thought-provoking critique of how the very construction of social science forces thinking processes, especially in terms of 'development', along very restricted pathways (Wallerstein, 2001).

Wallerstein was very much influenced by the French historian Fernand Braudel (1902–85), best known for establishing the *Annales* school of historical analysis which focused on *global* history as a totality rather than simply parts of it, and over long periods of time (the *longue durée*) rather than in discrete, self-contained periods. Braudel's approach was highly critical in its analysis of capitalism and its impact on ordinary people, and this is also central to Wallerstein's work. In addition, by taking his unit of analysis as nothing less than the entire world-system, and certainly transcending the nation-state, Wallerstein departed substantially from established social science approaches (see, generally, Wallerstein, Rojas, and Lemert, 2012).

> **KEY POINTS**
>
> - Historical sociology highlights the way in which complex, large-scale structure and patterns of human political and social organization emerge over time as the product of particular social forces rather than as naturally occurring phenomena.
> - Dependency theory and world-systems analysis draw on Marxist thought in critiquing theories of modernization and development, especially in relation to the Global South, and the exploitative structure of the global economic and political system.

SOCIAL THEORY AND CONSTRUCTIVISM

At the broadest level, **social constructivism** in global politics challenges the way in which both neorealism and neoliberalism take the essential components (states) and the character of the global or international system (anarchic) for granted, as if states and the system in which they operate were 'just there' rather than emerging as products of human **agency** and in historically contingent circumstances. These insights are drawn from the more general field of social theory which investigates the extent to which realities are in fact 'socially constructed'. Although it is claimed that constructivism has no direct antecedents in traditional international theories, English School approaches, in so far as these have a definite social orientation, have provided useful insights for the contemporary constructivist project in international thought (Ruggie, 1998: p. 11). There is also a significant tradition of European social theory, developed in earlier periods by classical sociologists such as Emile Durkheim, Max Weber, and Karl Mannheim, from which contemporary constructivists have drawn. Berger and Luckman's influential work, *The Social Construction of Reality* (1966) also broke significant ground in showing how social orders (which embody beliefs, norms, values, interests, rules, institutions, and so on) are an ongoing human production. And if we consider the sphere of global politics through the lens of social constructivist theory, we can see the extent to which it really is a 'world of our making' (Onuf, 1989).

The Ideational and the Material

Some constructivist approaches have been especially critical of the tendency in traditional IR theories to focus largely on *material* forces (e.g. guns and bombs), arguing that *ideational* forces are equally if not more important. Ideational forces are formed through social interaction and consist of norms, values, rules, and symbols that influence how agents come to acquire identities and interests and act in the world on the basis of those identities and interests (see, generally, James, Bertucci, and Hayes, eds, 2018). It is also within the realm of ideas that *meaning* is created, including the meaning of material objects. Alexander Wendt points out, for example, that a gun in the hands of an enemy is a very different thing from the same object in the hands of a friend or ally, adding that 'enmity is a social, not material, relation' (Wendt, 1996: p. 50). The impact or effect of material objects and forces therefore derives ultimately from social factors and the ways in which actors or agents come to assume identities as enemies or friends (or neither). The issue of *state* identity is discussed further below.

Wendt's version of constructivism does not deny the importance of material force. Rather, it establishes the important connection between material *and* ideational forces, thus providing a better understanding of how 'social facts' are produced. It follows that fundamental institutions, such as states and their sovereign properties, are social rather than material facts, constructed at an intersubjective level by agents (us!). Anarchy or **sovereignty**—or any other concept invented by humans—has no existence or meaning outside of those who think and believe in them. Thus anarchy is simply 'what states make of it' (Wendt, 1992: pp. 391–425). And the same must apply to sovereignty. The things we take for granted as the 'reality' of the world around us possess the same character—the market, the government, the EU, the UN, the US, in fact virtually any entity created and sustained by human agency. One cannot see, feel, hear, smell, taste, or choke on any of these 'things' precisely because they are not material. But they are nonetheless very real in these consequences.

All this casts a different light on the relationship between *agents* and *structures* (people and institutions), with many constructivists emphasizing that agents and structures are *mutually constituted*. Put another way, people are born into an existing world—one which has both material and ideational aspects—and are shaped by that world as they grow and mature and develop their own ideational perspectives. Existing structures, which always already embody a set of norms and values, shape each emerging generation of agents. But agents also act on existing structures and can change them. After all, these structures were put in place by previous generations rather than set in concrete by nature and can in principle be remade or replaced provided there is a sufficient level of *norm change* among relevant actors (see Katzenstein, 1996; Wiener, 2018).

The role of power in the construction of norms, values, and institutions is clearly key to understanding their capacity to endure. Here is where the idea of *social* power is all-important. Again, although it may well be related to material power, social power is much more subtle, reflecting 'the ability to set standards, and create norms and values that are deemed legitimate and desirable, without resorting to coercion or payment' (Van Ham, 2010: p. 8). The definition of social power provided here resonates with Gramsci's analysis of the role of cultural power in 'winning hearts and minds' as well as with the idea of 'soft power', which we consider in relation to diplomacy and foreign policy in Chapter 9.

State Identity

The issue of state identity, or more especially how states *construct* identities, which in turn inform—and are informed by—their interests and preferences in the sphere of global politics, has featured prominently in constructivist scholarship. State identity is similar to national identity, but there are differences. National identity may be understood as emerging from affective, intersubjective dynamics operating within a broad group which conceives of itself as a 'nation' (that is, 'a people'), on the basis of one or more of the following factors—a shared history, language, religion, culture, ethnicity, and so on. 'The nation' may also lay claim to a particular territory and a right to statehood. As we have seen earlier, however, few states contain singular nations and a 'national culture' is usually either an amalgam or is based on the characteristics and values of a dominant group.

State identity, while perhaps drawing on certain national characteristics, is more of a political/institutional identity oriented to the global or international sphere and its position and interests in that sphere vis-à-vis other states. State identity is implicated in foreign policy choices, alliances, membership of international organizations, and so on, and generally shapes behaviour and interaction in the global sphere. These of course may change over time, sometimes very slowly and sometimes more rapidly, according to circumstances. Japan's identity as an international actor, for example, has changed from that of an aggressive, militaristic state in the earlier part of the twentieth century to a peaceful, democratic member of international society after 1945. China's emergence as a major actor in world affairs means that its identity has undergone rapid change over the last few decades. Russia's identity in contemporary global politics has also been reconstructed in the wake of the break-up of the Soviet Union and the rise to power of Vladimir Putin. The longer-term outcome for the identity of the US as a global actor, indeed *the* leading global actor, following the Trump presidency remains to be seen.

In addition to state identities, other entities may also acquire identities in the international sphere. The EU, for example, has acquired an identity as a global actor over time, projecting certain norms, values, and interests according to its self-image as a peaceful, democratic, and human rights protective entity that also operates as a large-scale open trading bloc. The African Union also promotes an identity for the continent through a notion of pan-Africanism based on a set of common interests and values which transcend the individual member states. Much the same the same may be said of other regional formations such as the Arab League and ASEAN.

FIGURE 4.4 **President of the People's Republic of China, Xi Jinping, during the G20 summit in Hangzhou, China, 2016** Gil Corzo/Shutterstock.com

BOX 4.4   KEY QUOTE

Yaqing Qin on Culture and Social Theory

A social theory tends to originate in a particular geo-cultural setting, which shapes the practices of the cultural community and thus defines the efforts to develop theory, too. Social theory is therefore from the very beginning imprinted with the characteristic features of the cultural community of its origin, for it is this community that shapes the background knowledge of its members and thus provides the menu for the theorist to choose throughout the process of her theoretical construction.

(Qin, 2018: p. 3)

A constructivist analysis would look to how all such identities are constructed and re-constructed over time through social processes in both the national and global spheres. One obvious point to be addressed, however, is the extent to which states, like individuals, actually have multiple identities or fluid forms of identification that come into play at different times and under different circumstances, and which can be invoked by state elites according to their interests and opportunities (see Lebow, 2016: p. 22).

There are ongoing developments in the broad field of social theory and constructivism which are incorporating insights from additional areas of social theory including 'actor network theory', which focuses, among other things, on the dynamics arising from *relations* between and among actors, rather than the intrinsic properties of actors themselves (whether these are individuals, groups, or institutions). A major work synthesizing aspects of Western social theory with Confucian/Chinese precepts of relationships and relationality is Yaqing Qin's *A Relational Theory of World Politics* (2018), a work which critiques assumptions of rationality and posits 'culture' as providing the background condition for generating social knowledge, interpretation, and practice (see Box 4.4).

See **Chapter 5** for a critique of culturalist approaches.

However defined, constructivism has become an increasingly popular approach to the study of global politics for those seeking more complex, socially oriented accounts of the contemporary world.

POSTMODERNISM AND POSTSTRUCTURALISM

Postmodernism names perhaps the most complex of theoretical fields in the human sciences and is manifest in an array of ideas that challenge, in one way or another, some of the key assumptions of modernity. In the study of global politics, some prefer to describe their approach as 'poststructuralist', which emphasizes the linguistic aspects of meaning and interpretation that produce knowledges (note the plural). For convenience I use the term 'postmodernism' in this chapter.

While sharing some important basic assumptions with Critical Theory and constructivism, postmodern approaches to global politics are more radical in their **epistemology**, rejecting the idea that we can ever have certain grounds for knowledge. Postmodernism therefore rejects more thoroughly the essentially *modernist* assumption that we can describe the world in rational, objective terms. The best we can hope for are fleeting 'moments of clarity' which might allow us to grasp transient truths, but never final, absolute truths resting on permanent and unassailable foundations. One scholar notes the extent to which postmodernism/poststructuralism 'focuses on the question of representation and explores the ways in which dominant framings of world politics produce and reproduce relations of power [and] how they legitimate certain forms of action while marginalizing other ways of being'. He goes on to pose key questions as to *how we are produced as political subjects*—subjects who accept certain forms of action and not others, and ask certain questions and not others. This is directly related to the question of how 'certain mechanisms of power—political technologies of inclusion/exclusion—become normalized and legitimized' (Çalkivik, 2017).

Postmodernism's greatest strength lies in its insights into the relationship between power and knowledge and its capacity for the critique of existing institutions, practices, and ideas. Its weakness lies in its inability to go much beyond critique and to map out a programme for positive social and political change. Some would say that, taken to its logical conclusion, postmodernism simply ends in absolute relativism, nihilism, and, ultimately, incoherence. For if 'there is no truth' the very claim that this is so cannot itself be true. As a further consequence of its relativism—the notion that no 'standard' can be regarded as superior to any other because there is no objective way of adjudicating between them—postmodern approaches also stand accused of creating a pernicious moral vacuum in which good and evil may be regarded simply as competing narratives.

Nonetheless, postmodern strategies provide valuable insights into the *contingent* status of knowledge and the uses to which it may be put in all spheres of politics. Armed with the insight that knowledge is very often a function of power, and that such power can be used to construct **metanarratives** of enormous importance—understood as embodying comprehensive accounts of history, experience, and knowledge—we can see how this might operate in concrete contexts. The 'war on terror' which followed the attacks of 11 September 2001 (otherwise known as '9/11'), although not as 'grand' a narrative as an entire theory of history, is a good example (see Box 4.5).

A principal figure in the rise of postmodern thought was Michel Foucault (1926–84), who pioneered a 'genealogical' form of analysis. This interrogates truth claims posing as objective knowledge about the world while concealing the machinations of power. Foucault argued that each society possesses its own 'regime of truth' that exists as a set of *discourses* and which is imposed on, but generally accepted by, society at large. Foucault further proposed that the human sciences have themselves played a leading role in this concealment, lending a mantle of authority to all kinds of knowledge claims which, in the end, can be exposed as serving power (Foucault, 1980: p. 13).

The postmodern problematization of 'truth', 'knowledge', and related issues has also been raised in contemporary discussions of many of former US President Trump's claims, the phenomenon of 'fake news', and 'alternative facts'. Trump attorney Rudi Giuliani's assertion that 'truth isn't truth' and the promulgation of ever more astounding conspiracy theories in recent years have added to the confusion. Some claim that Trump—and the phenomena that surround him—are the product of postmodern social and political thought. Others suggest that this is not so, but that he can be *explained* through the lens of a postmodern analysis (Hanlon, 2018). Box 4.6 raises some of the critical issues surrounding the debate in which Trump stands not just as an unusual individual in politics but as a political phenomenon.

BOX 4.5 CASE STUDY

Positioning Iraq in the Metanarrative of the 'War on Terror'

The 'war on terror' was initiated by the attacks of 11 September 2001 ('9/11') on landmark targets in New York and Washington, DC. Two war zones were subsequently occupied by the US and allies—Afghanistan (in October 2001) and Iraq (in March 2003)—as part of the war. It is widely accepted that Afghanistan was the base for the leader of the group responsible for planning and carrying out the 9/11 attacks—Osama bin Laden. But how did Iraq come to be part of the 'war on terror'?

The following are well established:

1 Al-Qaeda operatives, most of whom were Saudi nationals (*none were Iraqi*), were responsible for the 9/11 attacks in the US in 2001. Their leader, Osama bin Laden (also a Saudi national), was based in Afghanistan, which was governed by the Taliban. The Taliban is a Sunni Muslim fundamentalist political movement which had come to power in Afghanistan during a period of civil war. Although Al-Qaeda and the Taliban are quite separate organizations, they share a common religious ideology.

2 Saddam Hussein, then President of Iraq, had no connection with Afghanistan, Al-Qaeda, or the Taliban. While hostile to the US (although an ally in an earlier period), he actually repressed Islamic fundamentalism in Iraq and promoted secularism.

3 No weapons of mass destruction were ever found in Iraq, which obviously means that there was never any genuine evidence that they existed there prior to the US-led invasion.

4 The presence of terrorists in Iraq *following* the US-led invasion (as evidenced by a relentless campaign of suicide bombing by various factions) was due almost solely to the 'war on terror' itself, as is the rise of the so-called 'Islamic State' which formed in the chaos created by the Iraq War.

Despite the lack of any evidence linking Iraq to the 9/11 attacks, a widespread belief developed, at least among the US public, that Iraq, along with Afghanistan, was the source of the 9/11 attacks. A *Washington Post* poll taken almost two years after the attacks, and around six months after the invasion of Iraq, found that about 70 per cent of Americans believed there was a link between 9/11 and Iraq. How did that link get there? One answer is provided in the same newspaper report which quotes Bush on establishing the link, without explicitly telling falsehoods:

> If the world fails to confront the threat posed by the Iraqi regime, refusing to use force, even as a last resort, free nations would assume immense and unacceptable risks. The attacks of September the 11th, 2001, showed what the enemies of America did with four airplanes. We will not wait to see what terrorists or terrorist states could do with weapons of mass destruction. (*Washington Post*, 2003)

Another speech reported just afterwards, declaring major combat in Iraq at an end, and linking the events of 9/11 more closely with Iraq, also claims that Iraq was allied with Al-Qaeda, which it was not.

> The battle of Iraq is one victory in a war on terror that began on September the 11th, 2001 . . . The liberation of Iraq is a crucial advance in the campaign against terror. We've removed an ally of al Qaeda, and cut off a source of terrorist funding . . . No terrorist network will gain weapons of mass destruction from the Iraqi regime, because the regime is no more . . . We have not forgotten the victims of September the 11th. . . .
> (quoted in Milbank and Deane, 2003: A1)

(Continued)

4

CRITICAL APPROACHES TO GLOBAL POLITICS

This suggests that the power of the presidential office in the US, supported by a largely uncritical media, succeeded in purveying a particular *metanarrative* about terrorism which was used to justify the war in Iraq despite the lack of evidence (either at the time or subsequently).

In contrast, support for the war in the UK was much weaker even though former Prime Minister Tony Blair used similar rhetoric. This may be attributed to greater scepticism about the link with 9/11, a more critical press, a more critical attitude towards political leaders, generally nurtured by a stronger system of government and opposition, and a less nationalistic political world view among the public at large, at least at that time. From a postmodern perspective, we might conclude that the power/knowledge nexus, which supports successful metanarratives, is not as strong in the UK as it is in the US.

Exactly why the US invaded Iraq, and why some important allies like the UK and Australia went along with it despite no evidence of links with terrorists or of weapons of mass destruction, has been a matter of much speculation, with various motives and interests being explored (see, for example, Cramer and Thrall, eds, 2012).

The widespread acceptance of the rhetoric behind the Iraq War may also be linked to a broader historical narrative that sees 'Islam' and 'the West' as essentially antagonistic. This narrative has been nurtured by figures on both 'sides'—that is, by those promoting anti-Westernism within the Islamic world as well as by those promoting anti-Islamism from within the West. Almost a decade before the events of 9/11, it was observed that a mass movement based on Islamic fundamentalist principles had 'erupted into the world political scene' to challenge 'Western economic, political, and cultural hegemony in its totality' (Mutman, 1992–93: p. 165).

Interestingly, this 'revolt against the West' may also be analysed through the lens of Hans Morgenthau's classical realism, which highlighted, among many other things, the forces driving a 'revolt against power'. As Morgenthau put it, '[T]he very threat of a world where power reigns not only supreme, but without rival, engenders that revolt against power which is as universal as the aspiration for power itself' (Morgenthau, 1978: p. 231).

More generally, the invasion of Iraq in 2003 must be understood against a wider historical background in which powerful narratives and discourses are embedded and which shape the identities and behaviours of actors in antagonistic relationships. Since 9/11 and the Iraq War, these narratives and discourses have fed into ongoing debates about terrorism and migration, and especially the assumption that 'Islamic terrorism' is a major security threat in Western societies.

QUESTIONS

1 If we accept that the metanarrative of the 'war on terror' as it pertained to Iraq was based on false premises, does this logically imply that there is, after all, a 'truth' about the Iraq War?

2 How does the controversy over the 'war on terror' illustrate the relationship between theory and practice?

The idea of the contingent status of knowledge resonates with Gramscian thought but differs from the latter (and other CT approaches) in its refusal to illuminate an alternative path for social life, for according to its own logic, this would simply end in another 'regime of truth' serving particular interests. Postmodernism does, however, raise awareness of the extent to which knowledge serves power and how the human sciences are themselves implicated in the production of power/knowledge. We must keep in mind, though, that power as such is not always a 'bad' thing; it can also be used for the 'good'—for example, in providing for a very significant range of public goods and services as well as regulating social institutions and practices.

BOX 4.6   KEY DEBATE

Truth, Reality, and the Trump Phenomenon

Many have proposed that the nature of reality and the status of truth have become open questions since Donald Trump decided to enter politics, and even more so after he was elected president. Almost any criticisms of Trump and his policies are decried by him and his loyal supporters as 'fake news' while factual information (such as the relatively smaller size of the crowd at his inauguration compared to that at Obama's) is countered with 'alternative facts'. The *Washington Post* maintains that Trump made 2,140 false or misleading claims in his first year (https://www.washingtonpost.com/news/fact-checker/wp/2018/01/20/president-trump-made-2140-false-or-misleading-claims-in-his-first-year/). And his 'base' is either in denial, or doesn't care.

Trump is also a supporter of a host of conspiracy theories. On climate change, for example, he once maintained that 'climate science was a hoax created by the Chinese to make US manufacturing uncompetitive', and that the polar ice caps were not melting but were instead 'at a record level' (quoted in Gabbatis, 2018). These claims are a direct repudiation of virtually all available scientific evidence on the subject, but the scientific consensus is explained away by accusing scientists of taking an opportunity 'to wield influence, secure funding or act out a green/Marxist agenda' (ibid.).

Not all claims about conspiracies, however, lack substance. It seems that there is plenty of evidence to implicate the Russian state in a conspiracy to interfere in the US elections of 2016. Moreover, Russia continued to interfere with the Mueller enquiry set up to investigate exactly who was involved. One news site reported that:

> The Russian operatives unloaded on Mueller through fake accounts on Facebook, Twitter and beyond, falsely claiming that the former FBI director was corrupt and that the allegations of Russian interference in the 2016 election were crackpot conspiracies. One post on Instagram—which emerged as an especially potent weapon in the Russian

FIGURE 4.5   President of the United States of America Donald J. Trump speaking at his Presidential Inauguration, 2017   GPA Photo Archive/DoD photo by US Marine Corps Lance Cpl. Cristian L. Ricardo

(Continued)

social media arsenal—claimed that Mueller had worked in the past with 'radical Islamic groups' (Denning, 2018).

In explaining the Trump phenomenon more generally, it has been suggested that 'one of the sharpest analytical tools available is the theory of postmodernism' (Heer, 2017) whose proponents 'describe a world where the visual has triumphed over the literary, where fragmented sound bites have replaced linear thinking, where nostalgia ("Make America Great Again") has replaced historical consciousness or felt experiences of the past, where simulacra is indistinguishable from reality, where an aesthetic of pastiche and kitsch (Trump Tower) replaces modernism's striving for purity and elitism, and where a shared plebeian culture of vulgarity papers over intensifying class disparities. In virtually every detail, Trump seems like the perfect manifestation of postmodernism' (ibid.).

The key question arising here is: How useful is postmodern theory—or any other theory—in analysing the 'Trump phenomenon'?

In summary, postmodern or poststructuralist analyses of international politics have interrogated various forms of the power/knowledge nexus, generally in a negative sense, as well as the grand narratives and discourses which purport to explain the nature and dynamics of the international sphere. Sovereignty, statecraft, anarchy, warfare, borders, identities and interests, and the interpretation of history are all subject to their critical gaze. Postmodernism has therefore gained a foothold in the study of global politics, highlighting the extent to which 'reality' exists, not as a concrete, unalterable state of affairs 'out there', but resides ultimately in our own mental structures.

KEY POINTS

- Postmodern/poststructural approaches to global politics share some common ground with CT and constructivism in IR but have a much more radical epistemology derived from the rejection of modernist assumptions about knowledge.

- A common criticism is that postmodernism's radical relativism deprives moral arguments in global politics, or any other sphere of social action, of any foundation and permits no adjudication between different standards.

- Despite these criticisms, postmodernism/poststructuralism is valuable in showing just how problematic 'truths' about global politics can be.

CONCLUSION

Whenever we think about the world around us, we do so through a certain set of assumptions concerning the reality of that world. Different theorists obviously see the world in different ways and will interpret facts accordingly. This highlights the point that facts do not simply speak for themselves. Certainly, the different theoretical approaches reviewed in this chapter, and in Chapter 3, often make them speak in very different ways. It follows that the study of global politics cannot be taken simply as a task requiring the unproblematic accumulation of the facts that we know (or think we know) about the world. A constructivist would be quick to point out that different theorists see the world in different ways because each has arranged and interpreted the facts about the world in a certain way. Similarly, we should not necessarily regard theory as an 'abstraction' from reality but as the means by which it is actually created. We might then ask whether each theory or way of seeing the world is as good as the next, or whether some are better than others. But rushing to endorse any one theory as the 'right' one is scarcely advisable for students in an early stage of their programme. The important thing is to give each of them serious attention and to allow one's existing beliefs to be challenged.

Some of the issues raised in this chapter also point to a wider debate about the relationship between social and political critique (and its methods), science, and the very idea of 'truth' and 'reality' itself. Good practice in social science requires high standards of evidence and argument. This does not require mimicking the methods of the natural sciences or relying solely on empirical and quantitative modes of research. But neither should hostility to these methods allow one's judgement to slip into a simple denial of certain 'realities' about the social and political world, whether these are 'socially constructed' or not. Different theories and approaches concerning how global politics may be best studied or analysed may well be at odds with each other, but it can also be said that methodological as well as theoretical pluralism is a strength rather than a weakness of the discipline.

The same considerations apply in 'decolonizing the curriculum'. This leads us to note that, if theory 'creates' the world, then the theories reviewed both here and in Chapter 3 can be seen as creating it from a largely 'Western' perspective, for virtually all of them are 'Western' in origin and orientation. It can scarcely be denied that theories in global politics do describe (as well as criticize) systems of knowledge and sets of practices created largely in Europe and North America and effectively globalized via processes of colonization and decolonization. Indeed, the theories are themselves products of that very same system. However, if we examine 'Western civilization' in detail, we find that it is the outcome of so many historical and cultural influences, many of which travelled from East Asia and the Pacific, South Asia, the Middle East, Africa, and the Americas, that it is difficult to call it an entirely European project. As the study of global politics and the way in which it is theorized continues to develop and change, and as centres of power themselves shift and change around the world, it will inevitably be enriched by insights from an ever wider intellectual community and set of perspectives.

KEY QUESTIONS

1 How has Marxism impacted on theoretical development in the study of global politics?

2 What are the main elements of Gramsci's notion of hegemony?

3 How does the idea of 'emancipation' contribute to the critical theorization of global politics?

4 In what ways does historical sociology contribute to understanding patterns of social and political change in global politics?

5   To what extent do dependency theory and world-systems theory overcome the problem of Eurocentrism in global political studies?

6   What do constructivists mean when they speak of the world as 'one of our making'?

7   What is the relationship between power and knowledge in postmodern approaches to global politics?

8   How useful are postmodern approaches to politics in analysing the Trump phenomenon?

FURTHER READING

Anievas, Alexander (ed.) (2010), *Marxism and World Politics: Contesting Global Capitalism* (London: Routledge).

An edited collection with authors approaching the topic from a variety of disciplinary perspectives. Topics include the logics of capitalism and critiques of Western hegemony and imperialism.

Dasgupta, Samir and Peter Kivisto (eds) (2014), *Postmodernism in a Global Perspective* (New Delhi: Sage).

An interesting set of interdisciplinary essays from leading authors on various themes which revolve around a notion of 'postmodern globalization theory' and include perspectives from feminism, social theory, risk analysis, religion, management studies, and literary criticism. Something for everyone!

Edkins, Jenny (2019), *Routledge Handbook of Critical International Relations* (Abingdon: Routledge).

Provides a wide-ranging collection of chapters by expert scholars which bring together critical theoretical perspectives with real-world problems.

Go, Julian and George Lawson (eds) (2017), *Global Historical Sociology* (Cambridge: Cambridge University Press).

Another collection by expert scholars providing a variety of cases in world historical change including such themes as revolution, warfare, empire, race, and sexuality.

Shannon, Thomas R. (2018), *An Introduction to the World-System Perspective* (2nd edn, New York: Routledge).

This book provides an overview of the historical emergence of the world system from AD 1400 through to the present time. It includes a critical assessment of world-systems theory itself, including both its strengths and weaknesses.

WEB LINKS

www.e-ir.info/2018/02/25/introducing-marxism-in-international-relations-theory/

www.e-ir.info/2013/05/05/historical-sociology-and-international-relations-the-question-of-genocide/

www.e-ir.info/2016/11/23/dependency-theory-a-useful-tool-for-analyzing-global-inequalities-today/

These three links are from the E-International Relations website.

www.marxists.org/archive/marx
www.marxists.org/archive/gramsci
www.marxists.org/subject/frankfurt-school/index.htm

These are related sites providing useful summaries as well as archives of key works for Marx, Gramsci, and the Frankfurt School.

https://plato.stanford.edu/entries/critical-theory/
https://plato.stanford.edu/entries/postmodernism/

These two sites are part of the online *Stanford Encyclopedia of Philosophy*.

 For additional material and resources please visit the **online resources** at: www.oup.com/he/lawson1e.

5

NEW WAVES OF THEORIZING IN GLOBAL POLITICS

- Feminism, Sexuality, and Gender Theory
- Racism, Ethnicity, and Cultural Theory
- Colonialism and Postcolonial Theory
- Conclusion

Reader's Guide

Most of the modes of theorizing discussed in this chapter are based on long-standing concerns in social and political theory and all of them involve identity politics in one way or another—a form of politics in which one's membership of a group, based on certain distinctive characteristics such as race, ethnicity, religion, gender, sexuality, etc., acquires significant political salience and is implicated in hierarchies of power. It follows that identity itself involves issues of both who one *is*, and who one is *not*. This does not just involve self-identification or self-definition, but is also mediated by the perceptions of others. In some cases there are connections with social movements concerned with issues of justice and equality in both domestic and global spheres. In almost all cases the specific issues of concern, and their theorization, have come relatively late to the agenda of global politics and so may be said to constitute a 'new wave' of theorizing in the discipline. Certainly, one will find little in earlier liberal, realist, or Marxist thought that addresses the concerns of gender theory, let alone sexuality, although Marxist thought has certainly addressed colonialism and related issues. Also, although the English School did raise issues to do with cultural pluralism in its early years, it did not probe the concept of culture itself in any depth. The earlier development of IR theory was therefore limited in the issues it considered of relevance to the international or global sphere. All the issues discussed in this chapter, however, are now firmly on the agenda and are likely to gain further prominence in both the theory and the practice of global politics in the foreseeable future.

FEMINISM, SEXUALITY, AND GENDER THEORY

There was a time when feminism, gender, and sexuality had almost zero visibility in the study of global politics. Times have changed, and so too has the way in which we approach the study of global politics. Since at least the 1980s, feminist approaches began to make an impact in the field, expanding in subsequent decades to take into account broader issues of gender and sexuality. Gender theory is linked to the rise of feminism but is more expansive in devoting serious attention to problems with the construction of masculinity and, increasingly, sexuality. For social and political theory generally, gendered roles, gendered hierarchies, sexuality and the very notion of a simple masculine/feminine binary gender divide are certainly issues in the analysis of power in any sphere. This section therefore highlights, first, the relationship between gender, sexuality, and power and the extent to which the personal really is the political, and then goes on to discuss the implications for global politics.

Feminism

Feminism, as a body of theory, reflects on and critiques specific social and political practices concerning the role and status of women vis-à-vis men, highlighting in particular the relations of inequality between them. These relations have been embedded historically in patriarchy which, like class relations, has been naturalized in conventional social and political thought. At its most basic, patriarchy is a pervasive system of control in which men possess superior social, political, economic, legal, and moral authority over women. For feminists, the theorization of patriarchy and associated mechanisms of female subordination is a necessary prelude to action. After all, as Marx famously stated, it is one thing to interpret the world—the point is to change it. Thus, 'Feminist perspectives on international relations seek to understand existing gender relations . . . in order to transform how they work at all levels of global social, economic, and political life' (True, 2017; see also Youngs, 2004: p. 82).

The quote in Box 5.1 illustrates the extent to which gender, from a feminist perspective, matters a great deal in the distribution of power and resources, from the level of the household (where in some places boys and men will receive preferential access to food resources) to the level of national and global governance where positions of power are controlled predominantly by men. Gender disparity is everywhere and reflected at all levels of social, political, and economic life.

BOX 5.1   KEY QUOTE

How Gender Matters

Across the globe, gender determines who goes hungry and who gets adequate nutrition and water, who can vote, run for office, marry, or have rights to children, who commands authority and respect and who is denigrated and dismissed, and who is most vulnerable to violence and abuse in their own homes and intimate relationships. . . . These norms shape more than personal and family relationships . . . they shape religious practice and the structure of markets and processes of governance.

(Celis et al., 2013: p. 2)

Although feminist scholars and activists had been contributing to political thought and to practical developments in women's rights from at least the nineteenth century onwards, it was not until the late 1980s that the apparent absence of women in global politics and economics began to be seriously scrutinized. Attention focused initially on how traditional discourses of IR effectively excluded women as participants. That the absence of women was made to appear 'normal' or 'natural'—even to many women themselves—was identified as a major problem, exemplifying just why the insights of critical social theory are so important. Many feminists have therefore adopted critical and postpositivist approaches, for as much as any group that finds itself marginalized by a dominant mainstream, feminists have interrogated the extent to which knowledge itself can be constructed to suit male interests and enhance male power.

A leading feminist scholar of global politics, Cynthia Enloe, puts the issue of power front and centre of her analysis, requiring a focus on what forms power takes, who gets to wield it in various contexts, and how gendered power is often camouflaged so that it doesn't even look like power (Enloe, 2014: p. 9). She insists that gender-blind analyses tend to attribute the relative invisibility of women in global affairs to tradition, cultural preferences, and timeless norms, 'as if each of these existed outside the realms where power is wielded' (Enloe, 2014: p. 11). Beyond that, Enloe says that any non-feminist analysis of the ways in which power operates is likely to be naïve (Enloe, 2013).

Feminism as a body of critical thought draws from, interacts with, and often critiques other schools of theory in analysing the problem of patriarchy and its power dynamics. 'Liberal feminists', for example, will apply certain insights of liberal theory—including the essential equality of all individuals—to critique the way in which conventional liberal theory has at best ignored, or at worst supported, patriarchal structures of authority. Box 5.2 contains a useful typology which categorizes some of the different theoretical approaches to feminism taken by scholars of global politics.

FIGURE 5.1 **Cynthia Enloe** Steven King, Clark University

5

NEW WAVES OF THEORIZING IN GLOBAL POLITICS

BOX 5.2

Varieties of Feminism

- **Liberal feminism** highlights the subordination of women in world politics but does not challenge the premises of traditional theories. It is similar to empirical feminism in that it investigates particular problems—say, of refugee women, gendered income inequalities, trafficking of women, rape in war, and so on—usually within a positivist framework. Liberal feminism seeks equality of women in a man's world rather than questioning the foundations of that world.

- **Critical feminism** builds explicitly on Critical Theory, subjecting relations of domination and subordination, the play of power in global politics, and the relationship between material and ideational factors to scrutiny through a gender-sensitive lens. As a theory seeking action and not just interpretation, it promotes a project of emancipation which takes explicit account of women's subordination.

- **Feminist constructivism** criss-crosses the terrain of constructivist theories of global politics. Some concede much methodological ground to positivism, in line with the predominant mode of American constructivism. Others lean towards a postpositivist questioning of the foundations of knowledge. Common themes in feminist constructivism are attention to ideational forces and the essentially social nature of the international sphere.

- **Feminist poststructuralism**, as with poststructuralism (or postmodernism) generally, highlights the construction of meaning through language and, in particular, the relationship between knowledge and power. Feminist poststructuralism critiques the way in which binary oppositions such as strong/weak, rational/emotional, and public/private, not to mention masculinity/femininity, have served to empower men at the expense of women.

- **Postcolonial feminism** often goes hand in hand with feminist poststructuralism in exposing certain relations of domination and subordination, but focuses critique on how these relations were established through imperialism and colonialism and persist through to the present period. Postcolonial feminists also often critique the way in which Western feminists construct knowledge about non-Western women and also tend to treat 'women' as a universal, homogeneous category regardless of differences in culture, social class, race, and geographical location. (adapted from Tickner and Sjoberg, 2010: pp. 198–203)

Notable for its absence from this typology is a 'realist IR feminism', perhaps because realism, at least as it has developed as a theory of international politics, is so irredeemably masculinist that it cannot accommodate feminist premises. One author, however, identifies a form of 'rationalist feminism' which is strongly empiricist and endorses the assumption that the state is the central actor in international politics and is essentially concerned with its own survival (see Hansen, 2014: pp. 15–16). Notwithstanding the absence of a 'realist' feminism, feminist scholarship certainly highlights the 'realities' of women's lives and their historical exclusion from positions of power, but regards none of these realities as fixed or natural (see Frazer, 2018: pp. 320–43).

Gender Theory

Gender theory focuses attention on the social or cultural construction of femininity and masculinity and related issues of sexuality. While one's sex is biologically given as either female or male, at least in most cases, gender theory looks to how various contextual factors, including social expectations, work to produce roles and behaviours that can be categorized as feminine or masculine. The critical distinction between sex and gender has therefore been used to challenge the notion that biology is necessarily destiny, and 'serves the argument that whatever biological intractability sex appears to have, gender is culturally constructed' (Butler, 1990: p. 8).

Gender theory also highlights that there is no one form of gendered behaviour that characterizes femininity or masculinity, and we must therefore speak of femininities and masculinities in the plural. So while the attention to gender issues forced by feminists has highlighted inequalities between men and women with respect to power and resources, gender theory extends the analysis and provides more nuance by variegating the concepts of femininity and masculinity (Blanchard, 2003: p. 1290). Work on masculinities, for example, has highlighted the fact that the 'rugged male warrior' type, often constructed as an ideal, is a stereotype which many 'real' men do not actually fit (Connell cited in Tickner, 1992: p. 6). Another scholar has investigated the male soldier's gendered construction of his own identity as masculine in relation to his ability to function as a combatant. Such constructions might explain not only the almost complete exclusion of women from warrior ranks—until recently, and then only in some armies—but also the way in which masculinity frequently depends on an 'other' constructed as feminine, and therefore opposite (Goldstein, 2001: pp. 251–2; see also Chisolm and Tidy, 2018). The perception of what constitutes a 'real man' has been analysed in terms of 'hegemonic masculinity'—a term indicating a dominant kind of masculinity which not all men conform to (Hooper, 2001: pp. 13–14). We therefore need to recognize the power relations between different kinds of masculinity 'constructed through practices that exclude and include, that intimidate and exploit' and which indicate 'a gender politics within masculinity' (Connell, 2005: p. 37).

FIGURE 5.2 **President of the United States of America Ronald Reagan with cowboy hat at a rally for Texas Republican candidates** Ronald Reagan Library, The US National Archives and Records Administration

Cynthia Enloe's work, cited above, also provides a powerful critique of 'manliness' and the notion that risk-taking and tough talking in foreign affairs demonstrate fitness to govern in a dangerous world. Writing at a time of Cold War tensions, and in the aftermath of the Vietnam War, she was among the first to highlight the extent to which discourses of manliness permeated the language of international politics. She noted in particular the impact that the humiliation of defeat in the Vietnam War in the mid-1970s had on white male identity in the US and which underpinned a certain 're-masculinization' of American politics under the conservative administration of former film cowboy Ronald Reagan. In contrast, liberal policies on such matters as civil rights for minorities tended to be 'feminized'.

Interestingly, we can find a concern with the consequences of a certain kind of manliness in the writings of Thucydides. As we saw in Chapter 3, his report of the Melian dialogue, in which muscular power trumps morality and justice, appears as a classic in the realist tradition of IR theory. But elsewhere he writes scathingly of a certain concept of manliness—what some might now call 'toxic masculinity'—that appeared in the context of civil warfare in the ancient Greek world.

> What used to be described as a thoughtless act of aggression was now regarded as the courage one would expect to find in a party member; to think of the future and wait was merely another way of saying one was a coward; any idea of moderation was just another attempt to disguise one's unmanly character; ability to understand a question meant that one was totally unfitted for action. Fanatical enthusiasm was the mark of a *real man* . . . (Thucydides, 1972: V, 82, emphasis added).

Gender and Political Violence

Political violence is often highly gendered, and this is most evident in the way that armies have traditionally placed men in combat roles, facing off in battle. But beneath the image of conventional warfare, there are forms of gendered political violence which involve sexual violence. The UN has defined 'conflict-related sexual violence' as including 'rape, sexual slavery, forced prostitution, forced pregnancy, forced abortion, enforced sterilization, forced marriage and any other form of sexual violence of comparable gravity perpetrated against women, men, girls or boys that is directly or indirectly linked to a conflict' (UN, 2019: p. 1). The war in Bosnia from 1992 to 1995 was just one conflict among many which saw rape used as a specific tactic of war. But men and boys were subject to another kind of treatment which brought into currency the term **ethnic cleansing** as set out in Box 5.3. This also relates to aspects of genocide, ethnicity, and nationalism discussed in the next section.

Sexuality

Sexuality refers to one's sexual orientation which, like gender, is not usually 'chosen'. It arises from complex biological and social processes which are still not well understood. Contemporary discourses on gender and sexuality have shown how categories of male/female and feminine/masculine are much more complicated than these simple binaries allow. The now widely recognized letters 'LGBT' or, even more extensively, 'LGBTQIA' (lesbian, gay, bisexual, transgender, queer or questioning, intersex, and asexual) indicates that each of these orientations differs from heterosexuality. Because

BOX 5.3 CASE STUDY

Gender and Genocide in the Bosnian War, 1992–95

With the end of the Cold War, the former communist Federal Republic of Yugoslavia began to disintegrate, generating bitter conflict between ethnic groups with identities based largely on religious affiliation. The province of Bosnia-Herzegovina, characterized by a multi-ethnic population of Catholic Croats, Orthodox Serbs, and Bosniak Muslims who had lived in relative harmony for years, became the scene of the most gruesome episodes after a referendum for independence in 1992. Some Bosnian Serbs (a minority within the province) dissented and were supported by nationalists in Serbia itself, including the arch-nationalist Serb leader, Slobodan Milošević, who backed Bosnian Serb militia.

The war that ensued saw several notorious episodes of ethnic cleansing now regarded as acts of genocide. The most serious occurred in Srebrenica in July 1995 when an estimated 8,000 Bosniak Muslim men and boys were slaughtered by units of the Army of Republika Srpska (VRS). The subsequent trial of one Serb leader, Radislav Krstić, produced a statement in the Appeals Chamber Judgment following his case before the International Criminal Tribunal for the former Yugoslavia or ICTY, which summed up the character of the incident. Bosnian Serb forces, he said,

> targeted for extinction the forty thousand Bosnian Muslims living in Srebrenica, a group which was emblematic of the Bosnian Muslims in general. They stripped all the male Muslim prisoners, military and civilian, elderly and young, of their personal belongings and identification, and deliberately and methodically killed them solely on the basis of their identity. . . . The Appeals Chamber . . . calls the massacre at Srebrenica by its proper name: genocide . . . (ICTY, 2004)

Female civilians among the Bosniak Muslims and some other groups were subjected to a different kind of treatment. Accounts emerged of women being raped as part of a systematic tactical pattern which included the phenomenon of rape camps where women were subjected to multiple rape, often with the intention of impregnating them with 'Serb' babies. This came to be seen as part of the wider pattern of genocide. In 1995, a charge of rape was brought in the ICTY, the first time that a sexual assault case had ever been prosecuted as a war crime by itself, and not as part of a larger case. The estimates of the number of women raped during the war run as high as 50,000.

The slaughter of men and boys on the one hand, and the systematic rape of women on the other, during this war, illustrate gendered aspects of warfare resulting in the most extreme forms of group political violence. In recent years, rape in war (which can also be perpetrated against men as an attack on their masculinity, although it is less common) has achieved much greater prominence as an issue in the narration of war histories generally.

In summary, this case illustrates complex links between gender, identity, sexual violence, and genocide.

heterosexuality is the dominant form of sexuality it is often described as 'normative sexuality' or 'heteronormativity', indicating that it has been 'naturalized as normal' whereas other sexualities are regarded as abnormal or deviant—some to the extent of being criminalized. Another term used to describe this general situation, which implies a certain power dynamic, is 'hegemonic heterosexuality' (see Lind, 2013: p. 189).

Movements promoting greater equality for sexual minorities around the globe have gained ground in recent years, at least in some countries. Generally speaking, LGBT rights (as human rights) are now associated with an emancipatory discourse of progress, secularism, and modernity (Langlois, 2015: p. 378). These rights have now also been incorporated within the UN human rights framework with the establishment of an office for an Independent Expert on Sexual Orientation and Gender Identity (ibid.). However, this has not led to a trend towards the convergence of global norms around the protection of non-heterosexual orientations and gender identities. Rather, a significant degree of 'norm polarization' has occurred with a line-up of conservative, often religious groups, opposing LGBT rights. Thus there has been 'a sustained, organized challenge in the name of "Orthodox", "Christian", "Islamic", and "African" values'. Russia has been especially proactive in promoting an international network supporting 'traditional values' in opposition to sexuality rights (Altman and Symons, 2015: p. 62).

Homophobia been historically exported to parts of the former colonial world by conservative Christian missionaries and colonial authorities, and it continues today. For example, a homophobic tradition is said to have been nurtured by British colonial authorities and missionaries in Uganda as part of their 'civilizing mission'. In the present period, some US evangelical groups have continued this mission by fomenting militant homophobia in Uganda and supporting anti-gay legislation which provides for life imprisonment for some sexual acts and even includes a prohibition on LGBT counselling. Acts of violence against the LGBT community in Uganda by both state and non-state actors has, not surprisingly, increased since then (see Boutchie, 2019).

KEY POINTS

- Studies in feminism, sexuality and gender theory provide a very different lens on global politics to those of traditional theories, incorporating more critical perspectives relevant to every aspect of the field.

- Gender theory in global politics critically analyses different forms of masculinity and femininity and their implications for issues ranging from political economy to political violence.

- Sexuality is now on the agenda of global politics with the UN having incorporated the issue within the broader framework of human rights.

RACISM, ETHNICITY, AND CULTURAL THEORY

Just as gender issues were once considered to be of little relevance in the wider world of power politics, so too were issues of race and racism. That has changed, with much more attention now directed to historic practices of racism in global politics and the ongoing salience of race in the contemporary period along with related issues of ethnicity and culture. The purpose of this section is to consider the basic concepts associated with these categories and how they are implicated in global politics in both theory and practice.

Prominent among the problems associated with race and/or ethnicity is the phenomenon of genocide. This has become a concern for the international community with the UN having instituted a policy of genocide prevention following horrific cases of genocide in Rwanda and the Balkans in the 1990s, both of which occurred in the context of civil war. Genocide prevention is linked in turn to the principle that the possession of sovereignty by a state confers on it the responsibility to protect its citizens from harm, as discussed in Chapter 2. If it fails to do so, then the responsibility to protect is incumbent on the international community which may engage in humanitarian intervention. Understanding genocide involves, first, an appreciation of how concepts such as 'race' and 'ethnicity' have been conceptualized in theorizing human difference.

Racism and Genocide

Racism exists as a mode of thought which assigns people to various categories, often (but not always) according to certain physical traits, and then assigns a higher or lesser value to people in these categories. This may be further reinforced by a power differential, where those who occupy a 'higher' racial status may in fact possess more power (social, economic, political) which, in turn, reinforces notions of superiority. As one scholar puts it, 'Racism . . . is not simply bigotry or prejudice, but beliefs, practices and policies reflective of and supported by institutional power, primarily state power' (Henderson, 2015: p. 20). The result is a racial hierarchy which lends itself readily to a process of naturalization—a process which, as we have seen earlier, has also been identified by critical class and gender theorists as operating in their particular spheres of concern.

But what of the concept of 'race' itself? Does it have any basis in biology? Are there really any significant genetic differences between categories perceived as 'racial'? The short answer is no. Modern genetics shows no significant differences between human population groups that could justify 'race' as a biological category, let alone the inherent superiority of one population group over another. Apart from a few superficial phenotypical characteristics such as skin colour, there is no biological basis on which people can be sorted into discrete 'race' categories, and certainly not with respect to intelligence, skills, or abilities.

Homo sapiens is, in fact, a single species which originated on the African continent, spread slowly throughout the world, acquired some genetic variation in response to environmental factors (e.g. mutations favouring paler skin in colder climates to enable better absorption of Vitamin D from the sun), but with many more similarities than differences. Race is therefore better understood as a *social* construct which fails as an analytical tool in understanding the scope of human genetic diversity (Gannon, 2016; see also Banton, 1998). It has therefore been argued that it is not actual (biological) racial differences that generate racism but rather 'racism that generates races' (Townley, 2007: p. 171).

Although race is a social construct, the impact of 'race thinking' in global history cannot be underestimated. It was a major factor in the justification of colonialism and the slave trade, the violence and other human rights abuses attending these, and the ongoing consequences for civil rights in the US in particular as well as in key aspects of global politics. The protests that erupted in the US, and which spread around the world following the murder of an unarmed black man, George Floyd, in Minnesota in the US, reflect the ongoing problems arising from historic practices. In fact, race thinking is said to have underpinned an entire world hierarchy in which imperial forces stood at the apex while 'subject races' and 'oppressed nationalities' languished at the bottom (Murray, 1910: p. 227).

FIGURE 5.3 Black Lives Matter protest in Minneapolis, Minnesota, USA, 2020
Justin Berken/Shutterstock.com

Racism underpinned Hitler's doctrine of 'Aryan supremacy' in Nazi Germany where Jews became the target of vicious racist propaganda campaigns, scapegoating them for all of Germany's economic ills. This was followed by a programme of extermination which saw around 6 million perish in death camps during the Holocaust of the Second World War. It was this programme that gave rise to the term 'genocide' (see Box 5.4). Given that anti-Semitic racism depended on notions of superiority/inferiority, one can only marvel at a mind-set that saw Nobel Laureate Albert Einstein effectively driven from Germany in the early 1930s, along with many other talented Jewish intellectuals.

Racist ideas and practices take many forms. Various types of superior/inferior formulations are evident in the hereditary Hindu caste system as well as in some tribal societies where members of other tribes may be considered less than human. One work focusing on attitudes in Japan, China, and Korea notes that Europeans 'have not been the sole producers of racial theories or the sole promulgators of racist agendas in modern times' (Kowner and Denel, 2015: p. 1). In Africa, 'racialized identities' have also come to the fore during various conflicts in Sudan where some groups based largely in the North regard themselves as 'Arab', and therefore superior, while those in the South, along with groups in the western region of Darfur, have been described as 'African' or 'Negroid' and therefore inferior. Darfuri people have also been subject to genocide (see Deng, 1995; Bassil, 2013).

Some types of prejudice may appear to be based on 'ethnic' rather than 'racial' difference. The term 'ethnic' comes from the (ancient) Greek *ethnos*, referring originally to an undifferentiated collectivity (as in a swarm of bees) and commonly used to denote 'a group of people with shared characteristics' (Chapman, McDonald, and Tonkin, 2016: p. 14). In addition to having a basis in common cultural practices (including language, religion, and arts), ethnicity is also often defined in terms of relatedness—that is, descent from a common ancestral group—thus endowing ethnicity with an element of biological

BOX 5.4 KEY CONCEPT

Genocide

In 1944, a Polish-Jewish lawyer, Raphael Lemkin, combined the ancient Greek word *genos* (race, tribe) with the Latin *cide* (derived from the Latin *caedere* to kill) to create a term capable of describing what had occurred in the death camps of Nazi Germany as well as other historic large-scale massacres aimed at destroying particular groups of people. The Convention on the Punishment and Prevention of Genocide adopted by the UN General Assembly in 1948 was the first of the UN's human rights treaties. It defines genocide as an act committed with the intent to destroy, in whole or in part, a national, ethnic, racial, or religious group by:

- killing members of the group;
- causing serious bodily or mental harm to members of the group;
- deliberately inflicting on the group conditions of life calculated to bring about its physical destruction in whole or in part;
- imposing measures intended to prevent births within the group and forcibly transferring children of the group to another group.

(see https://www.un.org/en/genocideprevention/genocide-convention.shtml)

FIGURE 5.4 **Raphael Lemkin** The History Collection/Alamy Stock Photo

relatedness. These factors contribute to a social identity invested with various meanings and attributes which, taken together, are invariably deployed as a marker of *difference* from other such groups. Ethnicity can therefore be used in social and political contexts in much the same way as 'race'.

Some political movements around the world have been described in terms of ethnic nationalism or ethnonationalism, bringing ethnicity and nationalism together to describe movements which aim to secure political autonomy for groups who identify as possessing a common ethnic heritage and who claim to form a legitimate nation. In a way, almost all forms of nationalism are 'ethnic', given that the ingredients of an ethnic group are virtually the same as those of a 'nation', as discussed in Chapter 2. But ethnic nationalism has more often been applied to describe minority groups within existing states. The quest for autonomy may aim for a completely new independent state for 'the nation' in

5

question and therefore entail secession from an existing state. Or it may aim for autonomous status within the existing state. Either way, they are often called 'separatist'. There are many examples of the phenomenon of ethnic nationalism, as understood in these terms, including the Basques and Catalans in Spain, the Quebecois in Canada, the Scots in the UK, the Chechens in Russia, the Kurds in various parts of the Middle East, Biafrans in eastern Nigeria, the Bougainvilleans of Papua New Guinea, and so on. Some ethnic nationalist claims have resulted in violent conflict, although that is not always the case. In recent times, Scotland and Quebec have had entirely peaceful referenda to decide whether they should stay as part of the UK and Canada respectively. And although a majority 'no' vote disappointed the pro-secession movements, the result was accepted—at least for the time being.

Even where there is no apparent difference in religion, culture, language, or physical appearance, the capacity of humans to 'construct' difference on a remarkably shallow basis—and then politicize that difference—is remarkable. This is well illustrated in the case of the Rwandan genocide (see Box 5.5) in the aftermath of which the UN developed a policy framework and guidelines for action in the form of humanitarian intervention in future cases.

BOX 5.5 CASE STUDY

The Rwandan Genocide

Rwanda is a country in East Africa with a current population of around 12.3 million people. It was colonized, first by Germany until the First World War and then by Belgium under a League of Nations mandate, and, following the Second World War, as a UN trust territory. It became independent in 1962. Its people have long been regarded as comprised of two main groups, Tutsi and Hutu. The Rwandan genocide of 1994 occurred when people identifying as Hutu slaughtered between 600,000 and 800,000 people identified as Tutsi as well as up to 30,000 moderate Hutu (including those who refused to support or participate in the slaughter).

A notable feature of this case is that Hutu and Tutsi are indistinguishable as far as religion, language, and general cultural practices go. Rather, the construction of 'difference' has been based on mytho-historical factors, including a belief that Tutsis are descended from pastoralists who had come from further north in an earlier historical period and settled alongside an existing population of agriculturalist Hutus. Whatever their origins, there was much intermingling over time, with the categories remaining quite fluid. Up to half the population in the contemporary period are probably descended from both groups.

Myths of origin nonetheless persisted in the popular imagination, reinforced by colonial authorities who promoted the idea of Tutsi racial superiority derived from their supposed origin in the north of Africa which made them seem closer to Europeans. Tutsi became even more privileged in education and the colonial system generally. Not surprisingly, this encouraged much resentment on the part of those classified as Hutu, thus providing a rich political resource for extremist leaders to draw on. Radical Hutu nationalism became imbued with a notion of entitlement that had been denied by Tutsis and which could only be realized by eradicating Tutsis.

The assassination of Hutu President Habyarimana in 1994 was the trigger for the massacre. Extremist Hutus in the media used their positions to purvey the most extraordinary hate speech against Tutsi 'cockroaches', urging 'loyal' Hutus to slaughter their Tutsi neighbours, almost as a moral duty. Even family members turned on other family members (there were any number of 'mixed marriages'). The genocide continued for 100 days until a Tutsi army put an end to the slaughter. The international community had stood by and done almost nothing.

For the most part, the basic facts of the genocide are not disputed, but attribution of blame is contested with some highlighting colonial factors while others note that intra-Hutu tensions and dynamics suggest otherwise (see Sharlett, 2001). Blame for failing to prevent the catastrophe has also been laid at the feet of various external actors including France (which had supported Habyarimana) and Belgium (the former colonial power), as well as the US and the UN.

The Rwandan genocide memorial in Kigali—an extensive complex which includes mass graves of some thousands of victims—highlights personal narratives of survival and loss, the continuing trauma of the event, and the efforts at reconciliation between survivors and *genocidaires*. It also has a section on other genocides and mass murders, including the Armenian genocide of 1915–17 during Ottoman Empire rule; the genocide of Herero and Namaqua people in Namibia under German rule from 1904 to 1908; the Holocaust of the Second World War; and the mass murder of Cambodians from 1975 to 1979 (which, strictly speaking, was not a genocide as there was no ethnic difference at all between killers and killed). To these we may add the genocides against indigenous people in many different places, from the Americas to Australia, and lesser known genocides in numerous locations around the world, from Myanmar to the former Soviet Union.

A comparative perspective enables an appreciation of the fact that such tragedies have occurred in very different places, at very different times, and under very different circumstances, making it difficult to make much more than broad analytic generalizations about the phenomenon. However, a basic common denominator in most cases may be found in the extent to which racialized identities of 'self' and 'other' can be constructed, manipulated, demonized, and strategized to serve whatever interests are at stake in any given case.

Racism, Colonialism, and Nationalism

The case of the Rwandan genocide, among others, shows how colonialism is historically implicated in certain cases with spillover effects in the postcolonial period. Colonialism itself has had very obvious racial elements, with European ideas of racial superiority providing a justification for the subjugation of people elsewhere, often resulting in large-scale violence, genocide, and mass murder as the fate of many indigenous populations attest. At the global level, one consequence of European colonialism and imperialism was the establishment of a racial global hierarchy, the effects of which are still discernible in the contemporary global system. More than a century ago, the African American scholar and activist, W. E. B. Du Bois (see Box 5.6), identified the problems posed by imperialism for the treatment of non-white populations around the world. Du Bois also challenged Woodrow Wilson not only on his failure to act in alleviating the rampant discrimination experienced by African Americans in the South but also on instituting policies and practices that nurtured prejudice even further, as discussed in Chapter 3.

It is clear that in the first part of the twentieth century—the period in which IR was becoming established as a discipline and its theorization was well under way—political thought in Europe and North America was imbued with racialist ideas which in turn

BOX 5.6 SHORT BIOGRAPHY

W. E. B. Du Bois (1868–1963)

William Edward Burghardt Du Bois was born in Massachusetts in the US in 1868. He gained his PhD from Harvard in 1895, the first African American to do so, with a thesis on the African slave trade. His subsequent works showed a concern to address both the problems facing African Americans in their home country as well as the challenge of racial politics in the world at large with a special focus on the plight of Africans and the depredations of European imperialism on the African continent.

Du Bois attended the 1919 Paris Peace Conference at which Wilson played a major role in establishing the League of Nations. At the same time, Du Bois was instrumental in convening a Pan-African Congress in Paris to press European delegates at the Peace Conference to allow greater participation by Africans in their own governments. Many Africans had served in the war for the Allies, but were excluded from the Peace Conference.

Throughout his life, his writings and his activism shone a light on cruelty and injustice and the insidious effects of racism wherever it occurred. In particular, he is said to have illuminated 'the crucial significance of race and racism as fundamental organising principles of international politics; axes of hierarchy and oppression structuring the logics of world politics as we know it' (Anievas, Manchanda, and Shilliam, 2015: p. 2).

FIGURE 5.5 **W. E. B. Du Bois** Library of Congress/photo by C. M. Battey

justified various imperial projects. This suggests that IR's theorization from this time is not simply Eurocentric but was tainted with elements of racism in the form of white supremacy (see Hobson, 2012: pp. 1–2). E. H. Carr had suggested that what IR was really about, at least in the Anglophone countries, was the study of 'how to run the world from positions of strength'. He added that it was 'little more than a rationalization for the exercise of power by the dominant nations over the weak', and 'an ideology of control' masquerading as 'a proper academic discipline' (quoted in Cox, 2016: p. xxix). Although not referring directly to the racial hierarchy of world politics in his time, the implication was clear.

Another study says that, in the US, 'international relations' in its earlier years actually meant 'race relations', and that early professors there 'wrestled with the prospect that a race war might lead to the end of the world hegemony of whites' (Vitalis, 2015: p. 1). This study also highlights the contributions of African American scholars located primarily at Howard University in Washington, DC who challenged the one-sided theorization of the IR discipline and illuminated alternatives to existing relations of dependency and domination in global politics.

In the contemporary period, the terms 'race' and 'racism' remain part of our everyday vocabulary and reflect attitudes and beliefs that are very real in their effects. They may also infuse certain expressions of nationalism, although this is not always explicit. One scholar notes that racist organizations often refuse that designation, claiming instead to be *nationalist*, although critics maintain that 'the discourses of race and nation are never very far apart' (Balibar, 1991: p. 37). Another scholar has also argued that nationalism gives racism the means through which it can become operationalized and that many expressions of nationalism have in fact allied themselves with racism (Mosse, 1995: p. 163).

Racism and nationalism, however, are not exactly the same. This is partly illustrated by the fact that there are many different forms of nationalism. Some, such as anti-colonial nationalism which was important in driving movements for independence in the former colonial world, is clearly emancipatory. Civic nationalism appears as an inclusive variety of the phenomenon where all citizens are treated on equal terms regardless of ethnic or cultural differences. Having said that, civic nationalism can also be associated with assimilationism, requiring the abandonment of valued aspects of cultural or ethnic identity among minorities, which is itself a form of discrimination. Other aspects of nationalism have been discussed in Chapter 2, along with aspects of the 'Alt-Right' movement which clearly combines nationalist/racist elements.

Culture and the Politics of Difference

If the perception of racial/ethnic difference has clear political salience, so too does the perception of cultural difference. We should note first that just as 'race' and 'ethnicity' often intersect with each other, they may also intersect with 'culture' and it is difficult to treat them as entirely separate categories. In this section, however, we look more closely at culture as a distinctive concept. Although never entirely absent from discourses in global politics, culture began to receive much more attention in the early post-Cold War period as part of a new wave of theorizing. Its importance in the study of global politics can be attributed in part to an influential thesis advanced by a prominent scholar of comparative politics, Samuel Huntington, who wrote of a looming 'clash of civilizations' in which culture—especially in the form of religion—would come to dominate the global landscape of political violence (Huntington, 1993).

Huntington's thesis was in direct response to the notion that, with the collapse of communism in its heartland (i.e. the USSR), liberal democracy appeared to have triumphed over its principal rival, thus signalling the 'end of history' (Fukuyama, 1989) in the sense that no other ideology could ever match the liberal democratic ideal. In contrast, Huntington saw no end to history in the realm of ideas, and certainly no end to political violence, but rather a future in which 'the West' would continue to confront various non-Wests in the battle for ideological supremacy. 'Islam' loomed large as a likely contender, pitching its own set of religious/cultural values against those of the liberal West. When the events of '9/11' occurred, Huntington's thesis appeared to come to life in the most dramatic way possible. This display of deadly extremism emerging from a group identifying as Islamic led the US and various allies to invade Afghanistan and later Iraq, as part of the 'war on terror', as discussed in Chapter 4. Of course most Muslims completely reject the legitimacy of 'Islamic' terrorism. We will not pursue the further details of these particular issues, but rather concentrate here on the idea of culture and its conceptualization in political thought.

The culture concept has a complex history, emerging out of nineteenth-century European thought along two distinct trajectories—one humanist (focusing largely on 'high culture' as expressed in art, music, and literature), with the other developing along anthropological lines. An early anthropological definition holds that 'Culture or Civilization, taken in its widest ethnographic sense, is that complex whole which includes knowledge, belief, art, morals, law, custom, and any other capabilities and habits acquired by man as a member of society' (Tylor, 1987: p. 37).

Of particular interest for global politics is a school of American cultural anthropology which emerged in the early twentieth century and through which the culture concept was initially developed as a means of countering racist ideas based on biological determinism which had been prominent in justifying imperialism and/or or slavery. A key argument was that the apparent differences between human groups were not determined by 'race' but rather by 'culture'—a set of beliefs, behaviours, and practices acquired through membership of particular social groups. From a normative perspective, each group was to be considered equal in status to any other, and of equal moral worth. Thus the practices of any one cultural group should not be considered morally superior or inferior to another.

The logic of this position follows that of sovereign equality which regards each state as no more, and no less, 'sovereign' than any other, regardless of size or status. In other words, all states are equally sovereign. On a similar logic, cultural anthropologists generally hold that all groups are equally 'cultured'. A further assumption is that the standards of one culture cannot be judged by the standards of another, and indeed *ought not* to be so judged. This is the basis of the doctrine of cultural relativism, which holds that moral and other standards are to be judged in their own context and not in relation to some absolute universal standard. For who can say what that standard might be, if not the standard of one dominant group imposed on others? For many cultural anthropologists, this position was a counter to the ethnocentrism of so many in their own society who judged non-Western societies as inferior. On the other hand, we might well want to judge practices such as human sacrifice, slavery, child marriage, and so on as morally wrong, even if they are part of 'a culture'.

The culture concept is also relevant to the issue of ethnocentrism. One prominent American cultural anthropologist, Melville J. Herskovits (1972: p. 98), described this phenomenon as 'the end result of a psychological process by which [people] center their world in their own group, seeing it in their own dimensions, judging conduct by their own standards, planning so as to achieve in terms of their own ambitions'. In this view, culture forms the total subjectivity of each and every person and ethnocentrism becomes one of its inescapable consequences. To the extent that this applies to all people at all times, however, it is ultimately an absolutist position. In other words, it promotes a totalizing concept of culture in explaining how *all* humans orient themselves to the world around them. But Herskovits's view may also be seen as embedded in a specific cultural milieu in a specific time in history—or more especially the view of an American cultural anthropologist of the mid-to-late twentieth century, and therefore ethnocentric itself!

The particular political context within which Herskovits wrote is of special interest here. Colonialism in many places had come to an end and the American audience which he was mainly addressing had been coming to terms with how they dealt with former European colonies. Herskovits pointed out that whereas American diplomats may have dealt previously with British diplomats in London on issues to do with India or the Sudan, or with the Dutch in the Hague with respect to Indonesia, who were at least culturally similar to themselves, they now needed to learn to deal directly with their counterparts in New Delhi, Khartoum, or Jakarta, whose world views were very different. This multicultural world, he said, was now one in which 'peoples with the most diverse modes of thought and behaviour are in continuous interaction' (ibid.: pp. 73–4).

Anthropological thought is of course complex and varied, and the features sketched above scarcely do full justice to the discipline's treatment of the culture concept. But it is clear enough that cultural theory as developed within the discipline of anthropology has some important implications for how we think about global politics, and in particular about the relationship between the West and non-West. Having said that, it becomes immediately obvious that even to state the relationship in such terms assumes something of a West/non-West dichotomy in global politics, as explored further in the next section.

KEY POINTS

- The idea of 'race' is based essentially on a discredited biological category and is best understood as a social construct.

- Racism and associated ideologies (including some forms of nationalism) have underscored significant aspects of global politics, from imperialism and colonialism in the nineteenth and twentieth centuries to the ideologies of far-right movements in various parts of the West today.

- The culture concept, as developed by cultural anthropologists in particular, plays an important role in explaining human difference and promoting understanding in a multicultural world, although the concept is not without its problems.

COLONIALISM AND POSTCOLONIAL THEORY

Postcolonial theory (and postcolonial studies more broadly) is an interdisciplinary enterprise aimed at critiquing the direct and indirect effects of colonization and its aftermath on subject people. It now sometimes appears under the rubric 'decolonialism'. Most of its proponents have tended to focus less on issues in political economy and much more on issues arising from culture. The 'culturalist' orientation of many postcolonial theorists has also seen a strong emphasis placed on critiques of Eurocentrism as well as Western versions of universalism. Thus one prominent postcolonial scholar notes that political modernity, which is embodied in the institutions of the state, the bureaucracy, and capitalist enterprise and expressed through concepts such as citizenship, human rights, legal equality, the individual, popular sovereignty, social and global justice, scientific rationality, and so on, 'all bear the burden of European thought and history' (Chakrabarty, 2008: p. 4).

Postcolonial theory is very explicitly normative, aiming to highlight the inherent injustices of colonial systems, or at least of European colonial systems. It is concerned not only with the past but also with manifestations of neocolonialism in the present with the critical emphasis usually on the West. The discourse of postcolonialism is therefore strongly *anti*colonial, constituting a discourse of opposition and resistance to colonial oppression and subordination. A relatively early critic was Franz Fanon (1925–61) who wrote in particular of the negative psychological consequences of racism in engendering feelings of inadequacy and inferiority in an anti-black world. He was also very much attuned to issues of socio-economic class, which often aligned with race and which he saw as having primacy over culture (see, generally, Haddour, 2019).

A key figure in the development of postcolonial thought with an emphasis on culture was Edward Said (1935–2003), a professor of comparative literature of Palestinian descent (but located in the US during most of his professional life). Said's critical work on Orientalism argued that Europeans—especially the English and French—had long treated the Orient as Europe's major 'cultural contestant'. By this he meant that Europeans defined *themselves* against, or in contrast with, the people of the Orient—and generally regarded themselves as superior. He further suggested that Orientalism is an *activity* dedicated to the production and dissemination of knowledge *about* the Orient and thereby a means of exercising authority over it (Said, 1978: pp. 1–30). In developing his ideas, Said drew on Gramscian notions of cultural hegemony as well as on Foucauldian insights into the power/knowledge nexus, which together inform his conception of Orientalism as a hegemonic discourse.

FIGURE 5.6 **Edward Said** CPA Media Pte Ltd/Alamy Stock Photo

Although Said's 'Orient' consisted largely of the Middle East, his ideas were generalized so that 'Orientalism' is now used to designate almost any construction of non-European 'Others' by Europeans or members of 'the West' more generally. Contemporary postcolonial analysis, to the extent that it embraces the framework provided by Said, is therefore associated largely with forms of resistance to European or Western imperialism and colonialism, the body of ideas which supported it, and its ongoing effects.

Postcolonial Critiques in Global Politics

Postcolonialism as an approach to global politics stands as the principal medium through which traditional theories, along with some other critical approaches to global politics, have been critiqued as largely Eurocentric. The implication is that they not only provide a very partial view of the wider reality of the world, but also are a vital aid in controlling it. 'As a social practice, IR constitutes a space in which certain understandings of the world dominate others, specific interests are privileged over others, and practices of power and domination acquire a normalized form' (Tickner, 2003: p. 300).

Another postcolonial critique holds that traditional IR approaches possess a 'wilful arrogance' in their basic assumptions about the state of nature, anarchy, and power politics. The focus of the hybrid beast, 'realism–liberalism', in particular, is said to have produced 'abstract, ahistorical conceptions of the state, the market, and the individual' which are in fact bound by particular cultural expressions that are essentially 'Western, white, male' (Agathangelou and Ling, 2004: pp. 24–5). But the critique of Western theory also extends to many Western feminists who stand accused of portraying the problems of women all over the world through the eyes of a Western female self.

While many alternative approaches to global politics accept the validity of these critiques, there is more to problems of power and domination in the postcolonial period than the almost exclusive focus on the West/non-West binary allows, as illustrated in Box 5.7.

BOX 5.7 KEY DEBATE

Debating Postcolonialism

While the era of decolonization is rightly seen as one of liberation from direct European domination for many colonized peoples, postcolonial critique tends to narrow the scope in analysing ongoing problems of domination, subordination, and exploitation in various locations around the world. One particular problem concerns the issue of 'internal colonialism' where some population groups in newly independent states have found themselves governed by postcolonial elites who are as alien to them as their former European colonizers, and sometimes even more destructive and exploitative.

A notable case is that of West Papua located on the western half of the island of New Guinea. The indigenous people are ethnically Melanesian. And their traditional lands are resource-rich. West Papua was effectively seized in the early 1960s by Indonesia which had gained independence from the Dutch in 1949. West Papua had also been a Dutch colony and this was used to legitimate Indonesia's claim. The UN at the time was heavily influenced by proponents of the decolonization movement—most of whom apparently did not see Indonesia as an agent of colonization itself. Indonesian occupation has since seen the massacre of thousands of West Papuans

(Continued)

along with episodes of torture and other human rights abuses. Together with policies supporting mass transmigration from other parts of Indonesia, the actions of the Indonesian state are said to constitute 'slow motion genocide' (see Lawson, 2017b).

To this day, the UN refuses to consider West Papua as colonized by Indonesia and, although its decolonization committee is still actively pursuing decolonization for some small territories still under US, UK, or French control (although most of these are not actually seeking decolonization), it will not consider listing West Papua for decolonization. To the extent that postcolonial scholarship focuses almost exclusively on European colonialism, cases such as West Papua tend to be neglected (ibid.).

Moving to the African continent, another question concerns how much responsibility for post-independence problems is attributable to colonialism and how much should be borne by local leaders. One Ugandan author argues that sole responsibility cannot simply be laid at the door of others. 'The irony of our recent history is that the agonies to which people have been subjected often did not start with the *arrival* of the European colonisers but with their *departure* in the 1960s. It is hard for us Africans to say this, and it is not to underestimate the evils of colonialism [but] . . . Ordinary Africans . . . are perplexed and angry when, having helped to achieve independence, they see around them oppression, coercion and mass murder' (Mutibwa, 1992, p. x, emphasis in original). With respect to the Rwandan genocide discussed earlier, we can trace some of the causative factors to the colonial period but, in the final analysis, it is not unreasonable to pin principal responsibility on those who actually planned and executed the genocide.

Edward Said himself notes that questions of power and authority once raised in relation to the classical empires of Britain and France may now be directed at despotic successor regimes from Kenya, Nigeria, Morocco, and Egypt to Pakistan, Burma (Myanmar), and Haiti, to name just a few, where 'the struggle on behalf of democracy and human rights continues' (Said, 1993: p. 21). Said's appeal to democracy and human rights is noteworthy because it is an appeal to universal ideals derived from European thought. Yet such 'universals' have been heavily critiqued in much postcolonial thought on the grounds that they are, once again, simply Eurocentric impositions on a culturally diverse, non-Western world. However, a recent work from an African perspective, which argues for a reconsideration of postcolonial approaches, 'rejects the usual hostility to universalism as an imperialist, Eurocentric hoax', and insists that only a universalist approach can supply the essential ground for necessary moral commitments (Sekyi-Otu, 2018: p. 1).

These examples further suggest that we may do well to move away from the tendency to over-invest in the binary opposition or dichotomy between the West and the non-West which risks oversimplifying many global problems and their possible solutions (Lawson, 2006; see also Katzenstein, 2016). At the same time, it would not do simply to dismiss the problematic legacies of European colonialism and their ongoing impact in significant parts of the former colonized world. Colonial rule was, in most cases, an oppressive, exploitative form of authoritarianism, and it is therefore unsurprising that many successor regimes have followed much the same path.

Questions raised by these issues include:

- Does the postcolonial ambit need to be extended to include cases such as West Papua?
- With respect to apportioning responsibility for violence, repression, and economic problems in the period since independence, how much can or should be attributed to colonial legacies, and what other factors should be taken into consideration?
- Even if concepts such as individual human rights are a product of European thought, does this mean they have little relevance outside of the West?

Decolonizing the Curriculum

Another issue of concern in recent postcolonial scholarship is the need to 'decolonize the curriculum'. Critics have pointed out that in global politics, as in many other fields of the humanities and social sciences, students are most likely to be exposed only to the ideas developed within a male-dominated Western tradition. Machiavelli, Hobbes, Marx, Gramsci, Foucault—to name just a few of the most prominent—are studied time and again, indeed as they are in the present volume. Rarely, if ever, do non-Western (or non-male) figures make an appearance. Accordingly, 'IR Theory' has been described as a 'Eurocentric monologue' employing methods and approaches 'marked by power relations, ideological agendas, class motivations, patriarchal considerations, imperial designs and other ethical challenges', with contestations occurring only within its own terms (Zondi, 2018: pp. 18, 29). Almost any critical theorist (Western or otherwise) would agree. But given that 'IR theory' has developed historically almost exclusively within the Western academy, it is scarcely surprising. It is no less surprising that Confucian thought is Sinocentric or that ideas generated by intellectuals in Africa are Afrocentric. And on the issue of 'patriarchal considerations', these are scarcely absent from other traditions of thought. Indeed, if there is one characteristic that Western and non-Western traditions share, it is the dominance of male figures and therefore male perspectives.

There is obviously much to be said for opening up discourses about how politics, and especially *global* politics, is studied and it is clear that a diversity of sources, methods, ideas, and approaches is a strength, not a weakness, in any discipline. As we have seen in previous chapters, IR scholarship has not been oblivious to the fact that non-European sources do not feature strongly in IR theory. Is the explanation for this because scholars have simply ignored what is available from other traditions of thought? Is part of the problem that access to sources other than those in English (or in English translation) is difficult for most scholars? Or is it because they have not been able to identify something that actually constitutes a body of theory that is distinctively 'IR' from a non-Western source?

Over a decade ago, some of these issues were examined in a multi-authored volume entitled *Why Is There No Non-Western International Relations Theory?* (Acharya and Buzan, eds, 2007). The title suggests that the problem lies in the fact that theorizing about 'international relations' has been largely absent in traditions of thought elsewhere. And although classical realism has been able to incorporate a handful of non-Western thinkers, and has been highly influential in places such as China, it still remains a 'Western theory'. One possible explanation for this state of affairs is the fact that the international system itself remains a Westphalian system of sovereign states, based squarely on a European model, and globalized through the processes of decolonization. But given that the rising centres of power are now in the Asia-Pacific, and if there is indeed a close nexus between power and knowledge, there may well be a shift in the sources of theorizing. Indeed, there is a very noticeable growth in scholarly output from China in particular, with works drawing increasingly on Chinese traditions of thought such as Confucianism, although the project is still in the early stages (see Qin, 2016). As we have seen in Chapter 3, one strand of this project has been conceived as a version of 'moral realism', which takes its cue, not surprisingly, from the rise of China as a global power and its challenge to global political leadership.

CONCLUSION

Traditional approaches to global politics have scarcely touched on the themes addressed in this chapter. But times have changed and these themes have attracted much more attention as the agenda for global politics has expanded over the last three decades or so to encompass a wider range of concerns. This is reflected both at a practical level, as exemplified by the UN's attention to such issues as gender and sexuality, as well as at the level of theory as scholars have sought to develop more sophisticated analytical tools to address the phenomena in question.

At the core of many of the issues discussed in this chapter are forms of identity politics in which membership of a group, or the possession of distinctive personal characteristics, acquires a certain political salience. Many people have been disadvantaged at various levels—socially, politically, and economically—by virtue of their membership of a group or their categorization by others. Women have been historically disadvantaged by virtue of their gender, LGBT people by virtue of their sexuality, African Americans by virtue of their race or colour, and so on. The broader history of imperialism and colonialism has also played a major role in producing the economic disadvantages experienced by many in the Global South. The demonstrable disadvantages experienced by members of particular groups are a reflection in turn of significant power imbalances, and this is what makes the issues *political*.

Attention to all these issues is now considered important to a more comprehensive approach to global politics. So too is addressing the extent to which Eurocentrism remains implicated in the production of knowledge at the expense of other knowledge systems and the insights they may contribute. At another level, it should also be evident from this chapter, as well as the previous theory chapters, that virtually all theorizing is prompted by 'real-world' issues and does not take place in a vacuum. This has scarcely led to a convergence of views about the state of the world and how its problems are best analysed. If anything, there is an even greater diversity of approaches in the present period. What may be said is that all the various theories discussed so far represent different ways of seeing the world, and that they all contribute something to enriching our understanding of the complex dynamics of global politics.

KEY QUESTIONS

1   How useful is a 'gender lens' in understanding the dynamics of power in global politics?

2   To what extent have gender and sexuality become global human rights issues?

3   If race is nothing more than a 'social construct', how can we explain its powerful historical effects?

4   What is the relationship between racism, nationalism, and genocide?

5   How have the legacies of imperialism and colonialism shaped the contemporary global system?

6   What are the key issues at stake in postcolonial theorizing?

7   Can postcolonial theories ever transcend the West/non-West dichotomy, or do they depend on it?

8 How might one go about 'decolonizing the curriculum' in IR theory?

9 Can we ever overcome ethnocentrism in the study of global politics?

FURTHER READING

Acharya, Amitav and Barry Buzan (eds) (2010), *Non-Western International Relations Theory: Perspectives On and Beyond Asia* (Abingdon: Routledge).
This book introduces non-Western IR traditions to a Western IR audience, challenging the dominance of Western theory and illuminating alternative perspectives.

de Jong, Sara, Rosalba Icaza, and Olivia U. Rutazibwa (eds) (2018), *Decolonization and Feminisms in Global Teaching and Learning* (Abingdon: Routledge).
There are 17 chapters in this very interesting edited collection dealing with a number of themes covered in this chapter, especially in the sections on feminism and postcolonialism.

Pearcey, Mark (2016), *The Exclusions of Civilization: Indigenous People in the Story of International Society* (New York: Palgrave Macmillan).
This book provides an assessment of the centrality of European colonialism and imperialism in the historical constitution of modern international relations while addressing the interconnections between the European and non-European sides of that history.

Persaud, Randolph and Alina Sajed (eds) (2018), *Race, Gender and Culture in International Relations: Postcolonial Perspectives* (London: Routledge).
Another edited collection which brings together many of the themes dealt with in this chapter including sexuality, nationalism, religion, and inequality analysed through a postcolonial lens.

Shepherd, Laura (ed.) (2015), *Gender Matters in Global Politics: A Feminist Introduction to International Relations* (London: Routledge, 2nd edn).
An edited collection with 31 substantive chapters on an extensive range of gender issues in topics ranging from violence and security to political economy, international institutions, and new technologies.

Wiener, Martin (2013), 'The Idea of "Colonial Legacy" and the Historiography of Empire', *Journal of the Historical Society*, 13(1): 1–32, https://onlinelibrary.wiley.com/doi/epdf/10.1111/jhis.12000.
This article reviews the literature on European colonial legacies and argues that trends in anti-colonial scholarship have tended to exaggerate their contribution to current problems.

WEB LINKS

https://www.cddc.vt.edu/feminism/enin.html
A very comprehensive site covering all aspects of feminist theory.

https://www.unaids.org/en/keywords/sexual-minorities
UN website with information on sexual minorities and various campaigns to eliminate persecution and prejudice.

https://www.antislavery.org/
Website of Anti-Slavery International, an organization dedicated to eliminating contemporary slavery which, according to the site, 'takes various forms and affects people of all ages, gender and races'.

https://www.youtube.com/watch?v=JncXpQQoZAo
Edward Said delivering the concluding lecture of an Orientalism conference.

 For additional material and resources please visit the **online resources** at: www.oup.com/he/lawson1e.

6

SECURITY AND INSECURITY

- Conceptualizing Security

- Security, Insecurity, and Power Politics

- The UN Security Council

- The UN and Intervention in the Post-Cold War Period

- Alternative Approaches to Security

- Human Security and the 'Responsibility to Protect'

- Security and Insecurity after '9/11'

- Conclusion

Reader's Guide

The security of the sovereign state, in a system of states, and existing under conditions of anarchy, has been the traditional focus of studies in global or international politics. Security in this context has therefore been concerned largely with the threats that states pose to each other. Over the last few decades, however, the agenda for security in global politics has expanded, and so too has its conceptualization. This chapter looks first at the general concept of security and the way in which issues come to be 'securitized'. We then move on to traditional approaches to security and insecurity, revisiting the Hobbesian state of nature and tracing security thinking in global politics through to the end of the Cold War. This is followed by a discussion of ideas about collective security as embodied in the UN, paying particular attention to the role of the Security Council and the issue of intervention in the post-Cold War period. This period has also seen the broadening of the security agenda to encompass concerns such as gender security, environmental security, cyber security, and the diffuse concept of 'human security'. The last section provides an overview of the 'war on terror', raising further questions concerning how best to deal with non-conventional security threats.

CONCEPTUALIZING SECURITY

'Security', like so many concepts in the social sciences, is multilayered and contested, as is its antonym, 'insecurity'. Security and insecurity possess objective and subjective, material and ideational dimensions, and one person's perception of threat may be another's idea of opportunity. Domestic security issues range from the maintenance of law and order to food security, energy security, health security, economic security, cyber security, biosecurity, gender security, identity security, and environmental security, among others. All of these may pose issues for personal security as well as for the security of particular groups or whole populations—from violence against women to the persecution of religious groups to outbreaks of infectious diseases, financial crises, terrorist attacks, cyber attacks, and so on. In the global sphere, security has traditionally been concerned mainly with the threats that states pose to each other, but many of the 'domestic' issues noted above overlap with those in the global sphere. Terrorism, for example, has historically taken different forms and poses problems for both the domestic and global spheres—spheres which are often difficult to disentangle.

Conceptualizing and theorizing security requires that we address three basic questions: first, what is being secured; second, what constitutes a condition of security; and third, in what circumstances do ideas about security (and insecurity) arise (Lipschutz, 1995: p. 1). Looking at the first question, we could enumerate various issue areas pertinent to security, starting with those referred to above. The problem here becomes one of an ever-expanding list with no limits on where one should draw the line. The second question concerning what constitutes a condition of security might seem more straightforward. Being able to walk down the street without fear of assault; to know that if one falls ill, one can access appropriate medical care; to be confident that adequate food, water, shelter, and energy is available on an ongoing basis; to trust that the air one breathes is not polluted by toxic particles; to know that one's assets are protected by law, or that the financial institutions on which one depends are adequately regulated; to be assured that one is not in danger of arbitrary arrest and detention by one's own government; or that one's own state is unlikely to be attacked or invaded by another or, just as disastrously, to lapse into civil war or even fall apart; and so on. But the 'and so on' entails the same problem of limits. Where does the list stop, how many different conditions must be met in order for one to be secure?

Another issue raised by both the first and second questions entails the delimiting of responsibility—that is, who is responsible for providing security? This has been seen primarily as the responsibility of the state, especially when it comes to law and order. The state establishes rules for human conduct in almost all spheres of life, many of which are designed to protect people from each other, and punishes those who transgress those rules. Beyond individual sovereign states, which by definition possess the authority to act in all the above areas, there is no 'world government' to enforce security in the international sphere. But there is the United Nations and a considerable body of international law which underpins a system of global governance and plays a key role in global security. These will be discussed in more detail in due course.

The third question entails investigation of the actual circumstances in which security issues arise. For example, at what point does the flow of people from one state to another appear to pose a threat (rather than a benefit, or even just a neutral issue) to the receiving state? Who decides whether immigrants—including both regular immigrants and asylum seekers—actually pose a threat at all, and on what basis? And why should 'state' or 'national' security be privileged over other types of security, including the 'human security' of those seeking refuge?

Securitization Theory

The analysis of security and insecurity also involves *securitization theory*. This offers conceptual tools drawn substantially from constructivist theory. To 'securitize' an issue—say, the flow of refugees from conflict zones or areas of severe economic deprivation into North America, Europe, and Australasia—is to designate these people as constituting an 'existential threat' requiring a special response. Securitization therefore goes beyond mere politicization of the issue, taking it to a level where it can be depicted as a matter of *national security* requiring emergency measures. The successful securitization of any given issue, however, depends ultimately on the force of the relevant 'speech act' performed to persuade the audience that it is in fact a security threat; in other words, where *saying so*, by someone with apparent authority and expertise, succeeds in rendering any given phenomenon a threat. Similar processes apply to the *de*securitization of an issue (see, generally, Buzan, Waever, and de Wilde, 1998). Box 6.1 summarizes how securitization works.

Critiques of securitization theory have come from both realist and critical perspectives. The former continue to defend a narrower conception of security in terms of military threats to the state whereas securitization theorists have placed a far greater range of issues affecting human well-being on the security agenda, which accords with a more liberal approach. Critical perspectives also endorse a broader conception of security, but regard securitization theory, as described above, as missing some crucial points and overemphasizing others. For example, Booth (2007: p. 167) says that securitization theory places too much importance on the audience and argues that even when there is unambiguous evidence of a particular security problem, the relevant audience may simply be unreceptive. Using the example of the 1994 Rwandan genocide, he notes that the UN Security Council, when confronted with overwhelming evidence of the massacre, chose not to interpret the event as requiring remedial action on their part. By disavowing responsibility, they chose

---

BOX 6.1 KEY CONCEPT

Securitization

Securitization theory suggests that national security policy is not 'a natural given' but is carefully designated by politicians and decision-makers. Accordingly, political issues are constituted as extreme security issues to be dealt with urgently when they have been labelled as 'dangerous', 'menacing', 'threatening', 'alarming'. The labelling is carried out by a 'securitizing actor' who has the social and institutional power to move the issue beyond ordinary politics. It follows that security issues are not simply 'out there' but must be articulated as problems by securitizing actors. Calling immigration a 'threat to national security', for instance, shifts immigration from a low priority political concern to a high priority issue that requires action, such as securing borders. Securitization theory challenges traditional approaches to security in IR and asserts that issues are not essentially threatening in themselves; rather, it is via the process of securitization that they become security 'problems' (Eroukhmanoff, 2018).

not to be a relevant audience. In addition, desecuritization may be used as a tactic to shift issues off a security agenda, or exclude them altogether, when in fact they should be on it. Institutionalized racism, for example, can flourish if racism (and the violence often associated with it) is 'desecuritized' (Booth, 2007: p. 168). The reaction to the murder of George Floyd in the US in 2020, mentioned in Chapter 5, however, has seen the issue become much more prominently securitized.

➡ See **Chapter 5** for a discussion of the Rwandan genocide and of racism.

KEY POINTS

- Security is a multilayered and contested concept raising issues of definition and scope.
- Splitting the study of security into domestic and global spheres is a conventional way of managing the field, but many issues cross over into both spheres.
- Securitization theory is based on the notion that issues become 'securitized' when those in positions of power and influence declare something to be a threat, and relevant audiences respond accordingly.

SECURITY, INSECURITY, AND POWER POLITICS

Traditional realist approaches to international relations are primarily concerned with the survival of the state, and a condition of *in*security arises whenever there is a threat to the state. Realists have generally taken their cue from a number of classic texts to construct an image of the **state of nature** characterized by a permanent condition of anarchy. Thomas Hobbes's famous account represents the state of nature as constituting a highly dangerous environment, lacking any effective civil structure. There is no authoritative ruler, no sense of justice or morality, and no security at all for the isolated individuals, who therefore exist within it in constant fear. The most powerful individuals prevail over the weaker, although even the powerful must watch their backs constantly. Thus the anarchic state of nature offers the most *in*secure existence imaginable. According to this viewpoint, the solution is to be found in the formation of bounded political communities—states—headed by a sovereign power. This arrangement works to banish anarchy within states, thus providing the conditions for a secure existence. But it does not banish anarchy in the sphere outside of or between states—that is, the international sphere where no sovereign power exists.

For neorealists in particular, the study of life *within* the state is regarded as the proper focus for political science, whereas their sole concern is with relations between states in the sphere of international anarchy, as discussed in Chapter 3. Given the nature of anarchy, the international sphere is necessarily the principal locus of insecurity for sovereign states and, therefore, ultimately for the people enclosed within them. Thus the primary concern should be how to maintain the *survival* of the sovereign state itself, for it is only when this is taken care of that people can effectively work to achieve 'the good life' within the state (see Box 6.2). We should also note, again, that for realists it is 'the international' rather than 'the global' that best describes their sphere of concern.

BOX 6.2 KEY QUOTE

John Mearsheimer on Security and State Survival

States seek to maintain their territorial integrity and the autonomy of their domestic political order. They can pursue other goals like prosperity and protecting human rights, but those aims must always take a back seat to survival, because if a state does not survive, it cannot pursue those other goals.
(Mearsheimer, 2010: p. 80)

None of this means that the international sphere is one of perpetual chaos or warfare. Realist approaches do not regard anarchy as precluding a degree of order and stability. But given its underlying dynamics, peace and security in the international sphere at any given time are tenuous. Perpetual anarchy thus ensures a state of continuous, underlying *in*security because, even in times of apparent peace, it is always ready to unleash its destructive forces when the fragile order weakens or breaks down. As we have seen, this kind of thinking crystallized in realist theory following the breakdown of international order in the lead-up to the Second World War, culminating in the turn to **power politics** in the post-war period. The power politics approach also involves considerations of both **balance of power** mechanisms and the **security dilemma** which ensures a perpetual, competitive struggle for security where, in the final analysis, states can depend only on their own resources. *Self-reliance* is therefore the watchword for security and the ultimate key to survival in the international sphere.

During the Cold War, the use of the term 'security' came to denote much more than simply protection against invasion. On the Soviet side, perceptions of security went hand in hand with imperial expansion in Eastern and Central Europe, while on the other side 'any state controlling large geographical areas containing significant quantities of natural resources in a way unacceptable to the US [presented] a threat to the "national security" of the United States' (Young and Kent, 2013: p. xxix). The evidence since the end of the Cold War, especially with respect to US intervention in Iraq, a country with vast oil resources, suggests that little has changed. Yet it is clear that a major humanitarian crisis was looming as Colonel Gaddafi's forces did not hesitate to target civilians, thus precipitating the UN-authorized intervention to establish a no-fly zone, as discussed in the next section. A statement issued by Canadian Prime Minister Stephen Harper in March 2011 set out a classic liberal idealist position on the humanitarian imperative in which moralizing themes were clearly evident (see Box 6.3). Interestingly, Harper was widely regarded as a 'hawk', a term reserved for those who need little persuasion to use military force rather than diplomacy and/or sanctions to achieve objectives. Indeed, Mearsheimer suggests that 'liberal interventionism' is actually far more hawkish than realism (see, generally, Mearsheimer, 2018).

Another prominent aspect of neorealism relates to the distribution of power in the international system and its effects on the security environment. Reflecting on the history of the state system in Europe from 1648 through to the Second World War, observers of international politics have generally agreed that the system during that period possessed a 'multipolar' character (Mearsheimer, 2010: pp. 85–7). In other words, significant power was distributed among three or more states within the system as a whole. The Cold War period, however, was described as 'bipolar' since power was divided largely

---

> **BOX 6.3 KEY QUOTE**
>
> **Canadian Prime Minister Stephen Harper, March 2011**
>
> One either believes in freedom, or one just says one believes in freedom. The Libyan people have shown by their sacrifice that they believe in it. Assisting them is a moral obligation upon those of us who profess this great ideal.
>
> (Harper, 2011, reported at https://www.ctvnews.ca/pm-heads-to-paris-for-emergency-summit-on-libya-1.620539)

between the US and its allies on the one hand, and the USSR and its allies on the other. The structure of **bipolarity**, together with the deterrent effect of nuclear weapons possessed by both sides, is often said to have produced the 'long peace' of the Cold War period in which major interstate warfare was threatened but did not actually occur. There is no agreement, however, as to whether a unipolar, bipolar, or multipolar system promotes greater security.

In the meantime, liberal approaches to security have challenged the premises of realism in terms of traditional issues of state security, with considerable success. This is despite the apparent failures of the interwar system—that is, the League of Nations. Indeed, the strong influence of **liberal institutionalism** is evident in the extent to which the immediate post-war period saw the re-establishment of overarching international organizations designed to ameliorate the negative effects of anarchy through collective security mechanisms. Foremost among these is of course the UN whose specific security functions we discuss next.

> **KEY POINTS**
>
> - Realists argue that anarchy ensures a state of continuous underlying *insecurity* even during times of apparent peace. Stability under conditions of anarchy is possible through balance of power mechanisms.
> - Liberals are inclined to support humanitarian intervention, which realists believe may do more harm than good, and rarely serves the interests of the intervening state.

THE UN SECURITY COUNCIL

The UN Charter establishes basic principles of order in support of international peace and security to which every new member must sign up. The Security Council, established under Chapter V, was originally composed of five permanent members—the UK, the US, the USSR, France, and China—and six non-permanent members. There are now ten non-permanent members who serve a two-year term. Each of the five permanent members—or 'P5'—retains veto power over any Security Council decision. This extraordinary power reflects a belief that the new UN would not function effectively without according a special place to the most prominent states, thereby rectifying a perceived weakness of the old League. The Security Council embodies the UN's aspirations to provide for 'collective

FIGURE 6.1 The United Nations Security Council, meeting in New York, USA, 2016
Golden Brown/Shutterstock.com

BOX 6.4 KEY CONCEPT

Collective Security

The anarchic character of the international political sphere, and some of the assumptions under-pinning realist approaches, may suggest that, in the final analysis, security is largely a matter of every state for itself. The best hope for peace and stability from this perspective is in achieving a balance of power. Liberals (and some constructivists), however, believe a superior approach may be found through a collective security arrangement. This means states joining together through a treaty which binds them to supporting each other in case of attack. The UN is the prime such trea-ty organization. Others include NATO as well as the Collective Security Treaty Organisation (CSTO) of which Armenia, Kazakhstan, Kyrgyzstan, Russia, Tajikistan, Uzbekistan, Azerbaijan, Belarus, and Georgia are members. The basic principle of such treaties is that an attack on one member state is regarded as an attack on all of them, and all must act collectively to defend against an aggressor.

---

security'—a term encapsulating the notion that true security cannot be obtained through the practice of 'every state for itself' but only by states operating collectively (see Box 6.4).

The composition and functioning of the UN Security Council has been subject to many criticisms over the years. Critics point to its failure to effectively mitigate serious conflicts, let alone resolve them, and highlight serious tensions within the Security Council itself where any of the five veto-wielding permanent members can prevent action being taken on a security issue if it is perceived as impacting on their own interests. Another criti-cism is that the five permanent members (the P5), which hold such a privileged position, reflects circumstances prevailing over seventy years ago in a world where decolonization had scarcely begun. The UN's membership has almost quadrupled since then, and many now see the permanent membership as skewed unfairly in favour of the developed world with none from Africa, the Middle East, South Asia, or South America.

Reform of the permanent membership, however, seems unlikely in the near future. If reform entailed an expanded permanent membership, the veto power would be extended further, making decisions on vexed issues even more difficult. And if one new member was admitted to make up the five, who would that be? Brazil, Japan, India, Nigeria, and Egypt are possible claimants, but none would be uncontroversial. On the other hand, if one of the permanent members was to give up their seat at the table, who should, or would, vacate their seat to make way for a new member? It's hard to imagine any agreeing to withdraw. If there were no permanent members at all, the dynamics of the Security Council would almost certainly change considerably but there is no guarantee that it would be for the better.

Although lack of reform is often thought to undermine the Security Council's legitimacy, the rotating tenure of the non-permanent membership does give an opportunity to all UN members to serve and its role and status remain important (see Hurd, 2008: pp. 199–217). It is also responsible for peace-keeping operations and, on occasion, can authorize and therefore legitimize the use of military force. Directives from the Security Council also carry strong normative force. During the Cold War, however, the bipolar character of global politics limited its efficacy, with the US and the USSR frequently using the veto to protect their own foreign policy interests and objectives. But the end of the Cold War introduced new dynamics, opening up the possibility of more robust intervention in the affairs of state.

THE UN AND INTERVENTION IN THE POST-COLD WAR PERIOD

When Iraq invaded Kuwait in August 1990, precipitating the Gulf War, the Security Council immediately condemned the action and demanded Iraq's unconditional withdrawal. Iraq under President Saddam Hussein remained intransigent. A further resolution set a deadline of 15 January 1991 for Iraq's withdrawal, after which member states would be authorized to use 'all necessary means' to expel Iraq from Kuwaiti territory. When Iraq failed to comply, the US led a coalition of more than thirty countries in 'Operation Desert Storm' and succeeded in its mandate to restore Kuwaiti sovereignty by expelling Iraq. UN authorization was key to the legitimacy of the operation. In addition, it appeared to herald a 'new world order' in which the Security Council, released from the constraints of the Cold War, could act in concert to enforce the most fundamental principles of international law. More generally, the UN was now seen as capable of taking genuinely effective cooperative security measures. The excerpt in Box 6.5 from US President George H. W. Bush's speech to a joint session of congress, sets out a classic liberal interpretation of the victory in strong moral terms.

The Iraq War, starting in 2003 with the US-led 'Operation Shock and Awe' and ongoing until 2011, was another story altogether. It was not authorized by the Security Council—of the P5 France, Russia, and China all opposed it although the UK was a strong supporter. The actions of the US-led coalition were far more controversial as a result, all the more so considering that the reason given for the war was that Iraq possessed weapons of mass destruction which, as we now know, it did not. Despite lack of authorization, the power of US hegemony enabled it to lead a 'coalition of the willing'

BOX 6.5 KEY QUOTE

Speech by President George H. W. Bush on End of Gulf War

This is a victory for every country in the coalition, for the United Nations. A victory for unprecedented international cooperation and diplomacy. . . . It is a victory for the rule of law and for what is right. . . .

Twice before in this century, an entire world was convulsed by war. Twice this century, out of the horrors of war hope emerged for enduring peace. Twice before, those hopes proved to be a distant dream, beyond the grasp of man.

Until now, the world we've known has been a world divided, a world of barbed wire and concrete block, conflict and cold war.

And now, we can see a new world coming into view. A world in which there is the very real prospect of a new world order. . . . A world where the United Nations, freed from cold war stalemate, is poised to fulfil the historic vision of its founders. A world in which freedom and respect for human rights find a home among all nations.   (*New York Times*, 1991)

(involving around forty-six other states although only three contributed ground troops) into a war completely outside of the purview of the UN and contrary to international law (see Lee, 2010).

Arguments that Saddam Hussein was a murderous dictator and needed to be eliminated had also featured strongly—an argument that realists regarded as moralistic liberal rhetoric justifying interventionism (Mearsheimer, 2010: p. 92). Realists also insisted, rightly, that the war was not in the US's own national interest (nor the UK's). But most liberal theorists were also opposed to intervention, at least partly on the grounds that the ends did not justify the means and also because intervention could well increase rather than reduce suffering. They were also highly critical of the way in which the Bush administration *misused* moral arguments and the idea of the democratic peace to justify the intervention and operate outside the UN system (see Russett, 2005: pp. 395–6). Thus neither realist nor liberal approaches could provide a solid basis for intervention.

The Libyan intervention in 2011, where civil war erupted in February of that year, illustrated another occasion when sufficient political will was mustered among Security Council members to authorize an intervention, although it was formally limited to establishing a no-fly zone to protect civilians who were being slaughtered in large numbers in rebel areas. The Security Council soon resolved to authorize a coalition of member states to take 'all necessary measures . . . to protect civilians and civilian populated areas' although it also excluded 'a foreign occupation force of any form'. This was a specifically *humanitarian* intervention and accorded with liberal principles of morality in global politics. The resolution went on to set out the terms of a no-fly zone (UN News, 2011).

Of the P5 members Russia and China abstained but did not veto the move. Soon after the commencement of operations, NATO officially assumed sole responsibility for international air operations to enforce the no-fly zone. Subsequent events illustrated that a limited, authorized intervention can rapidly expand. NATO forces went on to exceed their UN mandate and clearly acted to enforce regime change—that is, the total defeat of the Gaddafi regime. This succeeded in October 2011, when Gaddafi was killed by insurgents. Like Iraq, however, the security situation in Libya has scarcely improved. Rather, it remains wracked with political factionalism and civil violence and now also provides yet another theatre for Islamist extremism.

The Security Council has been criticized on other occasions for failures to intervene. The Rwandan genocide has been mentioned previously but another serious case occurred in the Darfur region of Sudan where the estimates of deaths from genocidal violence starting in 2003 have reached almost half a million. There are also failures with respect to both the civil war in Syria and the Ukraine crisis. The Syrian conflict erupted in 2011 when protests against the authoritarianism of President Bashar Al-Assad were met with violent repression. On this occasion both Russia and China used their veto to block Security Council resolutions on the Assad regime. This was influenced partly by what had happened in Libya with the Russian envoy stating that the international community should be alarmed by claims that the NATO interpretation of Security Council resolutions on Libya can serve as a model for the responsibility to protect, given what had happened there (cited in Kirsch and Helal, 2014: p. 431).

As for the conflict in eastern Ukraine which erupted in 2014, it is Russia that is seen as the major culprit, making a resolution difficult. Even so, the Security Council maintains an overview of efforts to bring peace to the region. The most recent genocidal activity has been in Myanmar where government forces are blamed for the slaughter and ethnic cleansing of Rohingya people who are Muslim, and ethnically distinct from the majority Buddhist population.

Accusations of UN failure in these and other situations of humanitarian crises show that there have been enormous, perhaps inflated, expectations concerning what the UN can achieve under contemporary conditions. The world today is very different from that which emerged at the end of the Second World War and in which the challenges of failing and fragile states, civil wars, and large-scale humanitarian disasters were not seen as the major concerns for the UN.

➡ See **Chapter 8** for further discussion of Russia and Ukraine and the Iraq War.

In the light of the reasoning behind the UN as a whole and the Security Council in particular, one might ask how different theoretical approaches to IR are reflected. On the one hand, the structure of the UN's central organ—the Security Council—and the dominance of the P5 reflect a realist concern for the accommodation of power politics even within an 'idealist institution'. In addition, the broader liberal vision for collective international security expressed through the UN remains tied to a traditional state-based vision of world order focused primarily on military issues. The issue of humanitarian intervention versus a strict interpretation of the doctrine of state sovereignty also illustrates the tensions between the positions characterized as pluralism and solidarism within English School theory, discussed in Chapter 3. The former resonates with realist and communitarian approaches while the latter reflects a more liberal, cosmopolitan view. In the 'real world' of Security Council deliberations, these views are likely to remain in tension with each other as hard cases continue to present themselves which, in practical terms, can only ever be considered on an individual basis (see Dunne, 2016).

➡ See **Chapter 7** for further discussion of the UN.

- The UN Security Council embodies the idea of collective security whereby an attack on one UN member is an attack on all—an eminently liberal notion—while the provision for five permanent members caters to a realist focus on the role of great powers and moderates its collective security function.

- Issues of humanitarian intervention are in direct tension with the traditional doctrine of state sovereignty, as played out in a number of cases in the post-Cold War period, requiring the Security Council to maintain a balancing act.

- The UN Security Council is the ultimate authority legitimating intervention although a hegemonic power can garner support for unauthorized interventions, as exemplified by the US in the case of the Iraq war.

ALTERNATIVE APPROACHES TO SECURITY

Since at least the 1960s, the peace movement had promoted the idea that genuine security was to be obtained not simply by defeating enemies in war but by working with them to resolve conflicts. Its proponents argued a case for rethinking security along the lines of 'positive peace', a concept which rejects peace as consisting merely in the absence of violent conflict and which focuses attention on the causes of conflict and their amelioration through cooperative social mechanisms. During the Cold War various peace activists campaigned against 'hot' warfare in Vietnam, Korea, and other parts of the Third World; against the advancement of nuclear technology for either military or non-military purposes; against poverty, underdevelopment, and neocolonialism in the Third World generally; and for the promotion of grass-roots democracy and social justice in industrialized nations. There were cross-cutting links as well to other social movements, including the women's movement and the environmental movement, both of which advanced their own particular conceptions of security and an alternative agenda for policy-makers. These moves led eventually to the conceptualization of 'human security' as a counter to the emphasis on traditional notions of state security, which we discuss in more detail shortly.

➲ See **Chapter 8** for further discussion of social movements.

Gender Approaches to Security

Feminism and gender theory have, not surprisingly, provided thoroughgoing critiques of conventional accounts of security. Although there are very different approaches, a common theme is that global politics in general, and security in particular, are not gender neutral and that a particular masculinist perspective has prevailed. As we saw previously, one issue that has received long overdue attention in recent years is that of rape in war as highlighted by the case of Bosnia-Herzegovina. Before this, there was enormous reluctance to recognize the extent to which rape is used as a widespread tactic in war and a manifestation of gross *in*security for its victims. The publicity surrounding the situation in the former Yugoslavia also brought long overdue attention to the widespread rape of German women at the end of the Second World War, mainly at the hands of the victorious Red Army, and of the forced prostitution of 'comfort women' by Japanese forces during the war in the Pacific. Instances of sexual assault in both cases ran into the millions.

These are clearly not the only historic cases—soldiers from many other countries and cultural backgrounds have engaged in rape, either en masse or individually, almost always with impunity. It has only very recently been treated seriously in international law. Indeed, the first time that sexual assault was treated separately as a war crime was in 1996 when eight Bosnian Serb military and police officers were indicted in The Hague in connection with the rape of Muslim women in the Bosnian war. A recent study of rape and forced marriage in the context of political violence, and the role of the International Criminal Court (ICC), traces how these actions have been defined and interpreted, and how progressive approaches have been resisted by states with strong patriarchal structures and where conservative religious beliefs underpin legal and social institutions (Baumeister, 2018). The criminalization of sexual violence in war has scarcely prevented the continuation of the practice, but it provides an indication that the practice of rape in war, as something that affects women in particular (although not exclusively), is now treated as an important security issue.

➡ See **Chapter 5** for a discussion of gender and rape in warfare.

➡ See **Chapter 8** for a discussion of the **International Criminal Court**.

Feminist security studies continue to contribute key insights into the extent to which violence frequently has a gendered aspect. But they also highlight the extent to which solutions may be gendered as well. For example, a 2015 UN report noted that women are almost universally portrayed, alongside children, as defenceless, vulnerable victims (see Davies and True, 2019: p. 7). This feeds into both policy and practice which therefore tend to focus on protecting women and girls *from* men, *by* men, thus perpetuating the inequalities of the gendered dimension, rather than looking to empower women and girls. A strategy based on social and political *empowerment* aimed at creating greater equality would see more positive outcomes in terms of prevention both nationally and globally.

Security and the North–South Gap

Another security concern in the post-Cold War period concerned with equality, or lack of it, has been the increasing gap between 'haves' and 'have-nots'—with the former consisting largely of the prosperous, industrialized countries of the northern hemisphere and the latter of underdeveloped countries, most of which lie in the **Global South**. This has produced a 'North–South' economic/developmental divide with significant security dimensions. Again, concerns about this pre-date the end of the Cold War, as the report of a UN-sponsored commission headed by former West German Chancellor and Nobel Peace Laureate Willy Brandt shows. Published in 1980, this influential report, entitled *North–South: A Programme for Survival* (UNESCO, 1980), examined in depth the range of problems arising from significant socio-economic disparities between countries.

The report emphasized the fact that both North and South had a strong mutual interest in putting an end to dependence, oppression, hunger, and general human distress. It proposed vastly increased aid flows, arguing that the transformation of the global economy would be in the long-term interests of all counties. Although some developed countries saw value in acting on its recommendations, others were tepid at best. US President Ronald Reagan evinced little interest in development issues except where aid was seen as a counter to Soviet influence. Even so, overall aid flows did increase. Just as importantly, the commission opened up new public discourses on the relationship between global development and security by highlighting that narrow military concerns were insufficient in an era of increasing global interdependence. Certainly, by 1989 it was clear that the Cold War had virtually collapsed and that the time for new security thinking in an increasingly globalized world had arrived. This occurred with the development of the multifaceted concept of human security, discussed shortly. Even so, millions remain in dire poverty in the Global South which, among other things, is a major factor in contemporary global migration patterns—something which better-off states very often see as threatening their border security. This has become a major political issue in Europe (including the UK), the US, and Australia in particular where right-wing populism has gathered strength, largely through depicting migrants and asylum seekers as a security threat.

Environmental Security

In addition to the plight of millions in the Global South and the multifaceted security threats they faced, attention has also turned to the natural environment. Again, concerns were raised well before the end of the Cold War and the UN had held its first major environmental summit in Stockholm in 1972. But the post-Cold War world has been more conducive to expressing environmental concerns explicitly in terms of *security*. The UN again took a lead, organizing an 'earth summit' in Rio de Janeiro in 1992. The latter produced the UN Convention on Climate Change (UNFCCC), which set up a framework for intergovernmental efforts to tackle global warming, followed by the Kyoto Protocol (1997) which strengthened the Convention by committing its signatories to binding targets for the reduction of greenhouse gas emissions (see https://unfccc.int/process/the-kyoto-protocol). The US under the Bush administration and Australia under the Howard government, however, subsequently pulled out, each claiming that the emissions reduction targets would damage their respective economies and both also claiming that developing countries, which included major emitters such as China and India, should not be given special treatment.

Further conferences were held in Copenhagen in 2009 and Cancún in 2010 with the latter establishing a Green Climate Fund intended to raise and disburse US$100 billion a year by 2020 to help poor nations deal with climate impacts and assist low-carbon development. A further 'Conference of the Parties' (COP 21), which refers to the countries that ratified the UNFCCC, was held in Paris in December 2015, which agreed 'to strengthen the global response to the threat of climate change by keeping a global temperature rise this century well below 2 degrees Celsius above pre-industrial levels and to pursue efforts to limit the temperature increase even further to 1.5 degrees Celsius' (UNFCCC, n.d.). In June 2017, President Trump announced that the US would cease all participation in the agreement to mitigate climate change (Whitehouse, 2017).

The consequences of global warming for security are potentially enormous. Rising sea levels—just one consequence—threaten not just the very existence of small island states, such as Tuvalu and Kiribati in the Pacific, the Maldives and Seychelles in the Indian Ocean, and low-lying countries like Holland and Bangladesh, but also the extensive

FIGURE 6.2 **Tuvalu** Romaine W/Shutterstock.com

coastal regions of countries like the US, Australia, China, and many more. Climate change will also impact adversely on food and water security, not to mention the considerable problems that will inevitably attend mass migration from low-lying areas, with implications for border security as new waves of 'environmental refugees' seek a safe place to live.

⊙ See **Chapter 11** for a discussion of environmentalism and related issues in IR.

Cyber Security

The increasing problem of cyber security has implications for a huge range of issues from the security of personal data to military operations, the conduct of diplomacy, energy installations, financial networks, communications, and so on. In the 1990s—the early days of the Internet—incidents involving hacking, malware, and denial-of-service attacks were more of a nuisance than a major security concern. But with Internet usage growing exponentially—reaching almost 4 billion users over the next two decades—cyber security has become a global issue (see, generally, Tikk and Kerttunen, 2020). As far as Western countries are concerned, some of the major threats to cyber security come from organized criminal groups as well as from state actors, especially Russia, China, and North Korea.

The extent of alleged Russian activity includes a wide range of cyber interventions aimed at undermining political and social stability in Western countries. Specific examples are interference in the 2016 US presidential elections which prompted the extraordinary Special Counsel investigation by former FBI Director Robert Mueller between 2017 and 2019 on links between Russia and the Trump campaign—an investigation which was itself hacked. President Trump consistently denied Russian involvement, denouncing the investigation as a 'witch-hunt' (Mueller, 2019). Other notable examples were the cyber attacks on the chemical weapons watchdog, the Organization for the Prohibition of Chemical Weapons, which was looking into the possible involvement of Russian agents in the poisoning of a former Russian double agent, Sergei Skripal, and his daughter in the UK in 2018 (discussed further in Chapter 9). Sports anti-doping authorities have also been targeted in the wake of alleged Russian state-sponsored doping of athletes in various sports.

China has been accused of cyber attacks and cyber spying, with high-tech companies and other big businesses as well as governments being targeted. Chinese hackers stand accused of stealing technology from industries including aviation, satellites, factory automation, finance and consumer electronics, which of course has been strongly denied by Chinese authorities. A report says that Chinese espionage threats have 'increasingly raised alarm bells among the so-called "five-eyes" countries that share intelligence—the US, the UK, Canada, New Zealand and Australia—in addition to non-western allies such as Japan' (*Financial Times*, 2018). Tensions have increased since the financial chief of Chinese tech giant Huawei was arrested in Canada in December 2018 on a US warrant relating to charges of fraud in connection with US sanctions on Iran, of providing misleading information to banks, and of stealing trade secrets from a US-based wi-fi operator (Felsenthal, 2019). China responded by arresting two Canadians in China, with Canada of course protesting in turn. China's ambassador to Canada has been quoted as saying that Canada's actions are 'due to western egotism and white supremacy' (*Guardian*, 2019).

➡ See **Chapter 9** for further discussion of Russia and China in the context of diplomacy and foreign policy.

Environmental security, cyber security, security issues arising from the North–South gap, and gender security are among the most prominent non-traditional security issues that have come to the fore in the post-Cold War period. Others include energy security, food and water security (not just in relation to climate change), biosecurity (protection of plants, animals and humans against pests and disease), and border security (with respect

FIGURE 6.3 **Director-General of the World Health Organization Tedros Adhanom Ghebreyesus at the Global Vaccination Summit, 2019** Alexandros Michailidis/Shutterstock.com

to refugees, illicit goods, diseases, etc.). Since the outbreak of the COVID-19 global pandemic, which was declared a Public Health Emergency of International Concern on 30 January 2020 by the World Health Organization (WHO), particular attention has also now been focused on *global health security*. The pandemic clearly has massive implications not just for public health but for national economies and, ultimately, for the global economy. A well-coordinated global response to the latter, based on reliable factual information, is best delivered through the WHO, for although we may find fault with such bureaucracies within the UN system, it would be difficult to set up another mechanism through which a proper global response could be carried out at all.

KEY POINTS

- Social movements such as the peace movement, the women's movement, and the environmental movement have all contributed to alternative conceptualizations of security.

- The 'North–South' developmental divide as well as crises generating millions of refugees in recent times have significant global security dimensions especially with respect to the border security of better-off states.

- Environmental security, cyber security, gender security, and global health security are among the major non-conventional security concerns of the twenty-first century, requiring both national and global responses.

HUMAN SECURITY AND THE 'RESPONSIBILITY TO PROTECT'

UN intervention and responses to other non-traditional security issues in the post-Cold War world have been supported conceptually by new security thinking first articulated explicitly in the UN's *Human Development Report: 1994* (UNDP, 1994). Opening with the claim that: 'The world can never be at peace unless people have security in their daily lives' (ibid.: p. 1), and a survey of the contrast between the unprecedented prosperity achieved by some and the deepening misery of so many others, the report went on to set out a case for redefining security in 'human' terms, implying a substantial shift away from security defined primarily as state/national security. The 'human' aspect here includes all those forms of security noted above under the rubric of alternative approaches and many more. Security itself is therefore defined in the broadest possible terms as 'safety from the constant threats of hunger, disease, crime and repression' and 'protection from sudden and hurtful disruptions in the pattern of our daily lives—whether in our homes, in our jobs, in our communities or in our environment' (ibid.: p. 3).

As with previous UN reports, there have been both supporters and critics. Among the latter, a common objection was that if virtually everything came under the rubric of 'security' then the term was meaningless. Furthermore, the broadening of the security agenda in this way meant that the important focus on *international* security may be lost. In theoretical terms, it is not hard to see that while realists would be concerned to maintain the international/domestic distinction as a matter of both practical and conceptual importance, those subscribing to alternative ideas about security would welcome the conceptual shift. This has resulted in efforts by policy-makers and others to tackle security at different levels. So while not neglecting traditional state security needs, more attention has been directed to the multiple levels at which security considerations operate. New security thinking has also prompted a questioning of state legitimacy and the inviolability of sovereignty when it comes to humanitarian crises, as Box 6.6 shows.

BOX 6.6 KEY DEBATE

The 'Responsibility to Protect'

An important report issued in 2001 by the International Commission on Intervention and State Sovereignty (ICISS), which was set up by the Canadian government, and entitled *The Responsibility to Protect*, was adopted by the UN World Summit in 2005. This followed from the experience of tragedies such as the Rwandan genocide when the UN had done nothing to prevent or mitigate the situation. A central claim is that, while it is the responsibility of sovereign states to protect their own citizens from avoidable catastrophe, if they are unwilling or unable to do so then that responsibility must be borne by the international community (ICISS, 2001). Thus the 'responsibility to protect'—commonly known as 'R2P'—is in the first instance the responsibility of states but may shift to the external realm—the international community—when any state fails in its essential responsibility. The 2005 UN World Summit outcome emphasized the obligations and responsibilities of both individual states and the international community collectively as per the following sections:

138. Each individual State has the responsibility to protect its populations from genocide, war crimes, ethnic cleansing and crimes against humanity. This responsibility entails the prevention of such crimes, including their incitement, through appropriate and necessary means. We accept that responsibility and will act in accordance with it. The international community should, as appropriate, encourage and help States to exercise this responsibility and support the United Nations in establishing an early warning capability.

139. The international community, through the United Nations, also has the responsibility to use appropriate diplomatic, humanitarian and other peaceful means, in accordance with Chapters VI and VIII of the Charter, to help protect populations from genocide, war crimes, ethnic cleansing and crimes against humanity. In this context, we are prepared to take collective action, in a timely and decisive manner, through the Security Council, in accordance with the Charter, including Chapter VII, on a case-by-case basis and in cooperation with relevant regional organizations as appropriate, should peaceful means be inadequate and national authorities manifestly fail to protect their populations from genocide, war crimes, ethnic cleansing and crimes against humanity. We stress the need for the General Assembly to continue consideration of the responsibility to protect populations from genocide, war crimes, ethnic cleansing and crimes against humanity and its implications, bearing in mind the principles of the Charter and international law. We also intend to commit ourselves, as necessary and appropriate, to helping States build capacity to protect their populations from genocide, war crimes, ethnic cleansing and crimes against humanity and to assisting those which are under stress before crises and conflicts break out. (United Nations, General Assembly, 2005)

Some have argued that the report did not go far enough in setting out a new framework for UN action in response to crises. A stronger framework would require, for example, limiting the veto

(Continued)

power of P5 members when extraordinary circumstances arose, and requiring the UN to do more than merely 'stand ready' to intervene, but actually oblige it to act (Bellamy, 2006).

As we have seen, however, stronger actions have not produced unambiguous goods in the global system. The Libyan intervention as a specific UN response in line with R2P scarcely produced the desired consequences. It destroyed the existing regime and did little to help set up a viable alternative regime, leaving the door open to a whole array of malign forces including jihadist violence, sectarianism, and tribalism (see Thakur, 2018: ch. 7). Some of the questions these issues raise are:

1 To what extent does the R2P doctrine set up a tension between the rights and responsibilities of individual sovereign states and the international community?

2 How does the debate about R2P reflect the respective positions taken in the English School debate over pluralism and solidarism, and in debates between realists and liberals?

KEY POINTS

- Traditional security paradigms have been challenged by the shift in emphasis from state security to human security and acknowledgement of the multiple levels at which insecurity occurs.

- The 'responsibility to protect' has highlighted the role that the international community (mainly through the UN) is expected to play when states cannot, or will not, protect their own citizens from harm, although there is no guarantee that well-intentioned intervention will do more good than harm.

SECURITY AND INSECURITY AFTER '9/11'

Developments in new security thinking in the twenty-first century have taken place against the background of a 'global war on terror', or GWOT, a term adopted by the Bush administration but officially dropped when President Obama came to power. The attacks on the World Trade Center in New York and the Pentagon in Washington by Al-Qaeda operatives on 11 September 2001 (widely referred to as '9/11') precipitated the US-led invasion of two sovereign states: Afghanistan and Iraq. The GWOT is not easily analysed in terms of traditional security paradigms even though the US response, in so far as it involved military force and interstate warfare, deployed traditional methods. The rise of Al-Qaeda and other organizations associated with 'militant Islam', together with the responses by the US and its allies, illustrates a number of twists and variations on the theme of security (see Box 6.7).

As we have seen in Chapter 4, Al-Qaeda, known to be based in Afghanistan with the blessing of the Taliban government, was the prime suspect in the 9/11 attacks. The US demanded that its leader, Osama bin Laden, be handed over by the Taliban government. When it refused to do so, the US and allies attacked just four weeks after. NATO had invoked Article 5 of NATO's founding charter which declares that an armed attack against

BOX 6.7 CASE STUDY

The Rise of Islamic Militancy

Islamic radicalism and militancy, which is deeply intertwined with politics in the Middle East region, has been on the rise since at least the 1970s, although the essential background to these developments can be traced back much further. The current geopolitical landscape has been shaped by the outcomes of the First and Second World Wars, colonialism, the authoritarianism of successor regimes in the postcolonial period, and the competing claims of Palestinian and Jewish groups to territory—claims which have acquired an increasing religiosity over the years, in turn fuelling the emergence of extremist, politically driven religious fundamentalism.

It was under the conditions of the Cold War, however, that Osama bin Laden's Al-Qaeda organization emerged in Afghanistan, a country with a long history of political instability and with strategic significance for the Soviet Union. It became a battleground for competing factions within the country from the early 1970s. While the Soviets supported a Marxist government, the US, along with Pakistan, Saudi Arabia, China, the UK, and other disparate regimes, generally supported an insurrection led by the Mujahidin, whose name means 'strugglers', also related to the word *jihad* or 'holy struggle'. Initially energized by and partially united in opposition to the Soviet presence in Afghanistan, any coherence the Mujahidin possessed largely dissipated after the Soviet withdrawal in 1989.

Violent conflict between contending factions as well as with the embattled central government continued until the strongest faction, the Taliban, gained control in 1996, imposing an uncompromising version of Islamic rule. Afghanistan thereafter became a haven for Al-Qaeda, originally formed in Afghanistan during the struggle against the Soviets, but for a time with its main base in Sudan. In 1996, bin Laden shifted to Afghanistan from where he planned attacks on two US embassies in East Africa in 1988 and a US Navy vessel in Yemen in 2000. But the most spectacular attacks, and those with the most far-reaching consequences, were those of 9/11. These attacks sparked the 'global war on terror'.

Related organizations operating in the contemporary period include Boko Haram, which emerged in Nigeria in 2002. Although undoubtedly inspired and supported by Al-Qaeda, the origins of Boko Haram may also be found in a sense of alienation and deprivation among Islamic communities in Nigeria's north. The organization achieved particular notoriety for its abduction of more than 200 schoolgirls in April 2014, many of whom may have been sold into slavery. Another Al-Qaeda-related organization in Africa is Somali-based Al Shabaab, which made headlines when it killed almost seventy people in an attack on a shopping mall in Nairobi in September 2013, and again in April 2015, with its attack on Garissa University College, in which 147 people were killed. It has been weakened by African Union forces, but continues with attacks in both Somalia and Kenya. Both Boko Haram and Al Shabaab are dedicated to the establishment of Islamic states and enmity against 'the West' and non-Muslims as well as any rival and/or moderate Muslim groups. Another group called Abu Sayyaf operates in the Philippines where it has been especially active since 2017, at one stage capturing a city in Mindanao in the south.

Even more infamous in recent times, especially in light of its gruesome execution of hostages, is the organization known variously as ISIL (Islamic State in Iraq and the Levant), ISIS (Islamic State in Iraq and Syria), or simply Islamic State (IS), which originally formed as an offshoot of Al-Qaeda in Iraq. It has attracted both Islamist enemies of the Syrian regime as well as Iraqi Sunnis, repressed under a Shia-dominated regime since the overthrow of Saddam Hussein. However, its targets also

(Continued)

include Kurds and Christian minorities. It is well known for attracting foreign militants from around the world, including Australians, Canadians, Americans, Britons, and other Europeans willing to fight, as well as Chechens, Jordanians, and Saudis, among others. Its activities in Iraq have drawn the US and some allies back to military engagement in the country. Abu Sayyaf in the Philippines is, incidentally, an affiliated movement.

IS has sought to establish a 'caliphate' which is, literally, a state governed by the principles of Islam and headed by a Caliph (a ruler understood to be a successor to the prophet Muhammad), although its use of this term, as with almost anything else claimed by IS and the other groups mentioned above, is opposed by moderate Muslims. Indeed the great majority of Muslims condemn all the acts of violence and intolerance perpetrated in the name of their religion. This has not prevented the demonization of Islam and its followers in non-Muslim majority countries (including but not limited to the West) by groups and individuals. These include not just right-wing minority groups and individuals who act out their own brands of extremism but also political leaders such as former US President Trump.

This case raises a range of questions, including:

1 To what extent does Islamic extremism represent an attack on 'modern' and/or 'Western' values?

2 How do moderate Muslims respond to extremist activities carried out in their name?

3 And what implications does this form of extremism hold for global politics?

one member is an attack on all, in accordance with the principle of collective security. 'Operation Enduring Freedom', as the initial intervention was called, eventually gave way to NATO's International Security Assistance Force (ISAF). Efforts in political reconstruction then saw elections held, a new government put in place, and a programme of infrastructure development commenced. Afghanistan, however, still barely functions as a state and insecurity at multiple levels is the order of the day while corruption is endemic. It took almost a decade to track bin Laden down. He was eventually found in hiding in Pakistan by US special forces in 2011 and executed on the spot.

The aftermath of the Iraq war, launched in March 2003 by the Bush administration as part of the GWOT, has gone badly by almost any measure. The years that followed the US-led invasion saw Iraq teetering on the brink of civil war between Shia and Sunni factions. And while Al-Qaeda had virtually no presence in Iraq before March 2003, the chaos engendered by the war saw it become another recruiting ground for both criminal and terrorist organizations. Eight years later, one highly critical report noted that the US suffered casualties of 4,400 soldiers dead and more than 32,000 seriously wounded; figures that nonetheless pale alongside an estimated 1 million Iraqi civilian deaths as a result of the invasion. The cost to the US economy has been around $3 trillion (more than sixty times the initial estimate) while the cost to Iraq in terms of infrastructure, environmental damage, and human capital is incalculable. In a 'liberated' Iraq, millions of Iraqis remain displaced, in both Iraq itself as well as around the region, and ordinary citizens remain politically oppressed in the post-war order (see Benjamin and Davis, 2011). The emergence of IS has also contributed to the worst refugee crisis in any region since the Second World War, although the Syrian government is no doubt the root cause of the problem there.

Another major lesson from the GWOT to date is that the use of conventional military tactics against a non-conventional enemy may not only be ineffectual in defeating that enemy but create many new problems. While bin Laden was finally killed in May 2011, Al-Qaeda and the Taliban have not only *not* been destroyed but have now been joined by other militant groups including IS; a seemingly never-ending supply of suicide bombers continues to pose a threat to civilian populations in countries around the world; and the prospects for peace and security for the people of both Afghanistan and Iraq remain bleak. It may be the case that terrorism is best dealt with by civil law enforcement agencies and the strengthening of national and international intelligence networks dedicated to the task. A simple news Internet search will usually give approximate numbers of attacks foiled each year in countries around the world by civil (police) agencies.

Military force is always a very blunt weapon and its consequences are often both unpredictable and uncontrollable. This led one of the most famous commentators on war, the Prussian military strategist Carl von Clausewitz (1780–1831), to observe that the planning and execution of war necessarily takes place in a kind of twilight where the effects of fog distort and obscure what is going on (see Clausewitz, 1993). The phrase 'the fog of war' is based on this observation. The Chinese Taoist thinker and strategist Sun Tzu, introduced in Chapter 3, advised more than 2,000 years ago that the best victory of all is gained without fighting, and outlined various strategies for achieving this end (see Sun, 2017). These observations point to the fact that much more subtle instruments of politics may be needed to achieve desirable security outcomes in the longer term, especially against highly unconventional threats.

6

KEY POINTS

- The 9/11 attacks prompted what may be seen as a conventional military response, but against a highly unconventional enemy.

- Although regime change was achieved in both Afghanistan and Iraq through military force, the long-term security outcomes for both countries, as well as the region more generally, remain highly problematic.

CONCLUSION

Security and insecurity in global politics are clearly multifaceted both conceptually and in practical terms. Various institutions, practices, and policies have been developed over the years to cope with different security challenges ranging from conventional threats to international peace and security from armed aggression by one or more states against others in the international system, to numerous other challenges arising from civil wars, terrorism, and the whole array of non-conventional security issues discussed in this chapter. The seriousness of these non-conventional threats has prompted an essential rethinking of what constitutes security and insecurity with the broad notion of human security now being promoted at all levels. Of particular concern have been large-scale threats arising *within* states—especially those associated with genocidal violence—prompting questions about the very nature of state sovereignty and the rights and responsibilities that go with it vis-à-vis the role of the international community in responding to large-scale suffering.

KEY QUESTIONS

1   How does traditional IR theory treat the concept of security and how does it relate to images of the 'state of nature'?

2   Should the nation-state remain central to how security is conceptualized in the present period with respect to both traditional and newer security issues?

3   How have social movements such as the peace movement, the women's movement and the environmental movement challenged traditional militarist approaches to security?

4   In what ways does a gender perspective illuminate non-traditional security issues in IR?

5   What are the main challenges posed for Western democracies by cyber attacks and interventions emanating from authoritarian states?

6   How does securitization theory enhance our critical understanding of the security agenda?

7   Does the concept of 'human security' offer a superior framework for addressing issues in the contemporary period?

8   Is the role of the UN in maintaining international peace and security likely to change significantly following the development of R2P?

9   Are terrorists best dealt with militarily or through law enforcement agencies (i.e. police and the courts) at both national and international levels?

6

GLOBAL POLITICS

FURTHER READING

Balzacq, Thierry (ed.) (2011), *Securitization Theory: How Security Problems Emerge and Dissolve* (Abingdon: Routledge).
Provides a new framework for analysing not just 'security' but the processes by which security issues emerge, evolve, and dissolve.

Bellamy, Alex J. (2014), *The Responsibility to Protect: A Defence* (Oxford: Oxford University Press).
A book-length study of the doctrine and the complex of issues driving the R2P agenda by a leading expert on the subject.

Dodds, Felix and Tim Pippard (eds) (2005), *Human and Environmental Security: An Agenda for Change* (London: Earthscan).
An edited collection by leading (mainly non-academic) commentators produced in advance of the UN's 2005 World Summit illustrating the complex links between human and environmental security.

Gentry, Caron E., Laura J. Shepherd, and Laura Sjoberg (eds) (2018), *Routledge Handbook of Gender and Security* (Abingdon: Routledge).
The core themes of this volume are that gender is conceptually necessary to thinking about central questions of security; analytically important for thinking about cause and effect in security; and politically important for considering possibilities of making the world better in the future.

Gheciu, Alexandra and William C. Wohlforth (eds) (2018), *The Oxford Handbook of International Security* (Oxford: Oxford University Press).
This presents itself as the definitive volume on the state of international security and the academic field of security studies, providing a *tour de force* of the most innovative areas of research as well as major developments in established lines of inquiry.

Peterson, Christian Philip, William M. Knoblauch, and Michael Loadenthal (eds) (2019), *The Routledge History of World Peace since 1750* (Abingdon: Routledge).

A very substantial collection of 34 individual chapters by expert contributors in the field of peace studies from across both the humanities and social sciences.

WEB LINKS

http://www.cfr.org

Website of the US-based Council on Foreign Relations containing numerous articles and commentary on contemporary security concerns around the world.

https://www.unwomen.org/en/news/in-focus/women-peace-security

This is the site for UN Women, a directorate within the UN dedicated to promoting gender equality and the empowerment of women.

https://www.terrorism-research.com

A useful general website containing articles and information about terrorism.

http://www.nato.int
https://www.un.org

These are the general websites for both the UN and NATO and will lead you through an enormous number of subsites with important documents and other interesting material.

https://russiaeu.ru/en

Website of the Permanent Mission of the Russian Federation to the European Union provides an alternative perspective which outlines, among other things, the emergence of a polycentric global order as a counter to claims of US hegemony.

 For additional material and resources please visit the **online resources** at: www.oup.com/he/lawson1e.

7

INTERNATIONAL ORGANIZATIONS IN GLOBAL POLITICS

- What Is an International Organization?
- The Emergence of International Organizations
- Intergovernmental Organizations (IGOs)
- Non-Governmental Organizations (NGOs)
- Social Movements and Global Civil Society
- Conclusion

Reader's Guide

This chapter first looks at the nature of international organizations and how they are generally theorized as participants in global politics and then reviews the rise of international organizations from a historical perspective, with particular reference to developments from the nineteenth century onwards. The chapter goes on to discuss the major intergovernmental institutions that emerged in the twentieth century and which have played such an important role in shaping global order. We look briefly at the League of Nations but most attention is given to its successor, the United Nations (UN), and its various appendages. Then there is the world of non-governmental organizations (NGOs), populated with a bewildering variety of bodies. Some possess significant status in the global sphere, others have little relevance, and still others pose dangers. Finally, we consider social movements and their relationship to the contemporary world of international organizations along with the idea of global civil society. In reviewing these institutions, actors, and ideas we should keep in mind that liberal international theory, especially in the form of liberal institutionalism, as well as proponents of international society, regard robust international organizations as essential building blocks of global order.

WHAT IS AN INTERNATIONAL ORGANIZATION?

International organizations (IOs), from the UN down to voluntary organizations with constituent members in just a few countries, operate in a sphere which transcends states and the state system in one way or another. This does not mean that they are necessarily more powerful or more important than states but, like states, IOs exist as tangible institutional products of social and political forces. Beyond that, they comprise clusters of ideas and coalitions of interest at a transnational level and generate purposeful activities in pursuit of certain desired outcomes. As we shall see, some have links with wider social movements. A prime example is the environmental movement which has generated numerous IOs.

IOs may be public or private organizations, depending on whether they are set up by state or non-state actors. Most are permanent, or at least aspire to an ongoing existence, even if many fall by the wayside. They invariably possess constitutional structures, although the extent to which they possess a legal personality is often unclear. Their power varies enormously, depending on their size and the resources at their disposal. And they come in such diverse forms that it is difficult to pin them down to one clear description.

The term 'international organization' also overlaps with international regime. The latter concept originated as a way of understanding international cooperation. As Keohane (1993: p. 23) explains, highly organized and systematic cooperation characterizes much of global politics, yet there are few rules that are hierarchically enforced. Rather, they are followed voluntarily and cooperatively, becoming embedded in relations of reciprocity. An international regime, though not itself an organization as such, usually incorporates one or more international organizations whose interests centre around a particular issue or theme. A prime example is the global human rights regime which revolves around a cluster of important norms and principles that give it its focus. It encompasses many organizations, including—but not limited to—the UN, and operates through processes and rules set up to promote and protect human rights at both national and international levels (see Rittberger and Zangl, 2006: pp. 6–7).

Some definitions encompass transnational and multinational corporations and these do fit a broad conception of what constitutes an IO. However, they are often treated separately from government and non-profit actors. The *Yearbook of International Organizations* does not include for-profit organizations such as transnational or multinational organizations but does list over 70,000 intergovernmental and non-governmental organizations. Around 40 per cent of these are dormant but, with around 1,200 new organizations being added each year, the field is obviously still growing (see https://uia.org/yearbook).

➡ See Chapter 2 for a discussion of transnational or multinational organizations.

Another category of IO, also excluded from most standard definitions, encompasses transnational criminal organizations or TCOs, but they are mentioned here because they are becoming increasingly important actors. Whereas organized crime has been very largely a concern for domestic policing agencies in earlier periods, the development of TCOs has required increased policing cooperation in the international sphere to deal with their various activities which include drug running, money laundering, people smuggling, and weapons smuggling. One author notes that the emergence of TCOs results at least partly from the same underlying changes in the global sphere that have proved conducive to the success of transnational corporations. Thus increased interdependence between states and the permeability of boundaries, developments in international travel and communications, and the globalization of international financial networks 'have facilitated the emergence of what is, in effect, a single global market for both licit and illicit commodities' (Williams, 1997: p. 316). We look briefly at how the UN has responded to TCOs and related activities in a later section.

This chapter focuses mainly on those IOs which are more conventionally recognized as such; namely, those set up by states through multilateral agreements, sometimes called intergovernmental organizations or IGOs. It also includes those set up by non-state or non-government actors whose primary business is not strictly commercial (or illicit)—these are the ubiquitous non-governmental organizations or NGOs. An important theme here is the interaction between different organizations in the international sphere that make a model of international politics, based almost exclusively on individual sovereign states acting on their own initiative and in their own interest, seem very inadequate. At the same time, those who lean heavily in the other direction by exaggerating the importance of IOs can too easily dismiss the crucial role that states play, not simply in organizing their own affairs but in creating the very world of IOs that may seem to make states less important in many areas. The quote in Box 7.1 suggests an approach which balances these views.

Theorizing International Organizations

Much of the theorization of IOs, or at least inter*governmental* organizations which produce institutions of formal global governance, is a product of liberal theory although constructivism makes a significant contribution as well. Realism may not dismiss the role of international organizations entirely, and may contribute to explaining governance at the global level in terms of the strategic choices made by sovereign states under conditions of anarchy, but it does not go much further than that. Given that the state is conceived as a

BOX 7.1 KEY QUOTE

International Organizations

There are two predominant views of international organizations among the general public. The first is a cynical view that emphasizes the dramatic rhetoric and seeming inability to deal with vital problems that are said to characterize international organizations generally and the United Nations in particular. According to this view, mirrored in some realist formulations, international organizations should be treated as insignificant actors on the international stage. The other view is an idealistic one. Those who hold this view envisage global solutions to the problems facing the world today, without recognition of the constraints imposed by state sovereignty. Most of the naïve calls for world government are products of this view. An understanding of international organizations and global governance probably requires that neither view be accepted in its entirety, nor be wholly rejected. International organizations are neither irrelevant nor omnipotent in global politics. They play important roles in international relations, but their influence varies according to the issue area and situation confronted.

(Diehl, 2005: p. 3)

unitary actor looking to secure its survival vis-à-vis other states in a highly competitive environment, a realist perspective sees IOs as limited in their utility and always subject to the dynamics of power politics. Liberals will agree that state survival and national sovereignty are highly valued, but they are not the only goals that motivate states. Liberal institutionalism provides insights into states as rational actors that address collective action problems arising from interdependence. Viewed in this light, IOs may be seen as a means reducing the transaction costs of cooperation in areas where states have overlapping of interests, thereby facilitating international governance under the structural constraints imposed by anarchy (Hooghe, Lenz, and Marks, 2019: pp. 3–4).

Constructivism sheds light on the social relations required to produce forms of international or global governance among sovereign states, and on how participants consider themselves vis-à-vis others. Constructivist theory therefore draws attention to the conditions under which the participants will be prepared to trade a measure of their sovereignty for a wider form of rule in the global sphere (Hooghe, Lenz, and Marks, 2019: p. 5). However, if the analysis is limited to a state-centric approach, this will not tell us much about the role and influence of NGOs in global governance. Having said that, both liberal and constructivist approaches are capable of incorporating an account of how NGOs, and the broader social movements with which they are often associated, work to influence developments in global governance as stakeholders, agenda setters, and 'norm entrepreneurs' (see, for example, De Mars and Dijkzeul, eds, 2015). Norm entrepreneurs are understood as people, groups, or organizations who work to change or guide social norms concerning a particular issue in a particular direction—for example, human rights organizations are concerned to strengthen and guide norms in such a way as to enhance human rights protection in a variety of ways. We consider human rights as well as the theorization of NGOs and global civil society later in this chapter.

➥ See **Chapter 3 for a discussion of liberalism and realism.**

➥ See **Chapter 4 for a discussion of constructivism.**

KEY POINTS

- IOs come in such a variety of forms that they are difficult to define, both with respect to their relationship with states and the state system as well as in terms of their constituent elements.

- Scholars of global politics interested in the contribution that IOs make to the international system as a whole tend to focus on IGOs and, to a lesser extent, NGOs.

- Liberalism and constructivism are the main bodies of theory applied to the analysis of IOs.

THE EMERGENCE OF INTERNATIONAL ORGANIZATIONS

'History, prior to the nineteenth century, affords relatively few examples of international organizations' (Gerbet, 1981: p. 28). Although this is a widely accepted view, the myriad IOs of the present era do have important precursors. Previous chapters have shown that certain structures, systems, activities, and ideas which are generally taken as characteristic of contemporary relations between political communities did not simply emerge out of nothing in Western Europe in the modern period and then spread to the rest of the world. So, just as recognizable diplomatic practices have been manifest in different times in different places, so too have recognizable IOs. The earliest known examples appear to have been defensive leagues set up among small neighbouring states. This was the case in at least one part of China between the seventh and the fifth centuries BC where assemblies met to organize their defences, while in ancient Greece rudimentary IOs were established to arbitrate on issues of mutual concern to a number of city-states (see, generally, Harle, 1998).

Examples of IOs in late medieval Europe include the Hanseatic League which operated between the fourteenth and sixteenth centuries and in which some fifty towns joined forces for the mutual protection of their trading interests, with representatives meeting in a general assembly to decide policy by majority voting. The Swiss confederation, dating from the late 1200s, and the United Provinces of the Netherlands, which emerged in the sixteenth century, although limited territorially, effectively started out as IOs (Gerbet, 1981: pp. 28–9; Klabbers, 2003: p. 16). Although it is not usually regarded as such, it is possible to look at the Catholic Church as an early IO, or rather a transnational organization which has been described as having special ties of authority to one country that were then extended to others (Lee and Lee, 2002: p. 147). It held sway throughout much of Europe for centuries, wielding considerable political and cultural power. It was also probably one of the first organizations to establish a near universal presence in the modern period to match its name—'catholic' meaning universal in the sense of 'all-embracing'.

The scale of IOs in earlier times was necessarily constrained by limitations on mobility and communications, as was the phenomenon of globalization itself. As communications and transport technologies developed, so too did the capacity to form ongoing associations which eventually gave rise to formal organizations on a much broader, more inclusive scale, and which were intended to have a more or less permanent existence. The rise of the modern state system, together with technological advances in transport and communications, therefore saw not only the enhancement of diplomatic networks and practices among states but also an accompanying growth of organizations designed to facilitate the business of international relations as such. State actors may well have looked first to their own interests, as realist theory suggests, but on a very wide range of matters those interests were likely to be enhanced by cooperation with other states, especially on issues concerning trade. And in turn, international cooperation was best achieved through certain kinds of organizations set up for particular purposes and through which rules and procedures agreed on by member states could be operationalized. This follows the logic of liberal theory.

A notable nineteenth-century development was the Concert of Europe which emerged among the great powers in post-Napoleonic Europe. This was not what we would call an IO in today's terms since it lacked a constitution, a permanent secretariat, and a headquarters, and did not meet on a regular basis (see Gerbet, 1981: p. 32). It may, nonetheless, be seen as a precursor to other major European developments in later years. The Concert system, as we saw in Chapter 2, started with the 1815 Congress of Vienna which provided a benchmark for interstate cooperation on setting international boundaries and managing waterways (vital for trade) on the continent as well as establishing certain diplomatic protocols. Subsequent conferences generated as part of the Concert system established a pattern of interaction which nurtured important ideas about collective responsibility and a mutual commitment to 'concert together' against threats to the system. Most important-ly, it established the idea that states' representatives should meet not merely to sign peace treaties at the end of a war, but also during peaceful periods to prevent war (Archer, 1983: p. 7). Thus IOs became a vital component of diplomatic processes as well as a system of international law as discussed in Chapters 8 and 9.

Although the Concert system virtually ceased to exist after the mid-nineteenth centu-ry, the second half of that century did see further ad hoc conferences held on important matters of mutual interest. For example, the 1878 Congress of Berlin met to settle issues in the Balkans following the Russo-Turkish war of 1877–78 and included delegates from the major European powers and observers from several smaller European states with interests in the region as well as representatives of the Ottoman Empire. With the inclusion of the lat-ter, the international element of such conferences was expanded beyond Europe into West Asia. Other treaties and conventions which reached beyond Europe were applied in relation to colonial territories and the US, often with respect to the navigation of waterways to facil-itate trade. The Hague Conferences of 1899 and 1907 established the principle of compul-sory arbitration of disputes, giving the development of international law a significant boost.

➲ See Chapter 8 for more on the Congress of Vienna, the Concert of Europe, and the Hague Peace Conferences.

The Congress of Vienna was the first significant international forum that took a stand on a broad humanitarian issue by condemning the slave trade as contrary to universal morality (Butler and MacCoby, 2003: p. 353). This was quite an unusual step for such a conference. But it is no coincidence that it occurred around the time that private organi-zations, many with a specific philanthropic mission, started to make their presence felt on the international scene as well. The anti-slavery movement in Britain, already active domestically and a prime force behind the Congress resolution, gave rise to an early NGO when its supporters coalesced into the 'Society for the Mitigation and Gradual Abolition of Slavery Throughout the British Dominions' in 1823. Anti-Slavery International, which operates today, was originally founded in 1839 and in 1840 a World Anti-Slavery Convention was held in London (see www.antislavery.org).

Anti-Slavery International is also associated with the International Labour Organization (ILO), itself established by the Treaty of Versailles in 1919 with the status of an autono-mous institution but in association with the League of Nations. It survived the demise of the League and is now a UN agency. The early anti-slavery efforts were underpinned by concerted activism on the part of British women who had formed their own local anti-slavery societies and went on to forge international links, especially across the Atlantic. So in these activities we also see an emergent women's movement which spread nationally and internationally to take up various causes, including their own liberation. The ILO has also been a Nobel Peace Prize winner, receiving the award on its fiftieth anniversary in 1969 (see, generally, Hughes and Haworth, 2011). We see in these developments an early example of norm entrepreneurship in the human rights field.

Transport and communications technologies, so essential to both globalization and the emergence of functioning IOs, were themselves among the most important subjects of international agreements and formal associations. For example, the year 1865 saw the foundation of the International Telegraph Union (now the International Telecommunications Union), followed in 1874 by the Universal Postal Union and in 1890 by the International Union of Railway Freight Transportation (Klabbers, 2003: p. 18).

The two former organizations are now UN specialized agencies, again illustrating continuities in the system of IOs despite the massive disruption of two world wars in the twentieth century. But improvements in transport technologies brought with them other problems, including the more rapid spread of disease, and so concerns about international public health were reflected in the 1853 International Sanitary Convention and subsequent conventions and international offices.

Equally, the rapid development of industry and trade saw the introduction of an International Bureau of Weights and Measures in 1875 while on the intellectual property front the Union for the Protection of the Rights of Authors over their Literary and Artistic Property was established in 1884. Private associations at an international level began to outstrip intergovernmental ones in this period, accelerating the trend in internationalism. Such associations were set up in connection with every kind of activity including the humanitarian, religious, ideological, scientific, and technological (Gerbet, 1981: p. 36).

At the first World Congress of International Organizations held in Brussels in 1910, convened under the auspices of the Union of International Associations, 132 international bodies and thirteen governments were represented. A second world congress in Ghent and Brussels in 1913 saw 169 international associations and twenty-two governments represented. The last world congress of this type (the seventh) was held in 1927 after which the League of Nations assumed responsibility (https://uia.org/history). The overall trend to internationalism in the century before the outbreak of the First World War might have indicated that a new era of peaceful international relations was about to dawn. But other forces, including those of nationalism, were also at work. The death and destruction of 1914–18 was, for a number of key actors, the clarion call for a permanent IGO supporting a strong framework for international law and designed above all to prevent further international conflict, a need reinforced rather than undermined by the Second World War.

KEY POINTS

- Although forms of IO existed before the nineteenth century, in Europe and elsewhere, the Congress of Vienna in 1815 acted as a catalyst for their rapid growth in the nineteenth century, which also helped underpin a nascent body of international law.

- Private organizations also achieved a significant international presence in the nineteenth and early twentieth centuries, those with philanthropic aims contributing to the development of humanitarian principles and the idea of international morality.

- Developments in transport and communications technologies provided a boost to the growth of IOs and themselves became the subject of international agreements and associations along with a host of other agreements.

INTERGOVERNMENTAL ORGANIZATIONS (IGOs)

The supremo of all IGOs is the UN—officially styled the United Nations Organization—with near universal membership of the world's states. Its founding commitment is to 'maintaining international peace and security, developing friendly relations among nations and promoting social progress, better living standards and human rights' (http://www.un.org/en/about-un/). The early development of the UN and the role of the Security Council have already been set out, so we focus here on other aspects of the UN's history, structure, and mission. But first it is useful to recall the key ideas behind the development of its predecessor organization, the League of Nations. These ideas were to come under attack from realists in later years for their vision of a peaceful global order founded on strong institutions of global governance and an explicit emphasis on the place of morality in the international sphere rather than naked self-interest. The preface to US President Woodrow Wilson's famous Fourteen Points address to the US Congress in January 1918 stands as one of the clearest statements of the idealist vision of global order in that period. The preface was followed by a 'program of the world's peace', the fourteenth point of which proposed the formation of a general association of nations, an idea given substance by the formation of the League of Nations in the immediate aftermath of the war.

⊙ See **Chapter 3** for a discussion of liberal theory and the League of Nations.

We have seen that the League of Nations has sometimes been described as a failed experiment because it did not prevent the Second World War. It could also be argued, however, that the Second World War illustrated just how important it is to have a strong, functioning IGO to provide for collective security as well as many other matters requiring international support and coordination. In any event, a number of key institutions and practices set up under the League's auspices survived and are enshrined in the present UN system (see Jackson and O'Malley, 2018). Certainly, the latter owes much to the previous experiment in global governance which, in turn, drew on the earlier experiences of the Concert system, thus demonstrating continuity over almost two centuries.

The UN emerged from the wartime cooperation between the major allied powers of the time, with many other states then joining in to create a more truly global body. The preamble to the UN Charter states the general principles and ideals on which the organization is based (Box 7.2). The main organs of the UN are set out in the UN's official organizational chart (see https://www.un.org/en/pdfs/un_system_chart.pdf).

The business of the first organ, the Trusteeship Council, set up for the purpose of dealing with eleven non-self-governing trust territories, which had formerly been League of

BOX 7.2

Preamble to the Charter of the United Nations

WE THE PEOPLES OF THE UNITED NATIONS DETERMINED

- to save succeeding generations from the scourge of war, which twice in our lifetime has brought untold sorrow to mankind, and
- to reaffirm faith in fundamental human rights, in the dignity and worth of the human person, in the equal rights of men and women and of nations large and small, and
- to establish conditions under which justice and respect for the obligations arising from treaties and other sources of international law can be maintained, and
- to promote social progress and better standards of life in larger freedom,

AND FOR THESE ENDS

- to practise tolerance and live together in peace with one another as good neighbours, and

- to unite our strength to maintain international peace and security, and

- to ensure, by the acceptance of principles and the institution of methods, that armed force shall not be used, save in the common interest, and

- to employ international machinery for the promotion of the economic and social advancement of all peoples.

(https://www.un.org/en/sections/un-charter/preamble/)

FIGURE 7.1 **The signing of the United Nations Charter, San Francisco, USA, 1945**
Pictures Now/Alamy Stock Photo

Nations mandate territories, was terminated in 1994 when the last trust territory, administered by the US, chose self-government and became an independent state. The second, and most powerful, of the UN's organs is, of course, the Security Council, discussed in Chapter 6. The third, and some may say the weakest, as well as being the largest, is the General Assembly. A common criticism is that it produces endless resolutions which are largely ineffective because there is no mechanism for enforcing them. This illustrates the fact that the UN General Assembly cannot be compared directly to a legislature because, although its resolutions may carry normative force, and guide policy, they cannot have the same legal status as legislation produced by a parliament within a national sphere. However, it would be a mistake to dismiss the significance of the General Assembly as a debating forum. It is the one place where representatives from all states can meet on a more or less equal footing, express views, and debate the full range of issues in international politics. It is, moreover, a key forum for both formal and informal diplomacy and strategic alliances on issues that come up for a vote. This does not necessarily produce desirable outcomes, let alone outcomes that satisfy everyone, but that is in the nature of any political body.

The Economic and Social Council (ECOSOC) has a mandate to initiate studies and reports and to formulate policy recommendations extending over an enormous range of economic and social issues covering living standards; full employment; international economic, social, and health problems; facilitating international cultural and educational cooperation; and encouraging universal respect for human rights and fundamental freedoms. Some of the best-known UN agencies, such as the World Health Organization (WHO), the Food and Agricultural Organization (FAO), the United Nations Educational, Scientific and Cultural Organization (UNESCO), and the World Bank group all fall under its rubric. It has a major role in organizing the many international conferences initiated by the UN and oversees the functional commissions, regional commissions, and other special bodies set out in the organizational chart. Given its scope and size, ECOSOC is by far the largest of the UN's principal organs and expends more than 70 per cent of the human and financial resources of the entire UN system (see https://www.un.org/ecosoc/en/about-us).

The UN and Human Rights

One of ECOSOC's most difficult and controversial functional commissions has been that dealing with human rights, and a brief account of developments in this area illustrates just how problematic it is to achieve coherence in regimes of global governance. The establishment of a Human Rights Commission (HRC) was mandated by the UN's Charter and reflected the abhorrence at the atrocities of the Second World War. Past wars had produced some appalling cases of cruelty and ill-treatment, but the nature of the genocide policies of Nazi Germany was unprecedented. Beginning with the Universal Declaration of Human Rights (UDHR), which was adopted by the General Assembly in 1948 (Box 7.3), the Commission produced a raft of human rights documents and treaties over a period of almost sixty years. The behaviour of many governments around the world over that period, however, demonstrates clearly that the existence of the Charter, or the fact that all members of the UN must endorse the UDHR, is no guarantee that basic human rights will be respected or protected.

Since the Charter was first drawn up, there has been a strong tendency to divide the broad concept of human rights into two distinct clusters: civil and political rights on the one hand, and economic, social, and cultural rights on the other. The division between the two groups, and whether one group is more important than the other, has been the subject of much debate in global politics, as illustrated in Box 7.4, along with recurrent issues of sovereignty and non-intervention. This raises themes of ethical universalism versus ethical relativism, discussed in Chapter 3 in the context of solidarism and pluralism in English School thought. It relates also to the doctrine of cultural relativism and issues of the West/non-West dichotomy in global politics, discussed in Chapter 5.

Other UN Organs and Agencies

The fifth main organ of the UN is the International Court of Justice (ICJ) located in The Hague, to be discussed in Chapter 8. The sixth and final organ comprises the UN Secretariat and the office of the Secretary-General. The organizational map of the General Assembly alone, which currently brings together 193 member states at least annually, as well as running important offices and conferences and providing services in six official languages (English, French, Arabic, Chinese, Russian, and Spanish), makes clear how extensive the demand for the services of a secretariat are (see, generally, Gordenker, 2010). The Secretary-General also seems to be expected to be everywhere at once, and possess

BOX 7.3

The Universal Declaration of Human Rights (UDHR)

The UDHR was adopted by the General Assembly of the United Nations on 10 December 1948, reflecting a moment in global history when all member states could agree, at least in principle, to a substantial list of human rights ranging from the basic right to life to a host of economic and social goods. All new members joining the UN must sign up to the UDHR.

The Preamble highlights ideals which 'recognize the inherent dignity and of the equal and inalienable rights of all members of the human family is the foundation of freedom, justice and peace in the world'; it notes the extent to which 'disregard and contempt for human rights have resulted in barbarous acts which have outraged the conscience of mankind'; and heralds 'the advent of a world in which human beings shall enjoy freedom of speech and belief and freedom from fear and want has been proclaimed as the highest aspiration of the common people'.

The Declaration itself contains thirty articles, the first ten of which are set out below:

Article 1:   All human beings are born free and equal in dignity and rights. They are endowed with reason and conscience and should act towards one another in a spirit of brotherhood.

Article 2:   Everyone is entitled to all the rights and freedoms set forth in this Declaration, without distinction of any kind, such as race, colour, sex, language, religion, political or other opinion, national or social origin, property, birth or other status. Furthermore, no distinction shall be made on the basis of the political, jurisdictional or international status of the country or territory to which a person belongs, whether it be independent, trust, non-self-governing or under any other limitation of sovereignty.

Article 3:   Everyone has the right to life, liberty and security of person.

Article 4:   No one shall be held in slavery or servitude; slavery and the slave trade shall be prohibited in all their forms.

Article 5:   No one shall be subjected to torture or to cruel, inhuman or degrading treatment or punishment.

Article 6:   Everyone has the right to recognition everywhere as a person before the law.

Article 7:   All are equal before the law and are entitled without any discrimination to equal protection of the law. All are entitled to equal protection against any discrimination in violation of this Declaration and against any incitement to such discrimination.

Article 8:   Everyone has the right to an effective remedy by the competent national tribunals for acts violating the fundamental rights granted him by the constitution or by law.

Article 9:   No one shall be subjected to arbitrary arrest, detention or exile.

Article 10: Everyone is entitled in full equality to a fair and public hearing by an independent and impartial tribunal, in the determination of his rights and obligations and of any criminal charge against him.

(http://www.un.org/en/universal-declaration-human-rights/index.html)

an encyclopaedic knowledge not only of the UN system itself but also of all the world's troubles, both current and potential. In practice, the Secretary-General will often appoint a representative for much routine committee work. One particularly important role for the Secretary-General is to bring matters likely to affect international peace and security

BOX 7.4 KEY DEBATE

The Politics of Human Rights in the UN

Civil and political rights are sometimes seen as possessing a typically 'Western' liberal character unsuited to the cultural context of non-Western countries. The most vocal proponents of this view have come from a number of Middle Eastern and African countries and parts of South East and East Asia, especially China. In addition, economic, social, and cultural rights are often regarded as more urgent for poorer, underdeveloped countries than the right to vote (although human rights activists in such countries generally do not support these kinds of 'culturalist' or 'developmentalist' arguments).

An early division of opinion on the two different clusters of rights gave rise to the development of separate covenants for each and so in 1976 the International Covenant on Civil and Political Rights (ICCPR) and the International Covenant on Economic, Social and Cultural Rights (ICESCR) entered into force. Apart from representing two broad approaches to rights, the covenants also embody a significant attempt to advance the codification of human rights as such and to introduce an international legal framework to support their advancement. Member states are not obliged to sign up to the covenants, but those that do so agree to accept their provisions as legal obligations as well as moral obligations.

The history of human rights issues in the UN has also been plagued by competing conceptions of what the UN can and cannot, or should and should not do, to advance the protection of human rights around the world. On the one hand, the UN is committed to respect for state sovereignty and therefore to the notion that each state is entitled to conduct its own affairs free from external interference. On the other hand, it is committed to the universality of human rights, which implies that it is not only entitled, but also actually enjoined, to act to promote and protect human rights wherever and whenever such action is needed. This is implicit in the responsibility to protect discussed in previous chapters. But any action—even mere criticism of state practices—can be construed as a violation of state sovereignty.

The HRC itself was frequently caught between these imperatives and contradictions. Apart from issues of state sovereignty versus universal human rights principles, some countries represented on the Commission at any one time were themselves countries where human rights abuses—usually perpetrated by the government itself—were being carried out. However, countries with poor human rights records—mainly outside the West—complained of being unfairly singled out for criticism. This also led to accusations of attempted interference in the internal affairs of sovereign states.

By 2006, the HRC was seen as an ineffectual and largely discredited body. It was replaced by a new Human Rights Council (HRC) which has revised terms for membership and functions. But it has so far failed to make any real difference due at least partly to the way in which the UN's human rights machinery is still manipulated and undermined by rights abusive regimes which are of course UN members themselves and are therefore eligible to hold seats on the new HRC (see Freedman, 2015). As of 2019, the HRC's forty-seven members included Saudi Arabia, Democratic Republic of Congo, Brazil, Egypt, Qatar, and Hungary—all with problematic human rights records. But with such a large membership, and the requirement that all regions be represented, it is almost inevitable that it will include such countries.

Some of the questions that arise from these issues are:

1 Can human rights really be divided into different categories?

2 Under what circumstances, if any, should state sovereignty be violated to protect human rights?

to the attention of the Security Council and to report regularly on operations that the UN is involved in. Although the Secretary-General has no authority beyond issuing formal warnings of trouble and delivering information, including anything gleaned from informal discussions, the importance of this function should not be underestimated.

The UN has also populated the sphere of IOs with a plethora of agencies and special programs; the WHO, the FAO, UNICEF, and UNESCO have already been mentioned above and the UN's organizational chart lists many more. Some, like UNICEF, are well known but others such as the United Nations Population Fund (UNFPA) are unlikely to register immediately in the minds of the general public. Others have emerged in more recent years to deal with problems unheard of in earlier periods. These include the joint United Nations Programme on HIV/AIDS (UNAIDS). Then there are regional commissions dealing with all the major regions of the world: Africa, Europe, Latin America and the Caribbean, Asia and the Pacific, and Western Asia (more commonly known as the Middle East).

The UN and its agencies do not have the IGO field entirely to themselves. There are also many regional organizations. The EU and ASEAN have been mentioned in previous chapters but there are others as well, from the African Union (AU) and the Pacific Islands Forum (PIF) to numerous trading blocs such as Mercado Común del Sur (Southern Common Market otherwise known as MERCOSUR) in Latin America and the North American Free Trade Agreement (NAFTA). These reflect another significant development in the world of IOs, and that is the trend to regionalization, which we examine in Chapter 10. For the moment, we may note that this trend, which has been gathering pace over the last few decades, is likely to have a significant impact in the future, but one which complements rather than undermines the role of the UN.

It is also worth mentioning here that IGOs, and multilateralism more generally, have proved useful for smaller, relatively less powerful states of the Global South which can and do, in certain contexts, engage in coalition-building behaviour to counter more

FIGURE 7.2 **26th African Union Summit in Addis Ababa, Ethiopia, 2016** Government Communication and Information System, Republic of South Africa

powerful states. This has been called a 'linkage strategy' and involves developing a collective identity based on similar circumstances and goals (thus reflecting an identity of *interests*). In turn, this enables them to 'counter the adverse effects of hierarchy, hegemony, inequality, and exclusion' (Braveboy-Wagner, 2009: p. 7).

The UN and Transnational Criminal Organizations

Although TCOs are not usually discussed under the rubric of 'international organizations', it is difficult to exclude them from some consideration, especially given their impact on issues of security and insecurity, discussed in Chapter 6. Certainly, they have become important enough for the UN to give them serious attention. Thus the UN Convention Against Transnational Organized Crime, otherwise known as the Palermo Convention (which has additional protocols on people trafficking and smuggling as well as on firearms), entered into force in 2003 (https://www.unodc.org/unodc/en/organized-crime/intro/UNTOC.html).

In addition to their sheer criminality, TCOs are also increasingly seen as threats to both national and international security. In the period after the 9/11 attacks, it was suggested that TCOs may facilitate terror networks through the provision of money-laundering facilities, false documents, and the procurement of weapons or other materials for terrorist purposes. There may also be a growing convergence between some terrorist organizations and organized crime networks (see Sanderson, 2004: pp. 49–61; Dishman, 2005: pp. 237–52). Major participants in the world of TCOs include Italian, Russian, and American mafia groups, Chinese Triads, motorcycle gangs like the Hell's Angels, drug cartels, and hybrid entities like the Taliban that merge crime, terrorism, and insurgency (see Sullivan, 2014: p. 161).

An important organization originating in 1923 to deal with criminality at a global level by providing a platform for cooperation between national agencies is the International Criminal Police Organization or Interpol. In the present period, it has had a particular focus on terrorism, cyber crime and organized crime. In carrying out its functions, Interpol's charter prohibits 'any intervention or activities of a political, military, religious or racial character' (Interpol, 1956–2017: p. 3). This has not prevented some governments from attempting to use it to pursue political objectives, including issuing a 'red notice' (a request to law enforcement agencies worldwide to provisionally arrest a person pending extradition, surrender, or similar legal action) for the apprehension of political opponents and critics. This is one among a number of strategies characterizing authoritarianism and which impacts on the operations of IGOs and their agencies.

KEY POINTS

- The League of Nations is often seen as a failure but it was nonetheless an important forerunner to the UN and a number of its institutions have been maintained as part of the latter system.

- The UN is the largest single IGO with five functioning main organs and a plethora of programmes, agencies, commissions, funds, courts, and tribunals involved in different aspects of global governance.

- Although the UN is the principal organ of global governance it does not possess the characteristics of a 'world government' in so far as its constituent members maintain sovereign authority within their own borders and do not form a 'world state'.

NON-GOVERNMENTAL ORGANIZATIONS (NGOs)

The non-state variety of international organization sometimes goes by the acronym INGO—which simply stands for *international* non-governmental organization—but for present purposes we shall make do with the more common term NGO. Like IOs in general, NGOs cannot be defined in a completely straightforward way. Generally speaking, however, they share the following characteristics: they are formal rather than ad hoc entities; they aspire to be self-governing according to their own constitutional set-up; they are private in the sense that they operate independently from governments; and they do not make or distribute profits. This describes both national and international bodies, so for those which operate outside of the national sphere, we need to add that they obviously have formal transnational links (see Gordenker and Weiss, 1996: p. 20).

GONGOs, QANGOs, and DONGOs

There are other types of organization which fall somewhere between the government and non-government spheres and, although they often claim to be NGOs, they do not really conform to the description above. Gordenker and Weiss (ibid.) identify three significant deviations. The first are 'government-organized non-government organizations' or GONGOs—entities created by governments usually as front organizations for their own purposes. These were typically produced by communist countries during the Cold War but the US and other Western countries sponsored some as well. Chinese GONGOs in the contemporary period are said to represent an aspect of state corporatism, and have little agency of their own (Marchetti, 2016: p. 22). In this scenario, the functions of civil society remain under state control and surveillance, which severely limits the extent to which they can be seen as part of civil society at all. Today, there is a wide variety of GONGOs, some of which serve dubious causes although others may be fairly benign. Examples range from the International Islamic Relief Organization based in Saudi Arabia and controlled by the government there, to the National Endowment for Democracy in the US which, although portrayed as a private, non-profit organization, is funded through Congress and is subject to its oversight. The excerpt in Box 7.5, taken from an article published in *Foreign Affairs* on the subject of GONGOS, and the dangers that some of them pose, is highly instructive as to their role in the sphere of IOs.

Another special type of organization is the quasi-autonomous NGO or QUANGO, which is typically funded largely by governments but operates autonomously. Unlike GONGOs, the relationship to government is a transparent one and no subterfuge is intended. The third type is the donor-organized NGO or DONGO. In this case, agencies such as the United Nations Development Program (UNDP) might organize and fund NGOs to coordinate or carry out projects (Gordenker and Weiss, 1996: pp. 20–1). A significant number of other NGOs enjoy consultative status with the UN or, more specifically, one of its councils or agencies. The UN's Economic and Social Council, for example, accords consultative status of some kind to more than 3,000 NGOs ranging from the Adventist Development Relief Agency to the World Press Freedom Committee. These are allied in turn to specific UN agencies such as UNESCO, the FAO, and the WHO.

BOX 7.5 KEY QUOTE

How Government-Sponsored Groups Masquerade as Civil Society

Behind this contradictory and almost laughable tongue twister [gongo] lies an important and growing global trend that deserves more scrutiny: governments funding and controlling non-governmental organizations (NGOs), often stealthily. Some gongos are benign, others irrelevant. But many . . . are dangerous. Some act as the thuggish arm of repressive governments. Others use the practices of democracy to subtly undermine democracy at home. Abroad, the gongos of repressive regimes lobby the United Nations and other international institutions, often posing as representatives of citizen groups with lofty aims when, in fact, they are nothing but agents of the governments that fund them. Some governments embed their gongos deep in the societies of other countries and use them to advance their interests abroad . . . The globalization and effectiveness of nongovernmental organizations will suffer if we don't find reliable ways of distinguishing organizations that truly represent democratic civil society from those that are tools of uncivil, undemocratic governments. (Naím, 2009)

NGOs and the UN

The practice of according UN consultative status to NGOs dates back to 1946 when ECOSOC granted such status to just over forty NGOs. Growth was steady over the next forty-five years and by 1992 there were more than 700 NGOs with consultative status. As indicated above, that number has since increased to more than 3,000. There are various rules and criteria governing eligibility. Among the most basic are:

1. the organization must have been in existence (officially registered with the appropriate government authorities as an NGO/non-profit) for at least two years;

2. it must have an established headquarters;

3. it must possess a democratically adopted constitution, authority to speak for its members, a representative structure, appropriate mechanisms of accountability, and democratic and transparent decision-making processes;

4. its basic resources must be derived mainly from contributions of the national affiliates or other components or from individual members; and

5. it must not have been established by governments or intergovernmental agreements (see http://csonet.org/index.php?menu=30).

NGOs, Philanthropy, and Humanitarianism

Many NGOs have a specific philanthropic or humanitarian purpose. Sometimes these are underpinned by religious beliefs but they are just as likely to be secular. Many are aligned with broader movements such as the environmental movement, the labour movement, the ecumenical movement, the peace movement, the indigenous rights movement, and the women's movement. More will be said about the role of these broader movements later in this chapter.

Examples of some of the better known NGOs reflecting the ideals of one or other of these movements, or sometimes two or more of them, are the Worldwide Fund for Nature, Greenpeace, the World Council of Churches, the World Peace Council, the International Women's Health Coalition, Médecins Sans Frontières, the Red Cross/Red Crescent, and Amnesty International, to name just a few. A brief account of the Red Cross/ Red Crescent Movement provides a case study of how one of the earliest NGOs operating in the international sphere has grown to be the largest humanitarian organization in the world. In addition, it was the prime mover behind the original Geneva Convention which has become the most important international convention relating to the conduct of warfare (see Box 7.6).

BOX 7.6 CASE STUDY

The Origins and Development of the International Red Cross/Red Crescent Movement

In 1859, Henry Dunant, a travelling Swiss businessman, witnessed one of the bloodiest battles of the nineteenth century in northern Italy when Napoleon III joined with local forces to drive Austrians from the country. Dunant subsequently published a small book which depicted, among other things, the battlefield after fighting had ceased, describing not just the dead but also the plight of the wounded and their desperate need for care. He went on to devise a plan for national relief societies to aid the wounded of war.

In February 1863, the Société Genevoise d'Utilité Publique (Geneva Society for Public Welfare) appointed a committee of five, including Dunant, to consider how the plan could be put into action. This committee, which effectively founded the Red Cross, called for an international conference to pursue Dunant's basic objectives. Dunant put his own time and money into the project, travelling throughout much of Europe to persuade governments to send representatives. The conference was held in October 1863 with thirty-nine delegates from sixteen nations.

Just under a year later, twelve nations signed the International Convention for the Amelioration of the Condition of the Wounded and Sick in Armed Forces in the Field, otherwise known as the Geneva Convention of 1864. The convention provided for guaranteed neutrality for medical personnel and officially adopted the red cross on a field of white as the identifying emblem (the red crescent was adopted in most Muslim countries).

Three other conventions were later added to cover naval warfare, prisoners of war, and civilians. Revisions of these conventions have been made periodically, the most extensive being in 1949 relating to the treatment of prisoners of war. The International Committee of the Red Cross remains based in Geneva and the International Federation of Red Cross and Red Crescent Societies has a presence in every country, although in Iran it operates as the Red Lion and Sun. The Red Cross has been associated with four Nobel Peace Prizes, with the very first Nobel Peace Prize being awarded to Henry Dunant himself in 1901 (see https://www.nobelprize.org/prizes/peace/1963/red-cross/history/).

As an example of how national branches work today in situations of violent conflict, 9,000 volunteers with the Syrian Red Crescent (known formally as the Syrian Arab Red Crescent and founded in 1942) have been working with the UN to deliver aid to thousands of internally displaced people in Syria (http://sarc.sy/category/sarc-news/).

(Continued)

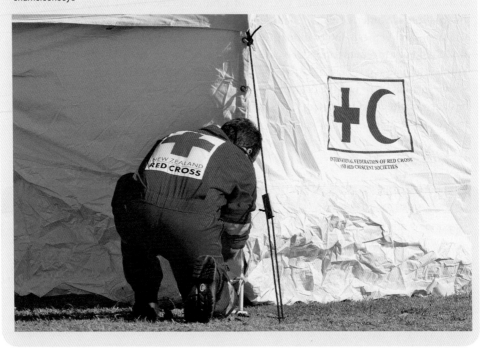

FIGURE 7.3 **Red Cross volunteer in Auckland, New Zealand, 2012** © iStock/ chameleonseye

---

KEY POINTS

- IGOs, especially the UN and its agencies, often have a close working relationship with NGOs and have established structures supporting the work of many NGOs.

- Not all NGOS are 'good' in the sense that they make a positive contribution. Some are merely fronts for nefarious activities by dictatorial governments and may work actively to undermine the efforts of other organizations with respect, for example, to human rights.

- Many NGOs are allied with broader movements, including philanthropic and humanitarian movements, thus contributing to a complex web of relationships between different kinds of actors, both state and non-state, in the global sphere.

SOCIAL MOVEMENTS AND GLOBAL CIVIL SOCIETY

As indicated above, many NGOs are involved in philanthropic or humanitarian causes, some of which are embedded in broader social movements. The term 'social movement' is generally understood to denote some kind of collective action, driven by a particular set of social concerns and emerging from society at large rather than through the governmental institutions of the state. Indeed, a feature of many social movements is an oppositional posture vis-à-vis certain aspects of state or governmental activity. In this respect they are often seen as a manifestation of grass-roots democracy expressing or articulating non-mainstream issues and agendas. As we have seen, social movements often transcend the domestic sphere, an early example being the anti-slavery movement. When a movement achieves a transnational profile and popular following, it obviously achieves the status of an international or global social movement. These often reflect shifting coalitions of interests around issue-oriented activities. But what social movements and the NGOs associated with them usually represent in one way or another is a 'cause', very often in relation to what is perceived as an injustice and/or a danger: poverty in the Global South, environmental degradation, nuclear weapons, the oppression of indigenous communities, and so on.

To take the latter example, the fact that the concept of indigenous rights has been firmly entrenched in the UN system—and given expression in a raft of measures adopted by some (mainly liberal Western) states with minority indigenous populations—has grown out of a general social movement that in turn gave rise to specific organized entities (NGOs) that have lobbied hard for recognition at local, national, and global levels. The origins of the movement are diffuse, but two general catalysts were the civil rights movement in the US from the 1950s and the anti-apartheid movement in South Africa, both of which attracted wider international sympathy and support, including that of the anti-slavery movement. That sympathy and support was soon extended to minority groups in many states around the world. One major NGO is the International Work Group for Indigenous Affairs (IWEIA). It was founded in 1968 in response to an alarm raised by anthropologists about the ongoing genocide of indigenous peoples in the Amazon. It has gone on to establish a network of researchers and activists to document the situation of indigenous peoples and advocate for their rights (see https://www.iwgia.org/en/about). There is also a World Council of Indigenous People founded in Canada in 1975 and dedicated to 'developing unity among Indigenous peoples throughout the world, strengthening their organizations, and battling the racism, injustice, and dangers they continue to face' (https://hashilthsa.com/news/2018-09-18/new-documentary-film-chronicles-politics-following-1975-world-indigenous-peoples). There is now a UN Permanent Forum on Indigenous Issues (UNPFII), established in 2000, which acts as a high-level advisory body to the Economic and Social Council, and a UN Declaration on the Rights of Indigenous Peoples adopted by the General Assembly in 2007 (https://www.human-rights.gov.au/our-work/un-declaration-rights-indigenous-peoples-1). This brief account illustrates the linkages within a diffuse movement, based on a rising social consciousness concerning a particular set of problematic issues, and leading in turn to the emergence of organized action in the form of NGOs and, eventually, to a global indigenous rights regime supported by the UN.

These broad social movements and the world of NGOs, taken together, are said to constitute a global civil society which has an important role in the general sphere of global governance. The idea of global civil society can also be understood initially in terms of its domestic counterpart. Civil society names a sphere of human association not mediated by the state, or at least not directly. Thus it signifies the activities of individuals as participants in groups or collectivities that have a private purpose—private in the sense that they are not part of the realm of formal state or governmental activity. They include professional associations, charities, interest groups, businesses, and so on. Their freedom of organization and articulation of interests is widely regarded as another important manifestation of democracy, and so the repression of genuine civil society organizations—i.e. *not* including GONGOs—and activities is seen as characteristic of authoritarian systems. Many civil

FIGURE 7.4 **President of Bolivia Evo Morales and principals of the UN Permanent Forum on Indigenous Issues, New York, USA, 2017** Pacific Press Media Production Corp./Alamy Stock Photo

society groups are obviously NGOs, but some do not fall easily into the definition of the latter. Also, not all NGOs are connected to social movements. It follows that, although we can often connect NGOs to social movements and in turn class these as part of civil society, we cannot simply conflate the lot into one seamless whole.

Just as domestic civil society names a sphere that is autonomous of direct government control, so global civil society may be understood as standing apart from the formal, inter-governmental structures of global governance. And as with social movements, global civil society may be regarded not merely as distinct from that sphere but sometimes positioned in opposition to the realm of formal state-based or state-generated activities. It is, therefore, another avenue through which democratic expression can take place. Certainly, those who look for democratic transformations in the international sphere and promote a form of cosmopolitan democracy—a project involving the extension of democratic account-ability to the global sphere—are broadly supportive of the positive role that global civil society has to play in such a process. How ideas of global civil society may be approached from different theoretical perspectives is set out briefly in Box 7.7.

Another point to consider is how the plurality of civil society groups around the world, and the notion of global civil society, have most often been analysed through the lens of Western scholarship, and whether this has limited understanding of how civil society groups operate in different contexts and what values they promote. In developing societies, understanding how local groups organize themselves, for example, around gender issues or aid programmes, may require a very different set of conceptualizations about civil society and how it operates, and these may also vary from one local context to the next (see, generally, Kamruzzaman, 2019). One must also take into account some of the power dynamics operating. When it comes to 'doing good', for example, women from the Global North (i.e. the West) who engage in NGO activities to aid and assist women in the Global South

BOX 7.7 KEY QUOTE

Theorizing Global Civil Society

Different theoretical perspectives can be used to interpret global civil society. Liberals may understand it as providing space for actors which then provide a bottom-up contribution to the effectiveness and legitimacy of the international system as a whole. In essence, it is democracy in action as power is being held to account by the populace. Realists, however, may interpret global civil society as a tool used by the most powerful states to advance their ultimate interests abroad, often promoting and popularizing ideas that are key to their national interest. Marxists may see global civil society as political vanguards that can spread a different world view that challenges the dominant order. But some may argue [along culturalist/postcolonial lines] that the concept of civil society as a sphere distinct from the family, state, and market remains a Western concept that does not apply easily to societies where the boundaries between these spheres are more blurred (excerpted from Marchetti, 2016).

➜ See **Chapter 3** for a discussion of liberalism and realism.

➜ See **Chapter 4** for a discussion of Marxism.

➜ See **Chapter 5** for a discussion of postcolonialism.

may not only fail to grasp the different context within which the latter must operate but generally do so from positions of power and privilege which can perpetuate continuities between the colonial 'civilizing mission' and development (de Jong, 2017: pp. 1–2).

At another level, we must also consider whether social movements and the broad sphere of global civil society, and the NGOs which are the principal vehicles of activity in these arenas, present a challenge to the traditional structures generated by state sovereignty and the state system. As we have seen, many NGOs have a close association with the UN and its programmes and agencies. So although we may distinguish NGOs from the UN as such, they have come to form an important part of the UN system as a whole. Social movements and global civil society are, therefore, enmeshed in a web of global relations constituted by IOs of all types, from the more formal intergovernmental institutions of global governance such as the UN to a plethora of other organizations and agencies.

KEY POINTS

- Global social movements reflect particular sets of concerns coalescing around issues such as the environment, indigenous rights, arms control, and so on, and which engender collective action on a global scale.

- Global civil society, as a sphere of action and interaction standing apart from formal intergovernmental structures and sometimes in opposition to it, constitutes the space within which both international NGOs and social movements more generally operate.

- Both social movements and global civil society are often regarded as enhancing the space and substance of democratic activity at a supranational level.

CONCLUSION

Realist views of how the international or global sphere is organized see states and the state system as the standard units around which almost everyone and everything else revolves, and with international activity of any real consequence being generated by state actors and with state interests firmly in mind. It follows from this view that the role of virtually all other institutions and actors is subordinate, including any form of IO. Indeed, some realists may dismiss the whole project of global governance, composed of the efforts of both state and non-state actors, as of little relevance in the 'real world' of power politics. But realist views comprise only one, admittedly influential, view of how the international system works. Liberal views, especially those described as liberal institutionalist, occupy a quite different general position. For liberals, it is largely through IOs that the dangerous aspects of international anarchy can be ameliorated, and all states have an interest in this. Both the League of Nations and the UN represent a practical manifestation of liberal international theory. Constructivists shed further light on how social processes, in response to both practical needs and the development of norms and values at the global level, have effectively created the world of IOs and global civil society. As for the fluid realm of NGOs and social movements, these may be seen as an important complement to the more formal sphere of IO and global governance, often acting in concert with it but sometimes opposing and resisting their policies and practices. However we may regard them, IOs have become such an integral part of the global system that it is difficult to imagine a world without them.

KEY QUESTIONS

1   What are the key characteristics of IOs?

2   How does an international regime differ from an IO?

3   How and why did IOs emerge in the modern period?

4   To what extent has there been a continuity of IOs over the last two centuries?

5   Was the League of Nations a complete failure?

6   On what general principles is the UN founded?

7   Is it possible for the UN to reconcile respect for state sovereignty and respect for universal human rights?

8   Could the UN do more as an IO, or is it expected to do too much as it is?

9   What role do NGOs and social movements play in the global system?

10   How can global civil society enhance opportunities for democratic expression?

11   How might concepts of civil society and social movements differ according to cultural context?

12   How can we deploy IR theory to interpret the role of IOs in global political order?

FURTHER READING

Breitmeier, Helmut (2016), *The Legitimacy of International Regimes* (Abingdon: Routledge).
> Explains and critically assesses the role of international regimes and non-state actors in contemporary global order with a particular focus on global environmental regimes and issues of legitimacy and efficacy.

Cogan, Jacob Katz, Ian Hurd, and Ian Johnstone (2016), *The Oxford Handbook of International Organizations* (Oxford: Oxford University Press).
> Covers a very wide range of issues concerning the evolution of IOs including the forces driving their formation, their accountability under international law, the multitude of forms they take, and the activities they pursue.

Karns, Margot P. and Karen A. Mingst (2009), *International Organizations: The Politics and Processes of Global Governance* (Boulder, CO: Lynne Rienner).
> Covers a wide range of IGOs and NGOs as well as norms and rules, issues of legitimacy and accountability, problems of human rights, development, and the environment relating to IOs. Included are case studies focusing on contemporary concerns such as conflict in the Congo and attempts to combat human trafficking.

Murdie, Amanda (2014), *Help or Harm: The Human Security Effects of International NGOs* (Stanford, CA: Stanford University Press).
> An interesting exploration, with numerous case-study illustrations, of the extent to which international NGOs such as Oxfam and Human Rights Watch make a difference to the cause of promoting human security around the world.

Youngs, Richard (2019), *Civic Activism Unleashed: New Hope or False Dawn for Democracy?* (Oxford: Oxford University Press).
> Examines the changing nature and increased intensity of civic activism around the world over the last decade with special attention to new types of civic or social movements that emerge without formal leadership and organization.

WEB LINKS

https://uia.org/
> Website of the Union of International Associations which publishes the *Yearbook of International Organizations*. It is a non-profit, apolitical, independent NGO which has pioneered research into, monitoring of, and provision of information on international organizations, international associations, and their global challenges since 1907. It also contains a link to a directory of major organizations.

http://www.un.org/en/
> Official website of the UN providing the initial point of navigation for the entire range of the organization's functions.

http://www.crwflags.com/fotw/flags/int.html#world
> Another useful directory of IOs which provides direct links to UN-linked websites as well as those of many regional organizations and NGOs.

 For additional material and resources please visit the **online resources** at: www.oup.com/he/lawson1e.

INTERNATIONAL ORGANIZATIONS IN GLOBAL POLITICS

7

8

INTERNATIONAL LAW

- The Rule of Law in Global Politics
- The Origins of International Law
- Key Concepts in the Development of International Law
- International Law in the Twentieth Century
- Treaties, Charters, and Covenants
- International Courts and Tribunals
- The Rules-Based Order in Contemporary Global Politics
- Conclusion

Reader's Guide

This chapter addresses the broad challenges involved in establishing global order under conditions of anarchy through international law. The fact that there is no world government with powers akin to national governments means that maintaining cooperative relations between and among states is always a careful balancing act, given the problem of enforcing international law in the absence of a single, overarching sovereign authority. The first substantive section looks at law in the global sphere through the notion of rule of law. We then consider the emergence of international law in broad historical perspective. Once again, we shall see that some important principles and practices in the present period have antecedents in a variety of settings in the ancient world. Natural law and the law of nations, the idea of 'just war', the secularization of law, and the notion of 'civilized nations' are all important themes here. Moving on to international law in the twentieth century, and up to the present period, we examine the nature of treaties, charters, and covenants which operate in multiple issue areas from postal services, trade, and aviation to communications, the environment, and human rights. Two major international courts—the International Court of Justice (ICJ) and the International Criminal Court (ICC) are also discussed in some detail. The final section looks at how the principles and practices of a rules-based international order are faring in the contemporary period with a focus on Russia, China, and the US.

THE RULE OF LAW IN GLOBAL POLITICS

Societies of all kinds are governed by a set of rules devised to regulate the conduct of their members in their dealings with each other. To the extent that it comprises an **international society**, this applies as much to the contemporary global sphere as it does to any other more limited sphere of human social activity. It is through the establishment of rules, and broad adherence to them, that an environment which is more or less predictable, stable, and orderly is established. These values are enhanced, and legitimacy is achieved, if the order is seen as more or less fair and just.

Whose influence is greatest in making the rules, and whose values and interests get to be represented in any given order, depends on a number of factors. Power obviously plays a significant role, but large, powerful states do not necessarily get everything their way. The fact that a rule of sovereign equality exists in a legal sense does make a difference to the way in which the dynamics of **power politics** operate. And to the extent that each **state** values, above all, its own **sovereignty**, it must logically allow that every other state in the global sphere is entitled to preserve the same sovereign rights. Also, despite the fact that the rule may be transgressed (for example, by Iraq invading Kuwait in 1990, and by the US and its allies invading Iraq in 2003) it holds good for most states most of the time. Military invasions, however, are just one way in which the legal sovereignty of states can be undermined. Cyber attacks, mentioned in Chapter 6, are now much more likely than brute force, and can be more readily denied.

International law has two major sources. First, there are laws arising from consistent state practices and norms of behaviour over a period of time which acquire legal status—hence, customary international law. The norm of diplomatic immunity is one area in which consistent practice was maintained over a considerable period of time before being codified in the Vienna Convention on Diplomatic Relations of 1961, as discussed in Chapter 9. The second major source derives from international treaties or conventions (treaty law). Treaties may be either bilateral—that is, between just two states, or **multilateral**—between three or more states. If a significant number of states consider themselves bound by the obligations of a multilateral treaty, then that may influence the behaviour of other states. The provisions of the treaty may gradually become established practice even by states that are not party to the original treaty, and such widespread established practice may then be considered as part of international customary law. So although customary law is distinct from treaty law, there is nonetheless a dynamic relationship between them. We consider the topic of treaties in more detail shortly.

The current global legal order is often seen as a product of the history of Western dominance and therefore **Eurocentric** in conception and tending to favour Western interests in practical terms. If so, this may raise questions about the overall legitimacy of the international legal system. On the other hand, the development of the substantial body of international law by the UN since 1945 has occurred with participation and input at a truly global level. Also, to depict non-Western states as 'passive objects of European domination' in the making of international law (Fassbender and Peters, 2012: p. 4), as in other spheres of global politics, is to gloss over their contributions. One study notes that in the early stages of UN law making, including human rights law, the 'levers of power were frequently operated by Arab, Asian, and African delegations' and that claims of 'Third World impotence would come as a surprise to both Western and Soviet foreign service officers who spent much of their time reacting to Afro-Asian bloc initiatives' (Burke, 2010: p. 5).

Another issue concerns effectiveness. It may be said that international law, and all the rules and regulations that constitute it, is rather feeble given that it cannot be enforced by a sovereign authority with coercive power. This is essentially a realist critique. But liberals would be quick to point out that states and other relevant actors do in fact follow most of the rules most of the time. This applies to an enormous range of activities from trade, diplomacy, security, and human rights to communications, navigation, and transport. One can only imagine a situation in which the international aviation industry, for example, was *not* heavily regulated and airline operators did *not* follow those regulations closely. This indicates a very high degree of international *cooperation*, and not mere *coexistence*. When it comes to issues like human rights, however, it is not uncommon to hear the invocation of the sovereign rights of the state and claims that such issues are a purely internal or domestic matter. Yet all recognized states are signatories to the UN's Universal Declaration of Human Rights, which sets standards that transcend individual states.

More generally, all states do have a strong interest in ensuring that the environment in which they operate *as* states is relatively stable and predictable. The same applies to other organizations that operate on a global scale, from business enterprises and financial institutions to sporting associations and charities. This does not mean that international law is not subverted by various actors. International criminal organizations, by definition, do so on a daily basis. And state actors frequently violate human rights law and engage in cheating behaviour. Nonetheless, we do have a rules-based international order, as explained in Box 8.1. When a state actor or other entity transgresses the rules, others in the international community can, through a variety of means, punish non-compliance and force behavioural change. These means include the weight of public opinion, self-help, intervention by a third party, sanctions by international organizations (for example, the UN, the Commonwealth, or regional entities), and, in the final resort, war (Alshdaifat, 2017: pp. 56–7).

BOX 8.1 KEY CONCEPT

The Rules-Based International Order

A rules-based international order refers to 'a shared commitment by all countries to conduct their activities in accordance with agreed rules that evolve over time, such as international law, regional security arrangements, trade agreements, immigration protocols, and cultural arrangements. . . . [It] is the only alternative to international coercion by competing great powers, spheres of influence, client states and terrorist organisations' (UNAA, 2017).

KEY POINTS

- Ideally, the international legal framework provides for an environment which is more or less predictable, stable, and orderly.
- International law is based on both customary practices emerging from the interaction of states over time and on formal treaties and conventions.
- International law cannot be enforced by a sovereign authority with coercive power but states and other relevant actors do in fact follow most of the rules most of the time.

THE ORIGINS OF INTERNATIONAL LAW

A conventional approach to the origins of contemporary international law would, once again, focus largely on the European experience with an emphasis on the emergence of the modern state system, with Westphalia as the key turning point. But there are many other historical precursors. Just as ancient political communities in all parts of the world needed to establish rules of behaviour within their own spheres, so it was necessary to regulate relations between such communities. Evidence for the establishment of formally recorded treaties between state entities can be traced back more than 4,000 years ago to ancient Mesopotamia where a boundary treaty between the kingdoms of Lagash and Umma was established. In this particular example, and in interstate relations of the time more generally, religious concepts played a decisive role. Those in power were believed to receive instructions from their deities concerning matters of state. Holding a certain territory was therefore justified as divinely sanctioned, and any trespass on that territory was a violation of a god-given order (see Altman, 2012: pp. 7–8). The involvement of divine beings in earlier times contrasts with what is understood to be a rational, secular, legal order in the present period.

Ancient tribute systems in the pre-modern imperial systems of Central and South America, Africa, the Middle East, and Asia also established rules for trade, diplomacy, and tax collection, and can be regarded as constituting international legal orders, albeit very hierarchical ones. And again, their legitimacy was usually based on the invocation of a divine authority. What the ancient systems also generally shared in common with each other, as well as with those of the contemporary period, was the desire to 'promote predictability and stability, to adequately channel state conduct in ways that were conducive to maintaining power relations, and to nourish the internal legitimacy and sovereignty of polities' (Bederman, 2008: p. 20).

Another early development in the conceptualization of international law is that it came to be understood as embodying not merely an assemblage of agreed upon practices but a set of principles reflecting notions of ethical behaviour in relations between state entities. The earliest evidence for this comes from China in the period from about 722 BC—the beginning of the 'Spring and Autumn' era—continuing through the 'Warring States' era from about 481 BC to the time China became a unified entity in 221 BC. Even before Confucius (551–479 BC), China's most prominent exponent of moral principles in all spheres of life, explicit notions of ethical conduct in interstate dealings had developed in at least a rudimentary form. Warfare generally required some principled justification while the conduct of war itself was subject to certain restraints, although in practice the principles were often breached (Neff, 2014: pp. 18–19). This is little different from the present period in which ethical norms find wide support in principle, but are often lacking in practice.

KEY POINTS

- Elements of international law concerning boundaries, warfare, treaty making, and diplomacy reach back nearly as far as written records can take us.
- Ancient sources of international law, evident in a variety of cultural or civilizational settings, were usually underpinned and legitimized by divine authority.
- There is also evidence for the emergence of principled conduct in relations between states, and in the conduct of warfare, from ancient times.

KEY CONCEPTS IN THE DEVELOPMENT OF INTERNATIONAL LAW

Natural Law and the Law of Nations

Although the contemporary international legal order appears to follow principles of **secularism**, religious thought played a major role in its development. Christian thought in Europe has some associations with the idea of 'natural law' which posits a form of moral universalism and is therefore **cosmopolitan** in orientation. The origins of the natural law tradition, however, are to be found in the thoroughly pagan traditions of thought in ancient Greece and Rome, some elements of which also influenced Arab and Islamic thought.

Natural law's most basic premise holds that there are laws derived from a 'natural' moral order—an order that transcends specific human communities and the particular rules and regulations they might invent for themselves. The latter rules are said to constitute 'positive law'—law made by human communities for certain purposes at certain times. In contrast, natural law, in transcending all such particularities, is applicable in all times and all places to all people—hence its universality.

As a logical corollary, natural law is cast as entirely objective, as opposed to the subjective character of positive, human-made law. People can gain knowledge of natural law, and readily grasp the difference between good and evil, just and unjust, through the application of reason which is itself 'natural'. A key figure in the development of the natural law tradition in Europe, St Thomas Aquinas (1225–74), saw in the human capacity for reasoned thought a 'divine spark'. He further observed that 'it is by naturally self-evident principles that we judge about the things we discover in the process of reasoning' (Aquinas, 2002: p. 2). It is noteworthy that Aquinas was well versed in both ancient Greek and Roman philosophy as well as Arab philosophy, and drew on all these sources for his insights, regardless of their non-Christian status.

The idea of natural law also gives rise to the idea of natural rights which, in turn, underpins the theorization of human rights, which we discuss later. For the moment we may note a fundamental problem with natural law ideas, as set out in Box 8.2. This problem was identified by Hedley Bull, a prominent member of the English School responsible for formulating the idea of **international society**, discussed in Chapter 3.

Along with the idea of natural law, there also arose the idea of *ius gentium*, the 'law of nations'. This had been conceptualized by the ancient Roman jurist Gaius, who wrote that 'All peoples who are ruled by laws and customs employ a law partly peculiar to themselves, partly common to all mankind' (quoted in McIlwain, 2005: p. 62). The *ius gentium*,

BOX 8.2 KEY QUOTE

Hedley Bull on Natural Law

The natural law theory, with its insistence that moral truth is apparent to all men by virtue of the light of reason, cannot readily accommodate the fact of moral disagreement, so prominent in the domain of international relations, or the clash of values and ways of life which it expresses.

(Bull, 1979: p. 181)

although not exactly the same as natural law, was nonetheless also conceptualized as deriving from the natural reason of all humankind, reflecting the need for practical rules of conduct between different human communities. Thus it dealt with the usual issues of interstate relations such as warfare, treaties, diplomacy, and trade. In contrast, the term *ius civile* (civil law) was used to denote law established by *particular* peoples (or **nations**) in application to their specific communities or states. So while the former is, like natural law, cosmopolitan in orientation, the latter accords with **communitarianism**. Again, these distinctions are important to conceptualizations of human rights.

➡ See **Chapters 1, 3, and 12** for discussion of cosmopolitanism and communitarianism.

The Idea of 'Just War'

One of the most significant developments in *ius gentium* came with the emergence of a 'just war' doctrine. As the term suggests, it came to specify the circumstances under which armed force could justifiably be used—usually as a measure to stop some form of evil-doing, or for the purpose of self-defence, or to come to the aid of an ally. Force must therefore be conducted by a legitimate authority (generally a state) pursuing a rightful cause with correct intentions, and not as an excuse for some other purpose such as theft of resources. It must also have a reasonable prospect of success, the *moral* benefits must outweigh the moral costs, and it must be prosecuted only as a last resort when other measures (such as diplomacy) have failed (see Lazar, 2016).

Taken together, these requirements underpin the right *to* war (*ius ad bellum*)—that is, the right to go to war against an adversary. The doctrine also came to embody moral precepts concerning *how* war ought to be conducted (*ius in bello*). Here, there must always be a distinction between military targets and civilian targets, and only military targets should be deliberately attacked; harm must be proportional to the military objectives and not exceed them; and violence and other harmful acts must be limited to those necessary to achieve the objectives, and not exceed them (see ibid.). If all this sounds more or less straightforward, the long and bitter experience of warfare in Europe where the doctrine arose suggests otherwise. Even so, much effort has gone into the attempt to establish an ethical basis for higher standards of conduct in warfare.

Elements of the just war doctrine which became part of the European *ius gentium* were formulated by another early Catholic figure, St Augustine of Hippo (354–430), who hailed from Numidia in North Africa (present-day Algeria). Augustine also drew on earlier Greek and Roman thought, citing Cicero's maxim that 'a war is never undertaken by the ideal State, except in defence of its honour and safety' (quoted in Mattox, 2018: p. 15). Many of these early ideas were further elaborated and tested in the work of Aquinas, referred to above, and later theorists of course have contributed to the tradition to the present time.

The history of thought on the issue of just war has scarcely been restricted to Europe. As we have seen, moral justifications for war were evident in early Chinese thought. The Confucian scholar Mencius (*c.*372–289 BC) discussed the issue of *yi zhan* (righteous war) and, well before him, Sun Tzu's *Art of War*—one among a number of Chinese classics on the topic—clearly regarded warfare as a last resort and advocated strategies that minimized harm to combatants on both sides (Lo, 2012: p. 440). Islamic thought too has grappled with complex issues in just war theory, including not just warfare conducted by formal state entities but 'irregular' wars including rebellions and civil war (see, generally, Kelsay, 1993).

In the context of global political issues of the time, and with the experience of Afghanistan and Iraq fresh in mind, an address by US President Obama to West Point graduates in 2014 referenced not only the defence of national interest but also basic just war principles: 'The United States will use military force, unilaterally if necessary, when our core interests demand it—when our people are threatened; when our livelihoods are at stake; when the security of our allies is in danger. *In these circumstances, we still need to ask tough questions about whether our actions are proportional and effective and just*' (Obama quoted in *Washington Post*, 2014).

But how, and by whom, military action is judged to be just is another issue. Elements of just war principles were invoked by US President George W. Bush and the UK Prime Minister Tony Blair in the invasion of Iraq with both adopting a highly moralistic posture in their emphasis on the evil nature of Saddam Hussein's regime and the threat posed by his weapons of mass destruction which, as it turns out, Iraq did not possess. As we have seen in previous chapters, realists have criticized the moralism that often accompanies justifications for war, although serious liberal theorists are also keenly aware of the hypocrisy that can attend the invocation of just war principles. Even so, this does not mean that issues of morality in the conduct of warfare can be dismissed and the substantial body of international law that deals with warfare attests to their importance.

Secularizing the Law of Nations

The gradual secularization of the law of nations in the European context entailed the separation of legal doctrine from religious doctrine. Natural law came to be linked to human reason alone, with no necessary connection to a 'divine spark'. A prominent figure in this development was Hugo Grotius, discussed in Chapter 3, who held that 'a theory of natural law does not presuppose the existence of God'—a bold assertion that has seen him cast as a principal secularizer of international law (von Ungern-Sterberg, 2012: p. 3).

The Peace of Westphalia represented an attempt to negate religious justifications for warfare in Europe and is often taken to mark the beginnings of the secularization of the international order in Europe. Others have argued, however, that because Westphalia was a 'Christian peace' (given the deep religiosity of both Catholic and Protestant parties to the conflict and subsequent treaties), it could not be described as a 'secular' peace (see, generally, Axworthy and Milton, 2016). This raises the question of how secularism is best understood. Many believe, mistakenly, that secularism simply equates to atheism. But this is not so, as explained in Box 8.3. Certainly, Christianity has left its imprint, but the legal system and its rules are now seen to operate independently of particular religious beliefs. Interestingly, another region in which religious differences have required a nuanced approach is South Asia where scholars have identified elements of a secularized conception of the 'family of nations' in the pre-British colonial period in India (Armitage and Pitts, 2017: p. 9).

In the trend to secularization in Europe, Grotius was followed by Emer de Vattel (1714–67), a Swiss jurist whose *Law of Nations* (first published in 1758) most effectively separated international law from religion. In so doing, he set out a substantial case for a body of international law derived from natural law. From the nineteenth century the emphasis on legal positivism grew, although natural law ideas have always remained an essential element in international law, providing it with a moral foundation on which the law works, at least in principle, to support the common good.

INTERNATIONAL LAW

8

> **BOX 8.3** KEY CONCEPT
>
> Secularism and Law
>
> Secularism is best understood as representing *neutrality* on religious matters, with no one religious belief system (or absence of belief) being favoured over another. Secularism therefore provides the basis not just for the coexistence of religions but for the equality of religions and, ultimately, freedom of religious thought, belief, and practice. When applied in a legal system, whether national or international, secularism therefore acknowledges both the fact of religious beliefs, and the right to practise them, as well as the right not to hold religious beliefs. It therefore supports a plurality of religions in any given sphere, but aims to transcend any *particular* religious belief system in the application of public law to ensure neutrality and equality before the law. Having said that, such rights are not absolute and there may be limits to certain practices. A religion requiring human sacrifice, to take an extreme example, would not be tolerated in any contemporary system.

A problem confronting legal positivism, however, was that because positive law was generally conceived as emanating from a sovereign will, it appeared to have no purchase in the anarchic international sphere. This remained so even if two or more sovereign powers had agreed among themselves on a particular set of rules to apply in their dealings with each other. The 'problem of anarchy' in this context accords with Thomas Hobbes's approach to sovereignty, and with realist approaches more generally, as discussed in Chapter 3. Nineteenth-century legal theorists, observing the increasing development of positive international law, certainly highlighted this problem. States nonetheless 'continued to regard international law as real law, they continued to abide by its rules in the vast majority of cases, their diplomatic communications continued to bristle with claims and counter-claims of legal right, and they continued to sign treaties by which they regarded themselves and other states as legally bound' (Hall, 2001: p. 281). If legal positivism implies that international law has little effect in the sphere of anarchy, then clearly it does not provide a complete picture of international legal reality (ibid.: p. 301).

From the Law of Nations to International Law

The nineteenth century saw a shift in vocabulary from the 'law of nations' to 'international law', largely through the influence of English legal and political theorist Jeremy Bentham (1748–1832). This was also a period of rapid social and political change with global exploration (from the early fifteenth century), the industrial revolution (from about 1760), the French Revolution (1789–99), the Napoleonic Wars (1803–15), and imperialism (mainly from about 1870), contributing to the dynamics of the times. The Congress of Vienna of 1814–15, mentioned in previous chapters, established a new legal order for Europe underpinned by novel modes of diplomacy embodied in the **Concert of Europe**. The latter lasted more or less until the outbreak of the First World War in 1914 by maintaining a **balance of power** among the major powers and constraining the spread of warfare when it did break out. The violence of the Crimean War (1853–56), which saw Great Britain, France, and the Ottomans oppose Russian expansionism in the Bosphorus, was at least confined to that region. The 1856 Treaty of Paris that ended this war also saw the Ottoman Empire join the Concert system, a development which contradicted the

FIGURE 8.1 **Statue of Simon Bolivar in Funchal, Madeira, Portugal** Bildagentur Zoonar GmbH/Shutterstock.com

belief that Muslim and Christian nations could never establish such political relations (Bakircioglu, 2014: p. 152).

Another conference in 1864, initiated by the Swiss on the instigation of the founder of the Red Cross, Henry Dunant, gave rise to the first Geneva Convention governing the humane treatment of wounded soldiers in war, as discussed in Chapter 7. This conference was attended by delegates from sixteen countries, again mainly European but also including the US, Mexico, and Brazil. The Geneva conventions of the present period date from this time, with additions over the years including four Geneva Conventions of 1949 following the atrocities of the Second World War and another two protocols added in 1977 to deal with the increasing problem of civil wars.

Substantial progress in developing international law in the nineteenth century was also taking place in Latin America. In 1826, the Congress of Panama was convened by Simon Bolivar. Originally from Venezuela, Bolivar had been the major figure in the revolutions throughout the region to gain independence from Spain (and Bolivia is named after him). At the time, Bolivar proposed a Latin American League of Nations, and the Congress also proposed mechanisms for maintaining peace and promoting conciliation across the region when disputes arose.

Although none of these specific proposals were to come about in the immediate period, cooperation across the region, including cooperation with the US, gained strength throughout the nineteenth century and into the twentieth. Achievements included the abolition of slavery, settlement of most boundary disputes, general treaties on arbitration, the building of the Panama canal, joint resistance to European intrusion, and a Pan-American Union (Inman, 1923: p. 239). By the end of the 1920s, additional measures included rejection of territorial conquest—later codified in the Organization of American States (OAS) and the UN Charter, the naturalization of foreign individuals, rights to navigation in international waters, *ius in bellum*, the reduction of armed forces, the duties and rights of states in civil strife, and certain human rights protections (Abello-Galbis and Arévalo-Ramírez, 2017: p. 19).

The nineteenth century closed with the 1899 Hague Peace Conference which represented an attempt, not to bring about the end of an existing war but pre-emptively to prevent war. Initiated by Tsar Nicholas II of Russia and dominated mainly by European delegates, it nonetheless included Japan, China, Siam (now Thailand), Turkey, and Persia (now Iran). Three broad areas were specifically addressed. The first concerned the pacific settlement of international disputes and saw the establishment of the Permanent Court of Arbitration. A second concerned the actual conduct of hostilities and a new convention was adopted which set out extensive laws governing warfare. This incorporated the 1864 Geneva Convention but extended the scope to many other areas. A third issue area saw agreements reached on limiting the types of armaments used, including a prohibition on poisons and certain kinds of projectiles.

A second conference was convened in 1907 which saw extensive participation by Latin American countries, including Argentina, Bolivia, Brazil, Chile, Cuba, the Dominican Republic, Ecuador, Guatemala, Haiti, Mexico, Nicaragua, Panama, Peru, El Salvador, Uruguay, and Venezuela. Most of these were to ratify the 1907 Convention for the Pacific Settlement of International Disputes whereas most European states did not do so until after the Second World War (see Obregón, 2017: pp. 3–5). Given that Latin American countries had been active in developing international law in their own region from early in the nineteenth century, they brought to the Hague meetings considerable experience in formulating both principle and practice in the field.

A third Hague conference to further pursue mechanisms was envisaged, but never held. It was overtaken by the onset of the First World War which showed just how costly the failure to reach workable agreements was. Even so, the original Geneva and Hague Conventions provide the basis on which contemporary International Humanitarian Law (IHL) and the grounds for the prosecution of war crimes are largely founded. Just how effective they have been in actually constraining the behaviour of combatants, however, is a matter of debate (see, generally, Evangelista and Tannanwald: 2017).

The Concept of 'Civilized Nations' in International Law

The nineteenth century also saw certain key concepts reflecting religious and cultural identity achieve prominence in the theorization of international law. Christianity was seen to underpin the essential character of 'civilized nations', the latter concept having first emerged within Europe in opposition to slavery and what was seen as an immoral trade in human lives. As noted in Chapter 7, the Congress of Vienna had represented a significant milestone in the abolition of the slave trade. Eight leading European powers signed a declaration condemning it as 'repugnant to the principles of humanity and universal morality' while making direct reference to the public outcry against it in 'all civilised nations' (Lessafer, 2015). The declaration against slavery and the treaties that followed may also be seen more generally as establishing, for the first time, a major human rights issue in international law.

Another innovation introduced at Vienna, albeit among only a few countries at the time, was a stipulation that religious affiliation should have no bearing on appointments to public office. The neutrality of the state on matters concerning religious affiliation therefore reinforced the principle of secularism in public affairs and this principle also came to be regarded as the mark of a civilized nation (Vec, 2012: p. 651). In the wider world, however, the association of civilized nationhood with Christianity became important for Europeans in distinguishing themselves from non-Europeans who did not share the Christian faith. This provided the basis on which an international law governing relations between civilized nations could be developed to theorize inequality between European and non-European states, serving in turn to justify imperialism and colonialism (see Kroll, 2015: pp. 238–49).

Conceptualizing international law through the prism of religion was obviously contrary to the trend in secularization. But the contradictions inherent in the concept of a law of civilized nations which excluded non-Christians from its ambit could not be sustained over the longer term. In any case, as we have seen, the Ottomans had joined the Concert of Europe in the latter part of the nineteenth century. It may also seem something of an irony that the 'civilized' nations of Europe instigated the most barbaric wars of the twentieth century in their own heartland. When the League of Nations established the Permanent Court of International Justice (PCIJ) in 1920, the Statute of the Court included 'the general principles of international law recognized by civilized nations' as a source. Much of the non-Western world was still in the grip of colonial rule, although a significant number of non-Western (and non-Christian) countries were League members. The PCIJ was replaced in 1946 by the UN's International Court of Justice (ICJ) which retains, in Article 38 (c), the same wording to this day, but it is now assumed that all nations, as represented by the member states of the UN, are 'civilized'.

KEY POINTS

- Natural law holds that there is an objective 'natural' moral order that transcends specific human communities and the particular, subjective rules and regulations that these devise.
- 'Just war' doctrine specifies the circumstances under which armed force can be justified (*ius ad bellum*) as well as moral precepts concerning *how* war ought to be conducted (*ius in bello*).
- The nineteenth century saw a conceptual shift from the 'law of nations' to 'international law' accompanied by increased norm development and codification with input from state actors in the Americas, the Middle East, and Asia as well as Europe.
- Secularization entailed the separation of legal doctrine from religious doctrine to achieve neutrality and should not be equated with atheism.
- The concept of 'civilized nations' has a convoluted history, having been used in opposition to slavery, in justifications for European imperialism in non-Christian countries, and to distinguish secular from non-secular legal systems.

INTERNATIONAL LAW IN THE TWENTIETH CENTURY

Any hope that the agreements reached at the Hague Conferences would provide a basis for durable peace were drowned in the rising tide of nationalism that afflicted Europe in the late nineteenth and early twentieth centuries, culminating in the First World War.

This led of course to the establishment of the League of Nations and then, following the Second World War, the United Nations—arguably the most significant developments in the twentieth-century institutionalization of international law. It is through these institutions that unilateral war-making was outlawed and collective security arrangements established; that governments came to be held to account for the treatment of their own citizens; and that persons (and not just states) emerged as subjects of international law (Franck, 1997–98: p. 139).

➡ See **Chapters 3 and 7** for a discussion of the League of Nations and the United Nations.

International law also began to accommodate non-state actors, including both individuals and groups (Spiermann, 2007: p. 785). An International Law Commission was also established by the General Assembly in 1947 to 'initiate studies and make recommendations for the purpose of . . . encouraging the progressive development of international law and its codification' (http://legal.un.org/ilc/). As of 2020, some of the principal topics on the Commission's programme of work are: immunity of state officials from foreign criminal jurisdiction, crimes against humanity, provisional application of treaties, general principles of law, protection of the environment in relation to armed conflicts, protection of the atmosphere, and sea level rise in relation to international law (ibid.).

Colonialism and Decolonization

The League did little to undermine imperialism and, if anything, simply reinforced it with a mandate system that awarded former German colonies as well as large swathes of former Ottoman territory to the main victors of the First World War. But again, this was not an entirely European division of spoils. Japan was given a mandate over former German territories in Micronesia, which it held until the end of the Second World War. The system did not envisage colonialism as a permanent institution but rather saw colonial powers as charged with a 'sacred trust', as 'civilized nations', to 'assist and protect peoples who had not yet reached the same level of development' (Matz, 2005: p. 60). Even so, the overall effect of the mandate system was to 'internationalize' colonial policy as well as to give it some consistency (ibid.: p. 52). All this was to change in the aftermath of the Second World War as the decolonization movement made rapid advances. One notable event accompanying these changes was the Bandung Conference, discussed in Box 8.4.

International Human Rights Law

Given the atrocities that had occurred during the Second World War, issues of human rights were to become a major focus for international law. The scope for human rights was widened with the adoption of the UN's Universal Declaration of Human Rights (UDHR) of 1948, on which much contemporary international human rights law is founded, although the UDHR itself carries a moral rather than a legal force. The subsequent Covenant on Civil and Political Rights and Covenant on Economic, Social, and Cultural Rights do, however, provide more specific legal force. Taken together, the UDHR and the two Covenants constitute the International Bill of Rights.

➡ See **Chapter 7** for a discussion of the UDHR, the Covenants, and the political issues surrounding them.

BOX 8.4   CASE STUDY

The Bandung Conference

In April 1955, the leaders of twenty-four Asian and African states met in the Indonesian city of Bandung. This is often considered as a founding moment in Global South solidarity, marking a shift in North–South relations while initiating South–South cooperation, promoting a discourse of developmentalism, and, in the context of the Cold War, providing the basis for the subsequent emergence of the Non-Aligned Movement (see, generally, Eslava, Fakhri, and Nesiah, 2017).

The core principles of the Bandung Conference were based on the 'Five Principles of Coexistence' agreed earlier by India's first prime minister, Jawaharlal Nehru, and China's first premier, Zhou Enlai, in 1954. These principles were embedded in the Panchsheel Treaty which was to serve as the basis of relations between their two countries as well as their approach to the wider world: political **self-determination**, mutual respect for sovereignty, non-aggression, non-interference in internal affairs, and equality (Panda, 2014). The Bandung Conference also declared its full support for human rights, emphasizing that national self-determination was a condition for the full expression of those rights. It also focused on **racism** and imperialism as a gross violation of human rights.

The final communiqué of the Bandung Conference included:

1   Respect for fundamental human rights and for the purposes and principles of the Charter of the United Nations.

2   Respect for the sovereignty and territorial integrity of all nations.

3   Recognition of the equality of all races and of the equality of all nations large and small.

4   Abstention from **intervention** or interference in the internal affairs of another country.

5   Respect for the right of each nation to defend itself singly or collectively, in conformity with the Charter of the United Nations.

6   (a) Abstention from the use of arrangements of collective defence to serve the particular interests of any of the big powers.

    (b) Abstention by any country from exerting pressures on other countries.

7   Refraining from acts or threats of aggression or the use of force against the territorial integrity or political independence of any country.

8   Settlement of all international disputes by peaceful means, such as negotiation, conciliation, arbitration, or judicial settlement as well as other peaceful means of the parties' own choice, in conformity with the Charter of the United Nations.

9   Promotion of mutual interests and cooperation.

10 Respect for justice and international obligations.

(Source: https://www.semanticscholar.org/paper/Final-Communiqu%C3%A9-of-the-Asian-African-conference-of-Bandung/a092de95d72c0b19a3594e6703f0488abbadab6f).

The communiqué affirmed the general principles of international law generated by the UN while giving an especially prominent place to the principle of racial equality. Most emphasis, however,

(Continued)

was placed on the values of sovereignty and, in turn, states' rights. Also, issues of racial equality were perceived almost exclusively through the prism of white/non-white relations. Given the recent experience of most participants with colonialism, and the fact that many countries were still colonized at the time, these emphases were to be expected. Indeed, the importance placed on these issues at Bandung presented a challenge to international law's relationship with European imperialism and all that this implied for the **Third World**.

Over the years that followed, the Bandung Conference was to acquire symbolic status as a Global South movement challenging the status quo not only at a particular moment in time but as an ongoing project. One commentary compares Bandung's status with another key moment in international legal history, suggesting that if 'Westphalia serves as the creation myth of international law, the myth of Bandung is its counterpoint', highlighting a vexed relationship and a critical grappling with world history as it has unfolded around the dynamics of colonialism and postcolonialism (Eslava, Fakhri, and Nesiah, 2017: p. 16).

Questions that continue to arise include:

1 How important was Bandung in consolidating an identity for the Third World/Global South through its mythical/symbolic status?

2 To what extent did Bandung achieve practical effects in international legal and political outcomes?

FIGURE 8.2 **Bandung Conference in Bandung, Indonesia, 1955** Photo 12/Alamy Stock Photo

There are now numerous additional human rights instruments dealing with specific issues. As well as the Genocide Convention, discussed in Chapter 5, there are treaties, covenants, and conventions dealing with torture, racial discrimination, discrimination against women, migrant workers and their families, the rights of the child, and the disabled, among others. Not all countries, however, are signatories to, or have ratified, each and every instrument. It has also been noted that international human rights treaties and humanitarian law may oblige states to protect and enforce human rights within their own territory and in the conduct of their activities abroad, but they do so without prescribing direct sanctions, legal consequences, or personal responsibility (Huikuri, 2019: p. 11). The setting up of the International Criminal Court (ICC) has been designed to address this problem, and will be discussed shortly.

KEY POINTS

- Developments since the early twentieth century have seen governments being held to account for the treatment of their own citizens with individuals and non-state actors emerging as subjects of international law as well.

- The decolonization movement and events such as the Bandung Conference gave an impetus to progressive stances on racism, developmentalism, and South–South cooperation while maintaining a conservative approach to doctrines of state sovereignty and non-intervention.

- Human rights came very much to the fore after the Second World War but, while there has been a significant growth in human rights law under UN auspices, enforcement has been difficult.

TREATIES, CHARTERS, AND COVENANTS

The term 'treaty' is the widely recognized generic term for a range of *written* international agreements including charters, covenants, declarations, protocols, statutes, and memoranda of understanding (MOUs). Treaties are a primary source of positive international law and are essential to international cooperation and coordination, not just between states but also between international organizations and other subjects of international law. Around 64,000 treaties have been registered with the UN, although not all treaties come under its auspices or are registered with it (Hollis, 2012: p. 8). The EU, for example, is set up under its own Treaty on European Union (otherwise known as the Maastricht Treaty), which came into effect in 1993 and which has numerous additional protocols and declarations. The EU also has over a thousand bilateral and multilateral treaties with other countries. Other regional organizations are similarly set up under treaties and also make other treaties.

Treaties are defined by the UN's 1969 Vienna Convention on the Law of Treaties (VCLT) —which is itself a treaty—as international agreements 'concluded between States in written form and governed by international law, whether embodied in a single instrument or in two or more related instruments and whatever particular designation'. The VCLT goes on to state that: 'Every treaty in force is binding upon the parties to it and must be performed by them in good faith' (see https://legal.un.org/ilc/texts/instruments/english/conventions/1_1_1969.pdf). This means that a treaty is a specific kind of international agreement, noting that not all such agreements take the form of treaties. Treaties may also comprise more than just a single text. For example, the original North American Free Trade Agreement (NAFTA) consisted of an original agreement along with a set of subsequent notes signed on four different dates in December 1992. As of 2019, NAFTA has been renegotiated as the United States-Mexico-Canada Agreement or USMCA (see https://jusmundi.com/en/document/treaty/en-north-american-free-trade-agreement-nafta-thursday-17th-december-1992).

FIGURE 8.3 Chancellor of Germany Angela Merkel and President of France Emmanuel Macron at a European Union press conference in Brussels, Belgium, 2018 Alexandros Michailidis/Shutterstock.com

Treaties not only regulate behaviour between states or other subjects of international law but may regulate how they behave in particular geographic spaces such as the seas and oceans, Antarctica, and outer space. They also regulate use of shared or common goods, such as fisheries and migratory birds, and atmospheric conditions, such as the ozone layer or greenhouse gas emissions (Hollis, 2012: p. 40). The adoption of treaties and similar instruments can be a rather complex and drawn-out process, as set out in Box 8.5.

BOX 8.5

Making International Treaties

Any given treaty is usually a response to an issue on which a consensus develops around the need for action at an international level. Depending on the body initiating action, it may then be referred to an expert group for investigation after which a draft text emerges and a process of negotiation and consultation commences. Assuming that a consensus is eventually achieved on the finer points of the instrument, it then moves to the adoption phase.

Even if adopted by the wider forum of the organization (e.g. the UN General Assembly), it may still be some considerable time before a treaty enters into force and even then not all members will have necessarily signed or ratified it. The current UN Convention on the Law of the Sea (UNCLOS), for example, had its origins in a UN conference in 1956 which resulted in four treaties dealing with some of the key issues. Further developments saw an almost decade-long conference process take place between 1973 and 1982, resulting in the current convention, although it did not enter into force until 1994 when the sixtieth state ratified it. Around twenty-five UN members still have not signed or ratified UNCLOS. But for those who have, it is legally binding.

'Ratification' denotes the formal consent of a state to be bound to a treaty. Initial signatures are usually subject to ratification by whatever domestic process is required. In the US, for example, an international treaty, even if negotiated by the President, must be approved by a two-thirds Senate majority. With bilateral treaties, ratification is usually accomplished by a simple exchange of instruments. In the case of multilateral treaties, the relevant body (e.g. the UN) will act as a depositary, collecting the ratifications of states while keeping all parties informed as it proceeds. This allows states time to gain the required approval at the domestic level and to enact whatever legislation is necessary to give the treaty effect (see, generally, https://treaties.un.org).

At the time a treaty is drawn up, it is usually agreed that a certain number of states must ratify it in order for it to enter into force. Some treaties can take years to enter into force, although states which have ratified it will generally abide by its terms in the meantime. Parties to a treaty can sometimes enter reservations concerning specific provisions to which it objects. Also, parties not involved in the process of treaty making may nonetheless accede to a treaty later, usually after it has already entered into force.

Even after signature or ratification, some states will nonetheless withdraw from treaties. The US, for example, has withdrawn unilaterally from a number of important treaties in recent times including the Paris climate change agreement of 2016, the 2015 Iran deal on nuclear issues, and the Trans-Pacific Partnership Agreement of 2016 on trade. These withdrawals occurred under the Trump administration, but there is a long record of relatively weak US participation in international treaties. Given the relative status of the US in the global sphere, its thin record on treaties, including human rights treaties, tends to undermine the integrity of a rules-based international order. In this respect, however, it is hardly alone among the great powers.

KEY POINTS

- Treaties, charters, covenants, declarations, protocols, statutes, and memoranda of understanding provide much of the basis for international cooperation between states as well as between international organizations and other subjects of international law.

- International treaties enhance elements of predictability and therefore stability in the global sphere, and enable the conduct of a wide range of activities, including the movement of goods and people, services, communications, the use of international spaces, care for the environment, the protection of people from harm, and so on.

- Despite the lack of enforcement mechanisms, the proliferation of treaties throughout the twentieth century and up to the present time attests to their efficacy in global politics and their key role in maintaining a rules-based international order.

INTERNATIONAL COURTS AND TRIBUNALS

Another major development in twentieth-century international law was the establishment of various international courts and tribunals. These are defined as 'permanent judicial bodies made up of independent judges who are entrusted with adjudicating international disputes on the basis of international law according to a pre-determined set of rules of procedure and rendering decisions which are binding on the parties' (Thomuschat, 2008: p. 19). Examples of regional courts include the African Court of Justice set up to interpret treaties established by the African Union; the Court of Justice of the Andean Community in Latin America which deals with trade disputes; and the European Court of Human Rights. There are many more around the world dealing with similar issues although Europe and Africa have been the most active regions in establishing various courts. The two main global courts now operating are the International Court of Justice (ICJ) and the International Criminal Court (ICC), both based in the Hague.

The International Court of Justice

The ICJ, often called the World Court, is part of the UN system although it operates on an independent basis. As with other institutions, its origins can be traced to much earlier periods and linked to the gradual development of methods of mediation and arbitration of disputes between states. Its immediate predecessor, the PCIJ, operated from 1922 until it was dissolved in 1946 to make way for the new UN-sponsored court.

The fifteen judges of the ICJ are elected for nine-year terms by both the UN General Assembly and the Security Council. They must be 'persons of high moral character, who possess the qualifications required in their respective countries for appointment to the highest judicial offices, or are jurisconsults of recognized competence in international law'. In addition, 'the Court as a whole must represent the main forms of civilization and the principal legal systems of the world'. In order to further guarantee their independence, no judge of the court can be dismissed unless, in the unanimous opinion of the other members, they no longer fulfil the required conditions. This has not happened to date (see https://www.icj-cij.org/en/members).

The ICJ has jurisdiction to decide legal disputes submitted to it by states and to give advisory opinions on legal questions at the request of UN organs or authorized agencies. Between May 1947 and July 2019, 177 cases had been entered into its General List. Examples of cases pending as of 2020 include Islamic Republic of Iran *v.* United States of America over certain Iranian assets; Ukraine *v.* the Russian Federation over both funding of terrorism and racial discrimination; and Palestine *v.* the United States of America over the relocation of the latter's embassy to Jerusalem (https://www.icj-cij.org/en/pending-cases).

It has been said that the ICJ, along with its predecessor, represents a 'unique twentieth-century move to international third-party decision making' (Franck, 1997: p. 146). This is so even though the ICJ can neither compel appearance before it nor enforce its decisions, at least not in a material sense. It is therefore remarkable that parties to proceedings almost always comply with its decisions, even when these go against them. For example, a long-standing dispute between Libya and Chad over a border area was submitted by both parties to the ICJ in 1990. In 1994, the court ruled in Chad's favour. Libya complied almost immediately by agreeing to a UN supervised withdrawal from the area.

A broader study of dispute settlement decisions under UNCLOS suggests that the overwhelming majority of the decisions have been implemented not only by small states but also by permanent members of the UN Security Council, even when they have lost in proceedings that have been unilaterally initiated against them (see Phan, 2019: pp. 70–90). This does not amount to the defeat of power politics as conceptualized in realist thought and evident in the play of international politics over the span of recorded history, but it does suggest that amelioration is possible. Cause and effect are often difficult to establish precisely, but the major reduction in interstate warfare since the end of the Second World War is at least partly due to the work of the ICJ.

The International Criminal Court

The ICC was established in 1998 under a treaty known as the Rome statute which entered into force in 2002. Like the ICJ, the ICC operates as a permanent court at a global level. Previously, serious criminal matters were usually dealt with by ad hoc criminal tribunals set up to deal with specific cases. Historically, the best-known of these were set up in the aftermath of the Second World War. The International Military Tribunal was established at Nuremberg to try major Nazi war criminals while the International Military Tribunal for the Far East (also known as the Tokyo War Crimes Tribunal) dealt with Japanese war criminals. More recently, the International Criminal Tribunal for the Former Yugoslavia (1993–2017) and the International Criminal Tribunal for Rwanda (1994–2015) have sought to bring the perpetrators of mass violence and **genocide** to justice.

The ICC's purpose is to prosecute the most serious of crimes committed by both state and non-state actors such as genocide, war crimes, and crimes against humanity, and thereby to give greater effect to human rights treaties. In 2017, the category of 'crimes of aggression' was added as a 'core crime' under the court's jurisdiction. The ICC is a court of 'last resort', which means that it assumes jurisdiction only when national legal systems are unable or unwilling to deal with such serious criminal acts. It also focuses on bringing high-level leaders involved in these crimes to justice, including heads of state.

The diplomatic conference which produced the Rome statute followed a decade of preparations and included an extraordinary number of participants—delegates from 160 states, 17 intergovernmental organizations, 14 UN agencies and funds, and 124 NGOs (Huikuri, 2019: p. 7). Seven countries—the US, China, Iraq, Israel, Libya, Qatar, and Yemen—voted against the statute in 1998. Overall, however, the high level of participation in, and support for, the process from all sectors is noteworthy. As of 2019, 138 states had signed, although only 123 are parties to the statute.

Having said that, a number of major powers—Russia, China, and the US in particular— have at times undermined the ICC. Not only have they declined to join, they have also obstructed its functioning through Security Council vetoes on referring cases, shielding both themselves and their allies from possible prosecution. The US has also withheld support for peacekeeping operations unless US citizens are exempted from proceedings arising out of their participation, and by cutting foreign aid to selected states unless they sign immunity agreements. The administration of George W. Bush was especially hostile to the court, although this was moderated during the Obama administration. The US did assist in bringing two suspects before the court from Democratic Republic of Congo and Uganda respectively. Most recently, however, the US under the Trump administration introduced a visa ban on ICC staff involved in the court's potential investigation of US citizens' activities in Afghanistan. The ban may also have been used to deter ICC investigations against citizens of US allies such as Israel (see Human Rights Watch, 2019).

For their part, Russia and China have vetoed referral of Syrian civil war issues by the Security Council to the ICC which the US had supported. Russia under Putin also withdrew its signature (although it had not in any case ratified the statute). This followed a report from the ICC describing Russia's annexation of Crimea as an 'occupation' and not

FIGURE 8.4 Fatou Bensouda, Prosecutor of the International Criminal Court, at a conference in The Hague, Netherlands, 2019 MikeChappazo/Shutterstock.com

a legitimate acquisition of territory. China has yet to engage substantially with the ICC, seemingly more concerned with maintaining state judicial sovereignty, although it supported the previous ad hoc international criminal tribunals as well as some of the ICC's indictment procedures (see, generally, Zhu, 2018).

The ICC has encountered some opposition from the African Union (AU) and the Arab League. As of 2020, all but one of the eleven cases before the court have been from Africa, giving rise to accusations that the court was unfairly targeting the continent and engaging in new forms of imperialism. On the other hand, African countries generally supported the establishment of the ICC, were among the first to join, and the first actually to refer cases to the ICC themselves. Moreover, African **civil society** organizations have been strongly supportive of the court and its attempts to bring justice to victims of severe human rights abuses in the continent, and regard objections by African leaders as largely specious (see, generally, Jalloh and Bantekas, eds, 2017). The ICC's chief prosecutor since 2012 (after serving from 2004 as a deputy prosecutor) is Fatou Bom Bensouda from Gambia. Other senior ICC positions are more or less representative of various parts of the globe and are not limited to Europe.

In this context it is also worth noting a preliminary enquiry conducted by the ICC into war crimes allegedly committed by Buddhist majority Myanmar against the minority Muslim Rohingya people of Rakhine state. In 2017, around 700,000 Rohingya had been forced to flee over the border into neighbouring Bangladesh in what appears to be a clear case of **ethnic cleansing**. A 2018 UN report found evidence of genocidal activity and other atrocities. Myanmar is not a signatory to the ICC but, in 2019, a case was brought by Gambia before the ICJ instead—a case supported by the Organization of Islamic Cooperation (OIC). The move has been spearheaded by Abubacarr Tambadou, Gambia's attorney general and minister of justice who previously worked for the International Criminal Tribunal for Rwanda (see https://www.bbc.com/news/world-asia-50375739).

These examples illustrate, among other things, the highly political nature of the international legal field, especially in criminal matters. The record of some major powers in undermining the ICC has been especially problematic but has not rendered it ineffective in all cases. A positive assessment sees the ICC as 'the last great institution of the twentieth century' and the 'highest point of a process that began in the wake of the Nuremberg judgement' (Islam, 2016: p. 1). But there is little doubt that revision of its processes and procedures will be ongoing as it continues to develop as another major institution of international law and of global order more generally.

KEY POINTS

- International courts and tribunals have been set up either by the UN or at a regional level to deal with a wide variety of issues and, despite the lack of enforcement mechanisms, have had significant success.

- The successes achieved by the ICJ to date do not amount to the defeat of power politics, but they do suggest that amelioration is possible.

- The ICC has faced particular difficulties in bringing the most egregious, high-level human rights violators before it but, despite attempts at sabotage by some of the most powerful actors, has made some headway.

THE RULES-BASED ORDER IN CONTEMPORARY GLOBAL POLITICS

The notion of a rules-based international order has been given greater prominence in recent discourses, mainly because it has been perceived to be under increasing threat due to the behaviour of powerful states seemingly determined to have their own way in global politics. Russia and China, in particular, have been criticized for operating unilaterally and with little regard for rules negotiated over many years. Russia's annexation of the Crimea in 2014, its backing of separatist forces in eastern Ukraine, and its alleged involvement in the poisoning of a former Russian double agent and his daughter in the UK in 2018, which violated both British sovereignty and the UN's Chemical Weapons Convention, as well as interference in US elections, have been major concerns. China has been accused of violations over its territorial claims in the South China Sea which include building a substantial military base on reefs in a contested area and threatening freedom of navigation under UNCLOS. China is also suspected of cyber spying and interference in the domestic politics of other countries. But, as set out in Box 8.6, the behaviour of the US has also come under much scrutiny over the past two decades, prompting debates about its own role in undermining the rules-based international order which, historically, it played such a key role in establishing.

Finally, on a quite different theme, we may ask from a critical perspective how the present rules-based international order has tended to work within, and further entrench, a system that is essentially unfair and unjust to many ordinary people. We may recall

BOX 8.6 KEY DEBATE

The US and the Rules-Based Order

The US is widely regarded as having played the leading role in the establishment of a robust rules-based international order in the post-Second World War period—an order under which a significant measure of peace, security, and stability has been achieved, at least relative to previous periods. In the contemporary period, however, the US, along with a number of key allies, appears to be playing a major role in undermining that order. The US stands accused of violating the UN's most basic rules and principles by invading Iraq in 2003 without UN Security Council authorization. Then in 2011, the US-led NATO mission far exceeded its mandate in the Libyan crisis in 2011 to force regime change, as discussed in previous chapters.

The US also has a very poor record on international treaties which are the foundation for much of the rules-based international order. It has rejected key multilateral agreements concerning global warming and nuclear issues in Iran while the Trump administration's **protectionism** is considered to be a threat to **multilateralism** in world trade.

A recent report from the UK's House of Lords, while highlighting problems posed by China and Russia, also looked at the role of US which, it said, had contributed to broader trends in **isolationism**, **unilateralism**, **populism**, and **identity politics**—all with implications for the traditional alliance between the UK and the US which has itself been a key factor in maintaining stability.

'We are living through a time of worldwide disruption and change. Trends including populism, identity politics, nationalism, isolationism, protectionism, and mass movements of people are putting considerable pressure on states and traditional structures of government. At the same time, the global balance of power is shifting and fragmenting in a way not experienced since the Second World War, undermining the rules-based international order. . . .

'The US Administration has taken a number of unilateral foreign policy decisions on high-profile issues, such as the Iran nuclear deal and trade policy, which undermine the UK's interests. The UK has struggled to influence the Administration, which is, in part, a reflection of a broader shift in the US towards a more inward-looking "America First" stance, with less focus on the transatlantic alliance or multilateralism. In future the Government will need to place less reliance on reaching a common US/UK approach to the main issues of the day than has often been the case in the past' (UK, 2018: p. 3).

We may recall here, however, that the UK under Tony Blair's prime ministership itself participated in the 2001 invasion of Iraq, contrary to international law.

The past record of the US is one thing, its future role is another. As rising powers acquire more prominence in global affairs, the relative decline in US power and influence will certainly change the dynamics surrounding the ongoing development of global order.

Key questions raised by the issues sketched above are:

1 To what extent has the US both contributed to, and undermined, the post-war rules-based international order?

2 Will the relative decline of US power necessarily lead to a concomitant decline in that order?

that critical theorists such as Robert Cox, discussed in Chapter 4, regard traditional theories such as liberalism as merely problem-solving—seeking amelioration of issues such as human rights abuses (including those arising from abject poverty) within the existing system rather than challenging the system itself. Critical theorists of international law certainly highlight the fact that human rights abuses, including, for example, the dispossession of indigenous people in the interests of economic 'development', are the product of a capitalist world system in which profit-making rather than human well-being is the primary motivation, but which so often goes unchallenged. According to this critical viewpoint, the current rules-based international order supports a **neoliberal** economic order in which key issues of justice and fairness are obscured and which, in its profit-seeking behaviour, works relentlessly in opposition to any project of **emancipation** (see, generally, Christodoulidis, Dukes, and Goldoni, eds, 2019). We revisit some of these issues in Chapter 10.

KEY POINTS

- Russia and China have been criticized for their unilateralism and apparent lack of regard for rules which they themselves have participated in making.

- The US has a relatively poor record on international treaties, which undermines its status as a leader in global politics.

- The rules-based international order remains effective in most instances but faces challenges from unilateralism and trends in 'anti-globalization'.

CONCLUSION

Global politics—encompassing a variety of actors and a multiplicity of relationships— is mediated by a complex legal framework consisting of both formal, positive law as well as law deriving from customary sources. These have been developed and negotiated over a considerable period of time and, although significant elements have been formulated in a European context, there have been significant influences from other parts of the globe. It is also worth emphasizing that while realist perspectives may critique the global legal system as a pale imitation of a national system in which a proper sovereign power can enforce law, the fact that most states and other relevant actors follow most of the rules most of the time suggests that it serves a vital purpose in underpinning a relatively more stable, predictable, and peaceful global order, as suggested by liberal approaches. Having said that, global order may nonetheless be subverted by powerful states or other actors intent on pursuing their own interests regardless of established rules. To that extent we can scarcely gloss over the fact that power politics is likely to remain a major dynamic in the global system and compromise the extent to which desirable outcomes can be achieved.

KEY QUESTIONS

1 What are the main elements of a rules-based international order?

2 How does international law differ from domestic law?

3 What are the main sources of international law?

4 How can violators of international law be punished?

5 What is natural law and how has it contributed to the development of international law?

6 What are the main precepts of 'just war'?

7 Is secularism important in the application of law?

8 Does religious or cultural identity still have associations with the concept of a 'civilized nation'?

9 How was international law implicated in European imperialism and colonialism in the nineteenth and twentieth centuries?

10 What role did the Bandung Conference play in the development of international law in the postcolonial period?

11 How do treaties, charters, and covenants come about, and what purposes do they serve?

12 How effective are the ICJ and the ICC?

13 What are the most useful theoretical tools in analysing international law?

FURTHER READING

Johns, Fleur, Richard Joyce, and Sundhya Pahuja (eds) (2011), *Events: The Force of International Law* (Abingdon: Routledge).
A fascinating collection of analyses of both historical and more recent events through which international law has acquired much of its force. Cases include Spanish colonization, Westphalia, the PCIJ, the release of Nelson Mandela, the Rwandan genocide, the WTO, and regime change in Iraq.

Kent, Avidan, Nikos Skoutaris, and Jamie Trinidad (eds) (2019), *The Future of International Courts: Regional, Institutional, and Procedural Challenges* (Abingdon: Routledge).
The process of international adjudication is examined by expert and emerging contributors from diverse perspectives. It examines some of the challenges that international courts face, from the rising influence of powerful states, the turn to populism, and the interplay between courts to the involvement of non-state actors and third parties in international proceedings.

Klabbers, Jan (2013), *International Law* (Cambridge: Cambridge University Press).
An excellent introductory textbook by a leading authority in the field, written clearly and concisely for readers new to the subject. It is organized around four key questions: Where does international law come from? To whom does it apply? How does it resolve conflict? And what does it say?

Roberts, Anthea (2017), *Is International Law International?* (Oxford: Oxford University Press).
A wide-ranging book posing critical questions about how some states and groups have dominated certain key aspects of international law. Not unexpectedly, the finger is pointed at Western actors. The analysis suggests that as global politics moves beyond the present period of Western dominance a deeper comparative understanding of an increasingly diverse range of actors will be required.

Yusuf, Abdulqawi A. (2014), *Pan-Africanism and International Law* (Leiden: Martinus Nijhoff).
A critical examination of Africa's encounters with international law, from when the continent's polities were excluded from the sphere of 'civilized nations' to the more recent period in which Africa has contributed to the development of law as a universal interstate normative system. Discussion includes the role of the Organization of African Unity and the African Union, set in the context of intra-African relations and the various stages in the evolution of Pan-Africanism.

WEB LINKS

https://www.un.org/en/sections/issues-depth/international-law-and-justice/index.html

Provides a broad overview of the UN's record in developing international law with links to additional relevant UN sites.

https://www.icj-cij.org/en
https://www.icc-cpi.int/

Home pages of the ICJ and ICC respectively, providing overviews of their activities including links to cases finalized and pending, media releases, publications, keynote speeches, and other resources.

https://www.achpr.org/

Site of the African Commission on Human and People's Rights with links to state parties, state reports, and mission reports.

https://www.oas.org/en/iachr/

Site of the Inter-American Commission on Human Rights with links to relevant items and other sites of interest.

 For additional material and resources please visit the **online resources** at: www.oup.com/he/lawson1e.

9

DIPLOMACY AND FOREIGN POLICY

- Diplomacy and Statecraft in Global History
- Diplomacy in Contemporary Global Politics
- Cold War Diplomacy
- Public Diplomacy and Soft Power
- Foreign Policy
- Diplomacy and Foreign Policy after Wikileaks
- Conclusion

Reader's Guide

Diplomacy and the conduct of foreign policy are fundamental to relations between political communities and have been practised for thousands of years. In the contemporary period, diplomatic and foreign policy practices usually involve fully professionalized state bureaucracies. But alongside formal state diplomacy, other important actors contribute as well, from non-government organizations (NGOs) to special envoys or third-party mediators tasked with specific missions. There are also special forms of diplomacy such as 'summit diplomacy' and 'public diplomacy', both of which have assumed increasing importance in contemporary practice. Foreign policy behaviour itself is a closely related but distinctive field of study focusing on the strategies that states adopt in their relations with each other and which reflect, in turn, the pressures that governments face in either the domestic or external sphere. In this chapter we also consider the foreign and security policy of the EU which now has a role and an identity as an international actor in its own right. This illustrates the fact that, while the state remains the most important entity in the international system, regional bodies are also key actors in diplomacy and foreign affairs. Finally, a brief account of Wikileaks illustrates another very different kind of actor in the field.

DIPLOMACY AND STATECRAFT IN GLOBAL HISTORY

If international relations in a conventional sense refer to the pattern of interactions between states in the international system of states, then diplomacy is the principal formal mechanism through which this takes place. Diplomacy is further characterized as embodying primarily peaceful means of conducting such interactions, although some diplomatic behaviour can be aggressive and threatening. Statecraft is an allied notion denoting the skilful conduct of state affairs or, as some may put it, 'steering the ship of state', usually in the context of external relations. The practice of diplomacy has a very long history, almost certainly reaching back beyond the earliest written records. One commentary suggests that the beginnings of diplomacy must have occurred when the first human societies decided it was better to hear the message than to devour the messenger (Hamilton and Langhorne, 2011: p. 7). To this observation we should add that it also had the advantage of being able to send the messenger back with a response, thereby establishing a basis for ongoing communications. A specific recorded reference to the utility of envoys or messengers may be found in Kautilya's ancient text, the *Arthasástra*, mentioned in Chapters 2 and 3, which states clearly the first principle of diplomacy: *don't shoot the messenger* (see Box 9.1).

Diplomacy is known to have existed in ancient China and indeed the pattern of interstate relations there has been compared directly with those of early modern Europe. For a time, Chinese city-states (called *guo*) enjoyed a certain autonomy, which saw alliances and diplomatic practices emerge in a multi-state system well before they did so in Europe, although in China this effectively ended with the establishment of an overarching imperial system in 221 BC (Hui, 2005: pp. 4–5). Other studies have investigated historical patterns of diplomacy and trade between China and India, illuminating the role of Buddhism in the process (see, generally, Sen, 2015), while evidence has also been found for the practice of alliance diplomacy in the regions covered by the ancient Inca, Aztec, and Mayan Empires in the Americas (see Cioffi-Revilla and Landman, 1999: pp. 559–98). There is also ample evidence for diplomatic relations between political communities in pre-modern Africa. A study of West African diplomatic traditions, for example, identifies the use of messengers, envoys, and ambassadors along with symbols of diplomatic office, ceremonials, and practices of immunity and safe-conduct (Smith, 1989: pp. 12–13). Many other examples of diplomatic practices, from Egypt to Byzantinium, the Greek states, and the Roman Empire can be cited to illustrate the extent and variety of diplomatic practices in the ancient world.

Formal diplomatic practices between state entities in early modern Europe emerged in Italy where resident embassies had developed by the 1450s. The Florentine political philosopher

BOX 9.1   KEY QUOTE

Kautilya on an Ancient Principle of Diplomacy

Messengers are the mouth-pieces of kings . . . hence messengers who, in the face of weapons raised against them, have to express their mission as exactly as they are entrusted with do not . . . deserve death.

(Shamasastry, n.d.: p. 41)

BOX 9.2 KEY QUOTE

Ermolao Barbaro on the First Duty of an Ambassador

The first duty of an ambassador is exactly the same as any other servant of a government, and that is, to do, say, advise, and think whatever may best serve the preservation and aggrandisement of his own state.

(Ermolao Barbaro (1454–93), Venetian noble, scholar, and ambassador at Naples and Rome, quoted in Langhorne, 2000: p. 35)

Niccolò Machiavelli, discussed in Chapter 3, was among the most experienced diplomats of his time as well as one of the best-known commentators on statecraft. The prime responsibility of an ambassador as a servant of the state was well understood by this time, as indicated by an oft-cited observation dating from the late fifteenth century (see Box 9.2).

The practice of maintaining embassies spread to other parts of Europe where, in due course, they became part and parcel of the sovereign state system (Mattingley, 1955: p. 10). In seventeenth-century France, the administrative machinery for managing foreign policy took on a more advanced form under the guidance of Cardinal de Richelieu (1585–1642) who implemented a system in which information flowed continuously both in and out of Paris, complemented by a method of record-keeping together with a unified and controlled system of management (Langhorne, 2000: p. 37).

Another significant development was the consolidation of the notion of *raison d'état* (**reason of state**). This expressed the idea that the state amounted to more than its ruler and the expression of his—or occasionally her—wishes (Craig and George, 1990: p. 5). The term became associated with realist ideas about *Machtpolitik* (**power politics**) which also implied the irrelevance of morality in the conduct of relations between states. In realist terms, *raison d'état* requires a statecraft attuned to the inevitability of conflict rather than one seeking justice and perpetual peace. It follows that, however much we might agree that these are highly desirable political goods, the *reality* is that peace and justice in the international sphere remain subordinate to the main business of diplomacy, statecraft, and foreign policy, which is the preservation of the state and the advancement of its interests through whatever means it is prudent to employ.

Raison d'état has been largely absorbed into the notion of **national interest** which is the more acceptable face of power politics in the contemporary period. Liberals and others concerned with the promotion of a more ethical approach to global politics, however, would not find 'national interest' cast in amoral terms acceptable. There is now much discussion of 'normative power', a quality attributed to the EU which proponents of the concept say has been developed precisely in order to escape 'great power mentality' (Manners, 2006: p. 183; see also Violakis, 2018).

In the wake of the Napoleonic wars, Europe achieved a relatively stable **balance of power** system, initially through the Congress of Vienna (1814–15), discussed in Chapters 2 and 8, at which the great powers were represented mainly by ambassadors and their diplomatic aides. As we have seen, they agreed to establish the **Concert of Europe**, an attempt to institute a formal structure for conducting relations between states. Diplomacy had previously consisted mainly in the representation of the interests of one sovereign state vis-à-vis another (bilateralism), and there was no mechanism for the cooperative management

FIGURE 9.1 **Illustration of the Congress of Vienna** Morphart Creation/Shutterstock.com

of state relations more generally. Thus in the Concert system we find the first glimmerings of the multilateralism that came to underpin the League of Nations and the UN.

The Concert system declined over the next half-century due at least partly to the rise of **nationalism** which became the principal vehicle of Europe's devastation in the next century. The years 1914–18 and 1939–45 can scarcely go down in the annals of history as bearing testimony to the capacity of European diplomacy and statecraft to ensure greater peace and stability, or as providing an exemplar of civilized behaviour. Nonetheless, the basic institutions of diplomacy and statecraft in Europe remained integral to the sovereign state system, and were carried along with the subsequent global spread of that system in the post-Second World War period. The 1961 Vienna Convention on Diplomatic Relations, which entered into force in April 1964, finally codified in international law well-established rules of diplomacy that all states observe today (for the full document see http://legal.un.org/ilc/texts/instruments/english/conventions/9_1_1961.pdf.).

KEY POINTS

- Diplomacy and statecraft have been a feature of relations between political communities from the earliest times, appearing in various forms in different parts of the world.

- Traditional views of diplomacy and statecraft in international relations incorporate elements of realist thought such as reason of state and power politics.

- Contemporary diplomatic methods developed largely within the modern European state system and were codified in international law through the 1961 Vienna Convention on Diplomatic Relations.

DIPLOMACY IN CONTEMPORARY GLOBAL POLITICS

Contemporary diplomatic processes cover virtually all aspects of a state's external or foreign relations from trade and aid to negotiations about territorial borders, international treaties of all kinds, the implementation of international law, the imposition of sanctions, the mediation of hostilities, boundary disputes, framework agreements on environmental protection and climate change, and so on. Diplomacy is not identical to foreign policy but is rather a means (although not the only means) by which foreign policy is carried out. Furthermore, diplomacy now extends beyond the pursuit of any given state's own foreign policy objectives, encompassing activities from third-party peace negotiations to earth summits which have seen extensive multilateral diplomatic activity involving a variety of actors, including numerous NGOs. We have also seen the emergence of 'track two diplomacy', otherwise known as 'backchannel diplomacy', which refers to informal or unofficial diplomatic efforts, sometimes undertaken by private citizens, business people, peace activists, religious figures, or NGOs as well as state actors. It is most commonly deployed in peace negotiations; for example, in preparing the ground for more formal talks by persuading parties in conflict to even agree to negotiate (see Jones, 2015). All these forms, and others, mean that diplomacy in the contemporary period is comprised of a complex of diverse and overlapping activities in pursuit of various goals.

Embassies, Consulates, and Professional Diplomatic Services

The routine business of external affairs is carried out by professional diplomatic services usually located within foreign ministries. In Britain, external affairs are conducted by the Foreign, Commonwealth and Development Office (FCDO) while in the US they are a function of the Department of State. Other countries may have a Department of Foreign Affairs and Trade (Australia), or a Ministry of Foreign Affairs with a separate ministry for trade and related matters (Japan). Whatever they are called, such departments run diplomatic missions, usually in the form of permanent embassies around the world. Within the Commonwealth, these are called High Commissions—a legacy of Britain's imperial system. Many small, relatively poor states, however, face particular problems in maintaining diplomatic missions abroad due to the high cost of premises and personnel, making it difficult for them to participate on equal terms. As in other spheres, the greater the resources, the greater the clout.

Embassies and consulates (the latter are generally subsidiary to a main embassy) carry out a range of functions from overseeing trade relations, liaising on military matters where there is an alliance with the host country, promoting cultural relations, issuing visas to prospective business people, immigrants, students or tourists, assisting their own nationals when problems arise, and other consular services. But embassies have, as often as not, also served as bases for intelligence gathering or, to put it more plainly, spying. Where an embassy lists a number of their personnel as 'cultural attachés', one or more are possibly spies. Such personnel may attempt to gather classified information about the host country, or they may in fact operate a surveillance regime focusing on their own nationals within the host country, as we see shortly.

The territory or building occupied by an embassy in a foreign country is sometimes regarded, mistakenly, as being effectively 'home soil' of the country concerned, with the same sovereign rights. Article 22 of the Vienna Convention on Diplomatic Relations deals with the inviolability of diplomatic missions, but this does not amount to awarding the premises they occupy the status of sovereign territory. The Article, however, prohibits agents of the receiving state from entering diplomatic premises, except with the consent of the head of the mission. It further provides that the premises of the mission, their furnishings, and any other property within it, as well as the means of transport of the mission, shall be immune from search, requisition, attachment, or execution The state in which a mission is located is also responsible for taking all appropriate measures to protect the premises of the mission.

Although it is not common practice for anyone claiming asylum to be able to do so at an embassy, and many embassies explicitly prohibit it, it has occurred. The best known case is that of Julian Assange, founder of Wikileaks—as discussed later in this chapter. Another recent incident on the premises of a diplomatic mission concerns the Saudi Arabian consulate in Istanbul, Turkey, where a dissident Saudi journalist, Jamal Khashoggi, was murdered in October 2018. After first denying he had been killed there, Saudi authorities, when confronted with the evidence, blamed it on a rogue intelligence agent. Other observers, including the US Central Intelligence Agency (CIA), believe it was on the orders of Saudi Crown Prince Mohammed bin Salman (otherwise known as MBS), who is the heir apparent to the Saudi crown and has a reputation for ruthless crackdowns on any critics.

In a quite separate account of the activities of the Saudi Arabian embassy in London, a long-time observer of diplomatic practices highlights the efforts of officials there to spy on Saudi students studying in the UK, making a useful case study of the link between a diplomatic presence and surveillance of their own nationals rather than of their host country (Box 9.3). The Saudis, however, are not the only ones to use their diplomatic missions abroad to monitor their students. China also keeps a close eye on student activity in the UK, the US, and Australia not only through embassy staff but also through 'loyal' Chinese students on university campuses who report on dissident activity (see Corr, 2017).

Summit Diplomacy

A relatively recent development in diplomatic practice is 'summit diplomacy', a phrase coined by Winston Churchill in the early **Cold War** period to describe top-level negotiations between key leaders. But it is only in the recent past that heads of government have met more regularly to discuss or negotiate directly (Melissen, 2003: p. 4). Summit diplomacy itself ranges from ad hoc bilateral summits, such as the summits between President Trump and North Korea's Kim Jong-un on the latter's nuclear weapons programme, to global multilateral summits which include not only heads of government and leading UN figures but in many cases parallel meetings for NGOs as well.

Among the largest have been the earth summits organized by the UN. Regional or inter-regional summits are now also part and parcel of the regular international scene, with organizations such the Asia-Pacific Economic Cooperation (APEC) forum, the Organization of American States (OAS), and the Asia-Europe Meeting process (ASEM) becoming solidly institutionalized. The Commonwealth, with fifty-four members, has reinvented itself as something of a diplomatic summit club in the postcolonial period, with the Commonwealth Heads of Government Meeting (CHOGM) being held every two years to discuss matters of mutual interest and concern, and formulate policies and initiatives at the highest level. Sometimes, these gatherings are seen as little more than

BOX 9.3 CASE STUDY

The London Embassy with Thirteen Cultural Attachés

The London embassy of Saudi Arabia has the third largest number of staff of any in the capital, exceeded only by China and the US. Of these, thirteen are cultural attachés—more than any other embassy.

What do all of these Saudi cultural attachés do? Helpfully, the section of which they are members, the 'Diplomatic Office of the Cultural Bureau' (aka Saudi Arabian Cultural Bureau or SACB), makes it clear that their core functions are exclusively concerned with university-level educational relationships.

In so far as this involves Saudi students studying at British universities, of which there are over 8,000 (as of 2018), it is also apparent that the SACB holds them in an iron grip. It is one thing to require reports at the end of every semester on their progress, and to urge them to participate in cultural activities that do not conflict with Islamic faith and Saudi traditions. But the Bureau's stated function also includes the supervision and monitoring of the activities of Saudi students and their club. No wonder Saudi Arabia's cultural attachés represent around a quarter of all diplomatic officers of this class in the British capital.

A report on the Saudi embassy in Washington also indicates that it has been intimidating Saudi students studying in the United States who voice criticisms of their government; for example, by severing grants, refusing to renew passports, and urging them to return home to an unknown fate.

(edited extract from Berridge, 2018)

The job of a Saudi cultural attaché is clearly not to promote what we may think of as 'culture' in the sense of art, music, literature, food, etc., which is the more conventional understanding associated with the role. Rather, the surveillance role that Saudi cultural attachés appear to perform in the UK is a reflection of a political culture steeped in **authoritarianism**, seeking to exert strict control over its own nationals while they are studying abroad in a **liberal democracy**. This is not exactly a 'diplomatic' activity as we would normally understand it. The case therefore illustrates another use to which the diplomatic infrastructure provided by embassies can be put.

opportunities for international socializing at the highest level. The acronym APEC, for example, has been recast as 'A Perfect Excuse for a Chat'. But one should never underestimate the value of high-level diplomatic socialization on a face-to-face basis and its role in building **international society**.

Culture and Diplomacy

Although diplomacy is governed by a universal set of rules, variations in diplomatic styles are often said to reflect local cultural or other differences. The Association of Southeast Asian Nations (ASEAN), for example, has promoted the 'ASEAN Way' as a distinctive style of regional diplomacy. Its emphasis on consensus decision-making and an almost absolute commitment to non-interference in the internal affairs of member states is said to differ from a 'Western' style of diplomacy. Certainly, the member states of the EU have given considerably less weight to state **sovereignty** in the interests of political and economic integration. But 'the West' is not a coherent cultural entity. The diplomatic style of the EU, for instance, has been contrasted very strongly with the hawkish approach evinced by the US under the administration of George W. Bush, although Obama subsequently adopted a less aggressive stance while diplomacy under the Trump administration followed no set path. It remains to be seen how the Biden administration fares.

Personal Diplomacy

Analysis of Trump's diplomatic style raises the issue of high-level 'personal diplomacy' which has developed over the years since the Second World War, enabled by the rapid development of transport and communications technologies. Box 9.4 both provides a brief overview of the personal diplomacy styles of US presidents, including a critical commentary on President Trump's approach, and raises some points for debate.

BOX 9.4 KEY DEBATE

Opportunities and Risk in Personal Diplomacy

History provides us with many examples of the value of leader-to-leader diplomacy. Roosevelt's connection with British Prime Minister Winston Churchill played a central role in the Allied victory during the Second World War. The bond between Jimmy Carter and Egyptian President Anwar Sadat was crucial to Egyptian–Israeli peace. And Ronald Reagan and Mikhail Gorbachev's relationship was key to the end of the Cold War. Presidents themselves have recognized the importance of leader-to-leader diplomacy.

But there are risks as well. Leaders don't always get along. Miscalculation and tension may be as likely as understanding and cooperation. In 1961, US–Soviet relations went from bad to worse after John F. Kennedy and Soviet Premier Nikita Khrushchev met. Khrushchev came away thinking Kennedy was weak and inexperienced. The following year, Khrushchev placed nuclear missiles in

FIGURE 9.2 President of the United States of America George W. Bush and President of Russia Vladimir Putin in Bratislava, Slovakia, 2005 Northfoto/Shutterstock.com

Cuba capable of reaching almost every corner of the continental United States. George W. Bush thought he could trust Russian leader Vladimir Putin because 'he looked the man in the eye'. But by the end of his presidency, it was clear that Bush had seriously misjudged the Russian leader.

In his first two years in office, Trump showed himself both following in his predecessors' personal diplomacy footsteps but also breaking from established norms. After becoming president, he continued to promote his personal relationships with world leaders. This is normal presidential behaviour. Where Trump differed from his predecessors is in the relationships he promoted and in his approach to personal diplomacy. Most striking was his praise of dictators. None have so publicly embraced brutal authoritarians such as Kim Jong-un, Vladimir Putin, and Saudi Crown Prince Mohammed bin Salman. This has a cost. Personal diplomacy is a form of theatre. It sends signals to domestic and international audiences. The leaders a president decides to meet with, praise, or attack is a statement of American values and policy. By effusively embracing dictators, Trump's personal diplomacy was at odds with traditional American foreign policy, and critics argued that this behaviour emboldens dictators.   (Edited extract from Chavez, 2019)

This analysis raises some interesting questions and debating points:

1 What risks are entailed in the conduct of personal diplomacy?

2 To what extent should leaders rely on their professional diplomatic and foreign policy personnel or trust their own intuitions?

3 To what extent did Trump's personal diplomatic style represent a departure from that of previous US presidents?

Science Diplomacy

Another important feature of the global diplomatic and foreign policy landscape involves science and, in particular, the importance of global scientific cooperation in a number of key issue areas—the environment, climate change, and public health being among the most prominent in the present period. The UN and its agencies have been especially active over the last few decades in promoting such cooperation under the rubric of environmental security, as discussed in Chapter 6. Environmental issues in general, and climate change in particular, will be examined in much more detail in Chapter 11. Here we may note that the urgency of such issues has seen a form of science diplomacy emerge to promote scientific collaboration at a global level. It is also worth noting that the internationalization of higher education and research, which has evolved so rapidly over the last two decades or so and has seen literally millions of students in all disciplines pursue studies abroad, has contributed much to the network of relations on which global scientific cooperation depends at its most basic level.

Science diplomacy also aims to promote understanding of the importance of evidence-based knowledge—a purpose made all the more important in a world in which conspiracy theories and fake news is disseminated so rapidly and to audiences in every corner of the globe, as discussed in Chapter 1. Science diplomacy is therefore often conducted along the lines of public diplomacy, although in this instance good science diplomacy is very far from propaganda (despite what some conspiracy theorists might claim).

In light of the global COVID-19 pandemic, there has obviously been much discussion about the importance of scientific and medical expertise along with the apparent lack of respect for scientific guidance. According to one report this factor, rather than weaknesses in international preparedness, is perhaps the most significant in the spread of COVID-19. 'In far too many places, science is either not trusted, not listened to, or not listened to quickly enough' (Cohen, 2020). This highlights both the vital role science diplomacy can play as well as the fact that it still has a long way to go in convincing relevant audiences when a global health threat really does need to be *securitized*.

→ See **Chapter 6** for a discussion of securitization theory.

> **KEY POINTS**
>
> - Contemporary diplomatic practice involves different actors including professional diplomatic services, special envoys, heads of government, the UN, NGOs, and regional bodies such as the EU and ASEAN. It may also involve a range of non-state actors in 'track-two diplomacy'.
> - Different countries and/or regions are said to possess certain diplomatic styles or orientations, although whether this is due to intrinsic cultural differences is a matter of debate. There were no 'intrinsic cultural differences' between US President Trump and his predecessors but his style was very different due to his unique personality.
> - Summit diplomacy and personal diplomacy have evolved since the end of the Second World War to become a regular feature of the global political landscape.
> - Science diplomacy has emerged as key to dealing with global threats such as climate change and pandemics.

COLD WAR DIPLOMACY

The study of Cold War diplomatic history is an extensive field dealing with a host of incidents, issues, and crises. These range from the expulsion of diplomats for alleged spying to major crises such as the blockade of West Berlin by the Soviets in 1948–49, and the Cuban missile crisis of 1962, the latter triggered when the Soviets attempted to deploy nuclear warheads in Cuba. The most serious crises were defused by diplomatic means, thus averting major overt conflict. It is commonly believed that the Cuban missile crisis was the closest the world has ever come to 'hot' nuclear warfare, and that the crisis was resolved largely because US President Kennedy and Soviet Premier Khrushchev both recognized that the consequences would be disastrous. Strategic thinking subsequently produced a theory of **deterrence** known as 'mutually assured destruction' (MAD) which assumed that the possession of incredibly destructive weapons served as the key to preventive strategy. This remains an essential aspect of US foreign and security policy.

Subsequent work on 'nuclear diplomacy' in the Cold War period has sought to answer the question: did the possession of nuclear weapons by both sides actually prevent a Third World War (Gaddis et al., 1999)? There is no clear-cut answer to this question, but what is certain is that, without systems of diplomacy operating, however clumsy they may have seemed at times, the Cold War may well have become the 'hottest' ever. Where diplomacy often did fail, however, was in relation to the Global South which bore the brunt of overt conflict conducted via conventional weaponry during the Cold War period.

Cold War diplomacy also introduced the term 'détente'—French for 'relaxation of tensions'—into the vocabulary of global politics. This applied to a period between 1969 and 1979 when tensions eased due to certain economic and geopolitical circumstances including the fiasco of the Vietnam War (from the US point of view), the souring of Soviet–Chinese relations accompanied by shifting attitudes towards China in the West, the huge cost of the arms race, and the desire to attend more to domestic matters.

Nuclear Diplomacy

The factors sketched above led to important summit meetings which resulted in the all-important Nuclear Non-Proliferation Treaty (NPT) which opened for signature in 1968. It was subsequently extended indefinitely and currently has 189 state parties as signatories, including five nuclear-weapon states—the US, France, the UK, Russia, and China—which are also the five permanent members of the UN Security Council. India, Pakistan, and North Korea—all known to possess nuclear weapons, plus Israel which does not publicly admit to its nuclear weapons—are not signatories.

The safeguards system set up by the NPT is administered by the International Atomic Energy Agency (IAEA) which conducts technical and safety reviews on an ongoing basis. One particularly noteworthy case it has dealt with concerns Iran—obviously a post-Cold War case but one which reflects its legacies. From around 2002, the IAEA began to express considerable concern over Iran's nuclear ambitions. Iran is a signatory to the NPT but is widely believed to have been developing a nuclear weapons programme under the cover of nuclear energy facilities. After more than a decade of sanctions, Iran agreed to a Joint Plan of Comprehensive Action (negotiated with the US, the UK, France, Russia, China, and Germany) in 2015 to limit its nuclear capacity in exchange for sanctions relief. The US under the Trump administration withdrew from the agreement in 2018 and reimposed sanctions, saying that the agreement was defective. There is no evidence, however, to point to any cheating behaviour on the part of Iran and the other countries remain party to the agreement (see https://www.nti.org/learn/countries/iran).

The NPT was complemented by other treaties and agreements including the Strategic Arms Limitation Treaty (SALT) dealing with a range of matters concerning missile deployment. The US under Reagan, however, withdrew from SALT and adopted a more confrontational approach which saw the end of détente. Nonetheless, the practices and procedures put in place during the Cold War continue as vital elements of contemporary diplomacy surrounding nuclear energy and weaponry, chemical and biological weapons, and the full range of conventional weapons from weapons of mass destruction to small arms and light weapons, land mines, and so on.

Continuities from Cold War Politics and Diplomacy

Other aspects of Cold War politics and diplomacy are familiar to us through popular culture, often in the form of fiction and cinema. Although the James Bond genre has been thoroughly reinvented for the post-Cold War world, its Cold War origins are unmistakable in its central theme of spying, an activity that developed close associations with Cold War diplomacy. Real-life dramas featured throughout the Cold War as intelligence gathering by both sides deployed almost any means available. And no better on-the-ground facilities existed than embassies and their diplomatic staff. A common feature of Cold War diplomacy was therefore the expulsion of embassy staff for alleged spying offences.

Post-Cold War episodes include the expulsion in July 2007 of four Russian diplomats from the UK following the alleged murder by radioactive isotope poisoning of former Russian agent, Alexander Litvinenko, who had become a UK citizen. Moscow's immediate response to the expulsion was a declaration of outrage and denial, followed by the summoning of the British ambassador in Moscow to the Russian foreign office, and then the 'tit-for-tat' expulsion of four British diplomats. A similar pattern was repeated following the March 2018 poisoning of the Skripals in Salisbury in the UK, mentioned in Chapter 6. The evidence points to the use of a deadly nerve agent called Novichok, known to have been developed in Russia, and the presence of Russian state agents in Salisbury at the time of the poisoning. In subsequent developments the UK expelled twenty-three Russian diplomats, following which Russia expelled the same number, and closed down British Council operations in Russia as well. Various of the UK's Western allies, convinced that the blame lay squarely with the Russian state, also responded with diplomatic sanctions. The symbolism and predictability of diplomatic gamesmanship, however, may be read as part and parcel of a system of structured interactions in which countries can express deep dissatisfaction with each other while confining it to a manageable arena.

> **KEY POINTS**
>
> - The Cold War was marked by various crises in which diplomacy played a key role in preventing what may have been a Third World War.
>
> - Cold War diplomacy saw the development of a system of treaties and conventions which continue to play an important role in the ongoing attempt to limit the production and distribution of a wide range of weapons.
>
> - Cold War continuities have been evident in certain diplomatic dramas involving Russia. These also illustrate, among other things, the extent to which diplomacy is at least partly a stage-managed performance albeit with very serious underpinnings.

PUBLIC DIPLOMACY AND SOFT POWER

Public diplomacy refers primarily to the ways in which governments attempt to influence public opinion abroad by utilizing the cultural power of ideas. Public diplomacy is implicated in the notion of 'soft power' formulated by the American liberal academic, Joseph Nye, who defines this form of power in terms of the ability to achieve one's end without the use of force or even coercion, effectively by winning 'hearts and minds' (see Box 9.5). Interestingly, this has some resonances with Antonio Gramsci's notion of cultural power and the way in which it supports **hegemony**, as discussed in Chapter 4.

Modes of Public Diplomacy

The two most prominent vehicles of public diplomacy in the UK are the British Council, which promotes British education and culture through offices around the world (see https://www.britishcouncil.org/), and the BBC World Service, which provides news and

> **BOX 9.5 KEY CONCEPT**
>
> 'Soft Power'
>
> [Soft power] is the ability to get what you want through attraction rather than coercion or payments. It arises from the attractiveness of a country's culture, political ideals, and policies. . . . When you can get others to admire your ideals and to want what you want, you do not have to spend as much on sticks and carrots to move them in your direction. Seduction is always more effective than coercion, and many values like democracy, human rights, and individual opportunity are deeply seductive . . . But attraction can turn to repulsion if we act in an arrogant manner and destroy the real message of deeper values.
>
> (Nye, 2004: p. x)

analysis in twenty-seven languages (see www.bbc.co.uk/news/world_radio_and_tv). Both receive funding from the FCDO, although both claim to enjoy substantial autonomy. The US State Department has a dedicated Under Secretary for Public Diplomacy and Public Affairs whose mission is 'to support the achievement of US foreign policy goals and objectives, advance national interests, and enhance national security by informing and influencing foreign publics and by expanding and strengthening the relationship between the people and government of the United States and citizens of the rest of the world' (www.state.gov/r). Broadcasting is also a major arm of public diplomacy with Voice of America (VOA), funded by Congress and administered by the US Agency for Global Media (USAGM) which oversees all non-military international broadcasting, reaching an estimated weekly global audience of 275 million with news, information, and cultural programming utilizing the Internet, mobile and social media, radio, and television (see https://www.insidevoa.com/).

As emerging powers, both India and China have also begun to engage in public diplomacy measures, although China has been far more proactive in raising its international profile over the last thirty years or so. This has been all the more important for a country with a poor human rights record and international image problems, especially following the Tiananmen Square massacre in 1989 when tanks confronted unarmed pro-democracy protestors. This incident left lasting impressions on a significant global audience through extensive media coverage.

To boost its image internationally, China in 2004 embarked on a project of developing 'Confucius Institutes' around the world. Modelled partly on the British Council, France's Alliance Française, and Germany's Goethe-Institut, these have been located mainly in established universities and, along with numerous 'Confucius classrooms' in schools, aim to promote learning of Chinese language and culture. As of 2019 there were 182 Institutes in European universities (including 29 in the UK alone), 160 in the US, 126 in Asia, 59 in Africa, and 29 in Oceania. Confucius classrooms in Europe and the US number around 650 (see http://english.hanban.org/node_10971.htm). A longer-standing institution, China Radio International, has been broadcasting since the 1940s. Its English broadcasting platform can (potentially) reach an audience of nearly 3 billion (see http://english.cri.cn/7146/2013/10/30/2203s795082.htm).

In recent years, concerns have been expressed about Confucius Institutes being used to promote the specific interests of the Chinese Communist Party (CCP) and to wield influence over such issues as Taiwan, Tibet, and China's record on human rights more generally. Accusations of espionage have also been made. Reporting on an FBI probe into their activities on American campuses, one media outlet opined that they had become centres for 'spreading pro-China propaganda and influence activities, including organizing Chinese communist student groups that challenge human rights activists and others' (https://www.washingtontimes.com/news/2018/feb/14/inside-the-ring-fbi-investigating-confucius-instit/).

Similar concerns have been expressed in Australia and the UK where the Institutes have also been branded by critics as 'Trojan horses' and a means by which the CCP can wield influence, not to mention maintaining, like Saudi Arabia, a watchful eye over its own students studying on those campuses and compromising freedom of expression, a value that is held very strongly in most Western universities and which is seen as threatened by authoritarian influences. Conversely, authoritarian governments often regard Western ideas of freedom of expression (along with the values of liberal democracy and human rights more generally) as a threat to their own values.

Cultural Diplomacy

The issue of advancing public diplomacy through cultural means, as exemplified by the provision of language instruction and accompanying cultural education, is often carried on under the specific label of 'cultural diplomacy' which relates to concepts of soft power. Cultural diplomacy, which can be practised by governments, the private sector and/or civil society, has been described as encompassing actions which are 'based on and utilize the exchange of ideas, values, traditions and other aspects of culture or identity, whether to strengthen relationships, enhance socio-cultural cooperation, promote national interests and beyond' (http://www.culturaldiplomacy.org/index.php?en_culturaldiplomacy). This rather bland description should be read together with a more clearly instrumental assessment of the value of cultural diplomacy set out in a 2005 US State Department report:

> [It] is in our cultural activities that a nation's idea of itself is best represented. And cultural diplomacy can enhance our national security in subtle, wide-ranging, and sustainable ways. Indeed, history may record that America's cultural riches played no less a role than military action in shaping our international leadership, including the war on terror. For the values embedded in our artistic and intellectual traditions form a bulwark against the forces of darkness.
>
> (Quoted in Ang, Isar, and Mar, 2016: p. 4)

New Public Diplomacy

Although public diplomacy is rarely a decisive factor in the success or otherwise of particular foreign policy initiatives, it functions as an important accessory service, especially in the contemporary period in which media and telecommunications have changed so radically. It has therefore been suggested that the 'new public diplomacy' of the contemporary period is shifting the focus from indirectly influencing other governments, which is essentially still a state-to-state interaction, to shaping the attitudes of other societies in a more direct state-to-society interaction (Henriksen, 2006: p. 1). It is interesting to note the extent to which President Obama started to use new social media as a tool of new public diplomacy. Concerted efforts were made to ensure that a major 'address to the Muslim World', delivered at Cairo University in June 2009, reached as large an audience as possible

FIGURE 9.3 **President of the United States of America Barack Obama at Cairo University in Cairo, Egypt, 2009** Official White House Photo by Pete Souza

by translating it into Arabic, Persian, Urdu, and around a dozen other languages and disseminating it through Twitter, Facebook, Myspace, YouTube, and other social networking sites as well as regular media outlets (Zeleny, 2009).

While on the subject of social media and new forms of public diplomacy, we must also consider briefly the phenomenon of Trump's 'Twitter diplomacy', which provoked much commentary during his tenure in office. One media article first described the concerns provoked by Trump's attachment to thinking out loud through Twitter, and the way in which he went against all the protocols of the formal diplomatic establishments, 'which regard such heedless commentary as, first, ill-advised in the extreme and, second, plain crass'. On the other hand, the article suggested that we may have been witnessing the end of spin and, if so, good riddance. 'Spin, and the degradation of language it entailed, is a large part of the reason people distrust politicians. They do not like politicians using words in ways ordinary people would not use them. Perhaps it takes the recklessness of Trump to yank language, politics and people back on to the same page, opening the way for a plain-speaking in public life that is less risky and rude than his is, but equally direct' (Dejevsky, 2017).

Public Diplomacy or Propaganda?

In more general terms, we may ask where one draws the line between public diplomacy (usually perceived as positive) and propaganda (usually seen as negative). Propaganda in a neutral sense simply denotes the dissemination or promotion of particular ideas and values. In a more instrumental sense, it implies an attempt to influence beliefs and behaviour rather than an objective presentation of 'the facts'. But it often conjures up images of deceit, distortion of facts, or even 'brainwashing'. Contemporary variations on the theme of propaganda include 'spin doctoring', otherwise known as 'news management', which has come in for much criticism over the last decade or so, as alluded to by the commentary on Trump's Twitter diplomacy which is, in some respects, almost the opposite of spin. Thus while his Twitter diplomacy can scarcely be described as carefully crafted, 'spin' is a conscious strategy of minimizing negative images of either politicians or political events while maximizing positive images (see Jowett and O'Donnell, 2006: pp. 2–3). And although spin is most often played to a domestic audience, it clearly has an important place in the international sphere of diplomacy and statecraft as well. All this suggests that public diplomacy and propaganda are simply different sides of the same coin.

KEY POINTS

- Public diplomacy involves attempts by governments to influence public opinion, mainly in other countries, by promoting positive images of one's country.

- Public diplomacy may be understood as an instrument of 'soft power' in contrast with the methods of power politics.

- Many acts of public diplomacy involve elements of propaganda and 'spin'.

FOREIGN POLICY

Foreign policy is generally framed in terms of the strategies that states, or rather those in control of a state at any given time, adopt in their dealings with other actors in the international system or with respect to relevant issues, such as the environment, aid, trade regimes, and so on. Foreign policy is often called a 'boundary activity' because it effectively straddles domestic and international spheres of politics and mediates between the two (Evans and Newnham, 1998: p. 179).

An important factor affecting a state's foreign policy behaviour is its regional or geopolitical location. For example, although much attention has recently focused on US behaviour in relation to the Middle East and East Asia, the history of US foreign policy shows how important the Americas have been for forging enduring patterns of foreign policy behaviour. It was in the context of the establishment of independent states in South America, and the attempts by European powers to maintain colonial systems there, that the US enunciated the 'Monroe doctrine', named after its initiator, President James Monroe. After safely concluding the purchase of Florida from Spain, Monroe announced to Congress in 1823 that the US would maintain an independent line on its interests in the Americas without reference to European interests. But this did not amount to a declaration of unqualified respect for the sovereignty of the new states emerging in the Americas.

The Monroe doctrine readily evolved into an attitude that political developments in the Americas were not just something that European powers should stay well out of. The US subsequently adopted policies of **unilateralism** and **interventionism** with respect to its southern neighbours as a matter of its own national interest. Subsequent interference by the US in the internal affairs of Central and South American states—including the undermining or outright overthrow of leftist governments, whether democratically elected or not—may be seen as the logical outcome of the doctrine. In 2005, a well-known right-wing Republican and religious conservative, Pat Robertson, actually declared publicly that the time had come to 'take out' (a euphemism for assassination) the elected socialist President of Venezuela, Hugo Chavez (see BBC, 2005). Robertson subsequently apologized, but the remark nonetheless reflected an important current of thinking among a sector of the US population.

US relations with its northern neighbour, Canada, stand in sharp contrast to those south of its border, despite strong elements of democratic socialism within Canadian politics—reflected in its universal health scheme and much stronger support for social welfare and public goods generally. One commentator suggests that many Canadians have a self-image as being less individualistic and more 'tolerant' and 'compassionate' than their US neighbours, while to the American left, Canada serves as a model of social democracy (Brooks, 2009: p. 45). More generally, Canada's foreign policy approach is often said to reflect its location in the global system as a 'middle power'—a status it shares with countries like Australia. Canadian and Australian approaches to diplomacy and foreign policy as middle powers, however, are not simply a function of their size and location in the global system but also of a particular self-image as 'good international citizens', strongly supporting multilateralism and international institutions like the UN, promoting the notion of a **rules-based international order**, and contributing substantially to activities such as peacekeeping.

The foreign policy of the UK has followed a different trajectory in its historical development, shaped both by the dynamics of the European region as well as by its historic colonizing enterprises. It has long been among the 'great powers' in global politics although there has been much talk about its declining status. Former Prime Minister David Cameron, however, insisted his country maintains the 'commercial, military and cultural clout to remain a significant global power' (quoted in Parker and Giles, 2010) while his successors, Theresa May and Boris Johnson, promoted the idea of 'Global Britain' in the wake of the Brexit vote, which means simply that the UK will need to work harder on its bilateral relations in the absence of the multilateral support network provided by the EU.

Special Relationships

The UK has been deeply enmeshed in 'special relationships' which have been decisive for its foreign policy. Although there are several 'special' relationships, such as the relationship with the former colonial empire through the Commonwealth as well as with the EU, *the* special relationship in recent years has been the Anglo-American relationship. This has ebbed and flowed according to whatever issues in global politics are salient and according to the personalities involved. The term 'special relationship' actually dates from the time when Roosevelt and Churchill forged a close personal alliance during the Second World War. Another strong personal alliance developed between Margaret Thatcher and Ronald Reagan during the latter stages of the Cold War, enhanced no doubt by their conservative dispositions and manifest in their shared loathing of communism.

The special relationship was put under intense scrutiny in the post-9/11 period when former Prime Minister Tony Blair offered unwavering support for George W. Bush in the GWOT and, especially, the invasion of Iraq which was cast by both parties as an integral part of that war even though there was no evidence linking Saddam with Al-Qaeda or the events of 9/11, as set out in Chapter 4. Blair came under much criticism at home for what seemed to be his uncritical endorsement of White House policy and support for a war that turned out to lack any justification. Early in his time in office, President Trump declared that the relationship had reached the 'highest level of special'. UK Prime Minister of the time, Theresa May, added that 'no two countries do more together to keep their people safe and prosperous'. But Trump was a little less than 'diplomatic' in saying, at the very same joint press conference with May, that Boris Johnson would also be a wonderful prime minister. 'I said he'll be a great prime minister. He's been very nice to me, he's been saying very good things about me as president. I think he thinks I'm doing a great job, I am doing a great job, that I can tell you, just in case you haven't noticed' (quoted in Walker, 2018).

Foreign Policy and Diplomacy in the Global South

If we look to other parts of the world, and especially the **Global South**, we may see very similar formal structures operating in terms of both diplomacy and foreign policy, but the challenges, concerns, and approaches may vary according to a range of historical, cultural, economic, and other factors. One will often find a particular emphasis on 'South–South' cooperation which may take place bilaterally as well as through regional and other multilateral forums, and cover a range of issues from trade to cultural exchanges. There are also efforts to enhance the profile of specific foreign policy approaches as situated in a more authentic cultural context. In South Africa, for example, an official White Paper makes reference to the country's liberation history and goes on to state that its evolving international engagement is based on two central tenets, namely, pan-Africanism and South–South solidarity. It therefore understands its national interest as being 'intrinsically linked to Africa's stability, unity, and prosperity'. There is a further specific reference to anti-colonialism in its foreign policy stance which accords with its liberation history and complements the emphasis on South–South relations (South Africa, 2011: p. 3).

South African foreign policy is also said to be guided by the values of Ubuntu—a word derived from a Bantu language that is understood as akin to a notion of shared humanity embracing positive values such as caring and kindness. It was popularized partly through the writings of Archbishop Desmond Tutu who, along with Nelson Mandela (1918–2013), was among the most prominent figures opposing apartheid in South Africa, which ended in 1993–94. More recently, Ubuntu has been used to frame both South African domestic and foreign policy approaches, at least at a rhetorical level, and is prominent in the White Paper mentioned above. In discussing the concept more critically, Qobo and Nyathi (2017) note first that foreign policies are, to a large extent, a projection of domestic values and policies. Thus the Ubuntu concept finds its way into the wider sphere of global politics where its values of pursuing 'common humanity, collaboration, cooperation and building partnership over conflict' chime with commonly accepted notions of 'good' politics.

As in many other cases, however, rhetoric is not always matched by performance either at home or abroad, and Ubuntu has been used to conceal corruption, especially under former President Jacob Zuma. Even so, the authors contend that Ubuntu remains necessary as a basis for a dialogue on exploring avenues for transformative change. 'This may mean renewal of both domestic and global institutions to better reflect the values associated with Ubuntu, and to facilitate a dialogue about the future of global governance' (ibid.).

FIGURE 9.4 **Archbishop Desmond Tutu in Cape Town, South Africa, 2011** © iStock/LightLock

The EU's Common Foreign and Security Policy

The EU as a foreign policy actor represents a significant departure from the traditional sovereign state model, although it is in Europe that the model was generated in the first place. The EU has been working to develop a Common Foreign and Security Policy (CFSP) in which is also embedded a European Security and Defence Policy (ESDP). A major factor contributing to the development of the CFSP/ESDP, and indeed to the consolidation of the European movement itself, was the end of the Cold War and the perceived need for coordination in regional affairs in the wake of the collapse of Soviet hegemony in Eastern Europe. Beyond the exigencies of these particular circumstances, it has also been suggested that the challenge for the European project was more fundamental: 'From its origins, the ideal or "vocation" of Europe has been to ensure peace between former warring European nation-states and to provide the conditions for geopolitical stability built on the foundations of a commitment to liberal democracy' (Dannreuther, 2004: pp. 1–2).

The CSFP was embedded in the 1993 Treaty on European Union (the Maastricht Treaty), subsequently refined in the 1999 Amsterdam Treaty and refined again in the Nice Treaty which came into effect in 2003, while the ESDP was given an operational capability in a 2001 meeting of the European Council. The CFSP's basic working profile is set out in Box 9.7.

These objectives clearly reflect a desire to export European political norms—especially in respect of human rights, democracy, and 'good governance'—to other parts of the world. The EU consciously projects itself as a qualitatively different kind of power in the international sphere—a 'normative power'—staking a claim 'to being a legitimate and thus a more effective international actor' (Farrell, 2005: p. 453). Further, while 'American unilateralism renews the legitimacy of power politics on the world stage, the normative approach in the European management of international relations sustains the relevance of the very notion of global governance' (ibid.). This illustrates once again the idea of soft power versus militarism and power politics more generally in achieving foreign policy objectives.

KEY POINTS

- Foreign policy refers to the strategies that governments adopt in their dealings with other actors in the international system.
- The foreign policy behaviour of states (and other actors) is influenced by size, capacity, geopolitical, and/or historical circumstances.
- Formerly colonized countries tend to place much emphasis on South–South cooperation as well as on the importance of local values.
- EU foreign policy is founded on a set of ideals which attempt to project 'normative power' and which is comparable in turn to 'soft power'.

DIPLOMACY AND FOREIGN POLICY AFTER WIKILEAKS

No account of diplomacy and foreign policy in the contemporary period would be complete without at least a brief account of Wikileaks. Launched in 2006, Wikileaks is self-described as a non-profit media organization providing 'an innovative, secure and anonymous way for independent sources around the world to leak information to our journalists' (https://wikileaks.org/About.html). By the end of 2010, Wikileaks had achieved extraordinary notoriety in global politics, due mainly to its release of classified material relating to the wars in Iraq and Afghanistan as well as the acquisition of more than 250,000 US diplomatic cables which it began releasing through a number of highly respected newspapers including the *Guardian*, the *New York Times*, *Le Monde*, *Der Spiegel*, and *El País*. In an editorial note accompanying the publication of some material from the confidential cables, the *New York Times* justified it on the basis that 'the documents serve an important public interest, illuminating the goals, successes, compromises and frustrations of American diplomacy in a way that other accounts cannot match' (*New York Times*, 2010).

Much of the documents' contents simply confirm what many already knew; for example, that the US administration believes—with good reason—that Russia is run like a 'mafia state'. Some documents are models of professional diplomatic reports providing frank, well-informed assessments of the situation in various countries. But more generally, Wikileaks has revealed the extent to which lies, deceit, and hypocrisy attend the pursuit of 'national interest' through diplomatic channels. And here the spotlight focuses squarely on the US. While it has engaged in a concerted campaign against Wikileaks for disseminating classified material, with some US figures even calling for the assassination of Julian Assange, the leaked material has revealed the extent to which the US is itself prepared to obtain intelligence illicitly (Lawson, 2011b).

A *Guardian* article also summarized aspects of a 'secret intelligence campaign targeted at the leadership of the UN' including the Secretary-General and the representatives of the other permanent Security Council members. One classified directive issued under Hillary Clinton's name in July 2009 sought forensic technical communications details relating to key UN officials, including passwords and personal encryption keys used in private and commercial networks for official communications as well as biometric information such as fingerprints and DNA. The article went on to note that a 1946 UN convention on privileges and immunities states, among other things, that the premises of the UN 'shall be inviolable' (Booth and Borger, 2010). The 1961 Vienna Convention on Diplomatic Relations also provides for the inviolability of a mission's premises, official documents, correspondence, and personnel (see United Nations, 1961).

Assange himself has paid a price for the leaks, having taken refuge in the Ecuadorian embassy in London between 2012 and 2019, following charges brought against him in Sweden for alleged sexual assault. Assange and supporters say these charges were trumped up and politically motivated, and opened up the possibility of him being extradited to the US on espionage charges.

In the meantime, Wikileaks also became implicated in the enquiry into alleged Russian interference in the US Presidential campaign. In January 2019, the *New York Times* claimed to have evidence of contact between at least seventeen Trump campaign officials and advisers, Wikileaks, and Russian nationals (Yourish and Buchanan, 2019) while another respected publication, *The Atlantic*, commented on collusion as 'highly likely', with Assange appearing to play an intermediate role (Graham, 2018).

In April 2019, Assange was eventually evicted from the Ecuadorian embassy in London and immediately arrested. He was jailed in the UK for evading his original bail conditions in 2012, and then faced extradition proceedings brought by the US with respect to at least eighteen charges including conspiring to hack into government computers and unlawfully disclosing classified information. These developments are themselves part and parcel of global diplomatic activity.

More generally, the 'feast of data' made available through Wikileaks has been described as an historian's dream and a diplomat's nightmare. 'Here, for all to see, are the confidences of friends, allies and rivals, garnished with American diplomats' frank, sometimes excoriating assessments of them' (Garton-Ash, 2010).

KEY POINTS

- Wikileaks has revealed the extent to which lies, deceit, and hypocrisy attend the pursuit of 'national interest' in diplomacy and foreign policy practice.
- State actors pursuing deceitful tactics would, if pressed, claim that they are essential to successful foreign policy.

CONCLUSION

Diplomacy implies peaceful or at least non-violent interactions between political actors and 'diplomatic solutions' are frequently contrasted with military ones. By the mid-twentieth century the traditional role of diplomacy was understood as a means of maintaining an international order in the interests of peace and stability (Butterfield, 1966: p. 190). The discussion of the various types of diplomacy further reinforces its image as a peaceful instrument of policy. But diplomacy is not always a process of negotiation between equals. States are not equal in their capacities or capabilities and stronger states are often in a superior bargaining position. Indeed, diplomacy can well be aggressive and coercive, as reflected in the phrase 'gunboat diplomacy' in which the threat of force accompanies negotiations.

Clausewitz famously proposed that war is simply 'the continuation of policy by other means' and a necessary instrument of foreign policy. But he also believed that if war had no specific, desirable political purpose, it was both stupid and wrong (Howard, 1966: p. 197). Diplomacy can certainly be accompanied by the proverbial sabre-rattling and shade into war. But diplomacy at its best is the very antithesis of war. It is a means by which conflicts and disagreements in the international sphere can be resolved peacefully via processes of negotiating, bargaining, and accommodation which spare all parties the prospect of death and destruction through direct violence. In the final analysis, foreign policies attuned to this end are much more likely to serve the national interest than the resort to the far cruder instruments of force.

KEY QUESTIONS

1   What distinguishes diplomacy and statecraft from other forms of political activity?

2   If states are no longer considered the only relevant actors in the international sphere, do they remain the most effective when it comes to diplomatic activity?

3   To what extent has diplomatic practice achieved uniformity throughout the international state system?

4   Are there genuinely different styles of diplomacy according to cultural factors or is the influence of culture in this sense sometimes exaggerated?

5   What role did deterrence play in 'nuclear diplomacy' during the Cold War?

6   Under what circumstances is summit diplomacy most effective?

7   What factors are likely to make personal diplomacy succeed or fail?

8   Is public diplomacy simply propaganda on an international scale?

9   To what extent has President Trump's 'Twitter diplomacy' represented a new phenomenon in US diplomacy and foreign policy?

10   What is the Monroe doctrine and how does it illustrate the historic importance of geopolitics in US foreign policy?

11   What is distinctive about South–South foreign relations?

12   Do you believe that the EU can be truly effective as a foreign policy actor in its own right?

13   What long-term impact is Wikileaks likely to have on diplomatic behaviour?

FURTHER READING

Berridge, G. R. (2015), *Diplomacy: Theory and Practice* (Basingstoke: Palgrave Macmillan, 5th edn).
   This text combines theoretical and historical perspectives on various styles and modes of diplomacy including discussion of key themes such as the art of negotiation, bilateral and multilateral diplomacy, summit diplomacy, and mediation. The author maintains a website on which he updates his work, which extends to many different aspects of diplomacy and diplomatic history. See https://grberridge.diplomacy.edu/.

Bjola, Corneliu and Markus Kornprobst (2018), *Understanding International Diplomacy: Theory, Practice and Ethics* (Abingdon: Routledge, 2nd edn).
   This up-to-date text sets out the major trends in the field of diplomacy together with a theoretical approach which understands diplomacy not as a collection of practices or a set of historical traditions

but rather as a form of institutionalized communication. Includes discussion of the Syrian and Ukraine crises as well as problems in the South China Sea.

Constantinou, Costas M., Pauline Kerr, and Paul Sharp (eds) (2016), *The Sage Handbook of Diplomacy* (Thousand Oaks, CA: Sage).
Another substantial edited collection with contributions on a variety of diplomatic activity from secret diplomacy, coercive diplomacy, and revolutionary diplomacy to celebrity diplomacy, sports diplomacy, and digital diplomacy.

Hill, Christopher (2016), *Foreign Policy in the Twenty-First Century* (London: Palgrave, 2nd edn).
Starting with definitions and general background, this book goes on to explore foreign policy issues, concepts, and approaches to the subject matter from a variety of perspectives.

Kerr, Pauline and Geoffrey Wiseman (eds) (2017), *Diplomacy in a Globalizing World* (Oxford: Oxford University Press).
The expert contributors to this edited volume of 23 chapters provide theoretical perspectives and historical background from a variety of Western and non-Western traditions as well as looking at contemporary issues and cases.

Shayam, Saran (2018), *How India Sees the World*: *Kautilya to the 21st Century* (New Delhi: Juggernaut Books).
Authored by a former Indian diplomat, this is a wide-ranging and very thoughtful book which provides both historical perspectives and contemporary insights on Indian statecraft with special reference to its neighbours in South Asia as well as China.

WEB LINKS

Below are web links for various foreign/external affairs departments around the world. The main pages, and various other pages within them, are examples of public diplomacy—the face they wish to show to the world. All websites listed are in English. Another website maintained by an Australian think tank provides additional sources of information on diplomacy. The last website is the Wikileaks site.

https://dfat.gov.au/pages/default.aspx: Australia's Department of Foreign Affairs and Trade
http://www.itamaraty.gov.br/en/: Brazil's Ministry of Foreign Affairs
https://www.international.gc.ca/international/index.aspx: Canada's Department of Foreign Affairs and International Trade (DFAIT)
http://www.dirco.gov.za/: South Africa's Department of International Relations and Cooperation
https://www.mfa.gov.cn/eng: China's Ministry of Foreign Affairs
https://eeas.europa.eu/diplomatic-network/foreign-affairs-council_en: EU Foreign Council website
https://www.mea.gov.in/: India's Ministry of External Affairs
https://www.mofa.go.jp: Japan's Ministry of Foreign Affairs
https://www.mofa.gov.sa/sites/mofaen/pages/default.aspx: Saudi Arabia's Ministry of Foreign Affairs
https://www.gov.uk/government/organisations/foreign-commonwealth-development-office: UK Foreign, Commonwealth and Development Office (FCDO)
https://www.state.gov: US Department of State
https://globaldiplomacyindex.lowyinstitute.org/: The 2019 Lowy Institute Global Diplomacy Index. Covering sixty-one countries and territories, the Index offers a comprehensive comparison of the world's most significant diplomatic networks across three years—2016, 2017, and 2019
https://wikileaks.org/: The website of Wikileaks, one of the most reviled websites in the world (at least by governments), but containing a wealth of diplomatic documents for analysis by students of global politics

 For additional material and resources please visit the **online resources** at: www.oup.com/he/lawson1e.

10

GLOBAL POLITICAL ECONOMY

Reader's Guide

In providing an overview of the field of Global Political Economy (GPE)—also known as International Political Economy (IPE)—this chapter builds on themes introduced in previous sections, including connections with theories of global politics. Once again, these are discussed from a historical perspective to enable a better appreciation of how ideas, practices, and institutions develop and interact over time. And once again, it will be seen that these theories arose substantially within a European context, although the extent to which they may be applied uncritically to issues of political economy in all parts of the globe must be questioned. Significant issues for GPE include trade, labour, the interaction of states and markets, the nexus between wealth and power, and the problems of development and underdevelopment in the global economy, taking partic-ular account of the North/South divide. The final section discusses the twin phen-ena of globalization and regionalization and the way in which these are shapi global economy and challenging the traditional role of the state. An underlyir of the chapter is the link between economic and political power.

THE STUDY OF GLOBAL POLITICAL ECONOMY

The study of politics has long been entwined with economic issues, as reflected in the specialist field of political economy, a term which suggests the merging of two significant aspects of social life and which can be traced as far back at least as the moral philosopher Adam Smith (1723–90), who produced an early account of modern industrial society. Since then, the very meaning of political economy has been contested. A recent commentary notes that, for Smith, political economy denoted 'the science of managing a nation's resources so as to generate wealth', while for Karl Marx (1818–83) it was concerned with 'how the ownership of the means of production influenced historic processes' (Weingast and Whitman, 2006: p. 3). In the twentieth century it was sometimes taken simply as the interrelationship between economics and politics on the one hand, or a particular methodological approach on the other (ibid.). For present purposes, political economy is taken to be a field of study which lies at the intersection of politics and economics and which is concerned primarily, although not exclusively, with the relationship between states and markets. GPE attempts to make sense of the state/market nexus and the dynamic complex of actors, issues, and processes that are involved on a global scale (see Smith, El-Anis, and Farrands, 2017: p. 3).

The addition of the word 'global' or 'international' to 'political economy' scarcely occurred before the 1970s and, when it did so, it was partly in conjunction with the rise of both **neoliberalism** and **neorealism** in the theorization of global politics. This is not to suggest that those working in political economy had neglected the global dimensions of the field, but rather to say that scholars of traditional international relations on the one hand, and economists on the other, had evinced little interest in each other's work. A significant impetus in the development of GPE was provided by a seminal article published in 1970 by Susan Strange who pointed out that the reciprocal ignorance exhibited by the two disciplines impoverished efforts in both fields to understand the world. IR scholars, she said, had been far too preoccupied with the political and strategic relations between governments, to the exclusion of almost everything else (Strange, 1970: pp. 304–15). The field has grown enormously since then, reflecting not only increased academic awareness of its importance but also the substantial changes in the global sphere in that period.

As with politics more generally then, GPE cannot confine itself simply to the structural study of institutions or organizations but must also take account of the norms, values, and interests that they reflect. Any arrangement of the global system of production, distribution, and exchange reflects a mix of values and must therefore be understood neither as ̃inely ordained nor as the fortuitous outcome of mere chance but rather 'the result of ̃an decisions taken in the context of manmade institutions and . . . self-set rules and ̃ns' (Strange quoted in Balaam and Veseth, 2005: p. 5).

̃ggested above, many studies in the field take the state and the market to be the two ̃ties involved. Indeed, it is the 'parallel existence and mutual interaction' of these ̃ 'political economy' (Gilpin with Gilpin, 1987: p. 8). The state embodies political ̃an ̃the market, famously cast as 'the invisible hand' by Adam Smith, is defined as ̃betw̃ mechanism where sellers and buyers exchange goods and services at prices ̃'s determined by supply and demand' (Cohn, 2005: p. 7). The relationship ̃d markets is often depicted as one of permanent tension, since the efforts

FIGURE 10.1 **Susan Strange** LSE Library

of state actors are primarily concerned with preserving **sovereignty** and political unity while markets are assumed to thrive on openness and the absence of barriers to trade. But their relationship is also seen as complementary in that state action is required to protect property rights, provide infrastructure, and regulate transactions. In turn, where an economy is thriving, which it seems more likely to do where trade barriers are minimal, there is often a proportional strengthening of national political and military power (ibid.).

Students of GPE are obviously concerned mainly with the dynamics produced in the global sphere, and the interactions between states, transnational corporations, international organizations, financial institutions, **governance** arrangements, and so on. But it needs emphasizing once again that the distinction between the domestic and the international is difficult to maintain, especially in the highly **interdependent** world of the twenty-first century.

KEY POINTS

- GPE sits at the intersection of international politics and economics as well as incorporating other interdisciplinary insights and has developed as a major focus of study within the broader field of global politics over the last five decades.

- Studies in GPE focus mainly on states and markets with the relationship between these consisting in a tangle of complex interactions and processes involving key dynamics of power and wealth.

- GPE cannot be confined to the study of institutions or organizations but must also t account of the norms, values, and interests that they reflect.

GLOBAL POLITICAL E

THE AGE OF MERCANTILISM

The term **mercantilism** (from the Latin for 'merchant') denotes a certain cluster of ideas concerning the balance of trade that arose in seventeenth-century Europe. A basic premise of classical mercantilism is that national wealth and military power form a virtuous circle: wealth enhances military power vis-à-vis other states (and in early modern Europe this often meant superior naval power); substantial wealth is acquired through trade; trade is protected by naval power; the wealth generated by trade further enhances naval capacity; and so on. Mercantilism is therefore consistent with the **power politics** approach to international politics (Smith, El-Anis, and Farrands, 2017: p. 15).

The relentless pursuit of trade is justified by its positive contribution to national strength, and so mercantilism is a form of economic **nationalism** supporting, among other things, trade **protectionism**. In a post-feudal age of state-building in Europe, mercantilism therefore resonated with other ideas about national greatness. It also went hand in hand with justifications of **colonialism** while the grounds for legitimate warfare were enlarged to encompass commercial and market considerations. Overall, the legacy of early mercantilist policies was 'to concentrate physical wealth in a few European nation-states, and to create a network of global economic interdependence the remains of which can still be seen today' (Watson, 2004: p. 3). Box 10.1 provides an insightful comment on the historical trajectory of mercantilism as it relates to European **imperialism** and colonialism.

Mercantilism was at odds with emergent liberal ideas in both economics and politics more generally. Conservative economic historians depicted mercantilism as *rightly* subordinating economic to political considerations of **national interest**, in line with their belief in 'the subordination of the individual to the state and to the exaltation of vigorous nationalism characteristic of mercantilism' (Viner, 1949: p. 4). An early nineteenth-century defender of mercantilism argued along lines similar to classical **realism**. Rejecting the **cosmopolitanism** of economic liberals, which assumes peaceful relations in a politically stable environment, Friedrich List (1789–1846) argued that political economy must start from the premise that relations between states are inherently conflictual, that nationalist rivalries produce the major dynamics with which political economy must grapple, and that 'true political science' must see a world characterized by free trade as 'a very unnatural one' (List, 1991: p. 54).

Mercantilist thinking declined following the rise of liberal thought but enjoyed a resurgence from the late nineteenth century on into the early twentieth century when nationalism was rife. Liberal ideas supporting free trade then suffered a proportionate decline.

X 10.1   KEY QUOTE

ntilism and Colonialism

Europe, mercantilism solidified the control of national monarchs over the local power remained from earlier feudal societies. When these alliances between central government commercial interests were extended overseas, *mercantilism became colonialism*, entially the joint government-private conquest of foreign territory and resources.

(Van den Berg, 2016: p. 270, emphasis added)

But the extreme nationalism and trade protectionism of the interwar years, and their association with the Great Depression as well as the Second World War, gave the basic economic principles of **classical liberalism** in the post-war period a boost, even though mainstream thinking about global politics took a decidedly realist turn at the same time (Cohn, 2005: p. 71). Since realist theorists evinced little interest in economics, however, specific mercantilist ideas did not figure prominently in the early post-war period of theorizing of global politics, although they did gather some support in the 1970s and into the 1908s as the architecture of the liberal economic world order came under strain with a global recession, as discussed shortly.

Mercantilism appeared to enjoy another renaissance under President Trump. Indeed the slogan 'make America great again', and the policy of trade protection that accompanied it, was based squarely on mercantilist premises. This prompted some critical observers to suggest that his trade policy was stuck in the 80s—the 1680s (Rampell, 2018). We consider aspects of Trump's mercantilism later in this chapter.

KEY POINTS

- Mercantilism is a theory of global political economy based on certain balance of trade principles.
- Historically, mercantilism embodies nationalist, imperialist, and realist elements.
- Mercantilism opposes the ideology of the free market, favouring a strong state which not only provides security but also is actively involved in the economy by promoting protectionist measures.

THE RISE OF LIBERAL POLITICAL ECONOMY

By the late eighteenth century, liberal political economy had displaced mercantilism in prominence due largely to Adam Smith's influence. His free trade ideas were based on the division of labour, economic **interdependence**, and the notion that states in an unregulated global economy would find a productive niche based on absolute advantage. This meant that each state would find the greatest benefit in producing specialized goods most efficiently and trading these with other states. These ideas were further refined by David Ricardo (1772–1823) who expanded Smith's insights with the concept of *comparative* advantage, stating that: 'The same rule which regulates the relative value of commodities in one country, does not regulate the relative value of the commodities exchanged between two or more countries' (Ricardo, 1821: p. 99). This suggests that, even if one state has no absolute advantage in the production of any particular good, it can at least specialize in the production and export of those it can produce with a relative advantage (Cohn, 2005: p. 92). In the course of explaining the principle of comparative advantage under a regime of free trade, David Ricardo provided a succinct summation of classical liberal political economy ideas and their implications for the wider world (Box 10.2).

Another important concept underpinning early liberal political economy was *laissez-faire* (literally, 'let be'), meaning that the state should allow free rein to *individual*

BOX 10.2   KEY QUOTE

David Ricardo on Comparative Advantage

Under a system of perfectly free commerce, each country naturally devotes its capital and labour to such employments as are most beneficial to each. The pursuit of individual advantage is admirably connected with the universal good of the whole. By stimulating industry, by regarding ingenuity, and by using most efficaciously the peculiar powers bestowed by nature, it distributes labour most effectively and most economically: while, by increasing the general mass of production, it diffuses general benefit, and binds together, by one common tie of interest and intercourse, the universal society of nations throughout the civilized world.   (Ricardo, 1821: p. 99)

initiative, competition, the pursuit of self-interest, and the invisible hand of market forces— all elements of classic liberal political economy. While the pursuit of self-interest may seem attuned only to selfish individual ends, Smith and other liberals believed that the sum of such individual actions adds to overall wealth and prosperity for the community. Liberalism thus described is a theory of the individual *in society* rather than a theory of individual, self-regarding action without reference to a wider social sphere. But because liberal theorists were opposed to mercantilist state practices, and to the abuse of state power more generally, liberal thought acquired a certain anti-statist hue. Even so, most versions of liberalism recognize the state as essential for the organization of political life as well as for legislation to protect rights, especially property rights.

John Maynard Keynes (1883–1946) was undoubtedly among the most prominent liberal economic thinkers of the twentieth century. But he was certainly no anti-statist, and regarded the state as essential to producing the necessary social, political, and economic conditions for human well-being. He also believed that the sum of rational individual actions did not always add up to a rational outcome at the collective level, and so it was important for the state to regulate economic affairs and make adjustments. Certainly, to treat 'the market' as the infallible source of all wisdom was a mistake. Keynes's legacy was embodied to a considerable extent in the post-war global economic order supported in the US by economists such as John Kenneth Galbraith (1908–2006) who presented a liberal case for state involvement in economy and society and maintained a critical stance on simplistic market fundamentalism: 'The notion that [the market] is intrinsically and universally benign is an error of libertarians and unduly orthodox conservatives' (Galbraith, 1984: pp. 39–42).

From the early 1980s, and especially following the end of the Cold War and the apparent triumph of capitalism, a reinvigorated form of market fundamentalism commonly referred to as 'neoliberalism' gained ascendancy, and it has continued to dominate despite the global financial crisis (GFC) of 2008, which we consider in more detail later. As with most 'isms', the term is contested. It has also been associated with an array of quite different political figures, from Margaret Thatcher and Tony Blair in the UK, to Ronald Reagan and George W. Bush in the US, and to Boris Yeltsin and Jiang Zemin, in Russia and China respectively, among others (Steger and Roy, 2010: p. x). We should also note that neoliberalism in the context of political economy differs from the concept of neoliberalism in global political theory that developed after the Second World War and which is sometimes called pluralism for its emphasis on the plurality of actors in the global political sphere.

FIGURE 10.2 **John Maynard Keynes** Pictorial Press Ltd/Alamy Stock Photo

At minimum, neoliberal doctrine calls for the privatization of state resources and assets and deregulation of financial and other institutions in the belief that this will produce the conditions under which the market can operate most efficiently and on a self-regulating basis. Indeed, neoliberalism sees free markets as the essential organizing principle for economics, politics, *and* society. The dominance of market logic in virtually all spheres of life has given rise to the notion of 'market society' in which non-market forces and ideas are distinctly subordinate (see Birch, 2017: p. 2; Zsolnai, 2018: p. 1). Neoliberalism thus appears to be very different not only from the socially oriented liberalism of Keynes and Galbraith, which supported robust state institutions and a well-regulated form of capitalism, but also from the classical liberalism of Adam Smith and David Ricardo (see Harvey, 2007: p. 20). A critical perspective would discern the way in which market logic has become naturalized—as if its dominance over all spheres of life is somehow 'natural', and therefore right.

KEY POINTS

- Liberalism displaced mercantilism as the leading theory of political economy with the rise of free trade ideas revolving around the division of labour, interdependence, and comparative advantage although mercantilist ideas reappear from time to time to challenge liberal orthodoxies.

- Liberal political economy promotes individual initiative, competition, the pursuit of self-interest, and the 'invisible hand' of market forces. Liberals generally believe that the sum of individual actions adds to overall wealth and prosperity although 'social' liberals like Keynes and Galbraith were more sceptical.

- Neoliberalism has become a dominant ideology over the last four decades or so and has tended to subordinate all other economic, political, and social forces to a market logic which represents the 'natural' order of things.

MARXISM AND CRITICAL GPE

The third of the classical theories of political economy is Marxism which, in theorizing such key matters as class struggle, imperialism, exploitation, and technological change, 'contributes an essential critical approach to the operation of contemporary political economy' (Watson, 2004: pp. 9–10). Class analysis and the distribution of wealth are implicit in dependency theory and world system analysis, discussed in Chapter 4.

Marx's economic theory critiques the crises produced in capitalism and pays particular attention to the social and political circumstances in which economic development takes place and through which economic institutions emerge. He is especially concerned to expose how capitalism came to dominate production not just on a national scale but globally. His thought is extended to explain human development in general, including the phenomenon of 'class struggle', a term which highlights the essential conflict of interests between workers and the ruling class. Furthermore, as we saw in Chapter 4, Marx viewed the *material realities* of the human condition as mediating the whole approach people take to their existence, which in turn forms the basis for his **historical materialism** (Box 10.3).

Elsewhere, Marx wrote of a fallacy propagated by defenders of capitalism and liberal political economy which holds that the mode of production is 'encased in eternal *natural* laws independent of history, at which opportunity bourgeois relations are then quietly smuggled in as the inviolable *natural* laws on which society in the abstract is founded' (Marx, 1857; emphasis added). This once again highlights the 'naturalization' of ideas, and hence of power, by ruling classes—which was the focus of much of Gramsci's work discussed earlier—and resonates with the idea that the political structure of society always reflects 'the prevailing class interests and is never independent of them' (Morrison, 2006: p. 132). Neither Marx nor Gramsci considered gender and race as issues in the naturalization of power, but these are now much more prominent in contemporary critical GPE, as we see shortly.

➡ See **Chapter 4** for a discussion of Marxism, Gramsci, class analysis and the world system.

A neo-Gramscian perspective focusing on transnational **hegemony** and the dynamics of domination and subordination, coercion, and consent has been developed by Robert W. Cox (1926–2018). He suggested that we should not simply accept the global economic

BOX 10.3 KEY QUOTE

Marx's Materialist Conception of History

In the social production of their existence, men inevitably enter into definite relations which are independent of their will, namely relations of production appropriate to a given stage in the development of the material forces of production. The totality of these relations of production constitutes the economic structure of society, the real foundation, on which arises a legal and political superstructure and to which correspond definite forms of consciousness. The mode of production of material life conditions the general process of social, political and intellectual life. *It is not the consciousness of men that determines their existence, but their social existence that determines their consciousness.*

(Marx, 1859, emphasis added)

or political order as it is but rather question how it came into being and how it might be transformed altogether—into a more just and equitable one (see, generally, Cox, 1981). Thus critical GPE approaches do not take socio-economic or political structures as neutral or objective but as subject to change via human agency. Critical GPE's *normative* project is to make these changes *for the better* and so to contribute to human **emancipation** in a broad sense.

Critical GPE in the Contemporary World

Critical approaches to GPE in the contemporary period focus particular attention on the commodification of labour in international markets as part of the broader process of globalization. They are also attuned to gender discrimination and **racism** as well as traditional class analysis. But there is still a long way to go before these issues are brought into the mainstream of discussion. In relation to gender, Griffin (2007: p. 720) argues that while a gendered analysis is central to a proper understanding of the processes and practices of the global political economy, and while much high-quality work has been done in recent years, it is still seen as a 'women's issue' and therefore as marginal to more important traditional concerns.

➔ See **Chapter 5** for a discussion of feminism, gender, and race.

International labour migration is itself a massive industry with numerous facets. In addition to the Marxist focus on class, critical and feminist theorists now also emphasize its race and gender dimensions, which are considerable. Critical theory also highlights the extent to which international labour migration rests on wage inequalities between source and destination countries caused by highly uneven development, with labour migration controlled by an economic logic subordinating other social and political concerns (Goss and Lindquist, 1995: p. 317). The other side of the coin is the search by transnational corporations for ever cheaper sources of labour. Countries providing low-cost labour are ideal bases for manufacturing industries. While supporters of the capitalist system see this as bringing benefits to the poor on the grounds that any job is better than no job, its critics see it as perpetuating and profiting massively from relations of exploitation. Box 10.4 highlights significant class, race, and gender elements in contemporary international labour markets.

BOX 10.4 CASE STUDY

Class, Race, and Gender in International Labour Markets

The global economy depends ultimately on the exploitation of labour, and in particular on the availability of cheap labour in less developed countries which highlights both class and race differentials—the latter understood in this context as defined by nationality. Many of the labour markets are also heavily gendered. For example, while Bangladeshi and Indonesian males are employed as migrant workers in construction projects in the Middle East, Singapore, and Malaysia, females from the Philippines and Indonesia are employed as domestic workers. Regulations protecting all such migrants are often very weak, leaving many at the mercy of both

(Continued)

the companies who arrange the work contracts—itself an industry—as well as the companies or individuals who employ them. Even less protected are illegal immigrant workers who are often 'trafficked' into destination countries. 'Illegals' or 'undocumented' workers are found throughout the world wherever there is a demand for cheap labour, from the UK and other European countries to the United Arab Emirates and Kuwait, Singapore, Malaysia, and Japan. Undocumented immigrant labour has been a very significant part of the US economy for some time, and now makes up around 50 per cent of all farm workers, 15 per cent of construction workers, and 9 per cent of service and domestic workers—for example, maids, cleaners, aged care workers, and nannies (Mayes, 2019).

The 'feminization' of cheap labour is especially prominent in developing countries in South East and East Asia, parts of Latin America, the Caribbean, and North Africa where increasing numbers of women work in labour-intensive, low-wage occupations either as domestic workers or in such industries as textiles/garments. One report states that 'Although producing for some of the most profitable companies in the world [women] are working for poverty wages, under dreadful conditions . . . Health and safety are often neglected, workers are denied breaks, and abuses are common—to mention a few of the problems in the industry' (https://www.fashionrevolution.org/exploitation-or-emancipation-women-workers-in-the-garment-industry/).

There is also increased trafficking of women and children made possible under conditions of globalization in the post-Cold War era. It has been an increasing phenomenon in Europe where young women from poorer areas in Eastern Europe and Russia have been recruited for the sex industry. The UN has developed a protocol to prevent, suppress, and punish trafficking to supplement the UN Convention against Transnational Organized Crime. In highlighting these and other issues, a 2017 report from the International Labour Organization (ILO) provided the following data which indicates the extent of the problem for men, women, and children generally but also the disproportionate exploitation of women and girls.

- At any given time in 2016, an estimated 40.3 million people are in modern slavery, including 24.9 million in forced labour and 15.4 million in forced marriage.
- It means there are 5.4 victims of modern slavery for every 1,000 people in the world.
- 1 in 4 victims of modern slavery are children.
- Out of the 24.9 million people trapped in forced labour, 16 million people are exploited in the private sector such as domestic work, construction or agriculture; 4.8 million persons in forced sexual exploitation, and 4 million persons in forced labour imposed by state authorities.
- Women and girls are disproportionately affected by forced labour, accounting for 99 per cent of victims in the commercial sex industry, and 58 per cent in other sectors.

(https://www.ilo.org/global/topics/forced-labour/lang--en/index.htm)

Questions that arise from these issues include:

1 What are the principal forces behind the class, race, and gender dimensions of international labour markets?

2 How does a contemporary critical GPE approach differ from a more traditional Marxist approach to these issues?

- The Marxist tradition of critique is embedded in the social and political relations underscoring the economic sphere and emphasizes the extent to which the political structure of society reflects the interests of ruling classes and is never independent of them.

- Class analysis remains highly relevant in a global sphere where low-cost labour migrates or, alternatively, manufacturing industries locate themselves in countries providing cheap and more easily exploited labour.

- Critical GPE is sensitive to issues of class, race, and gender, thereby incorporating a wider range of institutions and practices into analysis.

THE POST-WAR INTERNATIONAL ECONOMIC ORDER

As the Second World War drew to an end, plans for a new international economic order to free up access to markets and raw materials were developed alongside those for new institutions of global governance. Delegates meeting at Bretton Woods, New Hampshire, in 1944 were also concerned to institute a system which stabilized exchange rates and avoided recreating the conditions which had triggered worldwide depression in the interwar years. However, contending national interests challenged pure liberal principles and the system which emerged reflected many compromises (Ruggie, 1998: pp. 62–84).

Institutionally, the result was the establishment of three major bodies collectively dubbed the 'Bretton Woods institutions': the International Monetary Fund (IMF), the

FIGURE 10.3 Kristalina Georgieva, former CEO of the World Bank (2017–19), became the Managing Director of the International Monetary Fund in 2019. Pictured here in Moscow, Russia, 2018 ID1974/Shutterstock.com

International Bank for Reconstruction and Development (IBRD—later called the World Bank), and the General Agreement on Tariffs and Trade (GATT) pending a more permanent institution. It took until 1995 to establish the World Trade Organization (WTO) (see Wilkinson, 2000). The WTO is now the only global international organization dealing with rules of trade between nations.

The IMF was charged with maintaining a stable exchange rate mechanism and balance of payments regime although it did little in its first few years due to the focus on European reconstruction as well as the rebuilding of Japan and aid packages to Greece and Turkey, also funded largely by the US. In the late 1950s and 1960s, the IMF's involvement in supplying credits increased, especially as decolonization progressed, and it became a major player in Global South economies. The US continues to dominate both the IMF and the World Bank, a reflection of its early role in global financial institutions as the major supplier of funds, despite its having become one of the world's largest debtor nations in the present period (see Schuman, 2011).

Although the Bretton Woods institutions remain an important part of global economic architecture, a breakdown nonetheless occurred in the exchange rate mechanism. By the early 1970s, the US was faced with rising imports and a significant trade imbalance. Huge dollar outflows providing liquidity for the global economy, although contributing to the US's considerable prosperity, could not be sustained. Increased interdependence and the recovery of the European and Japanese economies, along with vastly increased financial flows, made it almost impossible to control currency values, producing adverse dynamics (see, generally, Spero and Hart, 1997: pp. 16–21). In 1971, the US abandoned the dollar gold standard and raised tariffs on imports. Other industrialized countries reacted by strengthening protectionism themselves. This flew in the face of GATT principles supporting free trade, thus hampering reforms.

Further trouble was in store with rising inflation, commodity shortages, unaccustomed floating currencies, and then the 'oil shocks' of the mid-1970s when oil producers quadrupled the price of oil in a year, with multiple consequences for the global economy, including recession. In 1975, a meeting of seven leading industrial countries—the US, the UK, Canada, France, Germany, Italy, and Japan (subsequently called the G7)—met to consider reform of the international monetary system, and amendments to the Articles of Agreement of the IMF were put in place in early 1976. Although this appeared to signal a return to **multilateralism** in management, the reforms did little except codify the prevailing 'nonsystem' (Spero and Hart, 1997: p. 23).

By the early 1980s, in the wake of both global economic developments and the fiasco of the Vietnam War, the status of the US as the world's leading economic and military powerhouse seemed in decline (Keohane, 1984). A global recession hit most countries hard and the US was no exception. Liberal economics was identified by conservative commentators as the culprit. One US-based commentator, William R. Hawkins, deployed the term 'neomercantilism' in proposing a form of economic conservatism based more squarely on national interest and dismissing the 'utopianism' of liberal economists' visions of world order based on free trade principles (Hawkins, 1984: pp. 25–39). Five years later, however, the collapse of communism and the apparent triumph of **liberal democracy**, capitalism, and free market ideology saw neomercantilism and realist GPE overshadowed by strengthening discourses of neoliberal globalization. As we see shortly, however, the onset of the GFC in 2008 severely tested neoliberal economic principles.

THE NORTH–SOUTH GAP

The North-South developmental gap is a frequent topic of debate in GPE circles. It is sometimes equated with the West/non-West divide, but this can be misleading. In the contemporary period, almost 90 per cent of global wealth is heavily concentrated in North America and Europe, but an increasing share is held by high-income Asia-Pacific countries, which include Japan, South Korea, Taiwan, and Singapore as well as Australia and New Zealand (https://www.wider.unu.edu/publication/global-distribution-household-wealth). China, India, and the Philippines are not regarded as wealthy countries but their share of growth in billionaires is now outpacing all other regions (https://www.knightfrank.com/news/india-leads-global-growth-of-ultra-high-net-worth-individuals-knight-frank-wealth-report-2019-013011.aspx). Sub-Saharan Africa, in contrast, remains the poorest region in the world, and is likely to remain on the bottom of the ladder for some time to come.

In analysing the North–South gap, it is instructive to look back over the last half century to identify relevant trends. In the 1960s, developing countries had formed the Group of Seventy-Seven (G77) to lobby as a bloc in global forums, especially the UN and the GATT. It had limited success. Neither the oil-producing nations that formed their own Organization of Petroleum Exporting Countries (OPEC), nor the countries of the industrialized north, were prepared to contemplate significant concessions to ease the burden of poorer countries. This led to calls for a New International Economic Order (NIEO) under which meaningful reforms could be achieved in aid, foreign investment regimes, the terms of trade, financial arrangements including loans, and a fairer overall monetary system. But little actually happened. By the mid-1970s, there was a rise in protectionism in key industrialized states influenced by neomercantilist ideas, accompanied by soaring energy costs, inflation, and increasing indebtedness.

Structural Adjustment and the Washington Consensus

In the meantime, the World Bank and IMF began to promote **structural adjustment** programmes for poor, underperforming countries. Inspired by neoliberal economic orthodoxies, these included the privatization of state-owned industries and resources, deregulation, strict limitations on public spending, and other austerity measures.

Loans were made conditional on governments implementing such measures. The result in many cases was to limit access to health, education, and public utilities even further without significantly improving overall economic performance or alleviating poverty.

The policy measures imposed by the World Bank and IMF—both based in Washington, DC—became known as the 'Washington Consensus', a term originally indicating adherence to a set of broad policy measures which, in addition to privatization and deregulation, included public sector reform, tax reform, fiscal discipline, trade liberalization, property rights, and interest rate and exchange rate reforms. The way in which these were interpreted and implemented is often seen as reflecting the thoroughgoing market fundamentalism supported by neoliberal ideology which, in the wake of capitalism's triumph in the Cold War, seemed unchallengeable (see Williamson, 2009). The Washington Consensus had crumbled by the early 2000s in the wake of evidence that showed poorer economic performance under the policy measures imposed, and what remained of it was extinguished by the GFC of 2008. There is now a 'post-Washington Consensus consensus' among leading economists that the project failed in grasping even the basic economic structures characterizing developing countries and the nature of the market itself (see, generally, Serra and Stiglitz, 2008).

The spectacular economic growth achieved by countries in East Asia, South East Asia, and India in recent years has maintained broad faith in market principles by many policy-makers. The role of the state, however, has been prominent in regulation and planning, leading to a model of an interventionist developmental state, contrary to market fundamentalism, and has been far more successful as a result. Even so, the gap between rich and poor in countries such as India and China has been widening rather than narrowing as the wealth created through economic growth has by no means trickled down to alleviate the poverty of millions. This suggests that, while capitalism as an economic system certainly generates wealth, it does not distribute it effectively or equitably. Nor does the logic of capitalist profit-seeking attend to the adverse environmental consequences of industrialization, thus highlighting the case for sustainable development. Both issues indicate a crucial role for both governments and international organizations like the UN.

➔ See **Chapter 11** for a discussion of environmental issues.

The Millennium Development Goals

With respect to global inequalities, the UN adopted a set of 'Millennium Development Goals' (MDGs) in 2000, with 2015 set as the year by which the number of people living in extreme poverty would be halved—a goal requiring significant funding commitments from richer countries. A 2005 World Summit committed additional funding, although progress in many areas remained disappointing. Another five years on, a UN report indicated that very little had changed, especially in sub-Saharan Africa. Although there had been some growth before the GFC, this event hit the poor particularly hard, slowing progress significantly. By the time of the twentieth anniversary of the UN's World Summit for Social Development in 2015, however, reports were more upbeat. While acknowledging uneven progress, with sub-Saharan Africa remaining a major problem area, there had been a significant overall decline in world poverty. The UN has refreshed the MDG project with a post-2015 development agenda called the '2030 Agenda for Sustainable Development' which promises to continue efforts in key areas of concern such as poverty and hunger alleviation, combating disease, improving opportunities for youth, and environmental protection (https://www.un.org/millenniumgoals/).

A 2018 World Bank report claimed 'tremendous progress' in respect of poverty reduction, with those living in extreme poverty globally falling to a new low of 10 per cent by 2015 (the latest year for which figures are available). But rates remain stubbornly high in low-income countries and those affected by conflict and political upheaval. Indeed, the total number of poor in sub-Saharan Africa has been on the increase. 'In 2015, more extreme poor lived in that region than in the rest of the world combined. By 2030, under all but the most optimistic scenarios, poverty will remain in double digits in Sub-Saharan Africa' (https://www.worldbank.org/en/publication/poverty-and-shared-prosperity).

Theorizing the North–South Gap

A deeper understanding of the distribution of poverty around the world may be gained by looking at how the 'North–South gap' is theorized. In terms of dependency theory, the post-war order with its mixture of liberal and mercantile/realist institutions and principles was a recipe for exploitation. World-systems analysis also proposes that underdevelopment and a global division of labour are actually necessary conditions for the maintenance of global capitalism. Other analyses may also emphasize the history of imperialism and find causal factors in the legacy of Western colonialism. However, the record is rather mixed, with some former colonial states now among the world's richest. Singapore, for example, is currently ranked in the top ten countries for wealth. Former colonies such as India are home to a large proportion of the world's poor, but also have a fair share of the world's ultra-rich as well as a very large middle class. Indeed, India is now about the sixth wealthiest country in the world, although most of that wealth is privately held.

➔ See **Chapter 4** for a discussion of dependency theory and world-systems analysis.

In considering issues of income inequality, it is also instructive to look at those countries which have the most equal income. All of the top ten in this category are in the European region, but most are former members of the Soviet Union where a social welfare model developed under communism remains in place. The top ten also include Finland and Norway which have strong social democratic traditions. This suggests that redistributive mechanisms have a vital role to play and that social democratic approaches to the distribution of goods are reasonably effective in delivering a measure of distributive justice within countries.

➔ See **Chapter 12** for a discussion of global distributive justice.

Liberal theory has looked to other explanations for the poor performance of many countries of the **Global South**, particularly in sub-Saharan Africa where an earlier World Bank report found that the best economic performance had occurred in the two countries that had been able to maintain parliamentary democracy—Botswana and Mauritius— and that elsewhere on the continent a crisis of governance underlay a litany of political, social, and economic woes (cited in Williams and Young, 1994: p. 86). This report is said to have marked a watershed in World Bank thinking about the importance of **good governance**, where governance is understood generally as encompassing all the institutions through which authority is exercised in a country, and includes how governments manage resources and implement policies as well as how those in authority are elected, held accountable, and replaced. Overall, liberal theory suggests that democracy (and strong governance institutions) and development go hand in hand while dictatorship is often a recipe for continuing poor growth and maldistribution of resources. On the other hand, **authoritarianism** characterizes Singapore's political system while China, which has recorded spectacular economic growth over the past three decades, remains under authoritarian communist rule.

More generally, the North–South gap in the distribution of the world's wealth is due to a complex of causes and the problems it generates cannot be resolved simply by the application of good governance principles and practices, important though these are. Aid is often uncoordinated and misdirected and sometimes merely alleviates symptoms while failing to address causes. Health issues, such as HIV/AIDS, deplete human capital. Countries where women's rights are poorly protected undermine their health, limit their educational opportunities, impact on the life chances of their children, and contribute to continuing cycles of poverty for both men and women. Poverty and instability also go hand in hand, generating humanitarian crises as well as wider security issues which impinge on neighbouring countries as well.

No one theory seems capable of addressing all these issues and providing an overall analysis. Perhaps what is required is a multilevel approach combining theoretical insights from economic, political, sociological, philosophical, and cultural perspectives. Any such approach must also include the normative underpinning provided by a concept of **global justice** which would highlight the current *mal*distribution of those goods and resources which are essential for a life worth living.

> ### KEY POINTS
>
> - The North–South gap generates serious international political, economic, and social problems and although some markets thrive on the disparities, few actually defend it as fair or just.
>
> - Some programmes inspired by neoliberal economic thinking and formulated by the World Bank and IMF, such as structural adjustment programmes, have been criticized for compounding the problems.
>
> - Critical perspectives on the distribution of wealth and poverty in the world also look to disparities *within* the Global South.

GLOBALIZATION AND REGIONALIZATION IN THE POST-COLD WAR WORLD

Globalization is central to the study of GPE. Indeed, some analyses focus almost exclusively on the economic dimensions of the phenomenon, positing liberalizing global market forces as the key dynamic: 'The world economy has internationalized its basic dynamics, it is dominated by uncontrollable market forces, and it has as its principal economic actors and major agents of change truly transnational corporations that owe allegiance to no nation-state and locate wherever on the globe market advantage dictates' (Hirst and Thompson, 1999: p. 1).

Previous chapters have emphasized the extent to which globalization, in that it involves deepening trends in interconnectedness which transcend state boundaries and controls, challenges the traditional view of international order based on independent sovereign states. Even relatively strong developed states are seen as losing their autonomy and a fair measure of regulatory capacity. But what this means for the capacity of states to deliver a reasonable measure of prosperity and protection in terms of 'human security' to their citizens is a particularly vexed question in the Global South where, as we have seen, structural adjustment programmes have already had a negative impact on state capacity. Further, the 'market' is not geared to anything but producing profits and a strictly economistic approach to explaining and understanding the dynamics of globalized markets cannot address issues of justice, either within or between states. The pursuit of profit has also gone hand in hand with tax avoidance and evasion which is in turn associated with aspects of globalization in the contemporary period.

Contemporary Issues in Globalization and GPE

A major focus in recent years has been on the tax avoidance strategies of multinational corporations which many states have been unable to tackle effectively. A 2017 report estimated global revenue losses to be in the order of US$500 billion annually and noted that the most significant losses occurred in low and lower middle-income countries, as well as across sub-Saharan Africa, Latin America, the Caribbean, and South Asia (Cobham and Jansky, 2017: p. 1). Within the EU, corporations such as Google, Microsoft, Apple, Amazon, Starbucks, Gap, and IKEA have been identified as costing tax revenue alone up to US$76 billion a year (Chew, 2016).

There have also been significant revelations about the extent of offshore tax havens used by the super-rich, including celebrities, business people, sports stars, politicians, and public officials from around the world as well as fraudsters, money launderers, and dealers in illicit goods. The 'Panama Papers', which refer to some 11.5 million files leaked in April 2016 from the database of the world's fourth largest offshore financial services provider, Mossack Fonseca, based in Panama, have revealed details of tax havens and offshore companies set up to hide the assets of political, business, and other figures from Russia, China, the US, and the UK and dozens of other countries (Neate, 2016). Offshore schemes are not necessarily illegal, but they do offer ways and means of hiding assets from public scrutiny as well as simply avoiding paying tax and thereby holding back vast sums that could otherwise be used for public goods—schools and colleges, hospitals and health services, roads and bridges, environmental projects, etc.

Another aspect of contemporary global economic development is the enormous growth in some Asia-Pacific economies and the prospects for a 'Pacific Century'. Despite the setbacks of a regional financial crisis in the late 1990s, and some fallout from the GFC, the Asia-Pacific boom has continued, with the growth of China and India attracting particular attention. But what has been especially interesting about developments in the region is the extent to which many states, or rather their governments, have been proactive in creating the conditions for growth in the global economy. It has therefore hardly been a case of states versus markets but rather states *promoting* markets as part of a broader developmental strategy.

Regionalization

Regionalization is a complex integrative process incorporating cultural and social dimensions as well as political and economic ones although, as with globalization, the primary dynamic of regionalization is usually seen to be economic. However, many regionalizing processes have an important security dimension as well. For example, the Association of Southeast Asian Nations (ASEAN), one of the longest-standing regional organizations outside Europe, was founded primarily for the purpose of securing regional peace in the Cold War period and has only lately been concerned with economic issues. The African Union (AU), whose predecessor organization—the Organization of African Unity (OUA)—had a strong political emphasis with support for decolonization and opposition to apartheid in South Africa at the top of its agenda for many years, now looks to supporting integration and development across the continent, although there is still a strong political and security focus. One of Latin America's longest standing regional organizations, Mercosur, is focused specifically on promoting free trade among its members as well as greater ease of movement among people. The Gulf Cooperation Council (GCC) is an alliance of six countries in the Arabian peninsula (Bahrain, Kuwait, Oman, Qatar, Saudi Arabia, and the United Arab Emirates) promoting economic, security, cultural, and social cooperation to

FIGURE 10.4 A meeting of Gulf Cooperation Council members with US Secretary of State John Kerry in Qatar, 2015 US Department of State

their mutual advantage. They have a particular interest in oil, given that they hold about half of all the world's oil reserves between them, although they also have a strong interest in diversifying their resource base.

Outside the EU—and in addition to ASEAN, the AU, the GCC, and Mercosur— regionalization has been proceeding apace in the areas covered by the former USSR, South Asia, the Pacific, and the Caribbean. There are also organizations covering huge swathes of the globe. The Asia-Pacific Economic Cooperation (APEC) forum, for example, has grown from an initial twelve participants in 1989 to a current membership of twenty-one comprising Australia, Brunei, Canada, Chile, China, Hong Kong, Indonesia, Japan, Malaysia, Mexico, New Zealand, Papua New Guinea, Peru, Philippines, Russia, Singapore, South Korea, Taiwan, Thailand, the US, and Vietnam. Its 'region' reaches halfway round the world with its member countries being home to close to 3 billion people and their economies representing approximately 60 per cent of world GDP and nearly 50 per cent of world trade.

While regionalization is clearly occurring in most parts of the world, the extent to which it has become institutionalized varies considerably. It is usually held to be most advanced, but by no means complete, in Europe. The EU itself has been a long time in the making—almost five decades passed from the time of the founding of the European Movement in 1943 to the Maastricht Treaty of 1992. Brexit is no doubt a substantial setback for the European project, and perhaps for the UK itself. At the time of writing, however, the future of both the EU and the UK in a post-Brexit world is unclear and it will take several years before the consequences can be properly assessed.

Experiments in regional integration in other parts of the world are generally far less institutionalized and there is little evidence elsewhere of a willingness to compromise or 'pool' sovereignty to enhance integration, a factor which has been key to the EU's success, although it was also a factor in Brexit. While states in other regions may cooperate closely on a range of matters, integration is fairly superficial. National sovereignty is jealously guarded by many states, some of which were still colonies only a generation ago and which cling tenaciously to an almost absolute principle of non-interference in their sovereign affairs.

Although some have seen regionalization as leading to the consolidation of rival trading blocs which threaten global multilateralism, others see it as perfectly compatible with global integration (Haggard, 1997: p. 20). Indeed, in some parts of the world, it is regarded as a means of participating more effectively in a globalized economy by creating opportunities for economic growth via free trade and other arrangements within a regional framework. Regionalization on this account is part of the broader globalization process itself rather than a negative reaction against it.

Anti-Globalization

Dissent and critiques of globalization and regionalization have emanated from broad **social movements** manifest in 'anti-globalization' protests—now regular occurrences at various global or regional forums. Most participants are peaceful protesters, often gathering under the banners of various **non-governmental organizations** (NGOs) with concerns ranging from labour rights to environmental issues, consumer protection, gender issues, peace advocacy, and so on. Others are self-described anarchists whose tactics range from civil disobedience to violence, mainly against commercial property and security personnel.

An early manifestation of 'global protest' was the 'Battle for Seattle' in November 1999 when around half a million demonstrators converged on a WTO ministerial meeting. The 2007 APEC meeting in Sydney saw thousands of security personnel deployed to lock down the entire city centre for several days to forestall the vigorous protests which had become a feature at summit meetings of regional or global organizations since Seattle. Estimated costs for the G8 and G20 meetings held in Canada in 2010, bringing together leaders of the world's richest nations, were reported to be a staggering US$1.1 billion, with security by far the most expensive item. In Hamburg in 2017, in addition to the cost of hosting the summit and providing security, the destruction of property during riots at the G20 meeting, where up to 100,000 protesters gathered, ran to about 12 million euros (http://www.g20.utoronto.ca/factsheets/factsheet_costs-g20.html). Security at the 2019 meeting in Osaka was extremely tight, and violence minimal.

While anarchists—who are by definition anti-statist—get most of the media attention, many of the protesters are concerned with issues that have actually been the traditional preserve of the state, and see the processes of globalization and regionalization as undermining the rights and interests of ordinary people in a variety of ways. As mentioned above, these include labour rights and consumer protection as well as environmental issues. This has prompted much debate on the role of the state, and indeed the future of sovereignty, in a globalizing world. The role of the state has also come under scrutiny again in the wake of the GFC, which we consider in the final section.

KEY POINTS

- Globalization and regionalization are complex integrative processes driven predominantly by a liberal economic logic while incorporating social and political dimensions.

- Some critical GPE approaches welcome the openings provided by globalization for new social movements while remaining critical of adverse economic consequences for marginalized groups.

- Both globalization and regionalization have been seen as undermining the traditional role of the state, an unwelcome development from the perspective of neomercantilist/realist approaches as well as from traditional leftist perspectives concerned with the negative impact on state provision for social protection and welfare.

FINANCIAL CRISES IN THE GLOBAL SYSTEM

From the Great Depression of the interwar period, to the GFC of 2008 and subsequent crises in the Eurozone, the global economic system has been subject to significant fluctuations in its fortunes. The GFC followed a period of rapid growth in the US and the development of increasingly complex financial products. The latter products involved the securitization of high-risk loans, mainly in the form of mortgages which had encouraged people with insufficient means to buy into a fast-rising housing market. From around 2006, interest rates started to climb and many could not meet repayments, precipitating an increase in bank foreclosures. With an avalanche of defaults, the 'housing bubble' burst. Financial institutions were left holding significantly devalued assets, and from early 2007 a number faced collapse. One of the largest investment banks, Lehman Brothers, declared bankruptcy in September 2008. Institutional failure created a liquidity crisis and loans for thousands of businesses as well as mortgages became increasingly difficult to obtain. When banks stop lending, precipitating a 'credit crunch', the economy contracts, unemployment rises, and recession sets in.

Heavy exposure to the high-risk strategies of US loan schemes saw a number of European economies hit very hard. The UK banking industry was badly mauled and government bailouts followed. By 2010, a sovereign debt crisis in the Eurozone emerged with Greece, Portugal, Spain, Italy, and Ireland the hardest hit. Of course, a 'global' crisis generally means just that and few countries were spared adverse consequences. One of the very few developed economies to escape recession was Australia, as discussed in Box 10.5.

There have been numerous commentaries and critiques of the GFC and its impact on the global economy, probing both proximate and deeper causes as well as looking at lessons learnt. Well-known financier and businessman, turned liberal philanthropist, Hungarian-American George Soros, provided a sharp commentary on economic theory in the wake of the crisis (Box 10.6).

BOX 10.5 KEY DEBATE

Australia and the GFC

In 2008, when the GFC struck economies around the world, Australia's proved resilient. At the time, Australia had a population of 21.25 million, a GDP of almost US$50,000 per capita and zero debt. It had enjoyed a substantial period of economic growth attributable to a decade-long commodities boom, favourable terms of trade, and an immigration programme bringing skilled workers in particular into the country. Unemployment was at a 30-year low although inflation was relatively high at 4.2 per cent. Australian commodities are often emphasized in the success story of the economy, but the service sector in fact makes up around 65 per cent of the economy. The budget surplus for 2008/09 was projected to be just over AU$27 million.

As the GFC wrought havoc in other advanced economies, a combination of factors kept the Australian economy on a stable footing. These included continued strong commodity exports to China; continued population growth through immigration; prudential regulation of financial institutions, meaning relatively low levels of 'toxic debt' so that banks maintained a high credit rating; a well-timed announcement by the Labour government that it would guarantee bank deposits and keep credit flowing; a cut in interest rates by the Reserve Bank; and a fiscal stimulus package which included direct payments to households and a boost to the housing sector as well as public spending on infrastructure—the latter a typically Keynesian strategy. There was no talk of austerity but rather the opposite. The Labour government borrowed AU$52 billion to fund the stimulus package.

Australia's deficit increased significantly, due partly to the funding for stimulus measures, but also to falls in the demand for commodities. As of September 2019, however, there was a current account surplus of AU$7.9 billion. Australia also held a world record in continuous economic growth (i.e. with no technical recession) for over thirty years. Despite these figures, Australia has experienced very slow wages growth, the gap between rich and poor has widened, household debt is very high, and an ageing population poses problems for the future—all issues affecting most other advanced economies to varying degrees in the present period. We have yet to see the

(Continued)

full impact of the COVID-19 crisis, but government stimulus has again been key. Notwithstanding these problems, Australia's experience of the GST raises some interesting debating points:

1 How strong is the case for more rather than less regulation of financial institutions by the state?

2 How well do Keynesian stimulus strategies more generally hold up in times of financial crisis?

BOX 10.6   KEY QUOTE

'The Anatomy of a Crisis'

Economic theory has modelled itself on theoretical physics. It has sought to establish timelessly valid laws that govern economic behavior and can be used reversibly both to explain and to predict events. . . .

Rational expectations theory and the efficient market hypothesis are products of this approach. Unfortunately they proved to be unsound. To be useful, the axioms must resemble reality . . . rational expectations theory was pretty conclusively falsified by the crash of 2008 which caught most participants and most regulators unawares. The crash of 2008 also falsified the Efficient Market Hypothesis because it was generated by internal developments within the financial markets, not by external shocks, as the hypothesis postulates.

The failure of these theories brings the entire edifice of economic theory into question. Can economic phenomena be predicted by universally valid laws? I contend that they can't be, because the phenomena studied have a fundamentally different structure from natural phenomena. The difference lies in the role of thinking. Economic phenomena have thinking participants, natural phenomena don't. The thinking of the participants introduces an element of uncertainty that is absent in natural phenomena. The uncertainty arises because the participants' thinking does not accurately represent reality . . .

We really have to rethink our view of the financial markets quite profoundly; recognizing that instead of perfect knowledge and perfect information our understanding is inherently imperfect and that applies to market participants and regulators and social scientists alike.   (Soros, 2010)

FIGURE 10.5 **George Soros speaking in Brussels, Belgium, 2017** Alexandros Michailidis/ Shutterstock.com

- The GFC is the latest in a series of 'boom and bust' episodes in the global capitalist economy, the first of which was the Great Depression of the late 1920s and early 1930s which also started in the US. Both illustrate the phenomena of financial 'contagion' made possible by the interconnectedness of a globalized economy, although the case of Australia illustrates that domestic economic policy still matters.

- The GFC has tested neoliberal approaches to the relationship between states and markets in advanced industrialized economies and found them wanting, just as they have been in relation to economic development in the Global South.

GLOBALIZATION AND THE TRUMP PHENOMENON

The 'Trump phenomenon' is, in large measure, an expression of nationalism/neomercantilism embodied in the slogan 'America first'. The Trump administration's trade policies reflected a belief that protectionism—that is, shielding domestic industries and businesses from cheaper foreign imports or competition—would provide overall benefits to the US economy and 'make America great again'. Most economic theories do not support this belief but rather highlight the opposite effect which emerges when less efficient domestic industries are sheltered from competition and consumer goods become more expensive. The classic liberal theories of Adam Smith and David Ricardo, discussed earlier, highlighted the efficiencies of market liberalization in contrast with the fallacies of economic nationalism.

The Trump administration not only abandoned the Trans-Pacific Partnership (TPP)—a trade agreement between the US and eleven other countries around the Asia-Pacific which was on the point of being ratified—but also introduced tariffs on billions of dollars worth of goods from China, Mexico, the EU, and Canada. In turn, each of these countries imposed tariffs on exports from the US.

The idea that no one wins a trade war, least of all the country that starts one, is partly borne out by the fact the US trade deficit increased in 2018, although others may say that it would take more time to see the positive benefits accrue. But since US exports are overwhelmingly in the service sector rather than in goods, protectionism through tariffs still makes little sense. In addition, trade is not a zero-sum game in which there are only winners or losers. A well-regulated trade regime can produce gains for all, although that result is not automatic. Job losses caused by uncompetitive industries closing down clearly impact whole communities if alternative employment is not readily available. In this respect, government has a role to play in assisting such communities.

The overall legacy of the Trump phenomenon for the US economy—and the global economy with which it is so intimately connected—is still far from clear. That it has been a disruptive force in global trade and competition is certainly evident enough, but the longer-term consequences will take some years to play out. At another level, one commentator has pointed out that Trump's beliefs and actions highlight the extent to which politics and economics are so strongly entwined. 'For globalization is not a spontaneous economic process: it is built on a political foundation' (Oatley, 2019: p. i). This foundation has been built up over years of political interaction between governments on a global scale which has produced a raft of institutions, regulations, and practices enabling businesses to interact productively across national boundaries and within a rules-based framework (ibid.). The US has been one of the principal architects of that order, as well as one of its main beneficiaries. Yet it is the very foundation of this order that Trump sought to overturn.

Some elements of the Trump agenda have been evident elsewhere, especially in Europe and the UK where anti-immigrant, anti-EU, and anti-globalization sentiments have been on the rise. As with Trump's neomercantilist policies, any assessment of the long-term effects will obviously have to wait.

One thing is certain, though, and that is that the unfettered pace of liberalization—which is one of the essential underpinnings of globalization—cannot be taken for granted and the benefits that it is meant to deliver will need to be spread more equitably to avoid backlash from those who perceive themselves as the ultimate losers. Trump undertook to deliver more benefits to those missing out, although critics suggest that his tax cuts for the US's wealthiest classes were scarcely a good start for redistributing benefits.

KEY POINTS

- The Trump phenomenon is in some ways unique to the US, but its nationalist and anti-globalization underpinnings are evident elsewhere, especially in the UK and parts of Europe.

- The liberalizing aspects of globalization with respect to both trade and the movement of labour appear to have brought greater prosperity to many, yet these have produced much of the resentment now expressed in support for the Trump agenda.

CONCLUSION

It is evident that the proper study of politics at either the national or global level entails due attention to the relationship between states and markets and between political and economic power. We have also seen that theories of GPE developed over the last few centuries parallel those in the more general field of politics. Mercantilism and realism, together with doctrines of nationalism and sovereignty, form a theoretical cluster which, although not entirely coherent, nonetheless produce a distinctive world view in which nation-states are the ultimate repository of political, social, and economic life and ought to be defended as such. Many traditional social democrats as well as the more conservative proponents of communitarianism would agree.

Liberal perspectives, while acknowledging the importance of states, generally embrace a more cosmopolitan world view which shifts the focus from discrete social, political, and economic communities to the myriad overlapping ties between these communities and an overarching global community. Aided by the revolution in transport, communications, and other forms of technology, these ties have produced a thoroughly interdependent world which can only benefit from a continued softening of sovereign state boundaries to provide a truly global market for goods and services. The twin phenomena of globalization and regionalization both reflect and support a liberal view of world order.

Critical GPE challenges the assumptions of both realists and liberals, urging attention to the vested interests that lie behind them and the injustices they mask. While levels of socio-economic well-being vary considerably within countries, critical GPE sees the North–South gap in the global economy as a standing indictment of both mercantilist and liberal (especially neoliberal) approaches. The GFC has served to reinforce critiques of the latter. The challenge is to move from incremental problem-solving approaches to a stance on theory and practice which probes the deeper historical development of opportunities and constraints as well as future trajectories. Some critical approaches do not oppose all aspects of globalization and find much to be welcomed in the challenge to sovereignty. Underpinned by a normative **cosmopolitanism**, while also recognizing the claims of localism, critical GPE sees the emergence of global and regional social movements as vehicles for positive change as well as providing an ongoing practical critique of both liberal and realist approaches.

KEY QUESTIONS

1   In what sense does classical mercantilism see national wealth and military power forming a virtuous circle?

2   How does liberal theory justify the pursuit of economic self-interest?

3   How relevant is class analysis to contemporary GPE?

4   How do gender-sensitive studies contribute to GPE?

5   What are the main features of critical GPE and how does it add to traditional Marxist perspectives?

6   What does the North–South gap tell us about justice and injustice in the global economy?

7   What is meant by the terms 'structural adjustment' and 'good governance' and how do they reflect liberal political and economic principles?

8   What are some of the main concerns expressed through the 'global protest' movement?

9   Are globalization and/or regionalization genuine threats to the future of the nation-state as the foundation of world order?

10   What does the GFC tell us about the relationship between states and markets?

11   What are the basic features of the 'Trump phenomenon' and to what extent are these evident outside the US?

FURTHER READING

Amoore, Louise (ed.) (2005), *The Global Resistance Reader* (London: Routledge).
> Claims to be the first comprehensive account of the exponential rise of transnational social movements in opposition to the financial, economic, and political hegemony of major international organizations such as the WTO, World Bank, and IMF with discussion of conceptual issues, substantive themes, and case studies.

Cafruny, Alan, Leila Simona Talani, and Gonzalo Pozo Martin (eds) (2016), *The Palgrave Handbook of Critical International Political Economy* (London: Palgrave Macmillan).
> Challenges the assumptions of mainstream GPE through a critical theory approach to the subject matter, and seeks to expose how many apparently objective analyses mask the machinations of power and privilege.

Eagleton-Pierce, Matthew (2016), *Neoliberalism: The Key Concepts* (Abingdon: Routledge).
> Provides a critical guide to a whole vocabulary of political economy that has developed around the idea of 'neoliberalism' over the last four decades or so.

Engel, Ulf, Heidrun Zinecker, Frank Mattheis, Antje Dietze, and Thomas Plötze (eds) (2017), *The New Politics of Regionalism: Perspectives from Africa, Latin America and Asia-Pacific* (Abingdon: Routledge).
> The contributors approach regionalism as one pattern of transformation and territorialization in a changing global order engaged in by different actors under varying circumstances and challenging state-centric perspectives on a number of different levels.

Ravenhill, John (ed.) (2017), *Global Political Economy* (Oxford: Oxford University Press, 5th edn).
> A detailed introduction to the subject matter of GPE with expert contributors covering theoretical approaches, global trade, finance and production, the implications of globalization for the state, and issues concerning the environment, the Global South, and regionalism.

Van der Pijl, Kees (2015), *Handbook of the International Political Economy of Production* (Cheltenham: Edward Elgar).
> Provides an interesting and comprehensive overview of the changing world of global production including the geography of why and where jobs are moving in manufacturing and services. Specific topics include the human and natural basis on which production rests, the consequences of exploitation and marginalization on body and mind, sex work, biotechnology, and issues of ecological rebalancing.

WEB LINKS

https://www.brettonwoodsproject.org/2019/01/art-320747/
> A good brief summary of Bretton Woods institutions with links to other parts of the Bretton Woods website.

https://www.iisd.org/
> International Institute for Sustainable Development: contains wide-ranging information on the developing world.

http://www.oecd.org/
> Organization for Economic Cooperation and Development (OECD): an invaluable source of statistical data as well as more general discussion of current developments in the global economy.

https://europa.eu/european-union/index_en
> This is the (English-language) gateway to the EU website which contains an enormous amount of information. Note that all the regional organizations mentioned in this chapter have websites which are easily found with a search engine.

https://www.wto.org/
Site of the World Trade Organization with information on history, purpose, and functions as well as many useful documents and data sources.

 For additional material and resources please visit the **online resources** at: www.oup.com/he/lawson1e.

11

GLOBAL POLITICS IN THE ANTHROPOCENE

- The Idea of the Anthropocene
- The Environmental Movement
- Politics, Science, and Ideology
- Environmentalism, Ecologism, and Green Theory
- The Greening of Sovereignty?
- Conclusion

Reader's Guide

The scope of politics in the global sphere has been extended over the last half century or so to include the impact of human industrial activity on the environment. The environmental movement and 'green theory' have grown out of concerns with the deleterious impact of this activity and the capacity of the planet to carry the burden of 'business as usual' in a world driven by the imperatives of endless growth. Many now believe that the impact on the earth's systems is so significant that the present geological period should be recognized as the 'Anthropocene'. Climate change is probably the most prominent issue associated with the Anthropocene at present, but it is not the only one. This chapter examines a range of issues in global environment politics starting with the reconceptualization of the present period. It then moves on to an account of the environmental movement, the emergence of various 'green' ideologies and theories, and the politics of science. This is essential background for considering the role of the state and its sovereign powers in the context of global environmental politics.

THE IDEA OF THE ANTHROPOCENE

There has been a growing conviction that the effects of large-scale industrial activity—which comprises a set of interrelated practices ranging from vast mining operations, the damming of river systems, and the exploitation of forest resources to deleterious agricultural practices, widespread pollution by plastics and other waste products, and the extensive use of carbon-based energy sources—requires reconceptualizing the present epoch as the Anthropocene (see Box 11.1). This concept places humans front and centre of the changing dynamics of the entire physical planetary system of which **anthropogenic** climate change is but one factor, albeit a major one. Taken together, these changes are now said to be driving the sixth major extinction event in the earth's history, putting the planet's biodiversity at enormous risk.

The idea of the Anthropocene was first popularized by Paul J. Crutzen who shared the Nobel Prize in chemistry for his work on the formation and composition of ozone (Crutzen, 2010) and who proposed that data retrieved from ice cores from the late eighteenth century, around the same time that James Watt invented the steam engine, shows discernible changes in atmospheric concentrations of what we now call 'greenhouse gases' (Crutzen and Stoermer, 2000). Of course, humans have engaged in industrial and agricultural practices for thousands of years, but it is the sheer scale of activity over the last 250 years or so that has prompted the reconceptualization of the present geological epoch.

In their own time, more than a century and a half before our own, Marx and Engels described the enormous changes that had already taken place with the development of industrial society.

> The bourgeoisie, during its rule of scarce one hundred years, has created more massive and more colossal productive forces than have all preceding generations together. Subjection of Nature's forces to man, machinery, application of chemistry to industry and agriculture, steam-navigation, railways, electric telegraphs, clearing of whole continents for cultivation, canalisation of rivers, [and] whole populations conjured out of the ground . . .
>
> (Marx and Engels, 1848: p. 47)

GLOBAL POLITICS

11

BOX 11.1 KEY CONCEPT

The Anthropocene

The Anthropocene is the name of a proposed new geological epoch which combines the ancient Greek words 'anthropos' (human being) and 'kainos' (recent), and which indicates a transition from the Holocene—the geological period dating from between 11,000 and 12,000 years ago when the Palaeolithic ice age ended. This earlier transition ushered in a period of congenial climatic conditions under which a whole variety of human civilizations have flourished, including modern industrial civilization. The conceptualization of the current transition is based on the observation that the human impact on essential planetary processes have become so profound that the earth has moved out of the Holocene epoch. The knowledge that human activity now rivals geological forces in influencing the trajectory of the earth system is said to have major implications for both earth system science as well as societal decision making at all levels (see Steffen et al., 2018: p. 8252).

All this, they declared, was leading to an absurd 'epidemic of over-production' (Marx and Engels, 1848: p. 47). The current state of massive industrial production and throwaway goods would probably come as no surprise to them.

Nor would the phenomenon of global warming due to increased carbon emissions come as a surprise to some nineteenth-century scientists. As far back as 1859, Irish-born scientist John Tyndall discovered that carbon dioxide (CO_2), which had been emitted at much higher levels since the beginning of the industrial revolution a century earlier, was opaque rather than transparent and absorbed a certain percentage of infrared radiation as it rose from the earth rather than allowing it to escape the atmosphere. It was therefore capable of producing a 'greenhouse effect' as concentrations in the atmosphere increased (Weart, 2008: p. 3). All properly conducted scientific studies have confirmed this early finding and the consensus among climate scientists around the world that global warming is caused largely by carbon emissions from human industrial activity, along with a number of other gases, is now between 97 per cent and 99 per cent. A publication produced jointly by the Royal Society in the UK and the National Academy of Sciences in the US, the most respected scientific bodies in the English-speaking world, states that:

> Greenhouse gases such as carbon dioxide (CO_2) absorb heat (infrared radiation) emitted from Earth's surface. Increases in the atmospheric concentrations of these gases cause Earth to warm by trapping more of this heat. Human activities—especially the burning of fossil fuels since the start of the Industrial Revolution—have increased atmospheric CO_2 concentrations by about 40%, with more than half the increase occurring since 1970. Since 1900, the global average surface temperature has increased by about 0.8%C (1.4%F). This has been accompanied by warming of the ocean, a rise in sea level, a strong decline in Arctic sea ice, and many other associated climate effects. Much of this warming has occurred in the last four decades. Detailed analyses have shown that warming during this period is mainly a result of the increased concentrations of CO_2 and other greenhouse gases.
>
> (Royal Society and National Academy of Science, 2014: p. 1)

The science on which these and other aspects of global warming and climate change are based is scrutinized on a regular basis by the UN's Intergovernmental Panel on Climate Change (IPCC), established in 1988 and now with 195 member states participating. It aims 'to provide policymakers with regular scientific assessments concerning climate change, its implications and potential future risks, and to put forward adaptation and mitigation strategies' (https://www.ipcc.ch/2019/11/28/ipcc-at-cop-25/). The IPCC has no doubts about the strength of the scientific consensus and the need for global political action to curb emissions. Nor has it any doubt that humans have been the principal agents in shifting the world out of the relatively stable Holocene into a much more unpredictable Anthropocene which will require a response that 'integrates multiple levels of inter-connectivity across the global community' (https://report.ipcc.ch/sr15/pdf/sr15_chapter1.pdf).

Another of the issues mentioned by Marx and Engels in the passage quoted above—population growth—is a key factor in the emergence of the Anthropocene. At the beginning of the Holocene, the total human population is estimated to have stood at around five million. It took until the late eighteenth century to reach one billion. As of 2019, it was just over 7.7 billion and still increasing by 1.08 per cent a year, although growth had been slowing slightly (https://www.worldometers.info/world-population/world-population-by-year/). By the end of the present century, projected estimates are in the order of 10.9 billion, although there is expected to be a slow decline thereafter (https://www.pewresearch.org/fact-tank/2019/06/17/worlds-population-is-projected-to-nearly-stop-growing-by-the-end-of-the-century/).

The very rapid increase over the last two centuries is due mainly to advances in various areas of science and technology, from the development of vaccines against deadly diseases to the transformation of agricultural practices which now produce food on an industrial scale and which has itself had a massive impact on the earth's systems. And the more people, the greater the impact on the environment, and the more the idea of the Anthropocene comes into focus.

While the Holocene provided a relatively steady climatic and bio/geo/chemical environment, this is unlikely to continue. As earth systems become more unsettled and unpredictable, the consequences for all life on the planet are profound. For humans, the 'stability of our infrastructure, the reliability of our production systems and the liveability of our cities will all be much less certain in the future' (Gillings and Hagan-Lawson, 2014: p. 1). Under these circumstances, politics at all levels also becomes more fraught. Human communities thrive in a stable, predictable environment and the relative certainty provided under such conditions feed through into more settled social, economic, and political interactions. This is what is at risk both locally and globally in the Anthropocene.

Although environmental concerns have long been on the agenda for global politics, and have figured in the concerns of IR as a discipline, the broader conceptual and practical issues raised by the more extensive concept of the Anthropocene have only just started to make an appearance in the scholarly literature. The Anthropocene clearly presents major challenges for an array of human security concerns, discussed in Chapter 6, for issues in global political economy including the North–South divide, discussed in Chapter 10, and for the capacity of both sovereign states and the institutions of regional and global governance to manage the dangers it presents, among other things. It also requires fresh attention to theorizing, to the relationship between politics and science, and to the conceptualization of values in global environmental discourses. The sections that follow provide an essential background to the rise of environmental concerns in global politics and the various ways in which environmental issues have been theorized as well as practical policy issues raised by the advent of the Anthropocene.

KEY POINTS

- The 'Anthropocene' denotes a shift from the geological era known as the Holocene to a new era in which human activity—mainly modern industrial activity—is recognized as having had a massive impact on all the earth's natural systems.

- Anthropogenic change more generally is also associated with the substantial growth in world population since the beginning of the modern industrial era.

- Although global environmental politics is well established in the discipline of IR, the conceptualization of the Anthropocene has extended and amplified the importance of the field.

THE ENVIRONMENTAL MOVEMENT

Significant public consciousness about the impact of human industrial and agricultural activity on the environment, and its consequences for the long-term health of the planet, has been evident since at least the 1960s, although environmental concerns had been expressed from around the middle of the nineteenth century when industrialization was in full swing throughout much of the West. But it was not until after the Second World War, and especially from the 1960s, that there was an exponential growth in all aspects of **environmentalism** and green politics. Another major concern was the rapid proliferation of nuclear weapons as well as the dangers posed by nuclear energy, noting that this was also the Cold War period when pursuit of nuclear capabilities was intense.

The Rise of Green Politics

These developments marked the rise of 'green politics' and 'the environment' as a concept around which political theory and practice has developed (Dryzek, 2013: p. 4) as well as the beginnings of a broad **social movement**. Among the earliest organizations was the Campaign for Nuclear Disarmament (CND) founded in the UK in 1958 to oppose both nuclear (plus chemical and biological) weapons as well as nuclear energy. It was inspired largely by the peace movement but acquired a strong environmental focus as well, especially in view of the devastation that even a limited nuclear war would produce.

In the US, a highly influential work by biologist Rachel Carson, *Silent Spring* (first published in 1962), produced evidence of biosphere poisoning by the hugely increased release of toxic substances into the environment since the end of the Second World War. Chemical warfare research conducted during the war had produced numerous synthetic chemicals subsequently used as insecticides by agricultural industries on a large scale. Their bioaccumulative properties meant that they found their way through earth and water cycles into every living species, resulting in a significant destruction of wildlife as well as numerous illnesses and deaths among humans exposed to high concentrations (Carson, 2002: pp. 18–26). Carson's work soon led to environmental controls on the use of chemicals and other pollutants, and she is now regarded as one of the most important figures in twentieth-century environmentalism (see Box 11.2).

BOX 11.2 SHORT BIOGRAPHY

Rachel Carson (1907–64)

Rachel Carson, born in May 1907 in Pennsylvania in the US, took a major in marine biology at college, going on to work for the US Bureau of Fisheries and also to write articles and books on seas, oceans, and other waterways. These works, some of which attracted prizes, established her as a leading authority in her field. Her accessible style also meant that her works were available to a wide audience.

By the late 1950s, Carson had become increasingly concerned with the deleterious effects of the huge amounts of pesticides and herbicides used in industrial agriculture and this became her major focus. The impact of *Silent Spring* cannot be underestimated. In 2012, it was awarded recognition by the American Chemical Society as a National Historical Chemical Landmark. Notwithstanding her indisputable integrity as a scientist, Carson was subject to both personal and professional attacks by those with vested interests in the industries producing dangerous agricultural chemicals—including attacks from scientists employed by those industries.

Rachel Carson died of cancer only eighteen months after the publication of *Silent Spring*. But she lived long enough to see the release of the US President's Science Advisory Committee's report on

(Continued)

FIGURE 11.1 Statue of Rachel Carson in Woods Hole, Massachusetts, USA

Rosemarie Mosteller/Shutterstock.com

'Use of Pesticides', released May 1963, which confirmed her findings, and concluded that until the publication of *Silent Spring* 'the American public did not know that pesticides were toxic' (https://www.post-gazette.com/opinion/Op-Ed/2014/04/13/THE-NEXT-PAGE-Rachel-Carsons-silence/stories/201404130058). She was posthumously awarded the Presidential Medal of Freedom by President Jimmy Carter in 1980.

Environmental issues in this period were joined by concerns associated with the 'population explosion'. In 1968, biologist Paul Ehrlich's *The Population Bomb* was published (jointly authored by his wife, Anne, who was not acknowledged as a co-author at the time). The Ehrlichs' book contained dire warnings about looming worldwide famines due to over-population (Ehrlich, 1968). In this, they echoed a much earlier warning note from an early liberal thinker, Thomas Malthus (1766–1834), who had written of the problem of unchecked population growth outstripping the resources available to feed increasing numbers.

In 1970, the first Earth Day was organized in the US, finding support among both Democrats and Republicans. Shortly after, the US Environmental Protection Authority (EPA) was established along with the passing of legislation on clean air, clean water, and the protection of endangered species. The year 1970 is therefore said to mark the birth of the modern environmental movement. Within the next two years the UN Environment Program (UNEP) was established, the UN Conference on the Human Environment was convened in Stockholm, Friends of the Earth and Greenpeace were founded, Norwegian philosopher Arne Næss coined the term 'deep ecology', and the first Green political parties emerged in New Zealand and Australia. From around this time, environmental organizations were also forming in countries such as India, Brazil, and South Africa as well as in the former Soviet Union (Lawson, 2015: p. 222).

Carson's findings were initially regarded as a largely American problem with little applicability to agriculture in Europe where pesticides were not used on such a large scale. But other environmental issues soon came to the fore with a number of disasters. One was the first massive oil spill from a supertanker, the *Torrey Canyon*, off the coast of Cornwell in the UK in 1967 which devastated coastlines from southwest Britain to France. Another was an enormous chemical explosion in Italy in 1976 which spread toxic fumes over the surrounding area. 'Acid rain' became a serious concern in both Europe and North America from the 1970s as the rise in fossil fuel use was found to have increased the acidic content of precipitation.

At much the same time it was discovered that the ozone layer, which acts as a shield against harmful UV radiation in the upper atmosphere, had been badly damaged, mainly by widespread industrial use of chlorofluorocarbon gases. But here is one good news story on global policy action, as set out in Box 11.3.

BOX 11.3 CASE STUDY

The Montreal Protocol: A Success Story in Global Politics

From the 1940s, a number of synthetic chemicals, including chlorofluorocarbon gases (CFCs) were invented as non-toxic and non-flammable gases, mainly for use in refrigeration and aerosols. CFCs became widely used and by the early 1970s worldwide production of the compounds had reached nearly 1 million tons per year. In 1976, the US National Academy of Sciences issued a report on the destructive effects of CFCs on stratospheric ozone. The ozone layer is a naturally forming layer of gas in the earth's stratosphere, 15 to 30 kilometres above the surface, that protects life on earth from excessive ultraviolet radiation—the best-known consequence of which is skin cancer.

Initially, the chemical industry maintained that the evidence was inconclusive and did not warrant drastic action. But in a victory for solid scientific research, governments were persuaded to act and the US, Canada, and most Scandinavian countries began to take action domestically by the late 1970s. EU countries were initially sceptical but eventually came on board as the scientific evidence became more compelling. This soon fed into wider global action. The 1987 Montreal Protocol on Substances that Deplete the Ozone Layer was ratified by all UN member countries and acted on in their industrial sectors. In subsequent years, the protocol was strengthened to require an eventual worldwide phaseout of the production of CFCs and other ozone depleting chemicals. This is regarded as a milestone in the history of global environmental governance.

In the US alone, it is estimated that this action prevented an additional 280 million cases of skin cancer, 1.5 million skin cancer deaths, and 45 million cataracts. In addition, without such action, the world could have been 25 per cent hotter. More generally, studies have shown that the ozone layer would have collapsed by 2050 with catastrophic consequences for the entire planet (https://www.nationalgeographic.com/news/2017/09/montreal-protocol-ozone-treaty-30-climate-change-hcfs-hfcs/).

One commentator notes that successful global environmental agreements often require reconciliation of the inherent tension between narrow business interests and broad public benefits. In

(Continued)

the case of CFCs, the participation of industry, after initial denialism and obstructionism, helped to ensure the creation of international regulations that would in fact be implemented. However, this occurred at least partly because the major players in the industry had the capacity to develop substitutes—not because they had suddenly become more ethical actors willing to accept adverse independent scientific findings relating to their products (see Kauffman, 1997: pp. 74–5).

Questions that arise from these issues include:

1 How difficult is it for global environmental agreements based on solid scientific evidence to succeed if opposed by commercial interests?

2 What lessons does this case hold for the implementation of agreements on climate change?

Nuclear concerns also continued to grow, especially after the Chernobyl accident in Ukraine in 1986 when a reactor exploded at a nuclear power plant, spreading a radioactive cloud over most of Europe. Although killing only around sixty people in the immediate time period, many thousands are said to have been affected by increased cancer rates and birth defects in the years that followed. In the meantime, in the Indian city of Bhopal in 1984, an explosion at a Union Carbide pesticide plant released around 30,000 tons of toxic gases, with government estimates of around 15,000 deaths as well as widespread illness and birth defects in the period following.

These and numerous other industrial incidents, along with an increasingly alarming rate of species extinction and biodiversity loss, diffuse but clearly discernible patterns of climate change, and very high levels of plastics pollution, among other things, have seen green politics become a major phenomenon, with the environmental movement now one of the largest of social movements impacting on global politics. The most recent manifestation is the Extinction Rebellion (colloquially XR) which began in the UK in May 2018 and which aims to compel governments—through non-violent civil disobedience—to take serious action in response to the climate emergency and biodiversity loss before it reaches a tipping point, at which stage it will be too late to prevent ecological disaster (see https://rebellion.earth/). XR also takes a cue from the world's youngest and best-known climate activist at the present time, Swedish teenager Greta Thunberg, discussed in Chapter 12.

KEY POINTS

- The post-war period gave rise to significantly increased environmental hazards as the use of new industrial technologies developed during the war proliferated.

- 'The environment' emerged as a concept informing new developments in political thinking from the 1960s, giving rise to a large-scale environmental movement and the phenomenon of 'green politics' at both local and global levels.

POLITICS, SCIENCE, AND IDEOLOGY

The increased attention to environmental issues triggered by Carson's work and advocacy also triggered a backlash—one that involved the status of scientific evidence on the one hand, and ideology on the other. These relate to issues of knowledge, belief, and evidence discussed in

Chapter 1 and are clearly of prime importance in global environmental politics. The backlash came initially from commercial interests which stood to lose profits due to bans on products that had been shown to be toxic to the environment and to human health. Carson herself was subject not only to sexist attacks depicting her as emotional and hysterical, but also to claims that she was an environmental mysticist and a fanatic who simply used science for her own political purposes (Mooney, 2005: p. 31). This marked the beginning of a period in which commercial interests more generally began to resist scientific findings that might compromise profitability—interests which have significant implications for the politics of the environment.

The Politics of Science

In exploring these issues, it is instructive to start with the infamous case of the tobacco lobby, which was faced with mounting evidence of the link between smoking and a range of serious illnesses, including cancer. The goal of the lobby was 'to fight science with science', or to at least fight the substantial body of scientific evidence of tobacco's harmful effects with enough superficially plausible science to cast doubt on some of the evidence, thus giving tobacco companies grounds to defend lawsuits brought against it (Oreskes and Conway, 2010: p. 10). Industries producing other highly dangerous materials such as asbestos and dichlorodiphenyltrichloroethane (DDT), among others, were to adopt similar tactics.

The link between politically conservative (or right-wing) politics and general environmental scepticism—and the science that supports it—appears to be a strong one, especially in the US (see Mooney, 2005: 33–4). As a result, there has been a significant decline in environmental protection since the 1970s, mainly under Republican administrations. One study of conservative think tanks published in 2008 found that 90 per cent espouse environmental scepticism and that this had become a largely successful tactic adopted by 'an elite-driven counter-movement designed to combat environmentalism' (Jacques, Dunlap, and Freeman, 2008: pp. 349–85).

The assault on environmental protection, and science more generally, has been reported as having increased significantly under President Trump. In May 2019, the leading science journal in the US, *Scientific American*, reported more than 100 documented attacks on science since Trump's election—more than had occurred under any other administration in recent history. The article went on to note that during George W. Bush's presidency there had been 98 documented attacks on science. But while these had happened over an eight-year period, the Trump administration reached the same figure in just two and a half years. (https://blogs.scientificamerican.com/observations/the-trump-administration-has-attacked-science-100-times-and-counting/).

Does all this indicate that attitudes to science in general and environmental politics in particular consist simply in conservative or right-wing, pro-industrial, pro-capitalist ideologues opposing left-wing, anti-industrial, anti-capitalist, pro-environmental ideologues? The record of some communist authoritarian regimes suggests that the answer is not so straightforward. The former Soviet Union had an extremely poor environmental record while the legacy of the Mao era in China is equally grim. The present regime in China is also falling well short on basic pollution standards, especially carbon emissions which are the largest in the world at just over 27 per cent. Around 1 million people a year die of air pollution alone in China (https://www.nationalgeographic.com/news/2017/05/china-air-pollution-solutions-environment-tangshan/). Having said that, some communist regimes have relatively good records—Cuba being one example.

The trade union movement in Western countries also has a patchy record. Some trade unions have a history of participating in the more general movement to protect the environment, with historical 'green bans' used as mechanisms for preserving both natural and built environments of national and international significance. But trade unions are also ultimately concerned with the protection of jobs, including jobs in high-carbon industries such as coal mining. In one notable example, the Australian Labor Party (ALP) lost the 2019 federal election due at least partly to the fact that coal sector workers, and the communities depending on coal revenues, felt threatened by the prospect of a shift away from coal-generated energy to renewables and voted for conservative parties with a solid pro-mining record and an equally strong record of climate change scepticism. One conservative MP, a member of the coalition that defeated the ALP in that election, declared in early September 2019, in response to a 'climate strike' by Australian school students, that

> everything you are told is a lie . . . the facts are, there is no link between climate change and drought, polar bears are increasing in number . . . Today's generation is safer from extreme weather than at any other time in human history.
>
> (Craig Kelly quoted in https://www.sbs.com.au/news/
> everything-you-are-told-is-a-lie-craig-kelly-hits-out-at-climate-strike-students)

That statement was made at the beginning of the catastrophic fire season over the Australian summer of 2019/20, which followed a period of prolonged drought and record high temperatures across much of the continent. The fires themselves achieved unenviable world records on a number of counts, from the number of hectares burnt out to the loss of millions of native animals, destruction of human lives and property, not to mention the capital, Canberra, achieving the world's worst air quality rating early in the new year. Smoke pollution from the massive fires, clearly visible from space, spread all the way across the Tasman Sea to New Zealand and beyond (see https://www.space.com/

FIGURE 11.2 Fires in Canberra, Australia, 2020 © iStock/Daniiielc

australia-wildfires-satellite-images-2019-2020.html). Under these circumstances the claim that we are safer from extreme weather than at any other time in human history seems bizarre. And polar bear numbers, incidentally, are not increasing.

These examples of attitudes to environmental issues show that there is a complex spectrum of beliefs and values that shift and change in response to new developments. Back in 1970, *New Republic* magazine described the environmental movement in the US as 'the biggest assortment of ill-matched allies since the Crusades—young and old, radicals of left and right, liberals and conservatives, humanists and scientists, atheists and deists' (quoted in McCormick, 1991: p. ix). Elsewhere, it has been pointed out that concerns for the environment can be spoken in the language of socialism, or conservatism, or liberalism but can generally be done so in a manner that does not compromise their core beliefs (https://www.cairn.info/revue-natures-sciences-societes-2014-2-page-132.htm#).

If we look to the record in the US, we can find statements strongly supportive of science from leading Republicans. During the period of his own administration, George H. W. Bush, said:

> Science, like any field of endeavour, relies on freedom of inquiry; and one of the hallmarks of that freedom is objectivity. Now, more than ever, on issues ranging from climate change to AIDS research to genetic engineering to food additives, government relies on the impartial perspective of science for guidance.
>
> (https://www.ucsusa.org/resources/2004-scientist-statement-scientific-integrity)

In terms of policy action, George H. W. Bush's presidency saw the US federal government step up its work on global warming. His administration also oversaw the development of the Montreal Protocol, which drastically cut the chlorofluorocarbons that were destroying the ozone layer. In addition, it instituted the Global Change Research Program encompassing thirteen federal agencies that seek to understand the changing earth system, and it signed into law the Global Change Research Act of 1990 which mandated that the National Climate Assessment be produced every four years (https://www.scientificamerican.com/article/bush-had-a-lasting-impact-on-climate-and-air-policy/).

In more recent times, however, it does seem as if conservative, right-wing views, at least in some Western countries, are now much more likely to reject scientific findings on issues such as climate change and/or the need for serious policy measures. Margaret Thatcher, conservative prime minister from 1979 to 1990 (and a chemistry graduate), was once a strong supporter of climate action, but later performed a u-turn largely because of the implications for capitalism and free enterprise, and she came to associate the climate change lobby with socialism. The current Conservative Party in the UK, while apparently accepting the climate science, is nonetheless short on effective policy measures. In contrast, Germany's right-of-centre Christian Democrats, especially under the leadership of Angela Merkel (who has a doctorate in physics), has had a relatively strong record on environmental protection.

What of 'green parties'? It may seem that we should be able to take for granted that such parties are strongly supportive of scientific findings regarding any aspect of the environment. But this is not necessarily so. Green parties throughout much of the West, while completely supportive of the scientific consensus on climate change, have often repudiated the almost equally strong scientific consensus on the safety of genetically modified organisms (GMOs) which are now commonly used in food crop production as well as having medical applications. GMOs are heavily regulated to minimize the risk of adverse consequences for either the environment or human health and have been found to present no greater risk than more conventionally developed food crops. Insulin for treating diabetes, incidentally, is also produced by genetically modified bacteria, and has been for half a century (see Lawson, 2017: pp. 143–53). Another commentator notes that 'to maintain the position that GMOs are not adequately tested, or that they are harmful or risky, you have to either highly selectively cherry pick a few outliers of low scientific quality, or you have to simply deny the science' (https://www.forbes.com/sites/jonentine/2014/09/17/the-debate-about-gmo-safety-is-over-thanks-to-a-new-trillion-meal-study/#76eacef18a63).

One region in the world which is highly conservative politically by almost any standard, but whose politicians fully accept the science of contemporary global warming and have been at the forefront of global climate change activism, is the Pacific island region. This is due to very close personal experience of the adverse effects of climate change with respect to the frequency and intensity of natural disasters, and to the fact that rising sea levels threaten the very existence of small island countries made up of low-lying atoll islands, some of which are likely to disappear altogether over the next half-century or so. These include the Marshall Islands and Kiribati in Micronesia as well as Tuvalu and Tokelau in Polynesia.

The case of the Pacific islands raises the issue of 'climate justice', as explained in Box 11.4, where the focus is not just on the environment itself but also on the social and economic issues raised for people, and especially those most vulnerable to adverse climate events. This has a North–South dimension because those most affected but who lack the resources to meet the challenges are mainly in the **Global South**. Yet these people are the ones least responsible for actually producing greenhouse gases.

Pacific island leaders have been especially critical of Australia under the leadership of conservative Prime Minister Scott Morrison who has persisted in downplaying the threat posed by climate change to his island neighbours. Australia also stands accused of failing both its own people and the world more generally as it has actively undermined

FIGURE 11.3 **Kiritimati Island, Kiribati** Kyung Muk Lim/Shutterstock.com

BOX 11.4 KEY CONCEPT

Climate Justice

The idea of climate justice expands the discourse to include not just damage to the environment but the actual and potential damage to individuals and communities. It also recognizes that adverse effects will have a variable impact depending on factors such as poverty, age, gender, and so on. Richer countries are better able to respond to climate-related crises (heatwaves, droughts, fires, floods, hurricanes, rising sea levels, etc.). At the same time, they have been the main producers of the greenhouse gases responsible for climate change. Climate justice requires a recognition of the unfair burden placed on those who are the least responsible for climate change yet who will suffer its effects more acutely. The concept of climate justice therefore incorporates a strong human rights dimension.

the Paris Agreement. A meeting in Madrid in December 2019 failed to lock in the necessary rules on carbon market regulations that would have given substantial effect to the Paris Agreement on limiting global warming to 1.5 degrees. Australia was seen as blocking effective action, on the explicit instructions of Morrison, by claiming 'carbon credits' through an 'accounting trick'. This has provided two of the world's highest-emitting countries—India and China—which have also been major destinations for Australian coal exports, a rationale for continuing to generate huge quantities of greenhouse gases into the future (see https://www.internationalaffairs.org.au/australianoutlook/coping-it-in-madrid-why-australias-stance-at-cop25-was-so-widely-condemned/). It is something of an irony that even before the events of the 2019–20 summer, Australia itself was seen as 'the canary in the coal mine' as far as the effects of climate change were concerned.

It may be said that a scientific consensus on any particular matter does not represent an unassailable truth, nor is it immune from challenge on the basis of new evidence. Scientists after all deal with probabilities rather than absolute certainties. And among their ranks there are sometimes purveyors of 'bad science' who portray the findings of mainstream climate science as 'fake news' and may challenge the very concept of a scientific consensus as possessing any validity. A scientific consensus nonetheless remains the most reliable guide for non-scientists—that is, for the great majority of the public at large—on a range of issues from climate change to GMOs, to the safety of vaccines and the links between tobacco and numerous life-threatening diseases. We must all check our own ideologies from time to time to ensure that whatever political values we hold, these do not blind us to 'inconvenient truths'.

KEY POINTS

- There appears to be a correlation between conservative/right-wing politics on the one hand, and resistance by commercial interests to scientific findings on environmental and health concerns that compromise profitability on the other.

- Although pro-environment attitudes may appear to reflect a left-wing political orientation, the environmental record of some authoritarian communist governments is relatively poor.

- Science itself has become highly politicized in contemporary debates, with different ideological positions becoming evident on issues ranging from climate change to GMOs.

ENVIRONMENTALISM, ECOLOGISM, AND GREEN THEORY

We have seen in earlier chapters the relevance of a considerable array of theories in the study of global politics, from the conventional approaches of realism and liberalism to the critical approaches of Marxism, feminism and gender theory, postmodernism, postcolonialism, and so on. The conceptualization of the Anthropocene and the broad field of green theory add yet another dimension. Like any other field of theoretical thought in the social sciences, however, 'green theory' is multifaceted, with many different and often conflicting approaches to issues concerning the natural environment as well as to norms and values.

We should note first that the 'environment' itself encompasses every form of biological life along with all the soil, air, water, and minerals on the planet. It is the *interconnectedness* of all these elements—human and non-human, biological and non-biological—that is taken to constitute an 'ecosphere'. Thus ecology as a science—*not* an ideology—studies the interrelatedness and interactions of these elements. It is clear, however, that both 'the environment' and 'ecology' have been invested with normative meaning and incorporated in theories of politics and morality. These are reflected in two main strands of theorizing— 'environmentalism' and 'ecologism'. Within these strands, however, there are also nuances which further complicate the expression of green theory, as set out in Box 11.5.

BOX 11.5   KEY CONCEPTS

Environmentalism and Ecologism

A basic, catch-all definition of 'environmentalism' can be stated simply as '[t]he ideologies and practices which inform and flow from a concern with the environment' (Johnston quoted in Pepper, 2019: pp. 1–2). But the proliferation of ideas about environmental problems, their root causes, and the changes required to address them properly have seen a shift in meaning. From perspectives at the more radical end of the spectrum, environmentalism has come to stand for a largely managerial, piecemeal, problem-solving approach to environmental problems which seeks merely to ameliorate them, often through technical fixes or other superficial measures, rather than addressing them at a fundamental level.

Mainstream environmentalism is also seen as largely imbued with **anthropocentrism** (human centred), valuing nature less for its own sake than for its importance to human well-being. Thus, in a hierarchy of values, humans occupy the top position with the non-human world (nature) acting as a support system. This amounts to a value system which is instrumental or utilitarian in that its purpose is to achieve a particular end—in this case, to support humans.

Proponents of 'ecologism', on the other hand, generally support an ethics based very firmly on the inherent value of 'nature' rather than of humans, and are therefore **ecocentric** (some prefer biocentric) rather than anthropocentric. This amounts to a value system which holds that nature has *intrinsic* worth. It is valuable *in itself* rather than because it supports human interests. Humans themselves must be regarded as simply one among many living things that have value. This may be called the green theory of value (Goodin, 1992: p. 41). However, it can also be argued that attributing meaning and value is something done by humans, and only humans, and that ecocentrism cannot escape its own essential humanness.

At a practical level, ecologism holds that environmental problems cannot be addressed without radical changes to patterns of production and consumption, which in turn requires significant shifts in fundamental values, including attitudes to the non-human natural world (Dobson, 2012: p. 2).

Furthermore, rather than ad hoc management of particular problems, ecologism takes a 'whole earth' approach. Thus any specific environmental problem, from acid rain, ozone depletion, and toxic waste to species extinction, soil erosion, and climate change must be viewed as part of a more general pattern arising from human activity, which requires a holistic approach to deal adequately with them. This approach further requires recognition of the linkages between social, political, cultural, economic, geographic, biological, and other relevant factors which together form a highly complex pattern of global **interdependence** (see Lawson, 2015: pp. 228–9).

The different approaches to the concept of nature reflected in environmentalism and ecologism are also taken to represent 'light green' versus 'dark green' stances or 'shallow ecology' versus 'deep ecology'. Sometimes the term 'green theory' is taken to apply more to the 'darker' green variety of thought. The 'darker' and 'deeper' positions are also said to be more aligned with general critical theory approaches to politics, although the original formulations of the various critical theories, discussed in Chapters 4 and 5, are not especially attuned to green themes. Even so, 'dark green' theorizing in particular embodies a strong critique of capitalism, of the values underpinning it, and therefore of the foundations of the contemporary global economy.

Survivalism v. Prometheanism

Another set of opposing themes that emerges in discussions of environmentalism and ecologism, and which are therefore implicit in various forms of green theorizing, are 'survivalism' and 'Prometheanism'. The term 'survivalism' is perhaps the more ambiguous, and can refer to some quite disparate views—especially in terms of political orientation. At the broadest level, survivalism refers simply to a belief by individuals and/or groups that an existential threat to life and security is looming and that one must plan actively for survival. But beyond that catch-all definition there are some very different approaches to the issue of future survival.

A basic Internet search on the term 'survivalism' will usually bring up contemporary survivalist groups which are sometimes also called 'preppers' because they actively prepare for some major apocalyptic scenario in which there is a general breakdown in civic structures. They tend to build bunkers, store supplies, arm themselves, and sometimes even move to remote 'off-the-grid' locations. Based mainly in the US, such groups are often aligned with right-wing, anti-government, anti-UN, and pro-gun attitudes.

Although right-wing prepper groups may be motivated at least partly by 'eco-threats', an earlier set of survivalist themes emerged much more specifically in the context of the environmental concerns of the late 1960s and 1970s and were more broadly associated with a left-of-centre intellectual perspective although some, like the deep ecologists, eschewed conventional ideologies of the left/right type and indeed believed themselves to be 'above ideology'. It is these groups with which Prometheanism is usually contrasted.

Some of the earlier survivalist groups were responding to perceived threats to human survival posed by the possibility of nuclear warfare. They were also very much concerned with the long-term effects of the radiation produced by all kinds of nuclear technologies. The zone around the Chernobyl nuclear reactor site, for example, will be uninhabitable for about 20,000 years. Attention also turned to other environmental problems brought about not only by various kinds of pollution but overpopulation as well. One of the first studies in the survivalist genre was an influential essay by Garrett Hardin, 'The Tragedy of the Commons', which highlighted the fact that a finite world with finite resources can only carry a finite population (Hardin, 1968: pp. 1243–8). Another study, commissioned by a group of scientists, business people, and politicians called the Club of Rome, was concerned with lack of action on problems of population growth, depletion of non-renewable resources, widespread malnutrition, and environmental degradation (Meadows, Randers, and Meadows, 1972).

The policy changes required to effect radical changes, however, did not find sufficient support and from the 1970s a less ambitious approach was adopted in the form of **sustainable development**. This approach has been described as a reformist discourse 'that seeks to improve (rather than radically remake) existing economic and political structures to reconcile development and environmental concerns' (Dryzek cited in Hackett, 2011: p. 295).

Garrett Hardin, along with deep ecologists, among others, had also mounted a strong critique of a popular notion that whatever problems might emerge, technical solutions could be found, and that therefore little or nothing would be required in the way of changes in human values. This latter view represents the 'Promethean approach', named after the ancient mythical Greek figure, Prometheus, who stole fire from the gods to give to humankind and who initiated scientific learning and the ability to develop technology to solve problems. Prometheanism is allied with 'cornucopianism', a belief that there are virtually 'unlimited natural resources, unlimited ability of natural systems to absorb pollutants, and unlimited corrective capacity in natural systems' (Dryzek, 2013: p. 52).

The idea of self-correcting natural systems resonates closely with the **neoliberal** belief in the self-correcting capacity of markets, as discussed in Chapter 10, and so Prometheanism/cornucopianism has a strong following among neoliberal economists as it promises to deal with problems such as climate change without disrupting current economic models premised on continuing growth (Dryzek, 2013: p. 53). It should therefore come as no surprise that conservative governments in Western countries have been drawn to Promethean discourses and have implemented policy agendas accordingly. Over the last decade, these discourses have been used to counter a range of environmental concerns, suggesting that the earth is 'infinitely forgiving of what humans might do to it' (ibid.: p. 67).

A few moments of critical reflection may lead us to conclude that a simple survivalist *v.* Promethean divide obscures many mid-range or mixed positions. It would be absurd to suggest that all survivalists would oppose the adoption of at least some technological solutions to address environmental problems—technologies associated with solar and wind energy are strongly supported across the environmentalism/ecologism belief spectrum. Nor are all Promethean perspectives anti-environmentalist. Certainly, in the climate change debate, it does not make sense to associate those who propose technical solutions to global warming with anti-environmentalism in general, or climate change denial in particular. The US-based Breakthrough Institute is strongly aligned with key aspects of Promethean thought, but represents itself as environmentalist in the sense that it recognizes the value of nature and the dangers posed by industrialism—including global warming and the urgent need for a low carbon economy. But it has high confidence in the ability of technology to deliver a 'good Anthropocene' and sees itself as highly progressive (see https://thebreakthrough.org/about).

The kind of ideas promoted by the Breakthrough Institute are sometimes called 'bright green'. The latter term was coined by journalist Alex Steffen to distinguish this form of environmentalism from the pragmatic reformism of light greens and the radical ecologism of dark greens. Bright green thought draws from **ecological modernization** theory—now more often simply called 'ecomodernism'—which challenges the idea that we need to deindustrialize as well as fundamentally reorder the core institutions of modern society to ensure a sustainable future (see Mol and Spaargaren, 2000: pp. 17–49). Bright green approaches advocate a move away from the gloom and doom survivalist and 'eco-tragic' perspectives to much more optimistic framings of future possibilities (McGrail, 2011: p. 123).

On a practical level, in addition to renewable energy technologies, bright green approaches are manifest in another suite of technologies, currently in the development phase, which seeks to combat climate change caused by carbon emissions. These technologies go under the rubric of climate engineering, or sometimes geoengineering, which may be defined as 'deliberate and large-scale intervention in Earth's climatic system with the aim of reducing global warming' (https://www.sciencedaily.com/terms/climate_engineering.htm). Two basic geoengineering methods are (1) the removal and sequestration of carbon dioxide from the atmosphere and (2) solar radiation management to reduce heat reaching the earth. One key question is whether such technologies would be sufficient to deal with the current level of atmospheric carbon dioxide, which has almost doubled since the beginning of the industrial era, without also deploying measures to severely restrict carbon emissions in the first place.

This suggests that viable solutions might incorporate both carbon reduction measures (through, for example, renewables technology) *and* climate engineering to deal with already high carbon levels. It further suggests that, rather than dismissing Prometheanism altogether, there may be a place for 'Promethean environmentalism', although this is likely to be hotly contested by those more inclined to ecologism. One form of Promethean environmentalism which addresses the need to reduce carbon emissions may include technologies, in addition to renewables and geoengineering, such as advanced nuclear power generation, as set out in Box 11.6. Needless to say, this is also rather controversial and will no doubt be a matter of ongoing debate.

BOX 11.6 KEY DEBATE

Should Nuclear Energy Production Be Increased to Help Mitigate Global Warming?

In October 2018, the UN's IPCC released a report indicating that if global warming was to be limited to 1.5 degrees above pre-industrial levels, then a significant increase in nuclear energy production would be needed. Proponents of nuclear power generation had already pointed out that, in addition to being virtually carbon neutral, it is capable of producing very significant amounts of energy to supplement renewables and to enhance the reliability of the kind of large-scale energy grids which now form vital infrastructure in many countries. Although uranium, which is the basic fuel used in nuclear reactors, is not renewable, sufficient supplies are available to take nuclear energy well into the future, especially given that newer technologies use comparatively little in the nuclear fuel cycle. There are currently about 450 nuclear power stations operating in thirty countries, supplying about 10 per cent of electricity globally (compared with about 64 per cent produced by coal, gas, and oil). There are about fifty more under construction but many more would be needed to reduce carbon emissions.

Not surprisingly, the case for new nuclear energy projects received a setback following the accident at the Fukushima Daiichi nuclear power plant in Japan in 2011 when an earthquake and tsunami struck the plant, leading to the meltdown of three nuclear reactor core units and the

(Continued)

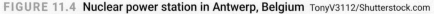

FIGURE 11.4 **Nuclear power station in Antwerp, Belgium** TonyV3112/Shutterstock.com

release of massive quantities of radioactive contaminants into the environment. This followed the Chernobyl disaster in 1986, mentioned earlier. In both cases, poor design and inadequate safety procedures played a key role in the disasters and, needless to say, lessons have been learned. Even so, nuclear power generation is perceived as dangerous, accidents and failures can and do occur at various levels, and concerns about highly hazardous waste remain. Those defending nuclear energy, however, would point out that many more die directly or suffer ill health from carbon pollution every year than from nuclear energy generation, and that this is likely to increase exponentially in future.

While recognizing the dangers of nuclear technology, some environmentalists now advocate the expansion of nuclear energy to replace coal and other carbon sources, not because they see nuclear as 'good' but simply because the dangers posed by global warming now far outweigh those that might arise from the expansion of nuclear energy programmes. Significant resources are currently being devoted by a number of countries to Generation III and IV technologies which are said to be far safer than the older technologies and much more efficient in their use of fuel as well as the minimization of waste. In the most recent development, Rolls-Royce announced early in 2020 that it was leading a consortium to build small modular reactors (SMRs), only about a sixteenth the size of a major power station and which could be installed in former nuclear sites in the UK. Regardless of how safe and efficient the new technologies are, however, the whole nuclear energy debate will undoubtedly remain highly contentious.

SOURCES

https://www.bbc.com/news/business-51233444

http://www.sfen.org/nuclear4climate/ipcc-report-more-nuclear-power-is-needed-to-meet-the-paris-agreement

https://www.world-nuclear.org/information-library/nuclear-fuel-cycle/nuclear-power-reactors/generation-iv-nuclear-reactors.aspx

Questions raised by the above issues include:

1 Does the IPCC's support for increased nuclear energy production represent a turning point in the debate over the future of energy and the global environment?

2 Does the case for nuclear energy in the context of global warming suggest a merging of survivalist and Promethean approaches to meet current challenges rather than irreconcilable postures?

KEY POINTS

- The growing importance of green politics at a practical level has seen an equally important growth of 'green theory' at an intellectual level as concerns about the global environment have strengthened.

- An important issue for both green theory and practice is the phenomenon of 'anti-science' in which highly credible scientific findings, for example on climate change, are cast as 'fake news', dismissed as 'alarmism', and portrayed as part of a socialist conspiracy to undermine capitalism.

- Survivalism and Prometheanism are often posited as opposing responses to contemporary environmental problems but, in practice, both may contribute to meeting the challenges of the Anthropocene.

THE GREENING OF SOVEREIGNTY?

What do the above issues raise for theory and practice in global politics? One response has been a focus on the capacity of states as arguably the most powerful actors in the global system and the only entities capable of bringing about effective action on environmental problems both individually and collectively. Some suggest that increasing state action indicates the 'greening of sovereignty' in the contemporary period. This requires that states use their sovereign power to limit the adverse environmental impact of industrialization by regulating a whole range of activities (including corporate activities) involved in resource exploitation, industrial production, infrastructure development, and waste management. Further, any decline in state power or sovereignty 'might even undermine the ability of the state to comply with international obligations and actually protect the environment' (Litfin, 1998: p. 4). This contrasts with earlier views, emanating mainly from the perspective of ecologism, not only that ecological holism and the division of the world into discrete territorial spaces appear to be mutually exclusive but also that the sovereign state has been deeply implicated in wreaking 'ecological havoc' in the present period (Litfin, 1998: p. 3).

Then there is the question of exactly what *kind* of state would be capable of ensuring that the most ecologically sustainable policies and practices are put into effect. One commentator suggests that most green political theorists (or at least those aligned with ecologism) would doubt that the liberal democratic state is really up to the task. She therefore proposes substituting 'liberal' with 'ecological' to produce an 'ecological democracy'.

This would not entail a complete rejection of liberal democratic ideals but would be far more attuned and responsive to the challenges of ecological sustainability (Eckersley, 2004: p. 2). It would, however, pose 'a fundamental challenge to traditional notions of the **nation**, of national sovereignty, and the organization of democracy in terms of an enclosed territorial space and polity'. Thus the project entails the reinvention of states rather than their rejection or circumvention (Eckersley, 2004: pp. 2–3). This approach is contrary to those who, in supporting 'global political ecology', often reject the statist framework 'through which international relations and world politics have been traditionally understood' (Eckersley, 2004: p. 4).

Another approach to the sovereign state stems from a pragmatic ecomodernism and proposes that the institutional power of the state be used much more effectively to develop radically better technologies to shift reliance away from highly polluting extractive industries such as coal and make them economically unviable. In fact, very significant low carbon innovation is essential—and the technologies need to be developed sooner rather than the later. Further, those who believe the answer lies in mounting a collective struggle against oppressive elites who benefit from the current high carbon economy are misguided, even though this belief fits the paradigm of previous social justice campaigns. 'Addressing climate change, however, is not like a civil rights movement—it calls into question the technical constitution as well as the political and cultural organization of human society' (Symons, 2019: pp. 7–8).

A broad suite of technologies would address not only energy industries but also the way in which people live on a daily basis. One key measure recommended follows the vision of the Breakthrough Institute—namely, the organization of communities into much denser, but highly liveable and sustainable spaces in cities along with intensive and sustainable agricultural practices. Taken together, these measures would substantially reduce the human footprint on the natural world. Furthermore, the relevant technologies should be transferred to poorer communities in the Global South to meet their development aspirations without resort to high carbon energy sources (Symons, 2019: p. 8). In fact, it is especially important for poorer communities that serious measures are taken to address carbon emissions because they will be the hardest hit by climate change. This links to the idea of climate justice, discussed above. Appropriate technological development should therefore make possible a 'good Anthropocene' at the global level, and not just for richer countries.

The approaches outlined here do not exhaust the alternatives for the reorganization of social and political life in the Anthropocene. There are ongoing debates about whether democracy is actually better at addressing environmental crises than **authoritarianism**. Some may say that democracies are given to 'huff and puff and, prey to vested interests and voters' distaste for hard choices, ultimately shirk the task'. Democratic Australia has been singled out for its 'failure to show the way in cutting emissions' and has 'only reinforced an argument which, increasingly, Asian environmentalists as well as self-serving autocrats make: that a crisis as severe (if man-made) as rising temperatures can be mitigated only by the firm smack of authoritarian rule' (*Economist*, 2019).

As we have seen, however, some major left-wing authoritarian regimes have had a poor record and that continues in present-day China and Russia—the latter having simply switched to right-wing authoritarianism. Supporters of social democracy approaches would point out that China and the former Soviet Union are, in any case, instances of 'state capitalism', and that capitalism in almost any form has always been a close ally of high carbon industrialism. Social democracy, one may argue, places much more emphasis on collective public goods than private or individual interests, which suggests that it is better placed to address the larger issues raised by climate change and other large-scale hazards in the Anthropocene (which will include significant public health issues). Social democracy does not require the abolition of capitalism but rather its regulation to ensure better outcomes for communities as a whole. These include not just redistributive mechanisms but robust environmental protections as well. Like ecomodernism, it is clearly prepared to use the power of the state to ensure desirable outcomes for communities at large.

One last approach that should be mentioned at least briefly is 'ecofascism'. This has been defined as 'a collectivist political regime that uses authoritarian measures to achieve its major goal—protecting nature' (Zimmerman and Toulouse, 2016: p. 64). No such regime actually exists at present but associations have been drawn between certain principles of Nazism and some of the more radical green activists who may favour authoritarian tactics to 'save the planet'. Contemporary right-wing supporters of individual rights have also labelled radical environmental activists who would undermine private property rights in the name of environmental justice as 'ecofascists' (Zimmerman and Toulouse, 2016: pp. 65–6).

Finally, under the broad rubric of **global governance**, there is the issue of global *environmental* governance which involves multiple actors from **civil society** groups engaging in advocacy and agenda setting, to knowledge brokers contributing expertise in political, social, economic, technical and scientific fields, and formal institutions and actors at local, regional, and global levels at both state and non-state levels. These many actors and institutions have emerged over the last half-century, born of the environmental concerns of the post-war period outlined earlier in the chapter, and constitute a complex field of activity in the global sphere.

We have also seen that the UN—as an organization of sovereign states, but engaged with all kinds of other actors—has been active on the environmental front at the global political level since the early 1970s. The UN has highlighted environmental issues as a major human security concern as well as promoting an agenda for the preservation of the earth's natural heritage for future generations. Indeed, consideration of the interests and well-being of future people (that is, people who do not even exist yet) adds another key normative dimension to the general field of green political theory in terms of intergenerational justice.

Just how effective global environmental governance is in addressing all the challenges that exist in the present period is an open question. Getting widespread agreement among key actors on particular issues, even in principle, is always difficult. Getting whatever practical measures are agreed on actually implemented at the local level is even harder. But the latter also depends very much on the willingness of ordinary people to accept the need for action and to support measures which may require some initial sacrifices for longer-term gain.

CONCLUSION

The agenda for global politics in the Anthropocene is complex, messy, and hotly contested. As a background to contemporary issues and debates, this chapter has provided an outline of the emergence of the broad environmental movement in the post-war period, which has become possibly the largest—and most diverse—of all contemporary social movements. It clearly involves very different views of nature and the environment on the one hand, and industrialism and capitalism on the other—views which have given rise to various schools of thought under the rubric of environmentalism, ecologism, green theory (in various shades), and ecomodernism. These evince different norms and value systems, which in turn inform different approaches to policy and practice on a spectrum which extends from reformism, managerialism, and faith in the capacity of technical innovation to produce much needed remedies for environmental problems to a rejection of key aspects of **modernity** and its central values—including anthropocentrism—in favour of a holistic, ecocentric world view.

The various positions taken in these debates have also been reflected in different views on the role of the state as a prime institution of politics in all spheres—of what the state can and should do to address the challenges of the Anthropocene at local, national, and international levels. But the multilateral governance of earth systems also involves the participation and coordination of a much wider range of actors from civil society to industry and to those professions on which we rely for relevant knowledge and expertise. The latter of course brings into focus the importance of scientific knowledge and the extent to which its findings can and have been politicized in ongoing debates, particularly but not exclusively in relation to climate science.

Finally, it is worth repeating one of the messages of Chapter 1, and that is that serious academic studies have a great deal of respect for well-established bodies of evidence on a range of phenomena, from the historical truth of events, such as the Holocaust and the dispossession of indigenous people, to scientific findings relating to vaccines and GMOs, to the reality and dangers of anthropogenic climate change. This does not mean that one does not continually question bodies of evidence on any subject—they are always subject to revision on the basis of new findings. But conspiracy theories, wishful thinking, dogmatic opinions, and the like do not count as evidence and are ill-suited as an ideational basis for meeting the challenges of living in the Anthropocene.

KEY QUESTIONS

1. What are the main factors implicated in the shift from the Holocene to the Anthropocene?

2. How does the idea of the Anthropocene challenge existing conceptions of the political, social, and economic conditions under which human communities organize themselves?

3. What were the major triggers for the rise of the environmental movement and 'green politics' in the post-war period?

4. How have commercial interests impacted on the science and politics of the environment?

5. Is the diversity of the environmental movement—and the different and sometimes antagonistic ideas and approaches emanating from it—a strength or a weakness?

6. Can one fruitfully combine survivalist and Promethean approaches to address environmental issues?

7. What is 'climate justice' and what measures need to be taken to achieve it?

8. To what extent does political ideology impact on beliefs and attitudes to environmental issues?

9. How reliable is a scientific consensus on any given environmental issue and what alternatives are there to guide the way we respond to such issues?

10. What kind of national and/or global political regime is best suited to meeting the challenges of the Anthropocene?

FURTHER READING

Dauvergne, Peter (ed.) (2012), *Handbook of Global Environmental Politics* (Cheltenham: Edward Elgar, 2nd edn).
   Contains forty short essays by various experts on both theoretical and practical aspects of global environmental politics and includes themes such as democracy, ethics, knowledge/power, sustainability, conflict, governance, regimes, global political economy, and so on.

Gillings, Michael R. and Elizabeth L. Hagan-Lawson (2014), 'The Cost of Living in the Anthropocene', *Earth Perspectives*, 1(2): 1–11. Available at: https://link.springer.com/article/10.1186/2194-6434-1-2
   Provides a broad overview of both the science of earth systems on which the reality of the Anthropocene is based as well as the impacts that it will have on social and economic systems.

Jacobsen, Stefan Gaarsmand (ed.) (2018), *Climate Justice and the Economy: Social Mobilization, Knowledge and the Political* (Abingdon: Routledge).
   Examines the economics of climate justice, addressing a diverse range of issues such as ecological debt, just transition, indigenous ecologies, social ecology, community economies and divestment. It also takes a transdisciplinary approach that synthesizes political economy, history, theory, and ethnography.

Mayer, Maximilian, Mariana Carpes, and Ruth Knoblich (eds) (2014), *The Global Politics of Science and Technology—Vol. 1: Concepts from International Relations and Other Disciplines* (Berlin: Springer).

Mayer, Maximilian, Mariana Carpes, and Ruth Knoblich (eds) (2016), *The Global Politics of Science and Technology—Vol. 2: Perspectives, Cases and Methods* (Berlin: Springer).
   These two volumes provide a comprehensive assessment of the impact of scientific and technological practices on international security, statehood, and global governance, bringing the study of science and international relations together in a novel analytical framework that transcends technological determinism and social constructivism. Within this framework, the second volume addresses issue areas, actors, and cases under the rubric of 'techno-politics'.

Nicholson, Simon and Paul Wapner (2016), *Global Environmental Politics: From Person to Planet* (Abingdon: Routledge).
   An introductory textbook that looks both at the nature of global environmental problems including climate change, species extinction, and freshwater scarcity as well as at what may be done about them. It seeks to provide a comprehensive, accessible account that is also balanced and forward-looking.

WEB LINKS

http://www.anthropocene.info/
   An educational web portal sponsored by a number of scientific and environmental organizations. It aims to 'inspire, educate and engage people about the interactions between humans and the planet'.

https://www.greenpeace.org/international/story/11658/a-brief-history-of-environmentalism/
   Website of one of the oldest and best-known organizations dedicated to environmental activism.

https://cei.org/issues/climate
   This link will take you directly to the climate change page of the Competitive Enterprise Institute, a conservative think tank that funds and supports climate change scepticism, among other things. The overall goal of the organization is to support free enterprise, individual liberty, and limited government.

https://www.skepticalscience.com/
   This website declares itself sceptical about climate change sceptics. It looks at a range of myths about climate change and contains many posts and articles on the subject of global warming.

 For additional material and resources please visit the **online resources** at:
www.oup.com/he/lawson1e.

12

CONCLUSION

Justice and the Future of Global Politics

- Normative Theory and Global Justice

- Cosmopolitanism, Communitarianism, and Human Rights

- Citizenship, Migration, and Refugees

- Intergenerational Justice

- Conclusion

Reader's Guide

In addressing some key issues of justice and the future of global politics, this final chapter draws together some of the themes running throughout the book. In addition to outlining the concept of global justice, the first section deals with two contrasting normative approaches to issues in global politics, namely cosmopolitanism and communitarianism, taking particular note of the debates that emerged in the post-Cold War period and which have been especially important for the analysis of human rights. We shall also see how these approaches map onto opposing strands of thought within the English School, namely solidarism and pluralism. The discussion here draws on other themes introduced in the earlier chapters on theory including liberal universalism, cultural theory, and postcolonialism. It then moves on to some specific issues in contemporary global politics involving the application of normative theory—citizenship, migration, and refugees. The final section considers issues of intergenerational justice with respect to the normative links between past, present, and future and the responsibilities these entail.

NORMATIVE THEORY AND GLOBAL JUSTICE

We saw in Chapter 1 that the field of political studies is often divided into two distinct approaches according to their aims and methods. First, political 'science' is concerned largely with observation and explanation—with ascertaining relevant facts about the world with a view to explaining political phenomena. It seeks to be as objective as possible, providing an account of the world *as it is* in empirical terms, rather than evaluating how *it ought to be* from some kind of moral or ethical standpoint. It therefore claims to produce *positive* knowledge. Political philosophy, on the other hand, poses questions about what is right and fair, good and bad, just and unjust, as well as about human freedom and flourishing, about the role of values, and about rights and obligations. It is therefore strongly *normative* in its focus not just on how the world is but also on how the world ought to be from an ethical viewpoint. *Normative theory* is therefore explicitly value-based and geared to addressing these kinds of questions and issues. In effect, it is explicitly concerned with making the world a better place through becoming a more *just* place. A broad observation of what justice implies is set out in the quotation in Box 12.1, illustrating that justice extends from the local or national to the global sphere, and from the past to the present and the future.

We may also recall that realist theories purport to describe and explain how the world *really* is while accusing liberals and others of wishful thinking about how the world could and should be. The latter theorists, however, would be quick to point out that realist thought is itself based on certain implicit values such as state sovereignty and national interest, as well as on premises that are questionable—for example, that certain structures or practices are 'natural' and cannot be changed. They may argue further that those working in liberal, Marxist, feminist, postcolonial, and other critical traditions at least make their normative positions clear. In addition, these critical approaches, along with constructivism, highlight the fact that what may be portrayed as 'natural' is not necessarily so but may simply be constructed in ways that reflect and legitimate certain power hierarchies.

Debates about whether studies of any kind can really be value-free have been perennial ones in the social sciences generally. The most radical positions on epistemology hold that there is no 'real world' out there that exists independently of subjective beliefs and interpretations, and that every view of the world is drenched in subjectivity. A more moderate view would recognize the reality of the material world, and its objective existence, while emphasizing the fact that ideational processes of interpretation mean that people experience reality in different ways (see Lawson, 2017c: p. 188). Perhaps the best that can be expected is that scholars and experts in any field will approach their task with a

---

BOX 12.1   KEY QUOTE

On Justice

Justice is about how benefits, burdens, responsibilities and entitlements should be distributed among members of a society—or among people of the world. It is about the rights people have, and what they owe to those whom they have harmed or could harm.   (Thompson, 2010: p. 5)

high degree of intellectual honesty, integrity, and professionalism and not 'cherry-pick' evidence to suit their arguments while ignoring inconvenient facts. In this respect, normative theorizing may be held to the same standards of integrity as positivist approaches.

What we can say with some confidence is that the purpose of the discipline of IR in its early years—especially after the First World War—was to study the causes of war and the conditions for peace in an attempt to reach an understanding of these matters and contribute to alleviating the enormous human suffering that attends large-scale violence. Thus the study of IR was, from the start, profoundly normative in its orientation and this has obviously fed into the contemporary study of global politics.

None of this is to suggest that norm change does not occur and that what it means to 'make the world a better place' does not vary over time. What may have been seen as right and fair at one point becomes ethically unacceptable at another. As we saw in Chapter 2, there was significant norm change after the Second World War concerning human rights and the legitimacy of colonial rule. The principle of self-determination of peoples, originally developed as a norm relating specifically to the European state system in the aftermath of the First World War, was now invoked as a right of people everywhere and was applied especially to the colonized world. In practical terms, it drove a large-scale decolonization movement which saw almost all former European colonies gain independence by the end of the twentieth century, although smaller indigenous minorities often did not benefit in the same way. But where it did occur, decolonization may be seen as achieving a measure of justice for formerly colonized peoples or nations.

The case of the decolonization of 'peoples' as collective entities may imply that global justice is concerned with collective rights—in this case the right of 'peoples' to self-determination and to form their own sovereign state. But global justice is more often defined in terms of individual rights, as set out in Box 12.2. This does not mean that

---

BOX 12.2 KEY CONCEPTS

Global Justice and International Justice

A distinction is often drawn between global and international justice. The key point of difference involves clarifying the entities among which justice is sought. In *international* justice, the nation or state is taken as the prime entity of concern and justice *among* nations or states is the focus. In the domain of *global* justice, by contrast, theorists do not seek primarily to define justice between states or nations. Rather they are concerned with justice *among human beings*. Global justice therefore takes individual human beings, and what constitutes fairness among them, as their primary object of concern.

Because many different kinds of interactions that affect human welfare and interests are not circumscribed by state membership, the global justice approach is able to raise significant issues of normative concern that may be neglected in international approaches. Global justice analyses do not preclude state and interstate obligations. In fact they often do, especially in the field of international law which may oblige states to act in ways that promote justice. But global justice is open to a much wider array of possible agents and organizations that might have duties and responsibilities in the global sphere.

Global justice and international justice have different strengths and can complement each other. In contemporary debates, however, they are often taken as rival approaches competing to provide the most plausible framework.   (Edited excerpt from Brock, 2015)

collective rights are necessarily incompatible with individual rights, but it does raises some important issues with respect to two important approaches to key issues in normative theory, namely cosmopolitanism and communitarianism, and how these inform different approaches to human rights, as discussed in the next section.

One further concept that comes under the broad rubric of global justice is global distributive justice, mentioned in Chapter 10. The quotation in Box 12.1 defined justice broadly in terms of how benefits, burdens, responsibilities, and entitlements should be distributed among members of a society or among people around the world. The idea of the *equitable distribution of goods and resources*—which includes political and social as well as economic goods—is therefore central to the very concept of justice. Where goods and resources are spread unevenly and unfairly, a case can be made for their redistribution. A conventional realist approach to global distributive justice holds that distributive justice is, or should be, limited to the domestic sphere and that efforts beyond borders are either futile or simply provide a pretext for advancing some other political agenda. Misgivings about effectiveness or hypocrisy, however, do not negate the moral worth of global distributive justice, but rather suggest that due caution be exercised in any practical project. Moreover, global distributive justice is such a pressing issue in the contemporary world that 'no one who takes international affairs seriously can ignore it' (Ip, 2017: p. 2). The issue of global distributive justice is central to debates between cosmopolitans, who see morality as transcending the boundaries of particular political communities to embrace the whole of humankind, and communitarians for whom morality is anchored precisely in such communities and for whom a transcendent universal morality makes no sense.

KEY POINTS

- Normative theory is explicitly value-based and is therefore concerned not just with how the world is, but with how it ought to be.
- Although it is value-laden, normative theorizing may be held to the same standards of integrity as positivist approaches.
- Global justice, which incorporates global distributive justice, is based on a conception of universal human rights and is concerned with the fair and just treatment of people wherever they are located.

COSMOPOLITANISM, COMMUNITARIANISM, AND HUMAN RIGHTS

Much of the debate about cosmopolitanism and communitarianism revolves around human rights and how the values that support such rights are grounded. The discussion of international organizations in Chapter 7 and international law in Chapter 8 noted the increased concern with human rights following the atrocities of the Second World War which resulted in the UN's Universal Declaration of Human Rights and the adoption of civil and political rights under one covenant and social, cultural, and economic rights in another. We also noted that critics of civil and political rights tended to associate these with a 'Western liberal tradition' and a cosmopolitan outlook that does not accord with the cultural context of many non-Western countries which are much more oriented to communitarianism. While there is some truth in this, it is also the case that this argument emanates largely from authoritarian regimes with poor human rights records. Thus there is a *political* context—as distinct from a cultural context—within which much of the debate about human rights and the relative merits of cosmopolitanism and communitarianism in the sphere of world politics has taken place.

Cosmopolitan Normative Theory

Cosmopolitanism in Western political philosophy may be traced to a school of thought in ancient Greece which opposed the distinction between Greeks and barbarians and whose followers declared themselves citizens of the world at large, and not just some particular part of it. This train of thought, which was also nurtured in Roman Stoic thought, became influential in early Christianity and, although contested by ideas which sought to emphasize local obligations, continued to exercise an influence over the ensuing centuries, including among those who laid the groundwork for international law (Kleingeld, 2019). Muslim intellectual thought, which shares with Christianity a universalist orientation as well as the legacies of ancient Greek thought, has distinct cosmopolitan elements while some African thinkers have also espoused cosmopolitan ideals, especially in responding to colonialism. Ghanaian independence leader Kwame Nkrumah (1912–72) proposed a style of cosmopolitan thought which merged 'the universal and the particular, the global (world at large) and the local (Africa), into a cosmopolitan whole of one humanity,' articulating a philosophy that was both egalitarian and generalizable (Nkrumah cited in

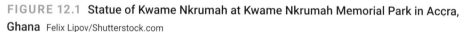

FIGURE 12.1 Statue of Kwame Nkrumah at Kwame Nkrumah Memorial Park in Accra, Ghana Felix Lipov/Shutterstock.com

Uimonen, 2020: p. 14). There is also the concept of *ubuntu* which embraces a notion of shared humanity, as discussed in Chapter 9.

The cosmopolitan idea may also be traced through the Chinese term *tian xia* which usually translates as 'all under heaven', although it has had various shades of meaning, some more restricted than others. The concept of 'Chinese cosmopolitan space' is said to have acquired the more abstract meaning of 'human-heartedness' which in turn represents 'a more universal humanitarianism' (Chun, 2009: p. 27). In India, cosmopolitanism defined as unity in diversity is readily grasped as an ideal on which the contemporary multicultural state is based, although that is under challenge from Hindu nationalism. In Japan, the notion of *kyosei* can include the idea of participation in a global community, the overcoming of prejudice, and the recognition of difference (Sugimoto cited in Delanty, 2014: p. 384).

These examples show that the cosmopolitan impulse is not restricted to any one time or place and, although it may be expressed in different ways according to context, it nonetheless embraces a notion of shared humanity that transcends local contexts. In the contemporary period, cosmopolitanism has developed as a normative theory with a distinctive orientation to global politics. In keeping with the historical trajectories sketched above, its moral scope transcends the boundaries of particular national groups or communities and embraces the whole of humankind. As we saw in Chapter 1 in the discussion of globalization, it emphasizes the notion that humans belong to 'one world' rather than simply one state or one nation, and that despite all the differences, humanity shares common problems, common interests, and a common fate. So whereas the idea of globalization—understood simply as a process through which goods and people, practices and ideas, transcend borders and spread around the world—has no necessary moral element, cosmopolitanism as a normative theory does.

Cosmopolitan normative theory aligns with contemporary theories of human rights and global justice, and in fact the terms 'cosmopolitan justice' and 'global justice' are virtually interchangeable. These generally take individual human beings as their primary object of concern, which is also a basic principle of liberal thought. Although it recognizes that national groups and other forms of human collectivities exist and are valuable to their members, it is the individual person who possesses moral standing, not the group as such. This is partly because individual people can just as easily suffer human rights abuses *within* a group, according to the rules of the group, and at the hands of those who hold power over the group.

At the same time, it is an individual's right to belong to a group. When it comes to citizenship or nationality, the right to belong is obviously an important one. Article 15 of the Universal Declaration of Human Rights (UDHR) stipulates first that: 'Everyone has the right to a nationality'; and second that: 'No one shall be arbitrarily deprived of his nationality nor denied the right to change [his/her] nationality' (https://www.un.org/en/universal-declaration-human-rights/). But to reiterate, this is not a group right, it is the right of an individual to belong to a group, as explained in Box 12.2.

Similar points can be made with respect to the difference between state security and human security, as discussed in Chapter 6. While the former is obviously all about states as collective entities, entitled to protect their sovereignty and interests in an international system of states, human security focuses on individual people within states—their rights to 'life, liberty, and security of person', and all the other rights set out in the UDHR, as discussed in Chapter 7. Further, it is the obligation of states to protect those rights. This is, after all, the point of sovereign authority. Where states fail in these obligations the doctrine of the 'responsibility to protect' may be invoked. Of course, there are considerable practical difficulties involved in maintaining these principles and humanitarian intervention can be highly problematic. The point here, however, is that the concept of human security resonates with principles of cosmopolitan normative theory and the idea of global justice. Again, this accords with basic liberal principles in which 'the individual' looms large as the basic bearer of rights.

None of this means that differences are not recognized or respected. Rather, it means that whatever differences there may be cannot be interpreted as providing grounds for unequal treatment when it comes to basic rights. Then there is the question of how much of a difference (cultural, national, religious, ethnic, etc.) really *makes* a difference and in what context. As the discussion in Chapter 5 on race, ethnicity, and culture showed, differences along these lines are not in themselves a cause of conflict. They need to be politicized— usually by agents acting in accord with some agenda of their own. Philosopher Anthony Kwame Appiah (2007: p. 8) has noted: 'The foreignness of foreigners, the strangeness of strangers; these things are real enough. It's just that we've been encouraged, not least by well-meaning intellectuals, to exaggerate their significance by an order of magnitude.' However, it is not just 'well-meaning intellectuals' who encourage this kind of thinking. It is evident in the rhetoric of nationalist politicians who promote xenophobia and exclusionary agendas based on 'them' and 'us'.

A cosmopolitan moral framework requires that people are not placed in a hierarchy which privileges any one kind of human over another: for example, males over females, high caste over low caste, American nationals over Iraqi nationals, or members of 'culture x' over 'culture y' with respect to basic rights (Lawson, 2015: p. 50). Nor does it mean that groups or communities are not valued. After all, individuals find membership in groups important for all kinds of reasons. At the same time, cosmopolitanism holds that groups are not more important than their individual members who should not be sacrificed for the greater good of the group.

While all this accords with liberal theory, most versions of critical theory, discussed in Chapter 4, subscribe to a similar normative framework in promoting a universal project of emancipation from unfair social, political, and economic arrangements. There is less emphasis on the individual but, to the extent that critical theorists share a cosmopolitan vision and subscribe to notions of global justice, the most basic bearer of rights remains the individual person.

At a practical level, the contemporary cosmopolitan impulse also gives rise to a sense of moral obligation which requires a response to humanitarian disasters of all kinds, regardless of where those who are suffering are located and what kind of community they belong to. As noted in Chapter 1, humanitarian disasters around the globe, whether they result from natural causes or are induced by human activity, invariably prompt state-sponsored as well as private aid to victims of floods, fires, earthquakes, tsunamis, epidemics, social and political violence, and outright warfare. And it's not just a matter of richer countries helping out people in poorer countries, although this is common enough. During the catastrophic Australian bush fire season of 2019–20, aid to Australian volunteer fire services, to victims who had lost everything, and to animal welfare organizations, was forthcoming from many different overseas sources, ranging from big business corporations like Apple to the Papua New Guinea Defence Forces, and to collections organized by ordinary villagers in Pacific island countries. The latter two are interesting examples of role reversal given that Australia is the Pacific island region's major aid donor.

But there is another side to cosmopolitanism which critics see as legitimating and perpetuating forms of hegemony in the global sphere. The humanitarian impulse can too easily be transformed into a justification for intervention in the affairs of states that do not measure up to certain standards. Needless to say, it is Western states that usually stand accused of meddling or more directly intervening in the affairs of non-Western states in the name of humanitarianism. There is therefore a need to recognize the 'increasingly close relationship between cosmopolitanism and power' and the fact that cosmopolitanism may reinforce the existing distribution of power in the international system (Rao, 2010: p. 11).

Communitarian Normative Theory

Cosmopolitanism is usually contrasted with both communitarianism and nationalism. As noted in Chapter 1, each of the latter have distinctive elements, but both express a much more focused concern with one's own community or national group, as explained in Box 12.3. The affinity with local groups or communities is portrayed as more 'natural' compared with the assumed artificiality of an 'abstract' cosmopolitanism (although the capacity for abstract thought is precisely what makes us human!). Communitarianism and nationalism can both take a form which is hostile to other groups, expressed in an antipathy to foreigners or people who do not share the same language, ethnicity, religion, or, more generally, 'culture', although this antipathy is more common in the modern ideology of nationalism, as discussed in Chapter 2. Communitarians may well reject the strong tendency in nationalism to construct a monolithic national identity at the expense of more localized forms of belonging, and so may support a form of multiculturalism within states where mutual tolerance and respect is the norm rather than antipathy or hostility. This approach is more difficult to maintain in the sphere of global politics where states are so often taken to encompass a 'national culture' in which local or minority differences become elided and 'state identity' assumes a more monolithic form.

BOX 12.3 KEY CONCEPTS

Cosmopolitanism and Communitarianism

Cosmopolitanism as a normative theory posits a universal moral framework within which all people are accorded equal moral status simply by virtue of their humanness and regardless of their abilities, socio-economic status, physical appearance, age or gender, or their membership of particular groups based on cultural, religious, ethnic, historical, or other particularities.

Communitarianism normative theory treats the concept of universally applicable moral values and human rights with suspicion. It focuses neither on the individual nor on humanity as a whole but sees life as intimately connected with those with whom we share immediate cultural or social bonds. The moral values said to arise from *within* such communities are taken to create bonds between its members that are far more meaningful than abstract notions of universal/individual rights. It follows that the claims of one's fellow community members take precedence over those of non-members.

Key aspects of communitarianism accord with classic conservative political thought which tends to privilege the community over the individual. A strong version of this thesis also accords more or less with the doctrine of cultural relativism, discussed in Chapter 5, which holds that moral standards are to be judged in their own context, relative to each cultural group, and not in relation to some absolute universal standard. As we saw earlier, this has its problems when we consider practices such as human sacrifice, slavery, and child marriage, not to mention 'fascist culture' and 'imperialist culture'.

Another point to consider is whether those promoting cosmopolitan approaches really do see universal rights only in an abstract sense—as emanating from some completely objective ethical truth, and as detached from the subjective contexts in which people actually live. As mentioned in Chapter 4, critical theorists such as Habermas reject the notion of objective ethical truths that exist independently of any social world. They are made *within* a social world, but one which is wide enough to embrace everyone. Furthermore, communities are not self-contained isolates but rather overlap and interact in all kinds of ways. Understood in this way, communities are dynamic rather than static entities, always shifting and changing according to a whole range of variables. Critical approaches of course include insights from Global Political Economy. As discussed in Chapter 10, critical GPE does not take socio-economic or political structures as neutral or objective. They are created via human agency and are always subject to change. Critical GPE's aim is to make changes *for the better* and, while it recognizes the importance of action at the local level, it is underpinned by a broad normative cosmopolitanism.

Chapter 5 also highlighted issues raised by postcolonial theory which, for the most part, rejects 'universals', at least partly because they derive from or represent European or Western thought. Yet those same universals convey the emancipatory ideas on which struggles against colonialism are largely based, including the right to self-determination which derives directly from European theory and practice. Similarly, the entire edifice of human rights theory rests ultimately on a universalist foundation, without which the very idea of *human* rights becomes meaningless. As noted earlier, the subject of human rights is not any particular *kind* of person but all or any persons regardless of whatever particularities they possess.

As a normative theory, communitarianism may also express important egalitarian elements. Here it is worth mentioning that socialist thought is strongly communitarian with respect to its emphasis on social justice and its orientation to the common good, which is usually expressed in opposition to liberal individualism. In this, it seems to share some common ground with conservative thought, but whereas conservatism tends to invest in 'natural' hierarchies—in which people are seen as 'naturally' unequal—socialist communities are envisaged as highly egalitarian. Then there is the issue of egalitarianism or equality *between* communities. In accordance with a communitarian logic, community x should be considered equally worthy, and as equally entitled to 'its rights', as community y. Where 'communities' take the form of nation-states with full sovereignty, equal to all others in a world of nation-states, the cosmopolitan/communitarian divide takes on another dimension. Box 12.4 sets out some key debating points in relation to the conceptualization of 'international society', as discussed in relation to the English School in Chapter 3, versus the conceptualization of a more cosmopolitan 'global society'.

BOX 12.4 KEY DEBATE

International Society *v.* Global Society

The different approaches evident in the cosmopolitan/communitarian divide map directly onto the debates about the nature of 'international society' among English School theorists. To recap, the 'pluralist' approach sees states in the international system as holding diverse values arising from their very different cultural, ethnic, religious, linguistic, and historical legacies. On this account, the state becomes the primary container of 'culture', and state identity is to a certain extent defined by 'its' culture. The idea of a common humanity gives way to a perception of a world of states each differentiated by, and holding values according to, their individual 'cultures'. It follows that the pluralist account of international society is a fairly minimalist one, held together not by a recognition of a common humanity but by an agreement among states on the importance of the international order itself, and a normative commitment to supporting peaceful coexistence among them.

This is a recipe for strict non-interference in the internal affairs of any given state, underscoring the 'rights' of sovereign states and, indeed, elevating such rights to universal status. The pluralist model really is an *international* society in the sense that it focuses on state-level relations and interactions and does not seek to transcend them. It certainly does not look to the nature of communities *within* states and the dynamics that attend these, but rather at states *as* communities. All this accords with realist approaches as well.

The 'solidarist' approach recognizes the inherent plurality of values among states in the international or global sphere. But at the same time it seeks a more robust commitment to shared norms of both domestic and international behaviour, especially when it comes to human rights. Solidarism therefore reflects not simply a solidarity among states forming a peaceful international society bound by a commitment to non-intervention, as required by the pluralist approach, but a much broader commitment to the solidarity of humankind itself.

It follows that while a norm of non-intervention may be taken as a standard feature of the society of states in the ordinary course of events, a solidarist position allows, in principle, for this norm to be overtaken by an *extra*ordinary turn of events, such as when a population group within a state becomes a target for genocide. And here we may note that in the 'real' world people's vital interests and well-being are usually most at risk from the very governments of the states that are supposed to protect and nurture them. The 'responsibility to protect', discussed in Chapter 6, sees sovereignty not just in terms of the *rights* that go with it but also in terms of the *duties and responsibilities* that states have to their own people. It also accords with a move from the notion of 'international' society, understood as a society *of states*, towards the idea of a 'global society' which transcends boundaries (although it does not erase them) and in turn underscores cosmopolitan principles of global justice.

The points of difference between communitarians and cosmopolitans over the role of culture, values, and the rights of states give rise to some interesting questions:

- Which set of cultural values gives rise to the notion of state sovereignty as a universal right?
- If the rights entailed in claims to sovereignty can be claimed as universal, then why not other rights?

- Much of the debate surrounding the cosmopolitan/communitarian divide in normative theory revolves around the issue of human rights and whether the values supporting these transcend the various states, nations, or communities that make up the human world.

- Cosmopolitanism, along with the concept of global justice, takes individuals as the most basic bearers of rights although the value of communities is not discounted.

- Communitarianism elevates the importance of communities as the primary source of value while challenging the idea that there can ever be an objective universal standard against which particular practices can be judged.

- The conceptualization of the solidarist and pluralist schools in English School theory maps more or less directly onto the cosmopolitan and communitarian positions.

CITIZENSHIP, MIGRATION, AND REFUGEES

Concepts of cosmopolitanism and communitarianism, global justice, human rights, and the nature of international society as distinct from global society, bear directly on the global politics of citizenship, migration, and refugees. While these are scarcely new issues, they are certainly at the forefront of contemporary global political concerns, presenting significant challenges to conventional assumptions about the extent to which the world can be divided unproblematically into discrete bounded entities with more or less fixed populations comprising a national citizenry and with large-scale movement from one place to another being the exception rather than the norm. In considering these matters, we start by looking more closely at the idea of citizenship, as set out in Box 12.5.

Citizenship is said to bring together the principles of individualism and collectivism in that it is an individual right which finds expression in the context of a national community. In other words, it 'recognises the dignity of the individual but at the same time reaffirms the social context in which the individual acts' (Faulks, 2000: p. 5). This is what sociologist Anthony Giddens calls a 'duality of structure' in which the individual and the community are conceived not as antagonistic or opposed. Rather, individual agency and social practices are mutually constituted and mutually dependent (Giddens cited in Faulks, 2000: p. 5). This particular point is an interesting one given that so much of the debate between cosmopolitanism and communitarianism tends to be stuck between the categories of the individual *v.* the community rather than exploring the ways in which they are interdependent.

This point becomes clearer when we consider that while citizenship is an individual right, that right automatically entails obligations and responsibilities to the national community. The US Department of Homeland Security, for example, advises that the responsibilities of citizenship range from supporting and defending the constitution, participating

BOX 12.5 KEY CONCEPT

Citizenship

According to one source, the concept of citizenship is composed of three main elements. First, it may be understood simply in terms of a legal status, defined by civil, political, and social rights. Second, it may cast citizens as political agents, actively participating in a society's political institutions. And third, it may entail membership in a political community that furnishes citizens with a distinct source of identity. There are, however, disagreements over the exact definition of each element, over their relative importance, and over the causal and/or conceptual relations between them (Leydet, 2017).

Another source highlights the variability of citizenship through time and space, noting the multiple forms of citizenship that have existed historically and still exist across different societies. It remains an unfinished institution, reflecting various historically produced presumptions and processes of change resulting from political contestation and periodic redefinition (Kostakopoulou, 2008: p. 14). Accordingly, it is unlikely to arrive at a final, fixed destination.

A third source also highlights the variability of the concept and notes the ramifications, in practice, for people around the world with citizens of wealthy democratic countries enjoying a high level of security of status both *de jure* and *de facto*. Many people are now able to possess citizenship of more than one country, or citizenship in one country plus permanent residence in another. At the other end of the spectrum there are stateless persons with no legal or practical standing anywhere in the world. In between, there are documented 'legal' migrants, undocumented 'illegal' migrants, individuals who are trafficked or smuggled, and recognized 'legal' refugees alongside unrecognized 'illegal' refugees (Howard-Hassman, 2015: p. 6).

FIGURE 12.2 **A naturalization ceremony in Portland, Oregon, USA, 2016** Diego G Diaz/ Shutterstock.com

in the democratic process and in one's local community, obeying all laws and paying taxes to defending the country if and when the need arises (https://www.uscis.gov/citizenship/learners/citizenship-rights-and-responsibilities).

There is also the cosmopolitan concept of 'global citizenship', mentioned in Chapter 1. While it does not negate one's state-based citizenship or national identity, it holds that we also have rights and responsibilities that transcend the state. In addition, the idea of global citizenship is associated with the concept of cosmopolitan democracy which holds that the principles of democratic governance can (and should) be extended beyond the state to the global sphere (see Archibugi, 2008). Ideas about both global citizenship and cosmopolitan democracy can be traced to early liberal thought, especially that of Immanuel Kant, discussed in Chapter 3, but they have been formulated afresh in the post-Cold War period when the challenges of globalization and problems generated by it appeared to call for new responses to problems of global justice.

One of the challenges presented by the intensification of globalization over the last thirty years or so has been the increased pace of migration. Millions of both skilled and unskilled workers, as well as refugees or asylum seekers, have been on the move—most seeking a better life for themselves and their families. In the case of refugees fleeing violence or persecution, it is often a case of sheer survival. A UN estimate of international migrants as of 2019 stood at 272 million, or 3.5 per cent of the global population. With respect to regional shares, Europe as a whole hosted the largest number of international migrants (82 million), followed by Northern America (59 million), and Northern Africa and Western Asia (49 million). As a share of international migrants in the total population, the highest proportions were recorded in Oceania (including Australia and New Zealand) (21.2 per cent) and Northern America (16 per cent) (https://www.un.org/development/desa/en/news/population/international-migrant-stock-2019.html).

The movement of refugees shows a different pattern, especially since the beginning of the Syrian civil war which alone has generated more than 6.7 million refugees. As of 2019, Turkey had hosted the largest number of refugees followed by Pakistan, Uganda, Sudan, and Germany, although Lebanon and Jordan have higher numbers as a proportion of their population. By the end of 2018, the global population of forcibly displaced people stood at 70.8 million, noting that some of these are internally displaced rather than seeking refuge in other countries. The largest proportion of refugees by far come from Syria, followed by Afghanistan, South Sudan, Myanmar, and Somalia. Another region experiencing significant refugee movement is South America where more than 3 million Venezuelans had left the country by the end of 2018, finding refuge mainly in Colombia, Brazil, Peru, Chile, and Ecuador (https://www.unhcr.org/globaltrends2018/). Box 12.6 provides the background to current provisions concerning the status of refugees in the global system and the duties owed to them by states in the international community.

Although critics of migration movements may see the benefits as accruing almost exclusively to the migrants themselves, and at the expense of the national communities that they seek to join, studies show that migrants bring essential skills and human capital, contribute to labour flexibility, boost working populations, contribute more in taxes and social contributions than they receive in benefits, and generally contribute substantially to the public purse. They have been especially important in countries with ageing

BOX 12.6

The 1951 Refugee Convention

The 1951 Refugee Convention, ratified by 145 state parties, defines the term 'refugee' and outlines the rights of the displaced, as well as the legal obligations of states to protect them. According to the Convention, a refugee is someone who is unable or unwilling to return to their country of origin owing to a well-founded fear of prosecution on the basis of their race, religion, nationality, membership of a particular social group, or political opinion.

The Convention further stipulates that, subject to certain specific exceptions, refugees should not be penalized for an illegal entry or stay. This recognizes that asylum seeking may require refugees to breach immigration rules. Asylum seekers may not be charged with immigration or criminal offences relating to the seeking of asylum, or be arbitrarily detained purely on the basis of seeking asylum. The Convention also contains various safeguards against the expulsion of refugees.

The core principle of the Convention is 'non-refoulement'. This means that a refugee should not be returned to a country where they face serious threats to their life or freedom. This is now considered a rule of customary international law. The principle of non-refoulement is so fundamental that no reservations or derogations may be made to it. It provides that no one shall expel or return ('refouler') a refugee against his or her will, in any manner whatsoever, to a territory where he or she fears threats to life or freedom. (https://www.unhcr.org/en-au/1951-refugee-convention.html)

populations and insufficient younger workers to support them (see https://www.oecd.org/migration/migration-policy-debates.htm). Similar considerations apply to refugees who very often bring valuable skill sets and a strong work ethic. Their economic contributions may take longer to become manifest, but this is often due to the fact that they are frequently denied the right to work for some time in host countries (see https://www.nature.com/articles/d41586-018-05507-0).

Despite the palpable benefits that migrants bring with them to the host country, there is nonetheless resistance and sometimes outright hostility from sectors of the host population, as discussed in Chapter 3 in the context of nationalism. The main political beneficiaries of generally hostile sentiments among host populations have been right-wing nationalist parties in Europe, the Trump administration in the US, pro-Brexit parties in the UK, and conservative nationalist groups in Australia where over 25 per cent of the current population were born overseas.

The predicament of refugees, in particular, obviously brings into focus certain questions pertaining to global justice and international justice. As we have seen, global justice takes individual human beings, and what constitutes fairness among them, as their primary object of concern. It is impartial in the sense that it does not discriminate on the basis of one's nationality (or gender, religion, ethnicity, age, etc.), and therefore reflects the most basic principles of the UDHR and of cosmopolitan normative theory. But does this mean that national borders play no positive role in situations of forced migration and asylum seeking? And does it mean that global justice, which transcends borders, must trump international justice? Box 12.7 sets out some key issues for debate in the context of the current refugee crisis.

BOX 12.7   KEY DEBATE

Global Justice, International Justice, and the Refugee Crisis

The nature of refugee crises might suggest that national borders are part of the problem, and play no part in the solution. Certainly, a simplistic take on cosmopolitanism and global justice would view national borders as setting up barriers to those seeking to escape great harm or even death. In some cases they do, but rather than seeing them as barriers in some absolute sense (which they rarely are), we can also see them as demarcating a safe zone from a danger zone. When Syrian nationals, for example, seek to escape life-threatening circumstances in their own country, the act of crossing from Syria into another country where asylum is possible means that the border delineates safety from danger. Similarly, Rohingya people escaping Myanmar into Bangladesh are moving from a national space which is highly dangerous to another national space which offers some protection. Many other examples could be cited to illustrate the point.

The act of crossing into a safer zone, however, raises many more issues for countries receiving refugees. If global justice demands that refugees be taken in and cared for regardless of who or what they are in terms of nationality, ethnic background, religion, etc., then *international* justice— that is, justice *between* nations—requires that the burden of caring for refugees is shared on the basis of proportionality and capability. In the case of Syrian refugees, the resources of Turkey, Jordan, and Lebanon to care for the millions now within their borders, even with UN assistance, are grossly inadequate. Bangladesh, itself one of the world's poorest countries, has a similar problem in caring for over a million Rohingya people as does Pakistan with around 1.4 million Afghan refugees. Countries in other regions—the Gulf, Northern Europe, North America, Australasia—have not taken on an adequate share of the burden, especially given that they are comparatively very well-resourced regions capable of accommodating and integrating many more refugees.

FIGURE 12.3 Kutupalong refugee camp near Cox's Bazar, Bangladesh, 2017 Russell Watkins/ UK Department for International Development

(Continued)

This illustrates the point that although they are often taken to be rival normative approaches, global justice and international justice have different strengths and can complement each other. Similarly, although cosmopolitanism and communitarianism are usually taken as almost completely opposed, they become complementary when *one community assists another* in a time of great need. Communitarianism, in principle, places great value on all communities and this can justify an obligation to assist. Both cosmopolitanism and communitarianism are, after all, both very much concerned with what humans need not just to survive but to thrive and prosper.

Questions arising from these issues include:

- Can national borders and national spaces be viewed as positive assets in dealing with refugee crises?
- Could theories of global justice and international justice be synthesized to produce a coherent normative approach to issues such as the refugee crisis?

KEY POINTS

- Citizenship is an individual right which finds expression in the context of a national community, and which therefore brings together the principles of individualism and collectivism.
- Although critics of migration usually see the benefits as accruing almost exclusively to the migrants themselves, and at the expense of the national communities they join, migrants bring essential skills and human capital that benefit the host community.
- The issue of sharing responsibility for refugees illustrates that norms of global justice and cosmopolitanism on the one hand, and international justice and communitarianism on the other, have different strengths and can complement each other.

INTERGENERATIONAL JUSTICE

The range of normative issues considered by students of global politics now extends to considerations of intergenerational justice. This applies not only to justice as between younger and older generations still living but also to people who no longer exist as well as to those who do not yet exist. It therefore applies to those whose future we hold in our hands, and whose well-being will be deeply affected by actions in the present, and to past injustices—slavery, colonialism, dispossession, genocide, etc. In the latter cases, those who suffered may no longer be alive, but their descendants may still experience adverse consequences. As one commentator notes, 'we are intensely vulnerable to what past generations have decided, and future generations are intensely vulnerable to us' (Vernon, 2016: p. 7).

Both past and future injustices involve people who are at some distance in time from the present. If we substitute this *temporal* dimension with a *spatial* dimension, it becomes apparent that the concept of intergenerational justice may be compared with global justice. As we have seen, the latter entails the notion that people suffering hunger, disease, or violence are entitled to a measure of justice from those able to help, even though they may be spatially distant. This is so regardless of whether the plight of those suffering is the direct or indirect fault of those in better-off countries. It is therefore not necessarily a matter of collective guilt but rather of collective responsibility which arises from shared membership in a society—in this case global society—rather than membership in a particular national group (see Vernon, 2016: p. 9). In certain cases, however, issues of collective guilt and responsibility do come into play. We consider this first in relation to historic injustices and some of the implications for global politics.

Historic Injustice and the Possibility of Redress

It is a fair question to ask whether members of particular communities in a current generation really do bear responsibility for acts perpetrated by predecessors to whom they may not even be related, at least as individuals. With respect to a national community which is said to bear some responsibility for injustices wrought by past acts, how is that to be expressed and by whom? Is any form of redress possible? And is it anachronistic to judge the past by the standards of the present?

The obvious candidates for issuing apologies for historic acts are political or institutional leaders who represent both a past generation of wrongdoers as well as a present generation that formally acknowledges the wrongs of their forebears. The last few decades have seen a spate of apologies for past wrongs—Pope John Paul II's apology for the Crusades on behalf of the Catholic Church; Japan's apologies to China and Korea in particular for war crimes committed during the Second World War; and the apologies of various German leaders, including Angela Merkel, for the Holocaust. On other occasions when there have been calls for apologies for shameful past acts, however, political leaders have refused. Former Australian Prime Minister John Howard, when called on to offer an apology to Aboriginal people for the wrongs experienced since British colonization, maintained that the current generation cannot and should not be held accountable for the behaviour of previous generations. This accords with versions of liberal theory which reject notions of collective guilt and deal only with individual responsibility (see Bentley, 2016).

As noted above, the judgement of past wrongs generally rests on standards applicable to the present time. It may therefore be anachronistic to deliver normative judgement based on the moral standards of the present rather than on those of the period in question. This argument is similar to the cultural relativist injunction which holds that one cannot and should not judge any given cultural group by the standards of another. However, it is simply not the case that we cannot judge 'others' by our own standards (which is itself a position based on a particular set of values). We can and do make value judgements all the time, and it is important that we do so. Having said that, we obviously need to be aware that our own judgements are indeed shaped by different circumstances, may reflect our own interests, and may be grounded in values that do not resonate everywhere. Because it is almost impossible to occupy a completely objective position, we must rely instead on imperfect inter-subjective agreements on basic standards such as those reflected in various human rights instruments adopted by the international community at large.

Two cases mentioned above in which apologies have been offered for historic wrongs during the Second World War—namely, German apologies for the Holocaust and Japanese apologies for gross human rights violations in China and Korea—bear further scrutiny for the issues they raise, as set out in Box 12.8.

BOX 12.8 CASE STUDY

Germany, Japan, and Historic Apologies

The war histories of Germany and Japan have been the subject of intense scrutiny in debates about responsibility for gross injustices during the Second World War. The facts of war crimes authorized by leaders of both countries are well established. In the case of Germany, the worst crime was the genocidal slaughter of around 6 million Jews from Germany as well as surrounding occupied countries, all civilians, along with many other 'undesirables'—gypsies, homosexuals, and political opponents. In the case of Japan, war crimes included mass atrocities in the form of rape, torture, and murder of civilians, especially in China; the extensive forced prostitution of women in Korea and elsewhere; and the gross mistreatment of prisoners of war, generally including torture, forced labour, and starvation. Many of the leaders directly responsible in both countries were later punished by special tribunals and either executed or imprisoned. But that was not the end of the matter and there have been ongoing issues of responsibility and redress.

The subsequent generation of political leaders, let alone the citizens at large, cannot be held personally responsible for the war crimes committed during that period. But in both cases *the state*, as represented by the later generation of political leaders, is held responsible for some measure of redress for the crimes of their predecessors: first, by current leaders openly recognizing that grave crimes were indeed committed by their predecessors; second, by acknowledging the victimhood of those who suffered; third, by adopting an attitude of remorse and offering an apology on behalf of the state; and fourth, by making reparations in the form of aid. This is notwithstanding that in the case of Japan in particular, conservative nationalist politicians have been rather more loath to acknowledge war criminality and maintain an apologetic stance. And of course there are also Holocaust deniers in Germany and among anti-Semitic elements elsewhere who refuse to accept irrefutable historical evidence and who offer 'alternative facts'.

Those issues aside, what do such acts of apology achieve? Are they just empty gestures or mere tokenism? Do they deliver some measure of intergenerational justice? And how do they impact on the dynamics of the broader global community? Apart from any material gestures that may accompany an act of apology, such as aid or reparations to the relevant communities, the symbolism embodied in a formal apology really is important, not least to surviving victims. In addition, it may be seen as the manifestation of a profoundly important normative shift in attitudes.

An act of apology also has practical implications for those states whose former leaders committed the atrocities. Although sensitivities and tensions over war histories remain and may never be fully reconciled, Germany and Japan have both been able more or less to 'normalize' their international relations rather than remain pariahs in the broader global community or 'society of states'. Allowing states to 'move on' is also important for the overall cohesion of global political relations.

Here it is also worth recalling a point made in Chapter 1 concerning the extent to which subjective emotions of love, hate, anger, joy, pride, and shame play a very real role in politics at all levels, and that humans cannot be seen simply as rational actors dealing with the world according to the objective calculation of interests. Certainly, normative issues of intergenerational justice raised by cases of historic wrongs illustrate the centrality of subjective emotions in how these scenarios play out.

Key points arising from these cases are:

- The significance that an official act of apology can have for communities whose past members suffered egregious human rights violations to have their suffering properly acknowledged should not be underestimated or discounted.

- It is equally important for global society more generally that states whose former political leaders carried out gross human rights violations are able to move on from such histories and participate as 'normal states' in the global sphere.

Of course, there are many other cases of historic injustice arising from warfare, colonialism, slavery, genocide, and other mass atrocities that remain unresolved and for which a measure of intergenerational justice may never be achieved.

The Rights of Future People

We now come, finally, to an issue that might seem odd at first glance—the rights of people who do not even exist—or rather, who do not exist *yet*. Barring a monumental catastrophe that would see virtually all life on the planet extinguished in a totally unexpected event, however, we know that new people will be born every day into a world not only of our making but of the making of our ancestors. In a hundred years' time, most of us living today will no longer be around, and the world will be occupied by up to 12 billion people who do not yet exist. Intergenerational justice in this context requires taking responsibility for the future in recognition that present actions may result in considerable harm to billions of future people.

Normative theorizing and philosophical debates involving the rights of future people is not entirely settled, but the general weight of serious discussion does come down on the side of those who support such rights (see Thompson, 2009). In ordinary discourse, only a moment's reflection is needed to recognize the extent to which we often talk about future generations and what kind of world we will be leaving them. But even if we don't fully recognize the rights of future people, we can nonetheless look to the rights and interests of children and young people who do already exist, but whose political rights (e.g. to vote) are as yet limited and whose fate is still largely determined by decisions taken by the present generation of adults.

Individuals are likely to be concerned first and foremost with the prospects for their own offspring, and will usually take some responsibility for even distant scenarios. At the same time, however, concern for one's own offspring, and their offspring after them, must also entail concern for what kind of broader society they will be living in at both the national and the global level. Even if we place greater value on the well-being of our local or national community, in accord with communitarian sentiments, that community is nonetheless inextricably tied into the fate of the larger global community. One cannot be separated from the other.

CONCLUSION

12

The most common concern expressed by those writing on issues of intergenerational justice for future people is the state of the environment in general and climate change in particular. This will impact, possibly in a very profound way, on virtually all spheres of life—the political, the social, and the economic. As we saw in Chapter 11, 'the environment' has been invested with normative meaning and incorporated in green theories of politics and morality that encompass the interests and well-being of both present and future generations. This is inherent in the concept of 'sustainable development' defined broadly as 'development that meets the needs of the present generation without compromising the ability of future generations to meet their own needs' (https://www.iisd.org/topic/sustainable-development).

This is the basis on which the UN has established a set of sustainable development goals (SDGs) which aim to eliminate poverty, hunger, and violent conflict and reduce inequalities while promoting well-being over a whole raft of goods in the areas of work, health, education, housing, infrastructure, and gender equity, all while ensuring adequate supplies of clean water, delivering energy, water and food security, and providing a clean, healthy environment for the benefit of both present and future generations (see https://www.un.org/sustainabledevelopment/sustainable-development-goals/). The extent to which sustainability is already compromised by environmental pollution of various kinds—from oceans of plastic waste to an atmosphere increasingly saturated by carbon emissions was illustrated in Chapter 11. And the extent to which it is compromising the prospects of the younger generation of the current period has prompted a groundswell among young people who are becoming increasingly concerned about their future.

Youth activism has been especially prominent in the politics of climate change in both national and global spheres, with 'climate strikes' organized by students to express frustration with lack of effective action by the current generation of political leaders on matters concerning their own futures. These were largely triggered by a single young individual, Greta Thunberg (see Box 12.9), who precipitated a groundswell of protest from young people all around the world, from Chile to Hong Kong, the Philippines, Australia, Lebanon, and Sudan, to name just a few.

One further matter, which brings together once again the normative link between past, present, and future, is the question of historic responsibility for harms *already generated* by carbon emissions and which will impact negatively on future generations. Wealthy industrialized countries (mainly in the West) have historically generated much of the carbon that is now saturating the atmosphere, notwithstanding that China is now the number one emitter, with the US second, and India third. To reduce future emissions obviously requires serious action from all three as well as other high-emitting countries. Nonetheless, if we consider the issue from the perspective of global distributive justice—which takes account not just of the distribution of goods and resources but also the distribution of duties and responsibilities—and the fact that advanced industrial countries are responsible for much of the carbon *already* in the atmosphere, then that suggests that they should take on a more significant share of the burden of carbon reduction. At the same time, it does not give *carte blanche* to countries such as China and India to just carry on business as usual, for they have duties and responsibilities to future generations as well, which includes a duty not to make things worse than they already are.

BOX 12.9 SHORT BIOGRAPHY

Greta Thunberg

Born on 3 January 2003 in Stockholm, Sweden, Greta Thunberg was only 15 years old when she sat alone outside the Swedish parliament in August 2018 with a placard proclaiming 'School Strike for the Climate'. Thunberg has since achieved worldwide recognition and has been invited to speak before world leaders at various forums, including the December 2018 UN Climate Change Conference and the 2019 UN Climate Action Summit. She was named *Time* magazine's 2019 person of the year—the youngest ever to hold that award.

Appearing before the US Congress in September 2019, she urged members to listen not so much to her as to the thousands of scientists whose findings, reported by the IPCC, so clearly spell out what the future holds for her generation, and those that will follow. Not surprisingly, those opposed to her views have often ridiculed and/or patronized her at a personal level. In return, Thunberg has highlighted the lack of maturity among world leaders who lack the will to act on climate change, or who even deny its necessity. She has been diagnosed with Asperger syndrome which she sees as an enabling condition—a 'superpower'—rather than a disability. Certainly, she has remarkable persistence and determination, and these qualities have won her huge numbers of followers and admirers around the world. She has become the face of youth activists in global environmental politics who are campaigning for their *right to a viable future*.

FIGURE 12.4 **Greta Thunberg addressing Members of the European Parliament, 2020**

> **KEY POINTS**
>
> - The concept of intergenerational justice highlights the strength of normative links between past, present, and future.
> - Cases of historic wrongs and possible means of redress at a later time raise complex questions of intergenerational responsibility and collective guilt while also illustrating the role of emotions in politics.
> - Intergenerational justice further requires taking responsibility for the future in recognition of the fact that present actions may result in considerable harm to billions in the future, including both the younger generation now living as well as those not yet born.

CONCLUSION

This final chapter has drawn together various themes emerging throughout the book through the prism of normative theory and the contrasting approaches offered by cosmopolitanism and communitarianism with particular reference to concepts of global justice and intergenerational justice. It has shown how these are implicated in many of the issues discussed throughout the book as well as more specifically in relation to citizenship, migration, and refugees, and to questions of historical redress for past wrongs and duties owed to future generations in terms of sustainability. In so doing, the chapter raises further important debating points which require not only a grasp of key developments in global politics, both past and present, but also an appreciation of the different conceptual and theoretical perspectives that may be brought to bear on their analysis.

Whatever else these and other issues discussed throughout the book have shown, they have illustrated above all the interconnectedness—political, social, economic, and environmental—of all people on the planet, whether we like it or not. One simply cannot maintain local or national isolation from the broader processes of global activity, whether these emanate from economic factors, social movements, or from physical changes to the environment. Even Andaman Islanders in the Indian Ocean and small indigenous communities deep in the Amazon rainforest, some of whom have no contact with the outside world at all, are not immune from global environmental changes. But although we do occupy a globalized world, the vast majority of us also live *within* communities—and we do generally value our community ties at both local and national levels.

The question is whether, from an ethical point of view, we actually have to choose between our local and national spaces *or* the broader community of humankind. Our thought processes are often drawn to adopting either/or positions where the choice of one seems to preclude the other. Is it possible to move beyond the cosmopolitan/communitarian divide? Is there some middle ground on which proponents of each can meet? Can we do justice both to those within our more immediate community with whom we share closer cultural and historical ties as well as to those who are both more distant and more different?

As noted earlier, addressing these difficult questions involves making value judgements and, in turn, questioning the basis on which we make such judgements. While this requires acknowledging our ethnocentric biases and our own subjective positions, it should not allow these to cripple our intellectual faculties when it comes to making judgements. The real problem for students of global politics is not how to avoid making value judgements but how to make value judgements that are well informed and reflexive, that have intellectual integrity and respect for evidence, and which take into account both general principles about the human condition as well as the particularities of any given situation or context (Lawson, 2006: p. 182). This is not the end point but rather the starting point for the study of global politics in a highly pluralistic, dynamic, and ever challenging world.

KEY QUESTIONS

1   What is the purpose of normative theory?

2   How can conceptions of global justice and international justice be viewed as complementary rather than opposed?

3   Is it possible to achieve global distributive justice or do those who promote it simply use it to serve another agenda?

4   How do cosmopolitans view the world of states?

5   Does communitarianism simply offer a justification for nationalism and xenophobia?

6   What issues do citizenship, migration, and refugees raise for normative theory in global politics?

7   How valid is the concept of intergenerational justice when it comes to redress of past wrongs?

8   Does the present generation have an obligation to avoid possible future harms to people who do not even exist?

9   How do questions of distributive justice bear on responsibility for historic carbon emissions?

10 What constitutes intellectual integrity in the study of global politics?

FURTHER READING

de Wilde, Pieter, Ruud Koopmans, Wolfgang Merkel, and Michael Zürn (eds) (2019), *The Struggle Over Borders: Cosmopolitanism and Communitarianism* (Cambridge: Cambridge University Press).
  A collection of essays discussing key issues in debates over immigration and refugees from cosmopolitan and communitarian perspectives and in the context of the rise of populism and the backlash against globalization, drawing on examples from Europe and the US as well as Turkey and Mexico.

Diprose, Christina, Gill Valentine, Robert M. Vanderbeck, Chen Liu, and Katie McQuaid (eds) (2019), *Climate Change, Consumption and Intergenerational Justice: Lived Experiences in China, Uganda and the UK* (Bristol: Policy Press).
  This is a short, concise, and accessible account of the links between climate change and consumption and the implications for intergenerational justice drawing on interesting examples from some very different locations and raising issues in 'moral geographies'.

Miller, David (2007), *National Responsibility and Global Justice* (Oxford: Oxford University Press).

It is interesting to see a book which presents a non-cosmopolitan account of global justice in which national responsibility goes beyond borders and extends liability for harms inflicted on other peoples. Global justice is to be understood, not in terms of equality but as a minimum set of basic rights belonging to humans everywhere. The account of collective responsibility also extends to the national past and provides for redress to those harmed by the actions of their predecessors.

Okeja, Uchenna B. (2013), *Normative Justification of a Global Ethic: A Perspective from African Philosophy* (Lanham MD: Lexington Books).

Makes a compelling case for redirecting the discourse on global justice through engagement with a broader range of traditions, such as African philosophy, and the lived experiences of those suffering poverty and violence. It addresses the most basic question of how humans should treat each other and promotes a global ethic based on the Golden Rule—do unto others as you would have them do unto you.

Tan, Kok-Chor (2017), *What Is This Thing Called Global Justice?* (Abingdon: Routledge).

An accessible text which introduces global justice as an important topic for both philosophical discussion as well as for a wide range of practical problems in the global political sphere, including poverty and inequality, nationalism, human rights, immigration, humanitarian intervention, and climate change.

WEB LINKS

https://plato.stanford.edu/entries/justice-global/

High-quality academic article on the theory/philosophy of global justice from the *Stanford Encyclopedia of Philosophy*.

https://www.carnegiecouncil.org/about/mission

Website of the Carnegie Council for Ethics in International Affairs whose mission is to 'inspire and guide debate, and to educate the public on ethical choices in matters related to global affairs'.

https://www.uscis.gov/us-citizenship/citizenship-through-naturalization/a-guide-naturalization

Webpage of US Citizenship and Immigration Services with all the requirements for citizenship by naturalization, giving insight into the rules and regulations, principles and practices, surrounding the process in the US.

https://www.unhcr.org/en-au/figures-at-a-glance.html

UNHCR website providing facts and figures relating to refugees around the world.

https://www.ted.com/speakers/peter_singer

One of the world's best-known figures in the field of applied ethics, Professor Peter Singer, delivers TED (Technology, Entertainment, Design) talks on a range of issues from animal welfare to global poverty. 'TED talks' promulgate 'ideas worth spreading'.

 For additional material and resources please visit the **online resources** at: www.oup.com/he/lawson1e.

GLOSSARY

Agency In social science literature denotes the fact of something happening or existing because of an actor's (agent's) action. The contrast is with a state of affairs that is chiefly determined by impersonal structural factors (historical, economic, etc.) over which human actors have little control.

Anarchy In its simplest sense anarchy denotes an absence of political rule or sovereign authority. In traditional international relations theory, **states** are said to exist in an anarchic international sphere because there is no sovereign authority standing above individual states.

Anthropocentrism An ethic which prioritizes the interests of humans over all other forms of life, often contrasted with **ecocentrism**.

Anthropogenic Something produced by human activity; for example, anthropogenic climate change is produced by fossil fuel consumption, industrial livestock production, large-scale deforestation, etc.

Anti-colonial nationalism This term refers to an ideology of resistance to European **colonialism** in which key elements of nationalist thought, **democracy**, and the principle of **self-determination** are combined and turned against colonizing powers in the quest for independence by subject nations. See also **nationalism** and **colonialism**.

Authoritarianism Refers to a style of rule which is generally unaccountable, restrictive of personal liberty, and which enforces strict obedience to political authority.

Authority A situation whereby an individual or group is regarded as having the right to exercise power and thereby acts legitimately.

Balance of payments Refers to a country's international economic transactions over a certain period showing the sum of all ingoing and outgoing sums between individuals, businesses, and government agencies in that country in relation to those in the rest of the world.

Balance of power A system of relations between **states** where the goal is to maintain an equilibrium of power, thus preventing the dominance of any one state.

Behaviouralism An approach that stresses a narrow view of scientific method in the study of social phenomena, aiming to produce objective, value-free measurement of the social world.

Bipolarity Describes a distribution of power in which two states possess a preponderance of economic, military, and political power and influence either globally or in a particular region. Bipolarity during the Cold War referred to the power and influence of the US vis-à-vis that of the USSR.

Bourgeoisie Term appearing frequently in Marxist analysis and referring to a merchant and/or propertied class possessing essential economic power and control.

Capitalism An economic system in which the means of production, distribution and exchange—which incorporates virtually all trade and industry—is privately owned and operated for profit.

Citizenship A legal status enjoyed by individuals within a **state** which grants them a range of social and political rights including participation in decision-making.

Civic nationalism Refers to loyalty to the institutions and values of a particular political community or **nation-state**—sometimes presented as a more moderate form of **nationalism**.

Civil society Consists of institutions, such as interest groups, which stand in an intermediary position between the individual and the state. See also **global civil society**.

Class analysis Associated with traditional Marxism which places socio-economic class (e.g. proletariat, peasantry, bourgeoisie, aristocracy) at the centre of virtually all political analysis.

Classical liberalism Emphasizes that the state's role should be limited to ensuring internal and external security and protecting individual rights, such as private property rights.

Cold War A term indicating a state of hostility and tension between the superpowers—i.e. the US and the Soviet Union—between the end of the Second World War in 1945 and the collapse of Soviet communism by the early 1990s.

Colonialism A mode of domination involving the subjugation of one population group and their territory to another, usually through settling the territory with sufficient people from the colonizing group to impose direct or indirect rule over the native population and to maintain control over resources and external relations. It is a common manifestation of **imperialism** but is not identical with it.

Communitarianism A strand of thought which argues that individuals gain their rights and duties within particular communities. It is often contrasted with **cosmopolitanism**.

Concert of Europe A largely informal agreement among the major powers of nineteenth-century Europe to act together—or 'concert' together—on matters of mutual concern. It was manifest principally in irregular diplomatic meetings and conferences aimed at the peaceful resolution of differences.

Constructivism Sometimes called *social* constructivism, it refers to the notion that the 'reality' of the world around us is constructed intersubjectively through social interaction which gives meaning to material objects and practices, thus 'reality' is not simply an objective truth detached from a social base.

Cosmopolitan democracy A system of popular control of supranational institutions and processes.

Cosmopolitanism A position which holds that humans ought to be regarded as a single moral community to which universal principles apply irrespective of national boundaries. It is often contrasted with **communitarianism**.

Deglobalization An assumed trend in reversing many integrative aspects of globalization, especially in the economic sphere.

Democratic peace A thesis which holds that countries that are **liberal democracies** do not go to war against each other.

Deterrence Both a theory and a strategy based on the notion that the possession of powerful weapons will deter aggression by other countries. During the Cold War, *nuclear* deterrence was a widely supported strategy.

Developmental state A state which prioritizes economic resources for rapid development, and which uses carrots and sticks to induce private economic institutions to comply.

Dichotomy A division into two apparently mutually exclusive or contradictory entities. For example, the West/non-West divide may be presented as such, although others may argue that it is a false dichotomy.

Ecocentricism An ethic which removes humans from the centre of the moral universe and accords intrinsic value to non-human parts of nature.

Ecological modernization A version of sustainable development which seeks to show how capitalist societies and their technologies can be reformed in an environmentally sustainable way—also called ecomodernism.

Ecologism An ideology that stresses the interdependence of all forms of life, and which is often used to denote the moral dethroning of humans.

Emancipation A common theme in critical theory which denotes a normative aspiration to liberate people from unfair economic, social, and political conditions.

Empire Shares a common etymology with **imperialism** and denotes a system in which one country or centre of power dominates and controls other weaker countries either directly or indirectly using force, the threat of force, or some other means of coercion.

Empirical Based on, concerned with, or verifiable by observation or experience rather than theory or pure logic.

Empirical analysis Refers to an evidence-based approach to the production of 'real-world' data—i.e. factual information about what *is* rather than what *ought* to be.

Enlightenment A seventeenth- and eighteenth-century intellectual and cultural movement that emphasized the application of reason to knowledge in a search for human progress.

Environmentalism A broad philosophy or ideology, also linked to a social movement, which evinces a concern for the environment and, especially, the negative impact of human industrial activity on it.

Epistemology Concerned with the theory of knowledge, including the methods through which we acquire knowledge about what exists, and how we justify claims to knowledge as distinct from opinion or belief.

Ethnic cleansing A term which emerged during the break-up of the former Yugoslavia and which referred to attempts to physically rid (i.e. 'cleanse') a particular area of people from a certain ethnic group by either driving them out or killing them.

Ethnic nationalism Also called ethnonationalism, refers to a form of nationalism in which 'the nation' is defined in terms of particular, distinctive ethnic characteristics such as culture, language, and/or religion as well as common descent.

Ethnocentrism The tendency to see and interpret the world primarily from the perspective of one's own cultural, ethnic, or national group. It often entails elements of hierarchy in that one tends to regard one's own culture as superior, or at least preferable, to others.

Eurocentrism Eurocentrism refers to a worldview that interprets the world essentially from the perspective of European civilization or, more generally, Western civilization. It is a specific form of the more general phenomenon of **ethnocentrism**.

Federal system The organization of a state into different substate territorial units which have the authority to make and implement certain policy decisions without interference from the national centre.

Genocide The deliberate and systematic destruction of people based on their racial, ethnic, national, or religious identity. The term was first coined in the wake of the **Holocaust** to describe the Nazi policy of exterminating the Jews of Europe.

Global civil society Refers broadly to the realm of non-state actors, including interest groups and NGOs in the global sphere.

Global governance This term extends the concept of **governance** to refer loosely to the 'architecture' constituted by various authoritative political, social, and economic structures and actors that interconnect and interact in the absence of actual 'government' in the global sphere.

Global justice The application of principles of justice at a global rather than a national level.

Global South This term corresponds more or less to what was commonly referred to as the 'Third World'. It designates poorer, underdeveloped countries most of which lie geographically south of the equator. Correspondingly, it requires a 'Global North', which is sometimes used as an alternate designation for 'the West'.

Globalism A belief that globalization is producing a transformation such that state boundaries and controls will become increasingly and inevitably meaningless.

Globalization A term used to describe the process of increasing economic, political, social, and cultural interdependence which has, for good or ill, reduced the autonomy of sovereign states.

Good governance A set of principles formulated by international financial institutions to make the government of developing states fair, effective, and free from corruption.

Governance Includes not just the traditional institutions of government but also broader inputs into decisions that steer society such as subnational and supranational institutions, the workings of the market and financial institutions, and the role of interest groups.

Hegemony Embodies the concept of political, social, and economic domination and control. It was developed as an important concept in the critical theory of Antonio Gramsci and is used to theorize relations of domination and subordination in both domestic and international spheres. In the global sphere it may refer to the general dominance of a particular country over others.

Hierarchy A hierarchy in global politics refers to a relationship of authority and a type of order in which a powerful state dominates and where other states are situated at various levels of subordination. An empire is a classic form of hierarchy. Even with a sovereign state system, however, a less formal structure of hierarchy may prevail.

Historical materialism Refers to Karl Marx's materialist conception of history which emphasizes, above all, the material aspects of human society and the way in which forms of societies rise and fall according to trends in human productivity over time. The material conditions of human life, and one's relation with the means of production, determine consciousness and therefore the ideational aspects of existence which include one's values, beliefs, and political principles.

Holocaust An ordinary dictionary meaning of 'holocaust' denotes large-scale destruction of people and property, usually by fire. A potential 'nuclear holocaust' illustrates one such usage. When capitalized, however, the Holocaust usually refers to the mass murder or genocide of around 6 million European Jews during the Second World War by Germany's Nazi regime. The preferred term for many Jews is the Hebrew word Shoah which derives from the biblical term for calamity. See also **genocide**.

Human nature Refers to innate and immutable human characteristics. Hobbes, for instance, regards the competitive and self-serving nature of humans as necessitating an all-powerful state. Other strands of thought regard human nature in a more positive light.

Humanitarian intervention Intervention by one country, or a group of countries, in the internal affairs of another country on the grounds that such intervention is justified by humanitarian concerns relating, for example, to **genocide**. See also **intervention** and **responsibility to protect**.

Idealism For the purposes of international relations theory, idealism refers to a school of liberal thought which emerged in the wake of the First World War and which envisaged opportunities for significant positive change in world affairs, aiming in particular at eliminating warfare. It remains an appropriate designation for any school of thought in global politics which promotes visions of a better world order in which peace and justice prevail. It is sometimes derided as 'utopianism' which implies the impossibility of a permanently peaceful and just global order.

Identity politics Sometimes referred to as the politics of difference, identity politics refers primarily to cultural movements which demand recognition and respect for particular groups of people based on their race, ethnicity, gender, sexual orientation, or nationality.

Imperialism Literally, 'to command', and denoting the exercise of power by one group over another. It is sometimes used synonymously with **colonialism** but is broader in its application because it does not necessarily involve actual physical occupation of the territory in question or direct rule over the subjugated people.

Industrial Revolution The term refers primarily to a period in the eighteenth and nineteenth century when the invention of new machines and methods of mass production in factories brought about significant social and economic change, beginning in the UK and then spreading to the rest of Europe and North America. A second such revolution followed in the late nineteenth and early twentieth centuries with further major developments including the invention of motorized vehicles, aeroplanes, and many other technological advances.

Interdependence The notion developed mainly in liberal theory which holds that states are interconnected through a web of relations, primarily in the economic field, which makes warfare less likely (and less desirable as a foreign policy strategy). *Complex* interdependence simply introduces more variables as relevant to the equation, therefore deepening the complexity of interdependence and strengthening the case for seeing the world as far more pluralistic than neorealist theories allow.

Intergenerational justice Principles of justice relating to non-contemporaries—that is, between those living now and those yet to be born.

International regime An idea encapsulating the way in which groups of actors in certain issue areas converge around a set of principles, norms, rules, and procedures. An example is the international human rights regime.

International society A concept associated with the English School of International Relations suggesting that the condition of anarchy in the international sphere does not preclude the development of a society of states characterized by peaceful working relations.

Internationalism Refers to both a belief in the benefits of international political and economic cooperation and a movement that advocates practical action in support of these objectives.

Intervention In global politics, usually refers to direct intervention by one or more states in the internal affairs of another, by either military or non-military means. See also **humanitarian intervention**.

Isolationism A foreign policy stance that attempts to isolate one's own nation from the problems and affairs of others. It has been applied historically to the US in the period after the First World War and especially during the 1930s when fascism was on the rise in Europe and the US sought to distance itself from such problems.

Liberal democracy Describes states—such as the US, the UK, and India—characterized by free and fair elections involving universal suffrage, together with a liberal political framework consisting of a relatively high degree of personal liberty and the protection of individual rights.

Liberal institutionalism Closely associated with **liberal internationalism**, this concept focuses more attention on the ability of international institutions to ameliorate the negative effects of **anarchy** in the international system.

Liberal internationalism A set of ideas revolving around a belief in the possibility of genuine progress in instituting peaceful and cooperative relations among states in the global or international sphere. These ideas are virtually synonymous with **liberal institutionalism**.

Machtpolitik See **power politics**.

Marxism The political and economic theories of Karl Marx and Friedrich Engels, later developed by their followers to form the basis of communism.

Mercantilism The economic theory that trade generates wealth and is stimulated by the accumulation of profitable balances, which a government should encourage by means of **protectionism**.

Metanarrative Sometimes called a 'grand narrative', this concept refers to a total philosophy or historical explanation of the social and political world, which is presented as an ultimate truth.

Metaphysics A branch of philosophy concerned with the nature of reality and existence, including the relationship between mind and matter (i.e. between the ideational and the material) and between potentiality and actuality. It is highly abstract, dealing with concepts such as knowing, being, identity, free will, determinism, and so on.

Methodology Refers primarily to the particular way(s) in which knowledge is produced. Methodologies vary considerably depending on the type of research being carried out to produce knowledge in different fields—historical, anthropological, linguistic, biological, medical, etc. Different methodologies invariably incorporate their own assumptions and rationales about the nature of knowledge, although these are not always stated explicitly.

Militarism An ideology that emphasizes the importance of military power in the belief that a state requires such power to preserve and expand its interests vis-à-vis other states. A strongly militaristic state tends to spend disproportionately on its defence forces and therefore subordinates other national goods to the military cause.

Modernity Modernity is a temporal and cultural phenomenon linked not only to the rise of industrialization in Europe and North America but also to profound changes in social and political thought which are closely associated with the intellectual movement known as the **Enlightenment**.

Multilateralism Multilateralism in global politics refers to a situation where three or more states cooperate in a certain policy area and/or on a particular course of action with respect to an issue of mutual concern. Global and regional institutions are essentially held together by a commitment to multilateral principles. Multilateralism contrasts with **unilateralism**.

Nation A named community, often referred to as 'a people', usually occupying a homeland and sharing one or more ethnic or cultural elements, such as a common history, language, religion, customs, etc. Nations may or may not have a state of their own.

National interest A concept closely associated with *raison d'état* (**reason of state**), **statecraft**, and **power politics**. It suggests that the interests of the **state** (or at least of one's own state) are paramount over any other consideration in the international sphere.

Nationalism In politics and international relations, nationalism refers to an ideology which holds that 'the **nation**' is more or less entitled to political autonomy, usually in a **state** of its own. See also **anti-colonial nationalism**, **civic nationalism**, and **ethnic nationalism**.

Nation-state A composite term bringing together two distinct entities—the **nation** understood as 'a people' and the **state** as a legal, territorial entity in which a structure of rule and authority over its people is embedded.

Natural law Law conceived as both universal and eternal, applying to all people in all places and at all times, because it derives from either 'nature' or God as distinct from local laws arising within specific communities.

Natural rights Rights which humans are said to possess irrespective of the particular legal or political system under which they live.

Neoliberalism This term has two distinct applications. First, it denotes a renewed school of liberal thought in international relations which emerged in the post-war period and which gave greater emphasis to the plurality of actors and institutions in the global sphere, Second, it refers to a powerful trend in economic liberal thought favouring free-market **capitalism** and a minimal role for the **state** in regulating economic activity and in providing services.

Neorealism A reformulation of **realism** in international relations in the post-war period which moves away from ideas about **human nature**, focusing rather on the *structure* of **anarchy** in the international sphere as the major determining factor in the play of **power politics**. For that reason it is also known as structural realism.

Non-governmental organization (NGO) A term applying to almost any organization that operates independently from government, whether at the local, national, or international level.

Normative analysis Refers to analysis which asks 'ought' rather than 'is' type questions, therefore forming the basis of political philosophy. It does not seek to ask, for example, whether **democracy**, or freedom, or a pluralist state exists, but whether these outcomes are desirable ones.

Ontology Relates to what exists. It asks what is there to know? Is there, for instance, an objective political world out there capable of being observed? Or is its reality, to at least some degree, actually created by the meanings or ideas we impose upon it?

Orientalism A term derived from the title of Edward Said's major work which denotes the means by which Europeans (or more generally Westerners) have often defined themselves and therefore assumed an identity vis-à-vis non-Western 'others', and in so doing have generally placed themselves in a position of relative superiority. Orientalism also involves the production of knowledge of non-Western others as a means of domination and control tantamount to **hegemony**.

Patriarchy Refers to male domination and corresponding female subordination and oppression.

Pluralism In global politics the concept is associated with one of two main approaches adopted by the English School in which the world is recognized as inherently pluralistic in terms of culture, interests, world views etc., as well as with **neoliberalism** which highlights the multiplicity, or plurality, of forces at work in the global sphere, including a variety of non-state actors.

Populism A political approach or strategy that aims to appeal emotionally to ordinary people who feel that their concerns are disregarded by established elite groups.

Positivism An approach which believes it is possible to generate empirical statements without any evaluative connotations. At an extreme level, 'logical positivists' argue that only empirical statements, together with those that are true by definition, are meaningful, thereby ruling out the value of normative statements altogether.

Postmodernism A multifaceted theoretical approach which challenges the certainties of modernism or **modernity**. It promotes **pluralism** and difference and can therefore be allied with projects of **identity politics**.

Power politics (*Machtpolitik*) A view of politics associated with realism and which generally takes morality and justice to be irrelevant to the conduct of international relations, a view predicated in turn on the notion that 'might is right'.

Protectionism An economic strategy, usually associated with a national policy of trade restriction in the form of tariffs and quotas, which attempts to protect domestic industries, businesses, and jobs from competition from abroad.

Racism Involves prejudice, discrimination, antagonism, and sometimes outright hatred directed against others perceived as belonging to a different racial, ethnic, cultural, or religious group, accompanied by a belief that one's own group is inherently superior.

Realism Denotes a complex array of theories and ideas in the human sciences, especially philosophy, sociology, politics, and international relations. In the latter, it names a general approach to theory which takes **power politics**, **national interest**, and similar concepts as foundational to action in the global sphere, and opposes what it sees as **idealism** in liberal and critical theories. See also **neorealism**.

Reason of state (*raison d'état*) Justification and rationalization of any action, mainly in foreign policy, that is presented as strictly and necessarily in the

national interest. It is allied closely with **realism** in international relations.

Regionalization A process in which a number of states in a given geographical area come together for mutually beneficial purposes, often forming a regional association. Some, like the EU, are highly institutionalized and have myriad economic, social, and political interconnections, while others may have minimal rules and less ambitious purposes.

Religious fundamentalism Refers to the belief of an individual or a group of individuals in the absolute authority of a sacred religious text or teachings of a particular religious leader, prophet, and/or God.

Responsibility to protect A relatively recent doctrine in global politics which modifies the **sovereignty** principle to allow **humanitarian intervention** in the internal affairs of a **state** in an attempt to alleviate gross human suffering.

Rule of law Refers mainly to the principle that everyone in a **state**, the executive included, is subject to the same impersonal laws. It may be extended to the global sphere in that every state, including the most powerful, is subject to international law. It is related to the concept of a **rules-based international order**.

Rules-based international order A global order characterized by a shared commitment, principally among UN member states and/or members of regional organizations, to act in accordance with agreed rules that have evolved over time and are encompassed in various bodies of international law and regional agreements.

Secession In global politics, secession refers to the withdrawal or breakaway by a distinctive group and their territory from an existing **state** to form a new state, or to re-establish an old one. The disintegration of the former Soviet Union and Yugoslavia provides many examples of the phenomenon in the post-Cold War period.

Secularism In political terms, it refers to the removal of religion from a privileged position in the **state**.

Security dilemma A concept developed principally in **realism**, in which the condition of **anarchy** is seen to prompt **states** to engage in self-regarding behaviour in order to survive. The dilemma arises when efforts by one state to enhance its own security (such as acquiring superior weaponry) provokes insecurity in another state, which may then respond by building up its own military capacity.

Self-determination A doctrine that emerged in the early twentieth century in relation to the right of 'peoples' (**nations**) to determine their own political future, thus embodying elements of both **democracy** and **nationalism**.

Social constructivism See **constructivism**.

Social democracy An approach which, after the Russian Revolution in 1917, became associated with **liberal democracies** which also engaged in redistributive policies and the creation of a welfare state.

Social justice The principle that goods ought to be distributed according to a principle based on need, merit, or pure equality.

Social movements Refers to largely informal broad-based movements composed of groups and individuals coalescing around key issue areas on a voluntary and often spontaneous basis. Examples include the environmental movement, the women's movement, the peace movement, and the anti-globalization movement.

Solidarism A term applied to a branch of thought in English School theory which seeks to promote greater protection of human rights internationally, even where this overrides, at least in principle, the rights of states to non-**intervention** in domestic politics. It is usually contrasted with the English School conceptualization of **pluralism**.

Sovereignty To say that a state is sovereign is to say that it is self-governing, subject to no other **state** in the global sphere, and possesses a monopoly of authority over the people and institutions in a given territorial area, including the exclusive right to use force.

State In the global sphere, the state refers specifically to the modern sovereign state—a legal entity recognized as possessing certain characteristics (namely, a legitimate claim over a territory and the people residing there) along with certain rights and duties vis-à-vis other states in the international system.

State of nature A concept with a long history in political and social thought which posits a hypothetical vision of how people lived before the institution of civil government and society. There are competing versions of the state of nature, some equating it with **anarchy** and therefore portraying it as dangerous while others see it in a more positive light.

Statecraft The skilful conduct of state affairs, usually in the context of external or foreign relations.

Structural adjustment Used in application to economic policies imposed on countries—usually poor and underdeveloped—by the World Bank and the International Monetary Fund as a condition for obtaining loans. Specific policies have included privatization, cuts in government expenditure on public services, devaluation, and tariff cuts.

Sustainable development A term denoting a mode of economic growth that aims to be compatible with environmental protection.

Third World See **Global South**.

Unilateralism Refers to the tendency of a state to pursue its preferred foreign policy strategies regardless of whether there is support from international bodies (such as the UN), or of any international law, or of the interests of other states. Unilateralism contrasts with **multilateralism.**

REFERENCES

Abello-Galbis, Ricardo and Walter Arévalo-Ramírez (2017), 'The Influence of the Latin American Doctrine on International Law', in Paula Wojcikiewicz Almeida and Jean-Marc Sorel (eds), *Latin America and the International Court of Justice: Contributions to International Law* (New York: Routledge), pp. 15–27.

Acharya, Amitav (2017), 'Towards a Global International Relations?', 10 December, *E-International Relations*, https://www.e-ir.info/2017/12/10/towards-a-global-international-relations/.

Acharya, Amitav and Barry Buzan (2019), *The Making of Global International Relations: Origins and Evolution of IR at its Centenary* (Cambridge: Cambridge University Press).

Agathangelou, Anna and Lily Ling (2004), 'The House of IR: From Family Power Politics to the *Poisies* of Worldism', *International Studies Review*, 6(1): 21–49.

Alatas, Syed Farid (2014), *Applying Ibn Khaldun: The Recovery of a Lost Tradition in Sociology* (Abingdon: Routledge).

Alshdaifat, Shadi Adnan (2017), *International Law and the Use of Force Against Terrorism* (Newcastle Upon Tyne: Cambridge Scholars Publishing).

Altman, Amnon (2012), *Tracing the Earliest Recorded Concepts of International Law: The Ancient Near East (2500–330 BCE)* (Leiden: Martinus Nijhoff).

Altman, Dennis and Jonathan Symons (2015), 'International Norm Polarization: Sexuality as a Subject of Human Rights Protection', *International Theory*, 7(1): 61–95.

Amoore, Louise (ed.) (2005), *The Global Resistance Reader* (London: Routledge).

Ang, Ien, Yudhishthir Raj Isar, and Phillip Mar (eds) (2016), *Cultural Diplomacy: Beyond the National Interest?* (Abingdon: Routledge).

Angell, Norman (1934), *The Great Illusion* (London: W. Heinemann).

Anievas, Alexander (ed.) (2010), *Marxism and World Politics: Contesting Global Capitalism* (London: Routledge).

Anievas, Alexander, Nivi Manchanda and Robbie Shilliam (2015), 'Confronting the Global Colour Line: An Introduction', in Alexander Anievas, Nivi Manchanda, and Robbie Shilliam (eds), *Race and Racism in International Relations: Confronting the Global Colour Line* (London: Routledge), pp. 1–15.

Anderson, Benedict (2006), *Imagined Communities: Reflections on the Origins and Spread of Nationalism* (London: Verso, rev. edn).

Anderson, James (2015), 'Nationalist Ideology and Territory', in R. J. Johnston, David Knight, and Eleonore Kofman (eds), *Nationalism, Self-Determination and Political Geography* (Abingdon: Routledge), pp. 18–39.

Appiah, Kwame Anthony (2007), *Cosmopolitanism: Ethics in a World of Strangers* (London: Penguin).

Aquinas, St Thomas (2002), *On Law, Morality, and Politics,* trans. Richard J. Regan, intr. William P. Baumgarth (Indianapolis: Hackett Publishing, 2nd edn).

Archer, Clive (1983), *International Organizations* (London: Allen & Unwin).

Archibugi, Daniele (2008), *The Global Commonwealth of Citizens: Toward Cosmopolitan Democracy* (Princeton, NJ: Princeton University Press).

Arendt, Hannah (1968), *Totalitarianism: Part Three of the Origins of Totalitarianism* (San Diego: Harvest Books).

Aristotle (1981), *The Politics*, trans. T. A. Sinclair, rev. T. J. Saunders (London: Penguin).

Armitage, David and Jennifer Pitts (2017), '"This Modern Grotius": An Introduction to the Life and Thought of C. H. Alexandrowicz', in C. H. Alexandrowicz, *The Law of Nations in Global History,* David Armitage and Jennifer Pitts (eds) (Oxford: Oxford University Press), pp. 1–34.

Ashworth, Lucian M. (2018), 'The Origins of International Relations', https://www.bisa.ac.uk/index.php/research-articles/539-the-origins-of-international-relations.

Axford, Barry (2013), *Theories of Globalization* (Cambridge: Polity Press).

Axworthy, Michael and Patrick Milton (2016), 'The Myth of Westphalia: Understanding Its True Legacy Might Help the Middle East', *Foreign Affairs,* 22 December, https://www.foreignaffairs.com/articles/europe/2016-12-22/myth-westphalia.

Bakircioglu, Onder (2014), *Islam and Warfare: Context and Compatibility with International Law* (Abingdon: Routledge).

Balaam, David N. and Michael Veseth (2005), *Introduction to International Political Economy* (Upper Saddle River, NJ: Pearson Prentice Hall, 3rd edn).

Balibar, Etienne (1991), 'Racism and Nationalism', in Etienne Balibar and Immanuel Wallerstein (eds), *Race, Nation, Class: Ambiguous Identities* (London: Verso), pp. 37–67.

Bangkok Declaration (1993), *Final Declaration of the Regional Meeting for Asia of the World Conference on Human Rights,* 29 March–2 April.

Banton, Michael (1998), *Racial Theories* (Cambridge: Cambridge University Press, 2nd edn).

Bassil, Noah R. (2013), *The Post-Colonial State and Civil War in Sudan: The Origins of Conflict in Darfur* (London: I.B. Tauris).

Baumeister, Hannah (2018), *Sexualised Crimes, Armed Conflict and the Law: The International Criminal Court and the Definitions of Rape and Forced Marriage* (Abingdon: Routledge).

BBC (2005), 'Apology Over Kill Chavez TV Call', 25 Aug., http://news.bbc.co.uk/2/hi/americas/4182294.stm

Bederman, David J. (2008), *International Law in the Ancient World* (Emory University School of Law, Public Law & Legal Theory Research Paper Series, Research Paper No. 08–32 available at <https://papers.ssrn.com/sol3/papers.cfm?abstract_id=1092442>).

Bell, Duncan (ed.) (2008), *Political Thought and International Relations: Variations on a Realist Theme* (Oxford: Oxford University Press).

Bellamy, Alex J. (2006), 'Whither the Responsibility to Protect? Humanitarian Intervention and the 2005 World Summit', *Ethics and International Affairs,* 20(2): 143–70.

Bentley, Tom (2016), 'Should a Nation Apologise for its Past', *The Conversation,* 18 October, https://theconversation.com/should-a-nation-apologise-for-the-crimes-of-its-past-66525.

Berridge, G. R. (2015), *Diplomacy: Theory and Practice* (Basingstoke: Palgrave Macmillan, 5th edn).

Berridge, G. R. (2018), 'Which London Embassy Needs 13 Cultural Attachés?', 10 December, https://grberridge.diplomacy.edu/.

Birch, Kean (2017), *A Research Agenda for Neoliberalism* (Cheltenham: Edward Elgar).

Bjola, Corneliu and Markus Kornprobst (2018), *Understanding International Diplomacy: Theory, Practice and Ethics* (Abingdon: Routledge, 2nd edn).

Blanchard, Eric M. (2003), 'Gender, International Relations, and the Development of Feminist Security Theory', *Signs: Journal of Women in Culture and Society,* 28(4): 1289–312.

Boesche, Roger (2002), 'Moderate Machiavelli? Contrasting The Prince with the Arthasastra of Kautilya', *Critical Horizons,* 3(2): 253–76.

Booth, Ken (2007), *Theory of World Security* (Cambridge: Cambridge University Press).

Booth, Robert and Julian Borger (2010), 'US Diplomats Spied on UN Leadership', *Guardian,* 29 November, https://www.theguardian.com/world/2010/nov/28/us-embassy-cables-spying-un.

Boucher, David (1998), *Political Theories of International Relations: From Thucydides to the Present* (Oxford: Oxford University Press).

Boutchie, Jessica (2019), 'Globalizing Hatred', *Harvard Political Review,* 15 March, https://harvardpolitics.com/covers/globalizing-hatred/.

Braveboy-Wagner, Jacqueline Anne (2009), *Institutions of the Global South* (Abingdon: Routledge).

Bremmer, Ian (2018), *Us vs Them: The Failure of Globalism* (London: Penguin).

Breuilly, John (ed.) (2013), *The Oxford Handbook of the History of Nationalism* (Oxford: Oxford University Press).

Brock, Gillian (2015), 'Global Justice', in Edward N. Zalta (ed.), *Stanford Encyclopedia of Philosophy,* https://plato.stanford.edu/entries/justice-global/.

Brooks, Stephen (2009), *Canadian Democracy* (Toronto: Oxford University Press, 6th edn).

Brown, Chris and Robyn Eckersley (eds) (2018), *The Oxford Handbook of International Political Theory* (Oxford: Oxford University Press).

Bull, Hedley (1979), 'Natural Law and International Relations', *British Journal of International Studies,* 5(2): 171–81.

Bull, Hedley (1997), *The Anarchic Society* (New York: Columbia University Press).

Burbank, Jane and Frederick Cooper (2010), *Empires in World History: Power and the Politics of Difference* (Princeton, NJ: Princeton University Press).

Burke, Roland (2010), *Decolonization and the Evolution of International Human Rights* (Philadelphia, PA: University of Pennsylvania Press).

Butler, Geoffrey G. and Simon MacCoby (2003), *Development of International Law* (Union, NJ: Lawbook Exchange).

Butler, Judith (2006), *Gender Trouble: Feminism and the Subversion of Identity* (New York: Routledge).

Butterfield, Herbert (1966), 'The New Diplomacy and Historical Diplomacy', in Herbert Butterfield and Martin Wight (eds), *Diplomatic Investigation: Essays in the Theory of International Politics* (London: George Allen & Unwin), pp. 181–92.

Buzan, Barry (2004), *From International to World Society: English School Theory and the Social Structure of Globalisation* (Cambridge: Cambridge University Press).

Buzan, Barry and Laust Schouenborg (2018), *Global International Society: A New Framework for Analysis* (Cambridge: Cambridge University Press).

Buzan, Barry, Ole Waever, and Jaap de Wilde (1998), *Security: A New Framework for Analysis* (Boulder: Lynne Rienner).

Cafruny, Alan, Leila Simona Talani, and Gonzalo Pozo Martin (eds) (2016), *The Palgrave Handbook of Critical International Political Economy* (London: Palgrave Macmillan).

Çalkivik, Asli (2017), *Poststructuralism and Postmodernism in International Relations* (Oxford: Oxford University Press).

Çalkivik, Asli (2020), 'Poststructuralism and Postmodernism in International Relations', *Oxford Research Encyclopedias* (Oxford: International Studies Association and Oxford University Press), 31 March, https://oxfordre.com/internationalstudies/view/10.1093/acrefore/9780190846626.001.0001/acrefore-9780190846626-e-102.

Callinicos, Alex (2018), 'Lenin and Imperialism', in Tom Rockmore and Norman Levine (eds), *Palgrave Handbook of Leninist Political Philosophy* (London: Palgrave Macmillan), pp. 457–82.

Carr, Edward Hallett (1948), *The Twenty Years' Crisis, 1919–1939: An Introduction to the Study of International Relations* (London: Macmillan).

Carson, Rachel (2002), *Silent Spring* (Boston, MA: Houghton Mifflin).

Celis, Karen, Johanna Kantola, Georgina Waylen, and S. Laurel (eds) (2013), 'Introduction: Gender and Politics: A Gendered World, A Gendered Discipline', in Georgina Waylen, Karen Celis, Johanna Kantola, and S. Laurel Weldon (eds), *The Oxford Handbook of Gender and Politics* (Oxford: Oxford University Press), pp. 1–26.

Chakrabarty, Dipesh (2008), *Provincializing Europe: Postcolonial Thought and Historical Difference* (Princeton, NJ: Princeton University Press, new edn).

Chan, Adrian (2003), *Chinese Marxism* (London: Continuum).

Chapman, Malcolm, Maryon McDonald, and Elizabeth Tonkin (2016), 'Introduction—History and Social Anthropology', in Elizabeth Tonkin, Maryon McDonald, and Malcolm Chapman (eds), *History and Ethnicity* (Abingdon: Routledge), pp. 1–21.

Chavez, Tizoc (2019), 'Personal Diplomacy Has Long Been a Presidential Tactic, But Trump Adds a Twist', *The Conversation,* 23 January, https://theconversation.com/personal-diplomacy-has-long-been-a-presidential-tactic-but-trump-adds-a-twist-105031.

Chen, Ching-Chang (2011), 'The Absence of Non-Western IR Theory in Asia Reconsidered', *International Relations of the Asia-Pacific,* 11(1): 1–23.

Chew, Jonathan (2016), '7 Corporate Giants Accused of Evading Billions in Taxes', *Fortune International*, 11 March, http://fortune.com/2016/03/11/apple-google-taxes-eu/.

Chisolm, Amanda and Joanna Tidy (eds) (2018), *Masculinities at the Margins: Beyond the Hegemonic in the Study of Militaries, Masculinities and War* (Abingdon: Routledge).

Christodoulidis, Emilios, Ruth Dukes, and Marco Goldoni (eds) (2019), *Research Handbook on Critical Legal Theory* (Cheltenham: Edward Elgar).

Chun, Shen (2009), 'On Chinese Cosmopolitanism: Tian Xia', *Culture Mandala: Bulletin of the Centre for East-West Cultural & Economic Studies,* 8(2): 20–9.

Clark, Ian (2005), *Legitimacy in International Society* (Oxford: Oxford University Press).

Cobham, Alex and Petr Jansky (2017), *Global Distribution of Revenue Loss from Tax Avoidance,* WIDER Working Paper 2017/55, March, UNU-WIDER, https://www.wider.unu.edu/sites/default/files/wp2017-55.pdf.

Cohen, Adam D. (2020), 'Experts Highlight How Science Diplomacy Combats Pandemics', *AAAS News,* 1 April, https://www.aaas.org/news/experts-highlight-how-science-diplomacy-combats-pandemics.

Cohn, Theodore H. (2005), *Global Political Economy: Theory and Practice* (New York: Pearson Longman, 3rd edn).

Colomer, Josep M. (2017), 'Empires Versus States', *Politics* (Oxford: Oxford Research Encyclopaedias).

Connell, R. W. (2005), *Masculinities* (Cambridge: Polity Press, 2nd edn).

Constantinou, Costas M., Pauline Kerr, and Paul Sharp (eds) (2016), *The Sage Handbook of Diplomacy* (Thousand Oaks, CA: Sage).

Corr, Anders (2017), 'Ban Official Chinese Student Organizations Abroad', *Forbes,* 4 June, https://www.forbes.com/sites/anderscorr/2017/06/04/ban-official-chinese-student-organizations-abroad/#6b3615f35bbc.

Cox, Michael (2016), 'Introduction by Michael Cox', in E. H. Carr, *The Twenty Years' Crisis, 1919–1939* (London: Palgrave Macmillan).

Cox, Robert (1981), 'Social Forces, States and World Orders: Beyond International Relations Theory', *Millennium: Journal of International Studies,* 10(2): 126–55.

Craig, Gordon A. and Alexander L. George (1990), *Force and Statecraft: Diplomatic Problems of our Times* (New York: Oxford University Press, 2nd edn).

Cramer, Jane K. and A. Trevor Thrall (eds) (2012), *Why Did the United States Invade Iraq?* (Abingdon: Routledge).

Crutzen, Paul J. (2010), 'Anthropocene Man', *Nature,* 467, 14(S10) October, http://www.nature.com/nature/journal/v467/n7317_supp/full/467S10a.html.

Crutzen, Paul J. and Eugene F. Stoermer (2000), 'The Anthropocene', Max Planck Institute for Chemistry, *IGBP Newsletter,* 41, May, http://www.mpic.de/en/honors-and-awards/the-anthropocene.html.

Dannreuther, Roland (2004), 'Introduction: Setting the Framework', in Roland Dannreuther (ed.), *European Union Foreign and Security Policy: Towards a Neighbourhood Strategy* (London: Routledge), pp. 1–11.

Darian-Smith, Eve and Philip C. McCarty (2017), *The Global Turn: Theories, Research Designs, and Methods for Global Studies* (Oakland, CA: University of California Press).

Dasgupta, Samir and Peter Kivisto (eds) (2014), *Postmodernism in a Global Perspective* (New Delhi: Sage).

Dauvergne, Peter (ed.) (2012), *Handbook of Global Environmental Politics* (Cheltenham: Edward Elgar, 2nd edn).

Davidson, Alastair (2018), *Antonio Gramsci: Towards an Intellectual Biography* (Chicago: Haymarket Books).

Davies, Sara and Jacqui True (eds) (2019), 'WPS: A Transformative Agenda', *The Oxford Handbook of Women, Peace and Security* (Oxford: Oxford University Press).

Dejevsky, Mary (2017), 'In Defence of Donald Trump's Twitter Diplomacy', *Guardian,* 6 February, https://www.theguardian.com/commentisfree/2017/feb/05/in-defence-of-twitter-diplomacy.

de Jong, Sara (2017), *Complicit Sisters: Gender and Women's Issues Across North-South Divides* (New York: Oxford University Press).

de Jong, Sara, Rosalba Icaza, and Olivia U. Rutazibwa (eds) (2018), *Decolonization and Feminisms in Global Teaching and Learning* (Abingdon: Routledge).

Delanty, Gerard (2014), 'Not All Is Lost in Translation: World Varieties of Cosmopolitanism', *Cultural Sociology,* 8(4): 374–91.

De Mars, William E. and Dennis Dijkzeul (eds) (2015), *The NGO Challenge for International Relations Theory* (Abingdon: Routledge).

Deng, Francis M. (1995), *War of Visions: Conflict of Identities in the Sudan* (Washington, DC: Brookings Institution).

Denning, Steve (2018), 'How Russia is Still Running Interference for Trump', *Forbes,* 19 December, https://www.forbes.com/sites/stevedenning/2018/12/19/how-putin-augments-trumps-disinformation-against-the-russia-probe/#6e66b58749a0.

de Wilde, Pieter, Ruud Koopmans, Wolfgang Merkel, and Michael Zürn (eds) (2019), *The Struggle Over Borders: Cosmopolitanism and Communitarianism* (Cambridge: Cambridge University Press).

Diehl, Paul F. (ed.) (2005), *The Politics of Global Governance: International Organizations in an Interdependent World* (Boulder, CO: Lynne Rienner, 3rd edn).

Diprose, Christina, Gill Valentine, Robert M. Vanderbeck, Chen Liu, and Katie McQuaid (eds) (2019), *Climate Change, Consumption and Intergenerational Justice: Lived Experiences in China, Uganda and the UK* (Bristol: Policy Press).

Dishman, Chris (2005), 'The Leaderless Nexus: When Crime and Terror Converge', *Studies in Conflict and Terrorism*, 28(3): 237–52.

Dobson, Andrew (2012), *Green Political Thought* (Abingdon: Routledge).

Dryzek, John (2013), *The Politics of the Earth: Environmental Discourses* (Oxford: Oxford University Press, 3rd edn).

Duducu, Jem (2018), *The Sultans: The Rise and Fall of the Ottoman Rulers and their World: A 600 Year History* (Stroud: Amberley Publishing).

Dunn, Kevin C. (2001), 'Introduction: Africa and International Relations Theory', in Kevin C. Dunn and Timothy M. Shaw (eds), *Africa's Challenge to International Relations Theory* (Basingstoke: Palgrave), pp. 1–10.

Dunne, Tim (1998), *Inventing International Society: A History of the English School* (Basingstoke: Macmillan).

Dunne, Tim (2016), *The English School and International Intervention*, E-International Relations, 17 February, https://www.e-ir.info/2016/02/17/the-english-school-and-humanitarian-intervention/

Eagleton-Pierce, Matthew (2016), *Neoliberalism: The Key Concepts* (Abingdon: Routledge).

Eckersley, Robyn (2004), *The Green State: Rethinking Democracy and Sovereignty* (Cambridge, MA: MIT Press).

Economist (2019), 'Are Dictatorships Better Than Democracies at Fighting Climate Change', 21 September, https://www.economist.com/asia/2019/09/21/are-dictatorships-better-than-democracies-at-fighting-climate-change.

Edkins, Jenny (2019), *Routledge Handbook of Critical International Relations* (Abingdon: Routledge).

Ehrlich, Paul (1968), *The Population Bomb* (New York: Ballantyne).

Engel, Ulf, Heidrun Zinecker, Frank Mattheis, Antje Dietze, and Thomas Plötze (eds) (2017), *The New Politics of Regionalism: Perspectives from Africa, Latin America and Asia-Pacific* (Abingdon: Routledge).

Enloe, Cynthia (2013), 'Interview', E-International Relations, 13 March, https://www.e-ir.info/2013/03/13/interview-cynthia-enloe/.

Enloe, Cynthia (2014), *Bananas, Beaches and Bases: Making Feminist Sense of International Politics* (Berkeley: University of California Press, 2nd edn).

Erikson, Thomas Hylland (2014), *Globalization: The Key Concepts* (London: Bloomsbury Academic, 2nd edn).

Eroukhmanoff, Clara (2018), 'Securitization Theory: An Introduction', *E-International Relations*, 14 January, https://www.e-ir.info/2018/01/14/securitisation-theory-an-introduction/.

Eslava, Luis, Michael Fakhri, and Vasuki Nesiah (2017), 'Introduction: The Spirit of Bandung', in Luis Eslava, Michael Fakhri, and Vasuki Nesiah (eds), *Bandung, Global History, International Law: Critical Pasts and Pending Futures* (Cambridge: Cambridge University Press), pp. 3–32.

EU (European Union) (2018), 'The EU In Brief', 4 July, https://europa.eu/european-union/about-eu/eu-in-brief_en.

Eun, Yong-Soo (2019), 'An Intellectual Confession from a Member of the "Non-White" IR Community: A Friendly Reply to David Lake's "White Man's IR"', *PS: Political Science and Politics*, 52(1): 78–84.

Evangelista, Matthew and Nina Tannenwald (eds) (2017), *Do the Geneva Conventions Matter?* (Oxford: Oxford University Press).

Evans, Graham and Jeffrey Newnham (1998), *The Penguin Dictionary of International Relations* (London: Penguin).

Farrell, Mary (2005), 'EU External Relations: Exporting the EU Model of Governance', *European Foreign Affairs Review*, 10(4): 451–62.

Fassbender, Bardo and Anne Peters (2012), 'Introduction: Towards a Global History of International Law', in Bardo Fassbender, Anne Peters, Simone Peter and Daniel Högger (eds), *The Oxford Handbook of the History of International Law* (Oxford: Oxford University Press), pp. 1–26.

Faulks, Keith (2000), *Citizenship* (London: Routledge).

Felsenthal, Edward (2019), 'Front Line Workers Tell Their Own Stories in the New Issue of TIME', *Time*, 28 January, http://time.com/5511960/charges-against-meng-wanzhou-huawei.

Ferguson, Niall (2003a), 'Hegemony or Empire', *Foreign Affairs*, 82(5): 154–61.

Ferguson, Niall (2003b), *Empire: How Britain Made the Modern World* (London: Allen Lane).

Financial Times (2018), 'US and UK Accuse China of Cyber Espionage Campaign', 21 December, https://www.ft.com/content/f5f0b42c-046c-11e9-99df-6183d3002ee.

Foucault, Michel (1980), *Power/Knowledge: Selected Interviews and Other Writings, 1972–1977, Part 2*, ed. Colin Gordon (Brighton: Harvester Press).

Franck, Thomas M. (1997–98), 'Three Major Innovations of International Law in the Twentieth Century', 17 QLR 139: 139–56.

Frank, Andre Gunder (1967), *Capitalism and Underdevelopment in Latin America: Historical Studies of Chile and Brazil* (New York: Monthly Review Press).

Frank, Andre Gunder and Barry K. Gills (eds) (1996), *The World System: Five Hundred Years or Five Thousand?* (London: Routledge).

Frazer, Elizabeth (2018), 'Feminism and Realism', in Matt Sleat (ed.), *Politics Recovered: Realist Thought in Theory and Practice* (New York: Columbia University Press).

Freedman, Rosa (2015), *Failing to Protect: The UN and the Politicization of Human Rights* (Oxford: Oxford University Press).

Fukuyama, Francis (1989), 'The End of History?', *The National Interest*, 16: 3–18.

Gabbatis, John (2018), 'Americans who believe in conspiracy theories about 9/11 and Princess Diana's death more likely to doubt climate change', *Independent*, 9 May, https://www.independent.co.uk/environment/climate-change-conspiracy-theory-new-world-order-jfk-princess-diana-a8343291.html.

Gaddis, John Lewis, Philip H. Gordon, Ernest R. May, and Jonathan Rosenberg (eds) (1999), *Cold War*

Statesmen Confront the Bomb: Nuclear Diplomacy since 1945 (New York: Oxford University Press).

Galbraith, J. K. (1984), 'Comment', *National Review*, 36 (6): 39–42.

Gannon, Megan (2016), 'Race is a Social Construct, Scientists Argue', *Scientific American*, 5 February, https://www.scientificamerican.com/article/race-is-a-social-construct-scientists-argue/.

Garton-Ash, Timothy (2010), 'US Embassy Cables: A Banquet of Secrets', *Guardian*, 29 November, https://www.theguardian.com/commentisfree/2010/nov/28/wikileaks-diplomacy-us-media-war.

Gerbet, Pierre (1981), 'Rise and Development of International Organizations', in Georges Abi-Saab (ed.), *The Concept of International Organization* (Paris: UNESCO).

Giddens, Anthony (1985), *The Nation-State and Violence* (Berkeley: University of California Press).

Gillings, Michael R. and Elizabeth L. Hagan-Lawson (2014), 'The Cost of Living in the Anthropocene', *Earth Perspectives*, 1(2): 1–11.

Gilpin, Robert with Jean Gilpin (1987), *The Political Economy of International Relations* (Princeton, NJ: Princeton University Press).

Go, Julian and George Lawson (eds) (2017), *Global Historical Sociology* (Cambridge: Cambridge University Press).

Goldenberg, Suzanne (2015), 'US Climate Deniers Call Paris Summit "A Threat to the World"', *Guardian*, 27 June 2015, http://www.theguardian.com/environment/2015/jun/26/us-climate-deniers-call-paris-summit-a-threat-to-the-world.

Goldstein Joshua S. (2001), *War and Gender: How Gender Shapes the War System and Vice Versa* (Cambridge: Cambridge University Press).

Goodin, Robert E. (1992), *Green Political Theory* (Cambridge: Polity Press).

Gordenker, Leon (2010), *The UN Secretary-General and Secretariat* (Abingdon: Routledge, 2nd edn).

Gordenker, Leon and Thomas G. Weiss (1996), 'Pluralizing Global Governance: Analytical Approaches and Dimensions', in Thomas G. Weiss and Leon Gordenker (eds), *NGOs, the UN and Global Governance* (Boulder, CO: Lynne Rienner), pp. 139–58.

Goss, Joss, and Bruce Lindquist (1995), 'Conceptualizing International Labor Migration: A Structuration Perspective', *International Migration Review*, 29(2): 317–51.

Graham, David A. (2018), 'Is Wikileaks a Russian Front?', *The Atlantic*, 29 November, https://www.theatlantic.com/politics/archive/2018/11/wikileaks-trump-mueller-roger-stone-jerome-corsi/576940/.

Gramsci, Antonio (1971), *Selections from Prison Notebooks* (London: Lawrence & Wishart).

Greer, Jed and Kavaljit Singh (2000), 'A Brief History of Transnational Corporations', *Global Policy Forum*, https://www.globalpolicy.org/empire/47068-a-brief-history-of-transnational-corporations.html.

Grieco, Joseph M. (1988), 'Anarchy and the Limits of Cooperation: A Realist Critique of the Newest Liberal Institutionalism', *International Organization*, 42(3): 485–507.

Griffin, Penny (2007), 'Refashioning IPE: What and How Gender Analysis Teaches International (Global), Political Economy', *Review of International Political Economy*, 14(4): 719–36.

Griffiths, Martin, Steven C. Roach, and M. Scott Sullivan (2009), *Fifty Key Thinkers in International Relations* (Abingdon: Routledge, 2nd edn).

Guardian (2019), 'China's Ambassador Accuses Canada of "White Supremacy" in Huawei CFO Arrest', 10 January, https://www.theguardian.com/world/2019/jan/09/china-ambassador-canada-white-supremacy-huawei.

Habermas, Jürgen (2003), 'Toward a Cosmopolitan Europe', *Journal of Democracy*, 14(4): 86–100.

Hackett, Steven C. (2011), *Environmental and Natural Resources Economics: Theory, Policy and the Sustainable Society* (Armonk, NY: M.E. Sharpe, 4th edn).

Haddour, Azzedine (2019), *Frantz Fanon, Postcolonialism and the Ethics of Difference* (Manchester: Manchester University Press).

Haggard, Stephan (1997), 'Regionalism in Asia and the Americas', in Edward D. Mans and Helen V. Milner (eds), *The Political Economy of Regionalism* (New York: Columbia University Press), pp. 20–49.

Hall, Stephen (2001), 'The Persistent Spectre: Natural Law, International Order and the Limits of Legal Positivism', *European Journal if International Law*, 12(2): 269–307.

Hamilton, Keith and Richard Langhorne (2011), *The Practice of Diplomacy: Its Evolution, Theory and Administration* (Abingdon: Routledge).

Hanlon, Aaron (2018), 'Postmodernism Didn't Cause Trump – It Explains Him', *Washington Post*, 30 August.

Hansen, Lene (2010), 'Ontologies, Epistemologies and Methodologies', in Laura J. Shepard (ed.), *Gender Matters in Global Politics: A Feminist Introduction to International Relations* (Abingdon: Routledge).

Hansen, Lene (2014), 'Ontologies, Epistemologies and Methodologies', in Laura J. Shepherd (ed.), *Gender Matters in Global Politics: A Feminist Introduction to International Relations* (Abingdon: Routledge, 2nd edn), pp. 14–23.

Hardin, Garrett (1968), 'The Tragedy of the Commons', *Science*, 162(3859): 1243–8.

Hardt, Michael and Negri Antonio (2000), *Empire* (Cambridge, MA: Harvard University Press).

Harle, Vilho (1988), *Ideas of Social Order in the Ancient World* (Westport, CT: Greenwood Press).

Harper, Stephen (2011), reported at https://www.ctvnews.ca/pm-heads-to-paris-for-emergency-summit-on-libya-1.620539.

Harvey, David (2007), *A Brief History of Neoliberalism* (Oxford: Oxford University Press).

Hawkins, William R. (1984), 'Neomercantilism: Is there a Case for Tariffs?', *National Review*, 36(6): 25–39.

Heer, Jeet (2017), 'America's First Postmodern President', *New Republic*, 8 July, https://newrepublic.com/article/143730/americas-first-postmodern-president.

Henderson, Errol A. (2015), 'Hidden in Plain Sight: Racism in International Relations Theory', in Alexander Anievas, Nivi Manchanda, and Robbie Shilliam (eds), *Race and Racism in International Relations: Confronting the Global Colour Line* (London: Routledge), pp. 19–43.

Henriksen, Alan K. (2006), *What Can Public Diplomacy Achieve?* (Discussion Papers in Diplomacy, The Hague: Institute of International Relations), https://www.clingendael.org/publication/what-can-public-diplomacy-achieve.

Herskovits, Melville J. (1972), *Cultural Relativism: Perspectives in Cultural Pluralism* (New York: Random House).

Herz, John H. (1950) 'Idealist Internationalism and the Security Dilemma', *World Politics*, 2(2): 157–80.

Hill, Christopher (2016), *Foreign Policy in the Twenty-First Century* (London: Palgrave, 2nd edn).

Hirst, Paul and Graeme Thompson (1999), *Globalization in Question* (Cambridge: Polity Press, 2nd edn).

Hobson, John M. (2012), *The Eurocentric Conception of World Politics: Western International Theory, 1760–2010* (Cambridge: Cambridge University Press).

Hollis, Duncan B. (2012), 'Introduction', in Duncan B. Hollis (ed.), *The Oxford Guide to Treaties* (Oxford: Oxford University Press).

Holslag, Jonathan (2018), *A Political History of the World: Three Thousand Years of War and Peace* (London: Penguin).

Hooghe, Liesbet, Tobias Lenz, and Gary Marks (2019), *A Theory of International Organization: A Postfunctionalist Theory of Governance,* Vol. IV (Oxford: Oxford University Press).

Hooper, Charlotte (2001), *Manly States: Masculinities, International Relations, and Gender Politics* (New York: Columbia University Press).

Howard, Michael (1966), 'War as an Instrument of Policy', in Herbert Butterfield and Martin Wight (eds), *Diplomatic Investigation: Essays in the Theory of International Politics* (London: George Allen & Unwin), pp. 193–205.

Howard-Hassman, Rhoda E. (2015), 'Introduction: The Human Right to Citizenship', in Rhoda E. Howard-Hassman and Margaret Walton-Roberts (eds), *The Human Right to Citizenship: A Slippery Concept* (Philadelphia: University of Pennsylvania Press), pp. 1–18.

Hughes, Steve and Nigel Haworth (2011), *International Labour Organization (ILO): Coming in from the Cold* (Abingdon: Routledge).

Hui, Victoria Tin-bor (2005), *War and State Formation in Ancient China and Early Modern Europe* (New York: Cambridge University Press).

Huikuri, Salla (2019), *The Institutionalization of the International Criminal Court* (London: Palgrave Macmillan).

Human Rights Watch (2019), 'US Threatens International Criminal Court', 15 March, https://www.hrw.org/news/2019/03/15/us-threatens-international-criminal-court.

Huntington, Samuel P. (1993), The Clash of Civilizations?', *Foreign Affairs,* 72(3): 22–49.

Huntley, Rebecca (2020), 'Climate Change Splits the Public into Six Groups: Understanding Them is the key to Future Action', *ABC News*, 31 January, https://www.abc.net.au/news/2020-01-29/climate-change-global-warming-six-groups-rebecca-huntley/11893384.

Hurd, Ian (2008), *After Anarchy: Legitimacy and Power in the United Nations Security Council* (Princeton, NJ: Princeton University Press).

Hutchison, Emma (2016), *Affective Communities in World Politics: Collective Emotions After Trauma* (Cambridge: Cambridge University Press).

ICISS (International Commission on Intervention and State Sovereignty) (2001), *The Responsibility to Protect: Report of the International Commission on Intervention and State Sovereignty, 2001,* https://www.globalr2p.org/resources/the-responsibility-to-protect-report-of-the-international-commission-on-intervention-and-state-sovereignty-2001/.

ICTY (International Criminal Tribunal for Former Yugoslavia), *Appeals Chamber Judgement in the Case of the Prosecutor v. Radislav Krstić*, ICTY, 19 Apr. 2004.

Ikenberry, G. John (2008), 'The Rise of China and the Future of the West: Can the Liberal System Survive?', *Foreign Affairs,* 87(1): 23–37.

Imamoto, Shizuka (2018), *Rejection of Racial Equality Bill* (Chennai: Notion Press).

Independent (2016), 'Hate Crimes Soar by 41% after Brexit Vote, Official Figures Reveal', 13 October, http://www.independent.co.uk/news/uk/crime/brexit-hate-crimes-racism-eu-referendum-vote-attacks-increase-police-figures-official-a7358866.html.

Inman, Samuel Guy (1923), 'Pan-American Conferences and Their Results', *Southwestern Political and Social Science Quarterly,* 4(3): 238–66.

International Labour Organization, 'Global Estimates of Modern Slavery: Forced Labour and Forced Marriage', Geneva, September 2017, www.ilo.org/global/topics/forced-labour/lang--en/index.htm.

Interpol (1956–2017), *Constitution of the ICPO-INTERPOL* (I/CONS/GA/1956 (2010).

Ip, Kevin K.W. (2017), 'Global Distributive Justice' in *Oxford Research Encyclopedias,* https://oxfordre.com/internationalstudies/view/10.1093/acrefore/9780190846626.001.0001/acrefore-9780190846626-e-89.

Islam, Mohammed Rabiul (2016), 'The International Criminal Court: Its Success and Limitations for Pursuing International Justice', *Journal of Civil and Legal Sciences*, 5(2): 1–6.

Jackson, Robert (2018), 'Sovereignty in World Politics: A Glance at the Conceptual and Historical Landscape', in Neil Walker (ed.), *Relocating Sovereignty* (Abingdon: Routledge).

Jackson, Simon and Alanna O'Malley (eds) (2018), *The Institution of International Order: From the League of Nations to the United Nations* (Abingdon: Routledge).

Jacobsen, Stefan Gaarsmand (ed.) (2018), *Climate Justice and the Economy: Social Mobilization, Knowledge and the Political* (Abingdon: Routledge).

Jacques, Peter J., Riley E. Dunlap, and Mark Freeman (2008), 'The Organisation of Denial: Conservative Think Tanks and Environmental Skepticism', *Environmental Politics*, 17(3): 349–85.

Jalloe, Charles and Ilias Bantekas (eds) (2017), *The International Criminal Court and Africa* (Oxford: Oxford University Press).

James, Patrick, Mariano E. Bertucci, and Jarrod Hayes (eds) (2018), *Constructivism Reconsidered: Past, Present and Future* (Ann Arbor, MI: University of Michigan Press).

Jeffery, Renee (2014), *Reason and Emotion in International Ethics* (Cambridge: Cambridge University Press).

Johns, Fleur, Richard Joyce, and Sundhya Pahuja (eds) (2011), *Events: The Force of International Law* (Abingdon: Routledge).

Jones, Martin, Rhys Jones, and Michael Woods (2014), *An Introduction to Political Geography: Space, Place and Politics* (Abingdon: Routledge).

Jones, Peter (2015), *Track Two Diplomacy in Theory and Practice* (Stanford: Stanford University Press).

Jowett, Garth S. and Victoria O'Donnell (2006), *Propaganda and Persuasion* (Thousand Oaks, CA: Sage).

Judis, John B. (2018), *The Nationalist Revival: Trade, Immigration, and the Revolt Against Globalization* (New York: Columbia Global Reports).

Kamruzzaman, Palash (2019), *Civil Society in the Global South* (Abingdon: Routledge).

Katzenstein, Peter J. (1996), *Cultural Norms and National Security: Police and Military in Postwar Japan* (Ithaca, NY: Cornell University Press).

Katzenstein, Peter J. (2016), 'Diversity and Empathy', *International Studies Review*, 18(1): 151–3.

Kauffman, Joanne (1997), 'Domestic and International Linkages in Global Environmental Politics: A Case-Study of the Montreal Protocol', in Miranda A. Schreurs and Elizabeth Economy (eds), *The Internationalization of Environmental Protection* (Cambridge: Cambridge University Press) pp. 262–82.

Kautilya (2016), *The Arthashatra* (London: Penguin).

Kelsay, John (1993), *Islam and War: A Study in Comparative Ethics* (Louisville, KY: John Knox Press).

Kennedy, Paul (1989), *The Rise and Fall of the Great Powers: Economic Change and Military Conflict from 1500 to 2000* (London: Fontana).

Kent, Avidan, Nikos Skoutaris, and Jamie Trinidad (eds) (2019), *The Future of International Courts: Regional, Institutional, and Procedural Challenges* (Abingdon: Routledge).

Keohane, Robert O. (1984), *After Hegemony: Cooperation and Discord in World Political Economy* (Princeton, NJ: Princeton University Press).

Keohane, Robert O. (1993), 'The Analysis of International Regimes: Towards a European-American Research Programme', in Volker Rittberger and Peter Mayer (eds), *Regime Theory and International Relations* (Oxford: Clarendon Press), pp. 23–48.

Keohane, Robert O. and Joseph S. Nye (1977), *Power and Interdependence: World Politics in Transition* (Boston, MA: Little, Brown).

Kerr, Pauline and Geoffrey Wiseman (eds) (2017), *Diplomacy in a Globalizing World* (Oxford: Oxford University Press).

Khaldun, Ibn (1969), *The Muqaddimah: An Introduction to History*, vol. 1, trans. Franz Rosenthal, ed. N. J. Dawood (Princeton, NJ: Princeton University Press).

Kinvall, Caterina and Jennifer Mitzen (2017), 'An Introduction to the Special Issue: Ontological Securities in World Politics', *Cooperation and Conflict*, 52(1): 3–11.

Kirsch, Philippe and Mohamed S. Helal (2014), 'Libya', in Jared Genser and Bruno Stagno Ugarte (eds), *The United Nations Security Council in the Age of Human Rights* (Cambridge: Cambridge University Press), pp. 396–433.

Kirshner, Jonathan (2010), 'The Tragedy of Offensive Realism: Classical Realism and the Rise of China', *European Journal of International Relations*, 18(1): 53–75.

Klabbers, Jan (2003), *An Introduction to International Institutional Law* (Cambridge: Cambridge University Press).

Klabbers, Jan (2013), *International Law* (Cambridge: Cambridge University Press).

Kleingeld, Pauline (2019), 'Cosmopolitanism', in *Stanford Encyclopedia of Philosophy*, https://plato.stanford.edu/entries/cosmopolitanism/.

Kostakopoulou, Dora (2008), *The Future Governance of Citizenship* (Cambridge: Cambridge University Press).

Kowner, Rotem and Walter Demel (2015), 'Introduction: The Synthesis of Foreign and Indigenous Constructions of Race in Modern East Asia and Its Actual Operation', in Rotem Kowner and Walter Demel (eds), *Race and Racism in Modern East Asia*, Vol. II: *Interactions, Nationalism, Gender and Lineage* (Leiden: Brill), pp. 1–22.

Kroll, Stefan (2015), 'The Illiberality of Liberal International Law: Religion, Science, and the Peaceful Violence of Civilization', in Thomas Hippler and Miloš Vec (eds), *Paradoxes of Peace in Nineteenth Century Europe* (Oxford: Oxford University Press), pp. 238–49.

Lamb, Peter and Fiona Robertson-Snape (2017), *Historical Dictionary of International Relations* (Lanham, MD: Rowman & Littlefield).

Langhorne, Richard (2000), 'Full Circle: New Principals and Old Consequences in the Modern Diplomatic System', *Diplomacy and Statecraft*, 11(1): 33–46.

Langlois, Anthony J. (2015), 'International Theory and LGBTQ Rights', in Chris Brown and Robyn Eckersley (eds), *The Oxford Handbook of International Political Theory* (Oxford: Oxford University Press), pp. 370–84.

Lawson, Stephanie (2006), *Culture and Context in World Politics* (Basingstoke: Palgrave).

Lawson, Stephanie (2011a) 'Cosmopolitan Pluralism: Beyond the Cultural Turn', *Cosmopolitan Civil Societies*, 3(3): 27–46.

Lawson, Stephanie (2011b), 'Diplomatic Bag's Pedagogic Pearls', *Times Higher Education*, 13–19 Jan, p. 19.

Lawson, Stephanie (2015), *Theories of International Relations: Contending Approaches to World Politics* (Cambridge: Polity).

Lawson, Stephanie (2017a), *International Relations* (Cambridge: Polity Press, 3rd edn).

Lawson, Stephanie (2017b), 'Regionalism and Colonialism in Contemporary Oceania', *Round Table*, 106(2): 143–53.

Lawson, Stephanie (2017c), 'IR Theory in the Anthropocene: Time for a Reality Check?', in Synne L. Dyvik, Jan Selby, and Rorden Wilkinson (eds), *What's the Point of International Relations?* (Abingdon: Routledge), pp. 182–92.

Lazar, Seth (2017), 'War', in Edward N. Zalta (ed.), *Stanford Encyclopedia of Philosophy* (Spring edn), https://plato.stanford.edu/archives/spr2017/entries/war/.

Lebow, Richard Ned (2007), 'Classical Realism', in Tim Dunne, Milja Kurki, and Steve Smith (eds), *International Relations Theories: Discipline and Diversity* (Oxford: Oxford University Press), pp. 52–70.

Lebow, Richard Ned (2016), *National Identities and International Relations* (Cambridge: Cambridge University Press).

Lee, Chung-He and Sang-Hwan Lee (2002), 'NGOs and International Society: Prospects on Their Roles in the 21st Century', *Pacific Focus*, XVIII(1): 147–62.

Lee, Lavina Rajendram (2010), *US Hegemony and International Legitimacy: Norms, Power and Followership in the Wars on Iraq* (Abingdon: Routledge).

Lessafer, Randall (2015), 'Vienna and the Abolition of the Slave Trade', https://blog.oup.com/2015/06/vienna-abolition-slave-trade/.

Leydet, Dominique (2017), 'Citizenship', in Edward N. Zalta (ed.), *The Stanford Encyclopedia of Philosophy*, https://plato.stanford.edu/entries/citizenship/

Lind, Amy (2013), 'Heteronormativity and Sexuality', in Georgina Waylen, Karen Celis, Johanna Kantola, and S. Laurel Weldon (eds) *The Oxford Handbook of Gender and Politics* (Oxford: Oxford University Press), pp. 189–213.

Linklater, Andrew (1998), *The Transformation of Political Community: Ethical Foundations of the Post-Westphalian Era* (Cambridge: Polity Press).

Linklater, Andrew (2011), *The Problem of Harm in World Politics: Theoretical Investigations* (Cambridge: Cambridge University Press).

Linklater, Andrew and Hideo Suganami (2006), *The English School of International Relations: A Contemporary Reassessment* (Cambridge: Cambridge University Press).

Lipschutz, Ronnie D. (ed.) (1995), *On Security* (New York: Columbia University Press).

List, Frederich (1991), 'Political and Cosmopolitical Economy', in George T. Crane and Abla Amawi (eds), *The Theoretical Evolution of International Political Economy: A Reader* (Oxford: Oxford University Press), pp. 48–54.

Litfin, Karen T. (1998), 'The Greening of Sovereignty: An Introduction', in Karen T. Litfin (ed.), *The Greening of Sovereignty in World Politics* (Cambridge, MA: MIT Press), pp. 1–29.

Little, Richard (1996), 'The Growing Relevance of Pluralism?', in Steve Smith, Ken Booth, and Marysia Zalewski (eds), *International Theory: Positivism and Beyond* (Cambridge: Cambridge University Press), pp. 66–86.

Litvinova, Daria (2017), 'LGBT Hate Crimes Double in Russia after Ban on "Gay Propaganda"', *Reuters*, 22 November, https://www.reuters.com/article/us-russia-lgbt-crime/lgbt-hate-crimes-double-in-russia-after-ban-on-gay-propaganda-idUSKBN1DL2FM.

Lo, Ping-Cheun (2012), 'The "Art of War" Corpus and Chinese Just War Ethics Past and Present', *Journal of Religious Ethics*, 40(3): 404–46.

Lockard, Craig A. (2008), *Societies, Networks, and Transitions: A Global History*, i. *To 1500* (Florence, KY: Houghton Mifflin/Cengage Learning).

Luxemburg, Rosa (1976), *The National Question: Selected Writings*, ed. and intr. Horace B. Davis (New York: Monthly Review Press).

McCormick, John (1991), *Reclaiming Paradise: The Global Environmental Movement* (Bloomington, IN: Midland/Indiana University Press).

McGrail, Stephen (2011), 'Environment in Transition? Emerging Perspectives, Issues and Futures Practices in Contemporary Environmentalism', *Journal of Futures Studies*, 15(3): 117–44.

Machiavelli, Niccolò (2009), *The Prince*, trans. W. K. Marriott, ed. Randy Dillon (Plano, TX: Veroglyphic).

McIlwain, Charles Howard (2005), *Constitutionalism Ancient and Modern* (Clark, NJ: Lawbook Exchange).

McIntyre, Lee (2018), *Post-Truth* (Cambridge, MA: MIT Press).

McLeod, John (2000), *Beginning Postcolonialism* (Manchester: Manchester University Press).

Mann, Michael (1996), 'Authoritarian and Liberal Militarism: A Contribution from Historical and Comparative Sociology', in Steve Smith, Ken Booth and Marysia Zalewksi (eds), *International Theory: Positivism and Beyond* (Cambridge: Cambridge University Press), pp. 221–39.

Manners, Ian (2006), 'Normative Power Europe Reconsidered: Beyond the Crossroads', *Journal of European Public Policy*, 13(2): 182–99.

Marchetti, Raffaelle (2016), 'Global Civil Society', in Stephen McGlinchey (ed.), *International Relations* (E-International Relations: https://www.e-ir.info/publication/beginners-textbook-international-relations/).

Marik, Soma (2008), *Reinterrogating the Classical Marxist Discourses of Revolutionary Democracy* (Delhi: Aakar Books).

Martill, Benjamin and Uta Staiger (eds) (2018), *Brexit and Beyond: Rethinking the Futures of Europe* (London: UCL Press).

Marx, Karl (1857), *Grundisse: Foundations of A Critique of Political Economy*, https://www.marxists.org/archive/marx/works/1857/grundrisse/ch01.htm.

Marx, Karl (1859), *A Contribution to the Critique of Political Economy*, https://www.marxists.org/archive/marx/works/1859/critique-pol-economy/preface.htm.

Marx, Karl (1950), 'Preface to A Contribution to the Critique of Political Economy', in Karl Marx and Frederick Engels, *Selected Works, Vol 1*. Moscow, Foreign Languages Publishing House available at https://www.marxists.org/archive/marx/works/1859/critique-pol-economy/preface.htm.

Marx, Karl and Friedrich Engels (1848), *The Manifesto of the Communist Party*, reproduced at www.marxists.org/archive/marx/works/1848/communist-manifesto/ch01.htm.

Mattingley, Garrett (1955), *Renaissance Diplomacy* (Boston, MA: Houghton Mifflin).

Mattox, John Mark (2018), 'The Just War Tradition in Late Antiquity and the Middle Ages', in Larry May (ed.), *The Cambridge Handbook of Just War* (Cambridge: Cambridge University Press), pp. 13–32.

Matz, Nele (2005), 'Civilization and the Mandate System under the League of Nations as Origin of Trusteeship', in A. von Bogdandy and R. Wolfrum (eds), *Max Planck Yearbook of United Nations Law*, vol. 9 (Leiden: Brill), pp. 47–95.

Mayer, Maximilian, Mariana Carpes, and Ruth Knoblich (eds) (2014), *The Global Politics of Science and Technology—Vol. 1: Concepts from International Relations and Other Disciplines* (Berlin: Springer).

Mayer, Maximilian, Mariana Carpes, and Ruth Knoblich (eds) (2016), *The Global Politics of Science and Technology—Vol. 2: Perspectives, Cases and Methods* (Berlin: Springer).

Mayes, Suzanne (2019), 'Why Care About Undocumented Immigrants? For One Thing They've Become Vital to Key Sectors of the US Economy', *The Conversation*, 15 January, https://theconversation.com/why-care-about-undocumented-immigrants-for-one-thing-they've-become-vital-to-key-sectors-of-the-us-economy-98790.

Meadows, Donella, Jorgen Randers, and Dennis L. Meadows (1972), *The Limits to Growth: The 30-Year Update* (New York: Universe Books).

Mearsheimer, John J. (2010), 'Structural Realism', in Tim Dunne (ed.), *International Relations Theory: Discipline and Diversity* (Oxford: Oxford University Press, 2nd edn), pp. 77–94.

Mearsheimer, John J. (2013), 'Structural Realism', in Tim Dunne, Milja Kurki and Steve Smith (eds), *Theories of International Relations: Discipline and Diversity* (Oxford: Oxford University Press, 3rd edn), pp. 77–93.

Mearsheimer, John (2014), 'Can China Rise Peacefully?', *The National Interest,* 25 October, https://nationalinterest.org/commentary/can-china-rise-peacefully-10204.

Mearsheimer, John (2018), *The Great Delusion: Liberal Dreams and International Realities* (New Haven, CT: Yale University Press).

Melissen, Jan (2003), *Summit Diplomacy Coming of Age* (Discussion Papers in Diplomacy, The Hague: Netherlands Institute of International Relations), www.nbiz.nl/publications/2003/20030500_cli_paper_dip_issue86.pdf.

Mentan, Tatah (2010), *The State in Africa: An Analysis of Impacts of Historical Trajectories of Global Capitalist Expansion and Domination in the Continent* (Mankon: Langaa Research and Publishing).

Meyer, William B. (2016), *The Progressive Environmental Prometheans: Left-Wing Heralds of a 'Good Anthropocene'* (New York: Palgrave Macmillan).

Milbank, Dana and Claudia Deane (2003), 'Hussein Link to 9/11 Lingers in Many Minds', *Washington Post,* 6 September, A1.

Miller, David (ed.) (1991), *The Blackwell Encyclopaedia of Political Thought* (Oxford: Blackwell Publishers).

Miller, David (2007), *National Responsibility and Global Justice* (Oxford: Oxford University Press).

Mol, Arthur P. J. and Gert Spaargen (2000), 'Ecological Modernisation Theory: A Review', *Environmental Politics*, 9(1): 17–49.

Mooney, Chris (2005), *The Republican War on Science* (New York: Basic Books).

Morgenthau, Hans J. (1948), *Politics Among Nations: The Struggle for Power and Peace* (New York: Alfred A. Knopf).

Morgenthau, Hans J. (1978) *Politics Among Nations: The Struggle for Power and Peace,* 5th edn rev. (New York: Alfred A. Knopf).

Morrison, Ken (2006), *Marx, Durkheim, Weber: Foundations of Modern Social Thought* (London: Sage, 2nd edn).

Moses, Jeremy (2014), *Sovereignty and Responsibility: Power, Norms and Intervention in International Relations* (Basingstoke: Palgrave Macmillan).

Mosse, George L. (1995), 'Racism and Nationalism', *Nations and Nationalism*, 1(2): 163–73.

Mourdaukoutas, Panos (2018), 'What is China Doing in Africa?', *Forbes*, 4 August, https://www.forbes.com/sites/panosmourdoukoutas/2018/08/04/china-is-treating-africa-the-same-way-european-colonists-did/#5a343537298b.

Mueller, Robert S. (2019), *The Mueller Report: Report on the Investigation into Russian Interference in the 2016 Presidential Election* (Washington, DC: US Department of Justice/Creative Media Partners).

Murray, Gilbert (1910), 'Discussion: Empire and Subject Races', *Sociological Review*, 3(3): 227–32.

Mutibwa, Phares (1992), *Uganda Since Independence: A Story of Unfulfilled Hopes* (London: Hurst & Co.).

Mutman, Mahmut (1992–93), 'Under the Sign of Orientalism: The West vs. Islam', *Cultural Critique*, 23 (Winter): 165–97.

Naess, Arne (1995), 'The Shallow and the Deep, Long-Range Ecology Movement: A Summary', in Alan R. Drengson and Yuichi Inoue (eds), *The Deep Ecology Movement: An Introductory Ecology* (Berkeley, CA: North Atlantic Books), pp. 3–10.

Naím, Moisés (2009), 'What is a GONGO?' *Foreign Policy*, 13 October, https://foreignpolicy.com/2009/10/13/what-is-a-gongo/.

Naím, Moisés (2014), *The End of Power: From Boardrooms to Battlefields and Churches to States—Why Being in Charge Isn't What It Used to Be* (New York: Basic Books).

Neate, Rupert (2016), 'Panama Papers: US Launches Criminal Inquiry Into Tax Avoidance Claims', *Guardian,* 19 April, https://www.theguardian.com/business/2016/apr/19/panama-papers-us-justice-department-investigation-tax-avoidance.

Neff, Stephen C. (2014), *Justice Among Nations: A History of International Law* (Cambridge, MA: Harvard University Press).

Neiwert, David (2017), 'Trump's Fixation on Demonizing Islam Hides True Homegrown Terror Threat', 21 June, https://www.revealnews.org/article/home-is-where-the-hate-is/.

Nettl, J.P. (2019), *Rosa Luxemburg* (London: Verso).

New York Times (1991), 'After the War: The President; Transcript of President Bush's Address on End of Gulf War', 7 March, www.nytimes.com/1991/03/07/us/after-war-president-transcript-president-bush-s-address-end-gulf-war.html.

New York Times (2009), 'Adding up the Government's Total Bailout Tab', 4 Feb., www.nytimes.com/interactive/2009/02/04/business/20090205-bailout-totals-graphic.html.

New York Times (2010), 'A Note to Readers: The Decision to Publish Diplomatic Documents', 28 Nov., www.nytimes.com/2010/11/29/world/29editornote.html.

Nicholson, Simon and Paul Wapner (2016), *Global Environmental Politics: From Person to Planet* (Abingdon: Routledge).

Norloff, Carla (2015), 'Hegemony', *Oxford Bibliographies*, https://www.oxfordbibliographies.com/view/document/obo-9780199743292/obo-9780199743292-0122.xml.

Nye, Joseph S., Jr (2004), *Soft Power: The Means to Success in World Politics* (New York: Public Affairs).

Nye, Joseph S., Jr (2005), *Understanding International Conflicts: An Introduction to Theory and History* (New York: Pearson Longman, 5th edn).

Oatley, Thomas (2019), *International Political Economy* (Routledge: New York, 6th edn).

Obregón, Liliana (2017), 'Identity Formation, Theorization and Decline of a Latin American International Law', in Paula Wojcikiewicz Almeida and Jean-Marc Sorel (eds), *Latin America and the International Court of Justice: Contributions to International Law* (New York, NY: Routledge), pp. 3–14.

Okeja, Uchenna B. (2013), *Normative Justification of a Global Ethic: A Perspective from African Philosophy* (Lanham, MD: Lexington Books).

Onuf, Nicholas (1989), *World of our Making: Rules and Rule in Social Theory and International Relations* (Columbia, SC: University of South Carolina Press).

Oreskes, Naomi and Erik M. Conway (2010), *Merchants of Doubt: How a Handful of Scientists Obscured the Truth on Issues from Tobacco Smoke to Global Warming* (New York: Bloomsbury Press).

Panda, Ankit (2014), 'Reflecting on China's Five Principles, 60 Years Later', *The Diplomat,* 26 June, https://thediplomat.com/2014/06/reflecting-on-chinas-five-principles-60-years-later/.

Parker, George and Chris Giles (2010), 'Cameron Insists Britain Still Great Power', *Financial Times*, 15 November, https://www.ft.com/content/e145a5a6-f0fb-11df-bf4b-00144feab49a.

Pearcey, Mark (2016), *The Exclusions of Civilization: Indigenous People in the Story of International Society* (New York: Palgrave Macmillan).

Pederson, Susan (2015), *The Guardians: The League of Nations and the Crisis of Empire* (Oxford: Oxford University Press).

Pepper, David (2019), *The Roots of Modern Environmentalism* (Abingdon: Routledge).

Persaud, Randolph and Alina Sajed (eds) (2018), *Race, Gender and Culture in International Relations: Postcolonial Perspectives* (London: Routledge).

Phan, Hao Duy (2019), 'International Courts and State Compliance: An Investigation of the Law of the Sea Cases', *Ocean Development and International Law*, 50(1): 70–90.

Qin, Yang (2016), 'A Relational Theory of World Politics', *International Studies Review,* 18(1): 33–47.

Qin, Yang (2018), *A Relational Theory of World Politics* (Cambridge: Cambridge University Press).

Qobo, Mzukisi and Nceku Nyanthi (2017), 'Ubuntu, Foreign Policy and Radical Uncertainty in South Africa and the World', *Africa Portal*, 20 September, https://www.africaportal.org/features/ubuntu-foreign-policy-and-radical-uncertainty-south-africa-and-world/.

Rampell, Catherine (2018), 'Trump's Trade Policy is Stuck in the 80s—the 1680s', *NorthJersey.Com/USA Today,* 1 June, https://www.northjersey.com/story/opinion/columnists/2018/06/01/donald-trump-trade-policy-stuck-80-s-1680-s-opinion/663828002/.

Rao, Rahul (2010), *Third World Protest: Between Home and the World* (Oxford: Oxford University Press).

Ravenhill, John (ed.) (2017), *Global Political Economy* (Oxford: Oxford University Press, 5th edn).

Ricardo, David (1821), *On the Principles of Political Economy and Taxation* (London: John Murray, 3rd edn).

Rittberger, Volker and Bernhard Zangl (2006), *International Organization; Polity, Politics Policies* (Basingstoke: Palgrave).

Roach, Steven C., Martin Griffiths, and Terry O'Callaghan (2014), *International Relations: The Key Concepts* (Abingdon: Routledge).

Roberts, Anthea (2017), *Is International Law International?* (Oxford: Oxford University Press).

Rockmore, Tom (2018), 'Introduction', in Tom Rockmore and Norman Levine (eds), *Palgrave Handbook of Leninist Political Philosophy* (London: Palgrave Macmillan), pp. 1–62.

Ross-Smith, Nicholas (2018), 'Can Neo-Classical Realism Become a Genuine Theory of International Relations?', *Journal of Politics*, 80(2): 742–9.

Royal Society and National Academy of Science (2014), *Climate Change: Evidence and Causes* (Washington, DC: National Academies Press).

Ruggie, John Gerard (1998), *Constructing the World Polity: Essays on International Institutionalization* (London: Routledge).

Russett, Bruce (2005), 'Bushwacking the Democratic Peace', *International Studies Perspectives*, 6(4): 395–408.

Rÿser, Rudolph C. (2012), *Indigenous Nations and Modern States: The Political Emergence of Nations Challenging State Power* (New York: Routledge).

Said, Edward W. (1978), *Orientalism: Western Conceptions of the Orient* (London: Penguin).

Said, Edward W. (1993), *Culture and Imperialism* (London: Vintage Books).

Sanderson, Thomas M. (2004), 'Transnational Terror and Organized Crime: Blurring the Lines', *SAIS Review,* 24(1): 49–61.

Schifferes, Steve (2020), 'Will Coronavirus be the Turning Point for Globalisation?', *The Conversation*, 28 March, https://theconversation.com/will-coronavirus-be-the-turning-point-for-globalisation-134739.

Schroeder, Paul (2003), 'Is the US an Empire?', *History News Network*, 2 March, http://hnn.us/articles/1237.html.

Schuman, Michael (2011), *Time: What the US Debt Problem Means for the Global Economy* (Washington, DC: Council on Foreign Relations), 19 April, www.cfr.org/economics/time-us-debt-problem-means-global-economy/p24708.

Schwarzmantel, John (2009), 'Introduction: Gramsci in His Time and In Ours', in Mark McNally and John Schwarzmantel (eds), *Gramsci and Global Politics: Hegemony and Resistance* (Abingdon: Routledge), pp. 1–16.

Sekyi-Otu, Ato (2018), *Left Universalism: Africacentric Essays* (New York: Routledge).

Sen, Tansen (2015), *Buddhism, Diplomacy and Trade: The Realignment of India-China Relations 600–1400* (London: Rowman & Littlefield).

Serra, Narcís and Joseph E. Stiglitz (eds) (2008), *The Washington Consensus Reconsidered: Towards a New Global Governance* (Oxford: Oxford University Press).

Serwer, Adam (2019), 'The Terrorism that Doesn't Spark a Panic', *The Atlantic,* 28 January, https://www.theatlantic.com/ideas/archive/2019/01/homegrown-terrorists-2018-were-almost-all-right-wing/581284/.

Shamasastry, R. ed., trans. (n.d.), *Kautilya's Arthasástra*, www.hindujagaran.org/DigitalLibrary/ArthashastraofChanakyaEng.pdf.

Shannon, Thomas R. (2018), *An Introduction to the World-System Perspective* (New York: Routledge, 2nd edn).

Sharlet, Jeffrey (2011), 'Fierce Debates Divide Scholars of the 1994 Rwandan Genocide', *Chronicle of Higher Education,* 47, 3 August, https://www.chronicle.com/article/Fierce-Debate-Divides-Scholars/10327.

Shayam, Saran (2018), *How India Sees the World: Kautilya to the 21st Century* (New Delhi: Juggernaut Books).

Shepherd, Laura (ed.) (2015), *Gender Matters in Global Politics: A Feminist Introduction to International Relations* (London: Routledge, 2nd edn).

Shilliam, Robbie (2017), 'Modernity and Modernization', *Oxford Research Encyclopedias,* https://oxfordre.com/internationalstudies/view/10.1093/acrefore/9780190846626.001.0001/acrefore-9780190846626-e-56?rskey=o0Eag4&result=2.

Sleat, Matt (ed.) (2018), *Politics Recovered: Realist Thought in Theory and Practice* (New York: Columbia University Press).

Smith, Robert Sydney (1989), *Warfare and Diplomacy in Pre-Colonial West Africa* (Madison, WI: University of Wisconsin Press, 2nd edn).

Smith, Roy, Imad El-Anis, and Christopher Farrands (2017), *International Political Economy in the 21st Century: Contemporary Issues and Analyses* (Abingdon: Routledge, 2nd edn).

Smith, Steve (1996), 'Positivism and Beyond', in Steve Smith, Ken Booth, and Marysia Zalewski (eds), *International Theory: Positivism and Beyond* (Cambridge: Cambridge University Press), pp. 11–44.

Smith, Steve (2000), 'The Discipline of International Relations: Still an American Social Science?', *British Journal of Politics and International Relations,* 2(3): 374–402.

Smith, William S. (2018), 'Why Foreign Policy Realism Isn't Enough', *The American Conservative,* 5 June, https://www.theamericanconservative.com/articles/why-foreign-policy-realism-isnt-enough/.

Soros, George (2010), 'Anatomy of a Crisis', 9 April, www.georgesoros.com.

South Africa (2011), *Building a Better World: The Diplomacy of Ubuntu,* White Paper on South Africa's Foreign Policy, final draft 13 May, https://www.sahistory.org.za/archive/building-better-world-diplomacy-ubuntu.

Spencer, Phillip and Howard Wollman (eds) (2005), *Nations and Nationalism: A Reader* (New Brunswick, NJ: Rutgers University Press).

Spero, Joan E. and Jeffrey A. Hart (1997), *The Politics of International Economic Relations* (New York: St Martin's Press, 5th edn).

Spierman, Ole (2007), 'Twentieth Century Internationalism in Law', *European Journal of International Law,* 18(5): 785–814.

Steffen, Will, Johan Rockström, Katherine Richardson, et al. (2018), 'Trajectories of the Earth System in the Anthropocene', *Perspective,* 115(33): 8252–9.

Steger, Manfred B. (2010), *Globalization* (New York: Sterling).

Steger, Manfred B. and Ravi K. Roy (2010), *Neoliberalism: A Very Short Introduction* (Oxford: Oxford University Press).

Stern, Geoffrey (2000), *The Structure of International Society* (London: Pinter).

Strange, Susan (1970), 'International Economics and International Relations: A Case of Mutual Neglect', *International Affairs,* 46(2): 304–15.

Sullivan, John P. (2014), 'Transnational Crime', in Mary Kaldor and Iavor Rangelov (eds), *The Handbook of Global Security* (Malden, MA: John Wiley & Sons), pp. 160–74.

Sun Tzu (2017), *The Art of War* (New York: Quarto Publishing).

Sylvest, Casper (2004), 'Interwar Internationalism, the British Labour Party, and the Historiography of International Relations', *International Studies Quarterly,* 48(2): 409–32.

Symons, Jonathan (2019), *Ecomodernism: Technology, Politics and the Climate Crisis* (Cambridge: Polity Press).

Tan, Kok-Chor (2017), *What Is This Thing Called Global Justice?* (Abingdon: Routledge).

Teschke, Benno (2003), *The Myth of 1648: Class, Geopolitics, and the Making of Modern International Relations* (London: Verso).

Thakur, Ramesh (2018), *Reviewing the Responsibility to Protect: Origins, Implementation and Controversies* (Abingdon: Routledge).

Thompson, Janna (2009), *Intergenerational Justice: Rights and Responsibilities in an Intergenerational Polity* (New York: Routledge).

Thompson, Janna (2010), 'What is Intergenerational Justice?', *Future Justice,* http://www.futureleaders.com.au.

Thomuschat, Christian (2008/19), 'International Law and Tribunals', in Rüdiger Wolfram (ed.), *Max Planck Encyclopedia of Public International Law* (Heidelberg and Oxford: Max Planck Institute for Comparative and International Law and Oxford University Press), https://opil.ouplaw.com/view/10.1093/law:epil/9780199231690/law-9780199231690-e35.

Thucydides (1972), *History of the Peloponnesian War* (Harmondsworth: Penguin).

Thucydides (2009), *The Peloponnesian War,* trans. Martin Hammond, intr. P. J. Rhodes (Oxford: Oxford University Press).

Tickner, Arlene B. (2003), 'Seeing IR Differently: Notes from the Third World', *Millennium: Journal of International Studies,* 32(2): 295–324.

Tickner, J. Ann (1992), *Gender in International Relations: Feminist Perspectives on Achieving Global Security* (New York: Columbia University Press).

Tickner, J. Ann and Laura Sjoberg (2010), 'Feminism', in Tim Dunne, Milja Kurki, and Steve Smith (eds), *Theories of International Relations: Discipline and Diversity* (Oxford: Oxford University Press, 2nd edn), pp. 198–203.

Tikk, Eneken and Mika Kerttunen (eds) (2020), *Routledge Handbook of International Cybersecurity* (Abingdon: Routledge).

Townley, Cynthia (2007), 'Patriotism: Problems at Home', in Aleksandar Pavković and Igor Primoratz (eds), *Patriotism: Philosophical and Political Perspectives* (Aldershot, Ashgate), pp. 163–81.

True, Jacquie (2017), 'Feminism and Gender Studies in International Relations Theory', *Oxford Research Encyclopedias* (Oxford: International Studies

Association and Oxford University Press), https://oxfordre.com/internationalstudies/view/10.1093/acrefore/9780190846626.001.0001/acrefore-9780190846626-e-46?rskey=6GSBVv&result=3.

Tylor, Edward B. (1987), 'The Science of Culture', reproduced in Herbert Applebaum (ed.), *Perspectives in Cultural Anthropology* (Albany: State University of New York).

Uimonen, Paula (2020), 'Decolonizing Cosmopolitanism: An Anthropological Reading of Immanual Kant and Kwame Nkrumah on the World as One', *Critique of Anthropology*, published online https://journals.sagepub.com/doi/pdf/10.1177/0308275X19840412.

UK (2011), Foreign and Commonwealth Office, 'Public Diplomacy/Global Issues', http://www.fco.gov.uk/en/about-us/what-we-do/public-diplomacy.

UK (2018), House of Lords, Select Committee on International Relations, 5th Report of Session 2017–19, *UK Foreign Policy in a Shifting World,* 18 December, https://publications.parliament.uk/pa/ld201719/ldselect/ldintrel/250/250.pdf.

UNAA (United Nations Association of Australia) (2017), *The United Nations and the Rules-Based International Order*, https://www.unaa.org.au/wp-content/uploads/2015/07/UNAA_RulesBasedOrder_ARTweb3.pdf.

UNESCO (1980), *North-South: A Programme for Survival; Report of the Independent Commission on International Development Issues,* https://unesdoc.unesco.org/ark:/48223/pf0000039496.

UNFCCC (n.d.), 'What is the Paris Agreement', *c.*2016, https://unfccc.int/process-and-meetings/the-paris-agreement/what-is-the-paris-agreement.

United Nations (1961), 'Vienna Convention on Diplomatic Relations', http://untreaty.un.org/ilc/texts/instruments/english/conventions/9_1_1961.pdf.

United Nations, General Assembly (2005), '2005 World Summit Outcome Document', https://www.un.org/en/genocideprevention/about-responsibility-to-protect.shtml.

United Nations (2019), *Conflict Related Sexual Violence: Report of the United Nations Secretary-General,* S/2019/280, 29 March. UN News (2011), 'UN Security Council Authorizes "All Necessary Measures" to Protect Civilians in Libya', 17 March, https://news.un.org/en/story/2011/03/369382-security-council-authorizes-all-necessary-measures-protect-civilians-libya.

Van den Berg, Hendrik and Joshua J. Lewer (2015), *International Trade and Economic Growth* (Abingdon: Routledge).

Van der Pijl, Kees (2015), *Handbook of the International Political Economy of Production* (Cheltenham: Edward Elgar).

Van Ham, Peter (2010), *Social Power in International Politics* (Abingdon: Routledge).

Vec, Miloš (2012), 'From the Congress of Vienna to the Paris Peace Treaties of 1919', in Bardo Fassbender and Anne Peters (eds), *The Oxford Handbook of the History of International Law* (Oxford: Oxford University Press), pp. 654–78.

Vernon, Richard (2016), *Justice Back and Forth: Duties to the Past and the Future* (Toronto: University of Toronto Press).

Vincent, Andrew (2003), 'Green Political Theory', in Richard Bellamy and Andrew Mason (eds), *Political Concepts* (Manchester: Manchester University Press), pp. 182–95.

Viner, Jacob (1949), 'Power versus Plenty as Objectives of Foreign Policy in the Seventeenth and Eighteenth Centuries', *World Politics*, 1(2): 1–29.

Violakis, Petros (2018), *Europeanisation and the Transformation of EU Security Policy: Post-Cold War Developments in the Common Security and Defence Policy* (Abingdon: Routledge).

Vitalis, Robert (2015), *White World Order, Black Power Politics: The Birth of American International Relations* (Ithaca, NY: Cornell University Press).

von Ungern-Sternberg, Antje (2012), 'Religion and Religious Intervention', in Bardo Fassbender and Anne Peters (eds), *The Oxford Handbook of the History of International Law* (Oxford: Oxford University Press), pp. 294–316.

Walker, Peter (2018), '"The Highest Level of Special": Trump Praises US Relationship With UK', *Guardian,* 14 July, https://www.theguardian.com/us-news/2018/jul/13/the-highest-level-of-special-trump-praises-us-relationship-with-uk.

Wallerstein Immanuel (1976), *The Modern World-System: Capitalist Agriculture and the Origins of the European World-Economy in the Sixteenth Century* (New York: Academic Press).

Wallerstein Immanuel (2001), *Unthinking Social Science: The Limits of Nineteenth-Century Paradigms* (Philadelphia: Temple University Press, 2nd edn).

Wallerstein, Immanuel, Charles C. Lemert, and Carlos Aguirre Rojas (2012), *Uncertain Worlds: World-Systems Analysis in Changing Times* (Abingdon: Routledge).

Waltz, Kenneth N. (1959), *Man, the State and War* (New York: Columbia University Press).

Waltz, Kenneth N. (1979), *Theory of International Politics* (Reading, MA: Addison-Wesley).

Washington Post (2003), 'Administration Comments on Saddam Hussein and the Sept. 11 Attacks', https://www.washingtonpost.com/wp-srv/politics/polls/9-11_saddam_quotes.html.

Washington Post (2014), 'Full Transcript of President Obama's Address at West Point', 28 May, https://www.washingtonpost.com/politics/full-text-of-president-obamas-commencement-address-at-west-point/2014/05/28/cfbcdcaa-e670-11e3-afc6-a1dd9407abcf_story.html.

Watson, Alison M. S. (2004), *An Introduction to International Political Economy* (London: Continuum).

Weart, Spencer R. (2008), *The Discovery of Global Warming* (Cambridge, MA: Harvard University Press, rev. edn).

Weingast, Barry R. and Donald Whitman (eds) (2006), *The Oxford Handbook of Political Economy* (Oxford: Oxford University Press).

Wendt, Alexander (1992), 'Anarchy is What States Make of It: The Social Construction of Power Politics', *International Organization*, 46(2): 391–425.

Wendt, Alexander (1996), 'Identity and Structural Change in International Politics', in Yosef Lapid and Friedrich Kratochwil (eds), *The Return of Culture and Identity in IR Theory* (Boulder, CO: Lynne Rienner), pp. 47–64.

Whitehouse (2017), 'Statement by President Trump on the Paris Accord', 1 June, https://www.whitehouse.gov/briefings-statements/statement-president-trump-paris-climate-accord/.

Wiener, Antje (2018), *Contestation and Constitution of Norms in Global International Relations* (Cambridge: Cambridge University Press).

Wiener, Martin (2013), 'The Idea of "Colonial Legacy" and the Historiography of Empire', *Journal of the Historical Society*, 13(1): 1–32.

Wight, Martin (1966), 'Why Is There No International Theory?', in Herbert Butterfield and Martin Wight (eds), *Diplomatic Investigations* (London: George Allen & Unwin), pp. 17–34.

Wilkinson, Rorden (2000), *Multilateralism and the World Trade Organisation* (London: Routledge).

Williams, Colin and Anthony D. Smith (1983), 'The National Construction of Social Space', *Progress in Human Geography*, 7(4): 502–18.

Williams, David and Tom Young (1994), 'Governance, the World, Bank and Liberal Theory', *Political Studies*, 42(1): 84–100.

Williams, Phil (1997), 'Transnational Criminal Organizations and International Security', in John Arquilla and David Ronfeldt (eds), *In Athena's Camp: Preparing for Conflict in the Information Age* (Santa Monica, CA: Rand Corporation), pp. 315–37.

Williamson, John (2009), 'A Short History of the Washington Consensus', *Law and Business Review of the Americas*, 15(1): 7–26.

Worth, Owen (2012), '"Accumulating the Critical Spirit", Rosa Luxemburg and Critical IPE', *International Politics*, 49(2): 136–53.

Yan, Xuetong (2011), *Ancient Chinese Thought: Modern Chinese Power* (Princeton, NJ: Princeton University Press).

Yan, Xuetong (2012), 'Chinese Realism, the Tsinghua School of International Relations, and the Impossibility of Harmony', *Theory Talks #51* (Heidelberg: Max Planck Institute), https://www.files.ethz.ch/isn/155591/Theory%20Talk51_Xuetong.pdf.

Youngs, Gillian (2004), 'Feminist International Relations: A Contradiction in Terms? Or: Why Women and Gender Are Essential to Understanding the World "We" Live In', *International Affairs*, 80(1): 75–87.

Yourish, Karen and Larry Buchanan (2019), 'Trump and His Associates Had More Than 100 Contacts with Russians before the Inauguration', *New York Times*, 19 January, https://www.nytimes.com/interactive/2019/01/26/us/politics/trump-contacts-russians-wikileaks.html.

Yusuf, Abdulqawi A. (2014), *Pan-Africanism and International Law* (Leiden: Martinus Nijhoff).

Zeleny, Jeff (2009), 'Multiple Channels for Obama's Cairo Speech', *New York Times*, 3 June, http://thelede.blogs.nytimes.com/2009/06/03/multiple-channels-for-obamas-cairo-speech.

Zhu, Dan (2018), *China and the International Criminal Court* (London: Palgrave Macmillan).

Zielonka, Jan (2007), *Europe as Empire: The Nature of the Enlarged European Union* (Oxford: Oxford University Press).

Zimmerman, Michael E. and Theresa A. Toulouse (2016), 'Ecofascism', in Joni Adamson, William A. Gleason, and David N. Pellow (eds), *Keywords for Environmental Politics* (New York: New York University Press), pp. 64–8.

Zondi, Siphamandla (2018), 'Decolonising International Relations and Its Theory: A Critical Conceptual Meditation', *Politikon*, 45(1): 16–31.

Zsolnai, Laszlo (2018), *Ethics, Meaning, and Market Society* (New York: Routledge).

INDEX

Note: Figures and boxes are indicated by an italic *f* and *b* following the page number.